EARLY MUSIC HISTORY 9

EDITORIAL BOARD

EARLY MUSIC HISTORY 9

STUDIES IN MEDIEVAL
AND
EARLY MODERN MUSIC

Edited by

IAIN FENLON
Fellow of King's College, Cambridge

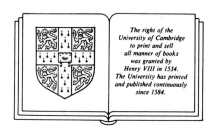

The right of the
University of Cambridge
to print and sell
all manner of books
was granted by
Henry VIII in 1534.
The University has printed
and published continuously
since 1584.

CAMBRIDGE UNIVERSITY PRESS

Cambridge

New York   Port Chester   Melbourne   Sydney

Published by the Press Syndicate of the University of Cambridge
The Pitt Building, Trumpington Street, Cambridge CB2 1RP
40 West 20th Street, New York, NY 10011, USA
10 Stamford Road, Oakleigh, Melbourne 3166, Australia

First published 1990

Phototypeset in Baskerville by Wyvern Typesetting Ltd, Bristol

Printed in Great Britain at the University Press, Cambridge

ISSN 0261-1279

ISBN 0 521 39051 6

SUBSCRIPTIONS The subscription price to volume 9, which includes postage, is
£35.00 for UK, and £38.00 elsewhere (US $71.00 in USA and Canada) for
institutions, £22.00 (US $39.00 in USA and Canada) for individuals ordering direct
from the Press and certifying that the annual is for their personal use. Airmail
(orders to Cambridge only) £8.00 extra. Copies of the annual for subscribers in the
USA and Canada are sent by air to New York to arrive with minimum delay.
Orders, which must be accompanied by payment, may be sent to a bookseller,
subscription agent or direct to the publishers: Cambridge University Press, The
Edinburgh Building, Shaftesbury Road, Cambridge CB2 2RU. Payment may be
made by any of the following methods: cheque (payable to Cambridge University
Press), UK postal order, bank draft, Post Office Giro (account no. 571 6055 GB
Bootle – advise CUP of payment), international money order, UNESCO coupons,
or any credit card bearing the Interbank symbol. Orders from the USA and Canada
should be sent to Cambridge University Press, 40 West 20th Street, New York, NY
10011.

BACK VOLUMES Volumes 1–8 are available from the publisher at £30.00 ($71.00 in
USA and Canada).

NOTE Each volume of *Early Music History* is now published in the year in which it is
subscribed. Volume 9 is therefore published in 1990. Readers should be aware,
however, that earlier volumes have been subscribed in the year *after* the copyright
and publication date given on this imprints page. Thus volume 8, the volume
received by 1989 subscribers, is dated 1988 on the imprints page.

CONTENTS

REVIEWS

v

NOTES FOR CONTRIBUTORS

PRESENTATION

Contributors should write in English, or be willing to have their articles translated. All typescripts must be double spaced with margins of at least 2.5 cm (1″). Footnotes, bibliographies, appendixes, tables and displayed quotations must also be double spaced. The 'top' (ribbon) copy of the typescript must be supplied. Scripts submitted for consideration will not normally be returned unless specifically requested.

Tables, graphs, diagrams and music examples must be supplied on separate sheets from the text of the article. Illustrations should be in the form of black and white prints, measuring 20.3 × 15.2 cm (8″ × 6″). All illustrative material should carry the contributor's name and should be numbered and carefully keyed into the typescript. Captions should be separately typed, double spaced.

SPELLING

English spelling, idiom and terminology should be used, e.g. bar (not measure), note (not tone), quaver (not eighth note). Where there is an option, '-ise' endings should be preferred to '-ize'.

PUNCTUATION

English punctuation practice should be followed: (1) single quotation marks, except for 'a "quote" within a quote'; (2) punctuation outside quotation marks, unless a complete sentence is quoted; (3) no comma before 'and' in a series; (4) footnote indicators follow punctuation; (5) square brackets [ ] only for interpolation in quoted matter; (6) no stop after abbreviations that include the last letter of a word, e.g. Dr, St (but Prof.).

Notes for Contributors

QUOTATIONS

A quotation of no more than 60 words of prose or one line of verse should be continuous within the text and enclosed in single quotation marks. Longer quotations should be displayed and quotation marks should not be used. For quotations from foreign languages, the English translation should be given in the text, the foreign-language original in the footnote.

NUMBERS

Numbers below 100 should be spelled out, except page, bar, folio numbers etc., sums of money and specific quantities, e.g. 20 ducats, 45 mm. Pairs of numbers should be elided as follows: 190–1, 198–9, 198–201, 212–13. Dates should be given in the following forms: 10 January 1983, the 1980s, sixteenth century (16th century in tables and lists), sixteenth-century polyphony.

CAPITALISATION

Incipits in all language (motets, songs, etc.), and titles except in English, should be capitalised as in running prose; titles in English should have all important words capitalised, e.g. *The Pavin of Delight*. Most offices should have a lower-case initial except in official titles, e.g. 'the Lord Chancellor entered the cathedral', 'Bishop Fisher entered the cathedral' (but 'the bishop entered the cathedral'). Names of institutions should have full (not prose-style) capitalisation, e.g. Liceo Musicale.

ITALICS

Titles and incipits of musical works in italic, but not genre titles or sections of the Mass/English Service, e.g. Kyrie, Magnificat. Italics for foreign words should be kept to a minimum; in general they should be used only for unusual words or if a word might be mistaken for English if not italicised. Titles of manuscripts should be roman in quotes, e.g. 'Rules How to Compose'. Names of institutions should be roman.

BIBLIOGRAPHICAL REFERENCES

Authors' and editors' forenames should not be given, only initials; where possible, editors should be given for Festschriften, conference proceedings, symposia, etc. In titles, all important words in English should be capitalised; all other languages should follow prose-style capitalisation, except for journal and series titles which should follow English capitalisation. Titles of series should be included, in roman, where relevant. Journal and series volume numbers should be given in arabic, volumes of a set in roman ('vol.' will not be used). Places and dates of publication should be included but not publishers' names. Dissertation titles should be given in roman and enclosed in quotation marks. Page numbers should be preceded by 'p.' or 'pp.' in all contexts. The first citation of a bibliographical reference should include full details; subsequent citations may use the author's surname, short title and relevant page numbers only. *Ibid.* and *op. cit.* may be used, but not *loc. cit.*

ABBREVIATIONS

Abbreviations for manuscript citations, libraries, periodicals, series, etc. should not be used without explanation; after the first full citation an abbreviation may be used throughout text and notes. Standard abbreviations may be used without explanation. In the text, 'Example', 'Figure' and 'bars' should be used (not 'Ex.', 'Fig.', 'bb.'). In references to manuscripts, 'fols.' should be used (not 'ff.') and 'v' (verso) and 'r' (recto) should be typed superscript where appropriate. The word for 'saint' should be spelled out or abbreviated according to language, e.g. San Andrea, SS. Pietro e Paolo, St Paul, St Agnes, St Denis, Ste Clothilde.

NOTE NAMES

Flats, sharps and naturals should be indicated by the conventional signs, not words. Note names should be roman and capitalised where general, e.g. C major, but should be italic and follow the Helmholtz code where specific ($C_{,,}$ $C_{,}$ $C\ c\ c'\ c''\ c'''$; c' = middle C). A simpler system may be used in discussions of repertories (e.g. chant) where different conventions are followed.

Notes for Contributors

Substantial changes in wording, other than corrections of printing errors, may be subject to a charge.

Early Music History (1989) Volume 9

CHARLES M. ATKINSON

FRANCO OF COLOGNE ON THE RHYTHM OF ORGANUM PURUM*

Thanks in part to a fine translation by Oliver Strunk,[1] the *Ars cantus mensurabilis* of Franco of Cologne is a treatise we all think we know. It is perhaps for this reason that Franco's treatise has been all but ignored in most of the recent discussions of the rhythm of Notre Dame organum.[2] The one noteworthy exception to this is Fritz Reckow's discussion of organum purum in his dissertation on Anonymous IV and in his various articles on organum and related topics in the *Handwörterbuch der musikalischen Terminologie*, in the Schrade *Gedenkschrift*, and elsewhere.[3] But for Reckow, and presum-

---

*This article is the revised version of a paper delivered at the Annual Meeting of the American Musicological Society, Baltimore, November 1988, and which was presented to Janet Knapp in an unpublished *Festgabe* on the occasion of her retirement from Vassar College.

[1] O. Strunk, *Source Readings in Music History* (New York, 1950), pp. 139–59.

[2] The interest of scholars has been focused more upon the ideas of Johannes de Garlandia, Anonymous IV and the St Emmeram Anonymous, among the Notre Dame theorists of the mid- to late thirteenth century, or upon the de la Fage Anonymous or the Vatican Organum Treatise in the earlier part of the century. See, for example, E. Roesner's discussion of 'Johannes de Garlandia on *organum in speciali*', *Early Music History*, 2 (1982), pp. 129–60, and his 'The Performance of Parisian Organum', *Early Music*, 7 (1979), pp. 174–89. (Roesner's discussion of Franco's term *floratura* will be reviewed later in this study.) See also E. H. Sanders, 'Consonance and Rhythm in the Organum of the 12th and 13th Centuries', *Journal of the American Musicological Society*, 33 (1980), pp. 264–86; J. Yudkin, 'The Rhythm of Organum Purum', *The Journal of Musicology*, 2 (1983), 355–76; *idem*, 'Notre Dame Theory: A Study of Terminology, including a New Translation of the Music Treatise of Anonymous IV' (Ph.D. dissertation, Stanford University, 1982); S. Fuller, 'Theoretical Foundations of Early Organum Theory', *Acta Musicologica*, 53 (1981), pp. 52–84; and S. Immel, 'The Vatican Organum Treatise Re-examined', *Abstracts of Papers Read at the Fiftieth Annual Meeting of the American Musicological Society* (Philadelphia, 1984), p. 18. For a more complete listing and assessment of recent scholarship on organum, see Yudkin's 'Notre Dame Theory', in particular his Introduction and Chapter 1 (pp. 1–48).

[3] F. Reckow, *Der Musiktraktat des Anonymus 4*, Beihefte zum Archiv für Musikwissenschaft 4 and 5 (Wiesbaden, 1967); 'Proprietas und perfectio: Zur Geschichte des Rhythmus, seiner Aufzeichnung und Terminologie im 13. Jahrhundert', *Acta Musicologica*, 39 (1967), pp. 115–43; 'Organum', *Handwörterbuch der musikalischen Terminologie* (Wiesbaden, 1971);

ably for most other scholars as well, Franco's description of organum is strongly coloured by his theories of mensuration, appearing to place even organum purum under the heading of 'mensurable music'.[4] This in turn seems to distance Franco from the earliest layer of organum composition at Notre Dame, rendering his ideas of little value in arriving at an interpretation of the rhythmic character of this music.[5]

The seeming neglect of Franco as a source of information about the rhythm of organum purum is thus in part a logical consequence of the very innovations for which his treatise is justifiably famous. As I hope to demonstrate, however, whatever neglect the treatise has been subject to vis-à-vis organum is not justifiable. The *Ars cantus mensurabilis* is in fact a treatise that can still offer us fresh perspectives not just on mensural notation, but also on the rhythm of organum purum – perspectives that heretofore may have been concealed from view under a veneer of translation.

The key to uncovering these perspectives is, I believe, the terminology Franco uses to describe the music with which he is dealing. Trying to gain access to the character of Notre Dame

---

Die Copula: Über einige Zusammenhänge zwischen Setzweise, Formbildung, Rhythmus und Vortrags-stil in der Mehrstimmigkeit von Notre Dame, Akademie der Wissenschaften und der Literatur zu Mainz: Abhandlungen der geistes- und sozialwissenschaftlichen Klasse, Jg. 1972, Nr. 13 (Wiesbaden, 1972); 'Das Organum', *Gattungen der Musik in Einzeldarstellungen: Gedenkschrift Leo Schrade*, 1. Folge, ed. W. Arlt, E. Lichtenhahn and H. Oesch (Bern, 1973), pp. 434–96; 'Organum', sections 1–5, *The New Grove Dictionary of Music and Musicians*, ed. S. Sadie, 20 vols. (London, 1980), XIII, pp. 796–803.

[4] See the discussion of this issue below, pp. 6–10. In his article 'Organum' for the *Handwörterbuch*, Reckow shows Franco as placing organum under the genus 'musica mensurabilis', stating: 'Bei Franco spielt bei der rhythmische Charakter bei der Mehrstimmigkeits-Klassifikation gar keine Rolle mehr, da für ihn alle Mehrstimmigkeit (von den Tenor-Haltetönen abgesehen) als rhythmisch-proportional gemessen gilt' (*op. cit.*, pp. 9–10). In *Der Musiktraktat des Anonymus 4*, II, pp. 40–5, Reckow hypothesises that Franco must already have been dealing with manuscript settings of organum purum in which the upper voice was written in modal, or perhaps even mensural notation: '[Franco's] Regelung setzt die Anwendung eines vom Zusammenklang zunächst völlig unabhängigen Rhythmisierungsverfahrens im Duplum voraus, und dieses Verfahren kann nur die modalrhythmische Lesung der Melismen sein, eventuell bereits nach mensuraler Umschrift' (*op. cit.*, p. 40).

[5] Franco's remarks on organum purum – a type of music that formed an important part of Leonin's *Magnus liber* – seem to form a sharp contrast with those of other thirteenth-century theorists. Whereas writers such as Johannes de Garlandia emphasise consonance or dissonance with the given tenor as the determinant of long and short note values in organum purum, Franco's stating that in organum purum 'Whatever is written as a *longa simplex* is long; as a breve, short; as a semibreve, still shorter', and 'Whatever is long requires concord with respect to the tenor,' does indeed seem to suggest that he was dealing with a later version of this type of music, just as Reckow hypothesised.

organum through the door of Franco's treatise brings us into the broader arena of terminological history and the relationships of terms to the concepts they describe. This is, of course, an area in which pioneering work has been done by Fritz Reckow, and which has been explored more recently by Edward Roesner and Jeremy Yudkin.[6] In approaching this topic I have therefore tried to follow the dictates of Franco himself: 'not hesitating to interpolate things well said by others or to eradicate and avert [their] errors and, if we have discovered something new, to uphold and prove it with good reasons'.[7]

Although he reserves his principal discussion of organum for the end of his work, two of the areas Franco touches upon in the first chapter lay important groundwork for the last one.[8] The first of these is his definition of mensurable music and *mensura*:

Excerpt 1. Franco, *Ars cantus mensurabilis*, chapter I
(1) Mensurabilis musica est cantus longis brevibusque temporibus mensuratus. (2) Gratia huius diffinitionis, videndum est quid sit mensura et quid tempus. (3) Mensura est habitudo quantitativa longitudinem et brevitatem cuiuslibet cantus mensurabilis manifestans. (4) Mensurabilis dico, quia in plana musica non attenditur talis mensura. (CSM 18, pp. 24–5)

In Franco's words, 'Mensurable music is *cantus* that is measured in long and short *tempora*' (or 'units of time'). He contrasts this with plainchant, in which, as he says, 'this kind of measure is not attendant' (sentence 4). Taking care to define his terms precisely, in the best Scholastic tradition, he goes on to define *mensura*, saying that 'Measure is a quantitative attribute making manifest the length and brevity of any mensurable melody' (sentence 3) or, using the version of the sentence as it appears in Jerome of Moravia's copy of Franco, 'Measure is an attribute showing the quantity, the length and brevity, of any mensurable *cantus*'.[9]

---

6   See the works cited in nn. 2 and 3 above.
7   'Proponimus igitur ipsam mensurabilem musicam sub compendio declarare; bene dictaque aliorum non recusabimus interponere, erroresque destruere et fugare; et si quid novi a nobis inventum fuerit, bonis rationibus sustinere et probare'; *Franconis de Colonia Ars cantus mensurabilis*, ed. G. Reaney and A. Gilles, Corpus Scriptorum de Musica [hereafter CSM] 18 ([Rome], 1974), p. 24. All translations are mine unless otherwise indicated.
8   The division and numbering of chapters is that given in CSM 18.
9   Jerome's version reads: 'Mensura est habitudo quantitatem, longitudinem et brevitatem cujuslibet cantus mensurabilis manifestans'. For the complete text see *Hieronymus de Moravia O.P.: Tractatus de musica*, ed. S. Cserba O.P., Freiburger Studien zur Musikwissenschaft 2 (Regensburg, 1935).

Franco's use of the terms 'quantitative' or 'quantity' in this passage is, I think, important. These are terms not found in the parallel passages in Johannes de Garlandia or Anonymous IV,[10] and to my mind signal the striving for order, specificity and precision characteristic both of Franco's treatise and of Scholasticism in general.[11]

A second aspect of Franco's first chapter is pivotal both within the treatise and for the topic with which we are concerned:

Excerpt 2. Franco, *Ars cantus mensurabilis*, chapter I
(7) Dividitur autem mensurabilis musica in mensurabilem simpliciter et partim. (8) Mensurabilis simpliciter est discantus, eo quod in omni parte sua tempore mensuratur. (9) Partim mensurabilis dicitur organum pro tanto quod non in qualibet parte sua mensuratur. (10) Et sciendum quod organum dupliciter sumitur, proprie et communiter. (11) Est enim organum proprie sumptum organum duplum, quod purum organum appellatur. (CSM 18, p. 25)

Franco first subdivides mensurable music into two categories, namely, that which is wholly measurable and that which is only

---

[10] For the parallel passages in Johannes de Garlandia see Reimer, *Johannes de Garlandia*, Beihefte zum Archiv für Musikwissenschaft 10 (Wiesbaden, 1972), p. 35, lines 1–3 (*musica mensurabilis*), and p. 36, sent. 5–8, and p. 37, sent. 16–20 (*mensura*); for Anon. IV, see Reckow, *Der Musiktraktat des Anonymus 4*, I, p. 22, lines 3–6 (*mensura*). In Anon. IV, see also p. 76, lines 12–35, and p. 77, lines 1–6. Somewhat surprising, given his dependence upon Johannes de Garlandia for certain aspects of his theory, is the fact that the St Emmeram Anonymous also uses the word 'quantitas' to distinguish between non-mensurable and mensurable music: 'Et nota, quod inmensurabilis est illa, ubi non sunt longe uel breues uel aliqua *quantitas* temporum sub certo numero distributa. Mensurabilis est illa, in qua sua *quantitas* temporum reperitur', H. Sowa, ed., *Ein anonymer glossierter Mensuraltraktat 1279*, Königsberger Studien zur Musikwissenschaft 9 (Kassel, 1930), p. 5 (my italics).

[11] In his famous essay on *Gothic Architecture and Scholasticism* (Cleveland and New York, 1957) E. Panofsky pointed to the importance of the Scholastic *summa* as a conceptual model that could operate in architecture just as in the various types of philosophical, scientific and theological writings that were its primary manifestation. Its principal attributes were: (1) totality (sufficient enumeration), (2) arrangement according to a system of homologous parts and parts of parts (sufficient articulation), (3) distinctness and deductive cogency (sufficient interrelation) (see Panofsky, p. 31). In the *summa*, as in other Scholastic writing, the commanding ideal was a mode of expression that would make the orderliness and logic of the author's thought palpably explicit and clear. Although I would not go so far as to characterise Franco's *Ars cantus mensurabilis* as a 'summa' in the sense of Aquinas's *Summa theologica*, Franco himself refers to his work as a 'compendium', and it does exhibit a number of traits (e.g. its striving to be comprehensive, the logical, hierarchical arrangement of its parts, and the clarity and specificity of its treatment) that place it squarely in the Scholastic tradition as Panofsky and others have characterised it. (The classic treatment of Scholasticism is of course M. Grabmann's *Geschichte der scholastischen Methode*, 2 vols. [Freiburg, 1909–11; repr. 1957], and the subject is treated in almost any work on medieval intellectual history. Two recent treatments are those of M. De Wulf, *An Introduction to Scholastic Philosophy*, trans. P. Coffey [New York, 1956] and J. Pieper, *Scholasticism* [London, 1960].)

partly so. The former (*simpliciter*) is discant, Franco says in sentence 8, 'because it is measured by time in its every part'; 'partly mensurable', on the other hand, 'is [that] called organum, in so far as it is that which is not measured in its every part'. This sentence is important – important enough for Franco to return to it later on in his discussion. We shall do the same.

Yet another matter that should be mentioned here is a comment Franco makes about the formal relationship of discant to organum. At the very close of his chapter XI, 'On Discant and its Species', Franco makes the following statement: 'Be it observed also that in discant, as well as in tripla etc., the equivalence in the perfections of longs, breves, and semibreves ought always to be borne in mind, so that there may be as many perfections in the discant, triplum, etc., as there are in the tenor, or conversely, counting both actual sounds and their omissions as far as the *penultimate*, where such measure is not attendant, *there being rather a point of organum in that place*'.[12]

Let us now turn to Franco's last chapter to see what that organum should be like:

Excerpt 3. Franco, *Ars cantus mensurabilis*, chapter XIV (beginning) (1) Organum proprie sumptum est cantus non in omni parte sua mensuratus. (2) Sciendum quod purum organum haberi non potest, nisi supra tenorem ubi sola nota est in unisono, ita quod, quando tenor accipit plures notas simul, statim est discantus, ut hic:

[e - sto - te]

(CSM 18, p. 80)

Franco begins his treatment by recalling two sentences from the first chapter of his work.[13] His first sentence is 'Organum, taken in itself, is *cantus* not measured in its every part,' which in the earlier chapter was followed almost immediately by the statement that 'organum taken in itself is organum duplum, which is called organum purum'. He now goes on to describe the chief identifying feature of organum

---

[12] 'Notandum quod tam in discantu quam in triplicibus etc. inspicienda est aequipollentia in perfectionibus longarum, brevium et semibrevium, ita quod tot perfectiones in tenore habeantur quot in discantu vel in triplo etc., vel e converso, computando tam voces rectas quam obmissas usque ad *penultimam*, ubi non attenditur talis mensura, *sed magis est organicus ibi punctus*' (CSM 18, p. 75; my italics).

[13] The relevant sentences in chapter I are sentences 9 and 11. See Excerpt 2 above.

purum within a two-voice texture (Excerpt 3, sentence 2): 'Be it known that there can be no organum purum except over a tenor where there is a single note on a single pitch [i.e. a sustained note], for when the tenor takes several notes together, discant begins at once'.[14]

There are, of course, distant echoes of both the St Emmeram Anonymous and Johannes de Garlandia in the last sentence above. But it is in the second section of Franco's treatment of organum purum that one finds the closest ties with Johannes de Garlandia. At the same time, this section demonstrates a fundamental shift from Johannes's views:

Excerpt 4. Franco's 'Rules of Consonance'
(3) Ipsius organi longae et breves tribus regulis cognoscuntur. (4) Prima est: quicquid notatur in longa simplici nota longum est, et in brevi breve, et in semibrevi semibreve. (5) Secunda regula est: quicquid est longum indiget concordantia respectu tenoris; sed si in discordantia venerit, tenor taceat vel se in concordantiam fingat, ut hic patet:

[Iu - - - dea et Iherusalem]

(6) Tertia regula est: quicquid accipitur immediate ante pausationem quae finis punctorum dicitur, est longum, quia omnis penultima longa est. (CSM 18, pp. 80–1)

Here, Franco presents his three 'rules of consonance', which follow

---

[14] Cf. the description of organum purum (=*organum speciale*) in the St Emmeram Anonymous's discussion of the four-note ligature with perfection and with opposite propriety: 'Ipsa figura quaternaria figurata per oppositum et perfecta semper in dispositione *organi specialis* nascitur sibi esse; id est quociensconque in cantu aliquo ordinatur, *supra burdonem tenoris* edificari cernitur a natura et sub dispositione organi specialis.' ('This quaternary figure, written *per oppositum* and perfect, always arises in the disposition of *organum speciale*; that is, whenever it is disposed in some melody [*cantus*] it is perceived to be erected *over a burdo of the tenor* by the nature and under the disposition of *organum speciale*'.) Sowa, ed., *Ein anonymer glossierter Mensuraltraktat*, p. 53, lines 2–6; my italics.) Franco's use of the phrase *in unisono* in this passage has a direct parallel in the treatise of Johannes de Garlandia. In his discussion of organum *cum alio*, Johannes states: 'eius aequipollentia tantum se tenet *in unisono* usque ad finem alicuius puncti, ut secum convenit secundum aliquam concordantiam' ('its equivalence is maintained *in unisono* [i.e. over a single pitch sustained in the tenor] as far as the end of a section, so that it might come together with it in some consonance'; Reimer, *Johannes de Garlandia*, I, pp. 88–9; my italics.) See also the discussion below, pp. 15–16.

Johannes de Garlandia's rules of consonance in number if not in content. (Johannes's rules appear in Excerpt 5.)

Excerpt 5. Johannes de Garlandia's 'Rules of Consonance'
(11) Longae et breves in organo tali modo dinoscuntur, scilicet per [concordantiam], per figuram, per paenultimam. (12) Unde regula: omne id, quod accidit in aliquo secundum virtutem [concordantiarum], dicitur longum. (13) Alia regula: quidquid figuratur longum secundum organa ante pausationem vel loco [concordantiae] dicitur longum. (14) Alia regula: quidquid accipitur ante longam pausationem vel ante perfectam concordantiam dicitur esse longum. (Reimer, *Johannes de Garlandia*, I, p. 89)

Both begin in a similar fashion, Johannes stating that the longs and breves in organum are distinguished by consonance, by *figura* (or note shape) and 'by the penultima'; Franco simply says that the longs and breves of organum purum can be understood by three rules. At this point, however, the two authors begin to diverge.

Johannes de Garlandia's first rule (sentence 12 in Excerpt 5) states: 'All that which falls anywhere [lit. 'somewhere'] in accord with the *virtus* of the consonances is said to be long.'[15] In other words, whatever creates a consonance should be long. Franco turns this rule on its head, as it were, stating (sentence 4 of Excerpt 4): 'Whatever is notated as a *longa simplex* note is long; [whatever is notated] as a breve is short; as a semibreve, even shorter.' This is actually closer to Johannes's second rule (sentence 13 in Excerpt 5): 'According to the precepts of organa, whatever is notated as a long before a rest, that is, in the position of a consonance, is said to be long.'[16]

---

[15] On the translation of the phrase 'omne id quod accidit' in this passage and the significance it holds for the interpretation of Johannes's ideas, see E. Sanders, 'Consonance and Rhythm in the Organum of the 12th and 13th Centuries', *Journal of the American Musicological Society*, 33 (1980), pp. 269–71, and the Communications of Professors Reckow and Sanders, *ibid.*, 34 (1981), pp. 588–91. On Johannes's 'rules of consonance' themselves, see W. Apel, 'From St. Martial to Notre Dame', *Journal of the American Musicological Society*, 2 (1949), pp. 145–58, and W. Waite, 'Discantus, Copula, Organum', *Journal of the American Musicological Society*, 5 (1952), pp. 77–87, and *The Rhythm of Twelfth-Century Polyphony* (New Haven and London, 1954), pp. 120–2. Both of these authors based their discussion on Coussemaker's edition (E. de Coussemaker, ed., *Scriptorum de musica medii aevi nova series* [hereafter *CS*], I, pp. 97–117 and 175–82). F. Reckow (*Der Musiktraktat des Anonymus 4*, II, pp. 35–9, 45) arrived at a new interpretation of Garlandia in part through a series of astute text-critical observations. He demonstrated clearly that the text in Coussemaker was faulty, and that a new edition was needed. For treatments based on the new edition by Reimer (*Johannes de Garlandia*, I–II) see Sanders, 'Consonance and Rhythm', pp. 267–74, Roesner, 'Johannes de Garlandia', pp. 153–6, and Yudkin, 'The Rhythm of Organum Purum'.

[16] As both Reckow and Roesner point out, Garlandia's second and third rules are 'codicils' to the first, addressing specific instances in which the general rule does not apply. The import

7

Charles M. Atkinson

Important here is that for Franco in this first rule, the rhythmically significant note-shape takes precedence over all else, presumably including consonance, as a determinant of length. Such a rule is quite in keeping with the innovative character of Franco's treatise, which perhaps for the first time defines precise mensural values and proportionate relationships for individual notes as well as for ligatures.[17] Indeed it may be these newly mensurated notes, the *notae simplices*, to which Franco is referring in this passage. His phrase is 'quicquid notatur in longa *simplici* nota'.[18] Whether the whole sentence is meant to refer to individual notes or to longs, breves, and semibreves in ligatures, it makes clear that it is note-shape, and not harmonic context, that dictates length.

This principle is reinforced further in Franco's second rule (sentence 5 in Excerpt 4): 'Whatever is long requires concord with respect to the tenor; but if it is in discord, the tenor should be silent or should form itself into a concord [*in concordantiam fingat*], as evident here.'

[Iu - - - dea et Iherusalem]

This rule has been discussed by Edward Roesner in his article 'The Performance of Parisian Organum' in the 1979 volume of *Early Music*. After quoting Strunk's translation, that if a long should occur as a discord, the singer should 'let the tenor remain silent or feign concord', Roesner states that 'what Franco had in mind by "feign concord" is equivocal. It seems highly unlikely that he meant the singer to change pitch'.[19] But as both the Latin 'se in concordantiam

of the second rule, in Roesner's words, is that 'the modal pattern takes precedence over the first rule at the ends of phrases' (Roesner, 'Johannes de Garlandia', p. 154). In Franco, the 'rule of the *figura*' has become the first one, and presumably applies anywhere in the course of the duplum melody.

17 On this point see A. Hughes, 'Franco of Cologne', *The New Grove Dictionary*, VI, pp. 794–7, and W. Apel, *The Notation of Polyphonic Music 900–1600*, 5th edn (Cambridge, MA, 1953), pp. 310–15. On the relationship of Franco's treatise to others in the thirteenth and early fourteenth centuries see W. Arlt and M. Haas, 'Pariser modale Mehrstimmigkeit in einem Fragment der Basler Universitätsbibliothek', *Forum Musicologicum*, Basler Studien zur Musikgeschichte 1 (Bern, 1975), pp. 231–41.

18 The example illustrating these rules, however, is written in modal, not mensural, notation in all manuscripts of the treatise except Paris, Bibliothèque Nationale, MS fonds lat. 16663. Cf. Reckow, *Der Musiktraktat des Anonymus 4*, II, p. 40 n. 9, and Cserba, ed., *Hieronymus de Moravia*, p. 258.

19 Roesner, 'The Performance of Parisian Organum', p. 176.

fingat' and the musical example following this sentence show, it is precisely a change of pitch in the tenor that Franco does intend. As Reckow had pointed out in his dissertation, no extant version of *Iudea et Iherusalem* exhibits the *E* that is the second tenor note in Franco's example.[20] The reason it is there must be to show how the tenor can 'form itself into a consonance' – in this case an octave – under the successive *e*'s in the duplum, which according to either a modal or a Franconian reading would sound for three *tempora*.[21]

Taken together, the two rules just discussed demonstrate how far Franco has moved away from Johannes de Garlandia in extending the sphere of influence of mensuration. Whereas in Johannes's work the notes of the upper voice of a section of organum were to be lengthened or shortened according to whether they were consonant or dissonant with the underlying tenor, Franco places the rhythmic component first, and then says that if the resultant interval under a long of the duplum happens to be a dissonance, then it is the tenor – not the duplum – that should make the adjustment.

Moving on to the third of Franco's rules (sentence 6 in Excerpt 4), we finally come back to territory shared by both Franco and Johannes. The latter had stated (sentence 14 of Excerpt 5): 'Whatever is taken before a long rest or before a perfect consonance is said to be long.' Franco, using wording that duplicates that of Johannes in large measure, says that 'Whatever is taken immediately before the rest which is called a *finis punctorum* is long, because every penultimate is long.'

[20]   Reckow, *Der Musiktraktat des Anonymus 4*, II, p. 41 n. 9.

[21]   As pointed out in n. 18 above, the example is written in modal notation in all manuscripts of the treatise except Paris, BN, fonds lat. 16663. Cf. the notation of *Iudea et Iherusalem* in Wolfenbüttel, Herzog August Bibliothek, MS 628 Helmst. (W₁), fol. 13, and Florence, Biblioteca Medicea-Laurenziana, MS Plut. 29.1, fol. 65, both readily available in C. Parrish, *The Notation of Medieval Music* (New York, 1959), plates xxvIIa and xxvIIb. The version in W₁ is particularly striking, since it begins with what looks like a Franconian *ternaria* without propriety and with perfection, but is in fact a *longa simplex* followed by a *binaria*.

      Although the sources for the *Magnus liber* show that singers were not willing to go so far as to follow Franco's suggestion of changing the notes of the plainchant in order to create a consonance with a newly composed duplum, there is nonetheless some evidence in practical sources to show that the successive *e*'s in the duplum of the first phrase of *Iudea et Iherusalem* did indeed create a problematic dissonance with the *F* in the tenor. Reckow (*Der Musiktraktat des Anonymus 4*, II, p. 41 n. 9) found that in a setting of *Benedicamus domino* on fol. 24ᵛ of the Las Huelgas manuscript – one with the same opening phrase as *Iudea et Iherusalem* – the last *binaria* of the phrase (with the pitches *e–c*) had been changed to a *ternaria* with the pitches *f–d–c*, followed by a *longa simplex* on *c*. Thus, instead of having an *e* of three *tempora* against the *F* in the tenor, the Las Huelgas setting forces the *e* of the penultimate ligature to sound for only one *tempus*.

As suggested earlier, Franco's three 'rules of consonance' give such weight to precise rhythmic denotation that one is virtually forced to assume that Franco is dealing with a duplum that is already 'rhythmisch streng festgelegt', as Fritz Reckow put it. This would in turn suggest, as it did for Reckow, that the 'part' referred to in Franco's definition of organum purum as a *'cantus* not measured in its every part' was the tenor.[22] This certainly seems logical, especially in as much as writers such as Anonymous VII and the St Emmeram Anonymous use the term *pars* in reference to a 'voice part', and beyond that in specific reference to the tenor.[23] It may be worth pointing out, however, that neither Johannes de Garlandia nor Franco himself in other parts of his treatise uses the term unequivocally in that way. Thus, before we simply accept Reckow's view and declare the case closed, let us see if Franco himself has anything further to say about the matter by turning our attention to the last sentence in his treatment – a sentence that to my mind is the most interesting and difficult of all.

The last sentence of Franco's treatment of organum purum reads as follows:

Excerpt 6. Franco, *Ars cantus mensurabilis*, chapter XIV, sentence 7
Item notandum, quod quotienscumque in organo puro plures figurae simul in unisono evenerint, sola prima debet percuti, reliquae vero omnes in floratura teneantur, ut hic.

(CSM 18, pp. 81–2)

[22] In Reckow's words: 'Infolgedessen [the statement quoted in n. 4 of the present article] kann sich die Einschränkung, daß das Organum purum ein *cantus non in omni parte sua mensuratus* sei . . ., nicht auf "Teile" (Abschnitte) der Oberstimmen-Melismen – diese sind nach Franco insgesamt rhythmisch streng festgelegt –, sondern nur auf die Tenor-"Stimme" und ihre Haltetöne selbst beziehen; denn diese allein sind (wenn auch nur der Schreibweise nach, nämlich als einfache *longae*) in ihrem Wert für Franco noch nicht exakt "gemessen".' (*Der Musiktraktat des Anonymus 4*, II, p. 41).
[23] Anon. VII: 'tenor est fundamentum motelli et dignior pars' (*CS* I, p. 379b); St Emmeram Anonymous: 'tenor . . . eo quod sit dignior pars' (Sowa, ed., *Ein anonymer glossierter Mensuraltraktat*, p. 92, lines 19f); Johannes de Grocheio: 'Tenor autem est illa pars, supra quam . . .' (E. Rohloff, *Der Musiktraktat des Johannes de Grocheo*, Media Latinitas Musica 2 [Leipzig, 1943], p. 57, line 12); Pseudo-Johannes de Muris: 'dum . . . pars una multum ascendit, reliqua vero multum descendit . . .' (*CS* III, p. 240b). These are cited after Reckow, *Der Musiktraktat des Anonymus 4*, II, p. 41 n. 11.

Strunk translates: 'Be it also observed that in organum purum, whenever several similar figures occur in unison, only the first is to be sounded; let all the rest observe the florid style' (Strunk, *Source Readings*, p. 159). He then transcribes the example as follows:

What is one to make of this? As a rendering of the Latin text, Strunk's translation is perfectly adequate. There is only one trouble with it: as far as I can determine, it makes somewhere from little to no sense.

In his article on 'The Performance of Parisian Organum' mentioned above, Edward Roesner places Franco's sentence in apposition to a statement by Anonymous IV dealing with the *longa florata*. In Roesner's words: 'Anonymous IV states that "two notes on the same pitch, whether consonant [with the tenor] or not, are rendered as a *longa florata*" (literally, a "long bedecked with flowers", or even a "fragrant long"). Franco agrees, noting that when several notes on the same pitch occur in succession, only the first is articulated and all together are sung *in floratura*.'[24]

Leaving aside for the time being the question of the relationship of the two passages – indeed, whether they have anything at all to do with each other – one can at least state that Roesner's paraphrase does no particular violence to the Latin. But again one has questions about what the passage should be taken to mean. Roesner cites Franco to make the point that the upper voice of organum purum was performed in a florid style – in a style, moreover, that was not just inherently florid, but one that 'appears to have been subjected to still greater embellishment in performance'.[25] In support of this view, Roesner follows his paraphrase of the problematic sentence in Franco with another passage in Anonymous IV, linked to the first two by the appearance of the word *florata*. Quoting Roesner again: 'Anonymous IV . . . recommends that the first, consonant tenor–duplum sonority in a piece be rendered as a *duplex longa florata* – that

---

[24] Roesner, 'The Performance of Parisian Organum', p. 176.   [25] *Ibid.*

is, held out, and executed with a flourish.'[26] Roesner then goes on to portray the outlines of what such embellished, 'floratura' performance might be like, drawing upon the supplement to the treatise of Johannes de Garlandia – presumably attributable to Jerome of Moravia[27] – and Jerome's own treatise on plainchant.

Roesner first discusses the *florificatio vocis* that appears in the section on *colores* in the supplement to Johannes de Garlandia,[28] explaining it by reference to Jerome's *flos harmonicus*, a slow *vibratio* or oscillation between the principal note and an ornamental note a semitone or whole tone above it.[29] Other ornaments Jerome mentions are the *reverberatio*, 'a short, rapid, appoggiatura-like ornament that approaches the main note from below',[30] and the *nota procellaris* ('agitated note'), 'in which the main note oscillates slowly with an ornamental one that appears to lie a half step away, and that has "the definite appearance of movement, but without interrupting the sound or the pitch"'.[31]

Roesner goes on to discuss in rich detail the possibilities for embellishment of organum purum, all presumably capable of being subsumed under Franco's term 'floratura'. Indeed, Roesner says of the *florificatio vocis* that 'Without doubt Jerome's example is also related to the devices mentioned by Franco and Anonymous IV'.[32]

Roesner may well be right, but I must admit to some doubts, at

---

[26]   *Ibid.*   [27]   I shall refer to the author of this supplement as 'Pseudo-Garlandia'.
[28]   Reimer, *Johannes de Garlandia*, I, p. 95.
[29]   For Jerome's discussion of the *flos harmonicus*, see Cserba, *Hieronymus de Moravia*, pp. 183–8. It is clear from Jerome's description of the *flos harmonicus* that it is indeed performed as Roesner ('The Performance of Parisian Organum', p. 177) states. What is not so clear is its connection with Pseudo-Garlandia's *florificatio vocis*. Roesner is convinced that the connection is close, and that the *florificatio vocis* 'is not an attempted graphic representation of some medieval ancestor of the early Baroque *trillo*' (p. 177). From his study of the term and concept of *color* in the thirteenth and fourteenth centuries, R. Voogt ('Repetition and Structure in the Three- and Four-Part Conductus of the Notre Dame School' [Ph.D. dissertation, The Ohio State University, 1982], pp. 23–67, esp. pp. 34–48) is equally convinced that the *florificatio vocis* is in fact what Roesner says it is not – namely, a series of repetitions of a single pitch, which in performance would probably sound rather like the Baroque *trillo*. Voogt feels that the model for Pseudo-Garlandia's *florificatio vocis* may have been the repercussive neumes of plainchant, examples of which also appear in the Aquitanian versus (cf. Voogt, Repetition and Structure', p. 40, and S. Fuller, 'Aquitanian Polyphony of the Eleventh and Twelfth Centuries' [Ph.D. dissertation, University of California at Berkeley, 1969], III, nos. 20–4).
[30]   Roesner, 'The Performance of Parisian Organum', p. 177. For Jerome's description of the *reverberatio* see Cserba, *Hieronymus de Moravia*, pp. 183–7.
[31]   'Nota procellaris in cantu fieri debet cum apparenti quidem motus absque tamen soni vel vocis interruptione' (Cserba, *Hieronymus de Moravia*, p. 185); translation from Roesner, 'The Performance of Parisian Organum', p. 177.
[32]   Roesner, 'The Performance of Parisian Organum', p. 177.

least vis-à-vis Franco. I am not at all sure that Franco's statement should be related to the types of embellishment Roesner discusses, nor am I sure that it should be placed in apposition to the statements by Anonymous IV on the *longa florata*. Why? To gain an answer, let us return to Franco's statement (Excerpt 6) and analyse it more closely with reference to the interpretations already suggested, and then see if there might not be available to us any alternative interpretative possibilities.

Franco states that whenever, in organum purum, several 'figurae' occur together 'in unisono', only the first ought to be 'percuti'; all of the remainder should be taken 'in floratura'.

Our first question here, I think, should be 'What is a *figura*?' The author of the *Discantus positio vulgaris*[33] does not use the term at all, preferring instead the term *nota*.[34] Johannes de Garlandia begins the second chapter of his work by saying: 'Sequitur de repraesentatione figurarum sive notularum, videlicet quomodo per huiusmodi figuras denotetur longitudo vel brevitas. Unde figura est repraesentatio soni secundum suum modum.' (Reimer, *Johannes de Garlandia*, I, p. 44; 'The following concerns the representation of the *figurae* or *notae*, that is, in what fashion length or brevity may be denoted by means of such figures. Whence, *figura* is the representation of sound according to its mode.')

In Jerome's version of John's treatise the corresponding version of the passage reads: '*Figura*, as it is taken here, is a sign denoting a sound – or sounds – in length and brevity according to its tempus.'[35] Finally, Franco himself had defined *figura* in the following manner at the beginning of his fourth chapter: 'Figura est repraesentatio vocis in aliquo modorum ordinatae, per quod patet quod figurae signifi-

---

[33] Cserba, *Hieronymus de Moravia*, pp. 189–94, and *CS* I, pp. 94b–97; translated by Janet Knapp in 'Two XIII-Century Treatises on Modal Rhythm and the Discant', *Journal of Music Theory*, 6 (1962), pp. 200–16.

[34] The word *nota* had, since Antiquity, carried the meaning of a 'graphic sign', 'mark' or 'character', and was used from late Antiquity (cf. Boethius, *De institutione musica*, bk IV, ch. 3) through the Middle Ages (cf. Jacques de Liège, *Speculum musicae*, bk VI, ch. 72) as the standard designation for the graphic signs representing music. For further discussion and bibliography see M. Huglo, 'Les noms des neumes et leur origine', *Études Grégoriennes*, 1 (1954), pp. 53–67; A.-M. Bautier-Régnier, 'A propos du sens de *neuma* et de *nota* en latin médiéval', *Revue Belge de Musicologie*, 18 (1964), pp. 1–9; B. Stäblein, *Schriftbild der einstimmigen Musik*, Musikgeschichte in Bildern, III: Musik des Mittelalters und der Renaissance, Lfg 4 (Leipzig, 1975), pp. 6–8, 19, 26, 30, and S. Corbin, *Die Neumen*, Paläographie der Musik, I/3 (Cologne, 1977), pp. 3.1–3.5.

[35] 'Figura, ut hic accipitur, est signum denotans sonum vel sonos secundum suum tempus longitudinis atque brevitatis' (Cserba, *Hieronymus de Moravia*, p. 197).

care debent modos, et non e converso.' (CSM 18, p. 29; '*Figura* is a representation of pitch disposed in some one of the modes, through which it is evident that figures ought to signify modes, and not the converse.') The term *figura* is one that for Franco seems to have the significance of a graphic notational sign conveying a fixed rhythmic value or values.[36]

---

[36] Franco and Johannes de Garlandia are not alone among thirteenth-century theorists in using the term *figura* in this way. Cf. the St Emmeram Anonymous: 'Cum ergo figura sit causa et principium omnis cantus, que et sub certa diminutione temporis seu temporum mensurata compositioni huius artis fons esse dicitur et origo' (Sowa, *Ein anonymer glossierter Mensuraltraktat*, p. 13, lines 9–12). What is unusual about this is that *figura* should have been used at all as a designation for a notational sign. As mentioned in n. 34, the standard medieval designation for the graphic signs used to represent music was *nota*, not *figura*. The most common use of the term *figura* in earlier treatises on music is to indicate a diagram (e.g. Aribo, *De musica* [c. 1070], ed. J. Smits van Waesberghe, CSM 2 [Rome, 1951], pp. 1–5; the *Quaestiones in musica* [c. 1120] attributed to Rudolf of St Trond [1070–1138], ed. R. Steglich, *Publikationen der Internationalen Musik-Gesellschaft*, Beihefte, II/10 [Leipzig, 1911], p. 18), although it is sometimes used to designate pitches, particularly in conjunction with the measurement of the monochord (e.g. Pseudo-Odo, *Dialogus in musica*, ed. M. Gerbert, *Scriptores Ecclesiastici de Musica*, I [St Blasien, 1784; repr. Milan, 1931], p. 253b; Guido, *Micrologus*, CSM 4 [1955], pp. 91–5; Wilhelm of Hirsau, *Musica*, ed. D. Harbinson, CSM 23 [1975], p. 74). As far as I have been able to determine, the earliest use of *figura* as a term designating practical notational signs seems to be in the thirteenth century, in treatises dealing with mensurable music. Although it is sometimes equated with *nota*, as in both Anon. VII and Anon. IV (cf. Reckow, *Der Musiktraktat des Anonymus 4*, I, pp. 40–1), *figura* – especially when used by itself – carries with it the connotation of a precise, measurable value. This usage must derive from its long tradition as a technical term in mathematics. (Cf. Bede's *De temporum ratione*, ed. C. W. Jones, *Bedae opera de temporibus* [Cambridge, MA, 1943], p. 181, lines 76–82, or the various mathematical works either by or attributed to Gerbert of Aurillac [later Pope Silvester II], ed. N. Bubnov, *Gerberti . . . Opera mathematica (972–1003)* [Berlin, 1899], *passim* [see Index].) Its association with mathematics may likewise have had something to do with use of *figura* in the theory of metrics, although the term already had a connection with poetry via rhetoric. (See, for example, the poem on metrical theory attributed to Walahfrid Strabo, ed. J. Huemer, *Neues Archiv der Gesellschaft für ältere deutsche Geschichtskunde*, 10 [1885], pp. 166–9, where *figura* seems to be synonymous with 'verse'. On rhetorical figures, see L. Arbusow, *Colores rhetorici* [Göttingen, 1948], E. Faral, *Les arts poétiques du XIIᵉ et du XIIIᵉ siècle* [Paris, 1924], and J. Murphy, *Rhetoric in the Middle Ages* [Berkeley, 1974].) It is worth noting here that the author of the *Summa musicae* (c. 1300), attributed to Johannes de Muris, comments that 'nota idem operatur in cantu, quod figura in metro', and goes on to say that 'Est enim intentio actoris in cantu & actoris in metro una in genere, scilicet ut vox cum materia dictaminis sui (concordet)' (Gerbert, *Scriptores*, III, p. 234b).

A terminological study of *figura* is still lacking; when done, it should provide fascinating insights into the relationships between music and its sister *artes* in the Middle Ages. M. Appel's *Terminologie in den mittelalterlichen Musiktraktaten* (Berlin, 1935), p. 9, and H. P. Gysin's *Studien zum Vokabular der Musiktheorie im Mittelalter* (Amsterdam, 1958), pp. 98–9, 104, are useful starting-points. I offer the above references – whose list is by no means complete – as a small additional contribution to such a study. I should here like to thank Dr Theresia Payr of the *Mittellateinisches Wörterbuch* and Dr Michael Bernhard of the *Lexicon musicum latinum* (both in Munich), and Dr Christoph von Blumröder of the *Handwörterbuch der musikalischen Terminologie* (Freiburg im Breisgau), for permission to work in their respective archives during the summers of 1982 and 1986 in preparation for this essay.

The next problematic phrase in Franco's sentence 7 (see Excerpt 6) is 'in unisono'. This could mean 'at the same pitch level' as it does in *Discantus positio vulgaris*: 'A ligature is the binding together of several successive notes – something which cannot be effected with notes of the same pitch' (*in unisono*).[37] If one applies this meaning to sentence 7 in Franco, the phrase would seem to refer to the iterations of the pitch f – four times altogether – in the musical example that follows this sentence.[38] Such a view is reinforced by the version of this example that appears in the manuscript Paris, Bibliothèque Nationale, fonds lat. 16663, the one containing Jerome of Moravia's compilation.[39] In that manuscript only the duplum is given, not the tenor, suggesting that it is primarily the duplum with which Franco is concerned here.

But there is yet another possible meaning for the phrase 'in unisono', one that is suggested by Johannes de Garlandia and even by Franco himself. The ninth sentence of Johannes's treatment of organum *in speciali*, in the section devoted to organum *cum alio*, contains the phrase *in unisono*: 'Et eius aequipollentia tantum se tenet *in unisono* usque ad finem alicuius puncti, ut secum convenit secundum aliquam concordantiam.' ('And its equivalence is maintained *in unisono* as far as the end of a section, so that it can come together with it in some consonance.')[40] All modern authors I know of have taken the phrase 'in unisono' here to be a reference to the sustained, single pitch in the tenor.[41] Franco, too, had used the phrase in a similar fashion in the second sentence of the present chapter (cf. Excerpt 3 above): 'Sciendum quod purum organum haberi non potest, nisi supra tenorem ubi sola nota est *in unisono* . . .' ('One should know that organum purum cannot obtain except over a tenor where there is a single note on a single pitch [*in unisono*]'.) Taking the phrase 'in unisono' to be a reference to a sustained pitch in the tenor, one might translate the first clause of Franco's now-familiar sentence 7 (Excerpt 6) as 'whenever several figures come

---

[37] 'Ligatura est plurium notarum invicem conjunctarum ligatio, quae quidem *in unisono* fieri non debet' (Cserba, *Hieronymus de Moravia*, p. 190; my italics). The translation is by Janet Knapp ('Two XIII-Century Treatises', p. 203).

[38] This interpretation is advanced by both Voogt ('Repetition and Structure', pp. 40–3) and Roesner ('The Performance of Parisian Organum', p. 176) in their respective interpretations of the passage in question here.

[39] See Cserba, *Hieronymus de Moravia*, p. 259.

[40] Cf. n. 14 above.

[41] See, for example, the works cited in n. 15 above.

together over a single pitch in the tenor'. Still, this interpretation is not one that I wish to push too far – at least, not yet.

This brings us to the final clause in the sentence (Excerpt 6) and to the last and most difficult pair of words of all: *percuti* and *floratura*. The clause reads as follows: 'sola prima debet percuti, reliquae vero omnes in floratura teneantur'.[42] As we saw earlier, Strunk translates this phrase 'only the first is to be sounded; let all the rest observe the florid style'.[43] Roesner's version is 'when several notes on the same pitch occur in succession, only the first is articulated and all together are sung in floratura'.[44] I should like to suggest that there is yet another way to read this passage.

Both *percuti* and *floratura* are words that are quite rare in writings on music, not only in the twelfth and thirteenth centuries, but virtually throughout the Middle Ages. Of the two, 'percuti', the passive infinitive of the verb *percutio* (to strike), and its nominative form, *percussio*, are the more common, being used in Boethius, Cassiodorus, Isidore and other writers to refer to either the striking or plucking of the strings of an instrument, or to the vibrations created by such striking.[45]

At the same time, though, there is another usage of these terms that has a venerable tradition of its own that starts in Antiquity and continues through the thirteenth century and beyond. Although it is most closely connected with the arts of grammar and rhetoric, this usage is at the same time intrinsically linked to music. I am referring here to the tradition of demarcating or 'beating' the temporal units of metric poetry, described not just via the words *percutio* or *percussio*, but also with the terms *ictus* and *plausus*.[46]

The fundamental principle of *percussio* is described well by the fourth-century grammarian Marius Victorinus: 'est autem *percussio* cuiuslibet metri in pedes divisio'[47] ('*Percussio* is the division of any

---

[42] CSM 18, pp. 81–2.

[43] Strunk, *Source Readings*, p. 159.

[44] Roesner, 'The Performance of Parisian Organum', p. 176.

[45] Cf. Boethius, *De institutione musica libri quinque*, ed. G. Friedlein (Leipzig, 1867), I, 3, p. 189, lines 15–19, 22–3, and I, 31, p. 222, lines 6–12; Cassiodorus, *Institutiones*, ed. R. A. B. Mynors (Oxford, 1937), II, 5, sections 6 and 7, also in Gerbert, *Scriptores*, I, pp. 16–17; Isidore, *Etymologiarum sive Originum libri xx*, ed. W. M. Lindsay, 2 vols. (Oxford, 1911), bk III, section 22, also in Gerbert, *Scriptores*, I, pp. 23–4.

[46] For a treatment of these terms in Antiquity, see R. Wagner, 'Der Berliner Notenpapyrus, nebst Untersuchungen zur rhythmischen Notierung und Theorie', *Philologus*, 77 (1921), pp. 256–310, esp. pp. 301–7.

[47] '*Percutitur* vero versus anapaestus praecipue per dipodian, interdum et per singulos pedes.

metre into feet'). Perhaps the earliest evidence for *percussio* as a *terminus technicus* is found in Cicero, *De oratore*: 'Among the variety of metres, the frequent use of the iambus and the tribrach is forbidden to the orator by Aristotle, the master of your school, Catulus. They nonetheless invade our oratory and conversational style by natural affinity; but the *percussiones* of their rhythms are (strongly) marked, and their feet are short.'[48] Quintilian's *Institutio oratoria* provides a number of instances. In book 9, for example, in urging the orator not to employ verse, such as iambic trimeter, in prose, he says: 'One can refer to [this verse] as either trimetrum or senarium, since it has six feet and three *percussiones*.'[49]

That these *percussiones* were actually beaten, and that their beating could at times be rather noisy, is suggested by a passage in Rufinus's commentary on the metres of Terence. Bassus says to Nero: 'Moreover the iambic: Whenever it assumes feet of the dactylic genus, the iambic appears to end unless you should dispose it by means of the *percussio* so that whenever you stamp your foot [*pedem supplodes*], you strike an iamb; therefore those places of the *percussio* do not receive anything other than the iamb and a tribrach equal to it, or they will have exhibited another species of metre.'[50]

The examples I have just cited are only a few among a great many that could be adduced to document the use of *percussio* in Antiquity. For the Middle Ages, however, the *locus classicus* for both the theory and practice of *percutio*, as well as *ictus* and *plausus*, is Augustine.[51] His

---

est autem *percussio* cuiuslibet metri in pedes divisio.' Marius Victorinus, *Artis grammaticae libri III*, in H. Keil, *Grammatici latini*, 8 vols. (Leipzig, 1855–80), VI, p. 75, lines 26–9 (my italics).

[48] 'Nam cum sint numeri plures, iambum et trochaeum frequentem segregat ab oratore Aristoteles, Catule, vester; qui natura tamen incurrunt ipsi in orationem sermonemque nostrum, sed sunt insignes *percussiones* eorum numerorum e minuti pedes.' Cicero, *De oratore*, ed. and trans. H. H. Rackham (Cambridge, MA, 1942), III, 182–3, pp. 144–5 (my italics; the translation is a modified version of Rackham's). See also *De oratore*, III, 185–6, and *Orator*, ed. and trans. H. M. Hubbell (London, 1952), 198–9.

[49] 'Trimetrum et senarium promisce dicere licet, sex enim pedes, tres *percussiones* habet.' Quintilian, *Institutio oratoria*, ed. and trans. H. E. Butler (London, 1953), IX, 4, 75, pp. 548–9 (my italics). See also *Institutio oratoria* IX, 4, 51–2, and XI, 3, 108–9.

[50] 'Jambicus autem, cum pedes etiam dactylici generis adsumat, desinit iambicus videri, nisi *percussione* ita moderaveris, ut, cum pedem supplodes, iambum ferias; ideoque illa loca *percussionis* non recipiunt alium quam iambum et ei parem tribrachyn, aut alterius exhibuerint metri speciem.' Rufinus, *Commentarium in metra Terentiana*, in Keil, *Grammatici latini*, VI, p. 555, lines 23–7 (my italics).

[51] Edition and French translation by G. Finaert and F.-J. Thonnard, *De musica libri sex*, Oeuvres de Saint Augustin, 1re série: Opuscules, VII: *Dialogues philosophiques*, IV: *La musique* (Bruges, 1947); English translation by R. C. Taliaferro in *Writings of Saint Augustine*, II, Fathers of the Church 4 (New York, 1947).

De musica abounds in references to these terms.[52] For our purposes two will have to suffice.

In book II, chapter 13, the master says that he will run through several poetic feet 'with the accompanying *plausus*' so that the disciple may see whether there is any flaw. He tells the student: 'Fix your ears on the sound and your eyes on the beat [*plausus*]. For the hand beating time is not to be heard but seen, and note must be taken of the amount of time given to the arsis and to the thesis.'[53] After this has been done, the student says: 'I certainly wonder how those feet with a division in a ratio of one to two could have been beaten [*percutio*] to this time.'[54]

In book IV, chapter 1, the following dialogue takes place between master and student: M. 'What quantity must the rest be when it is repeated? D. One tempus, the length of one short syllable [*brevis*]. M. Come now, beat [*percute*] this meter, not with the voice, but with the hand. D. I have. M. Then beat the anapest in the same way.'[55]

As mentioned, many more examples of the use of *percutio* and *plausus* in Augustine could be cited. For our purposes, though, it is necessary to ask whether any of this might have been known to Franco in the mid- to late thirteenth century. The answer, I believe, must be 'Yes'. Evidence for this comes from several aspects of Franco's treatise itself – such as his justification for the perfect long of three tempora[56] – and from at least two authors intimately involved

---

52 Since there is no *Index verborum* for the edition, I provide a list of these references here, listed by book, chapter, and section: *Percutio:* I, I, 1; II, XI, 20; II, XIII, 24; IV, I, 1; IV, VII, 8; VI, V, 11; VI, VIII, 20. *Percussio:* II, XI, 20; II, XI, 21; IV, II, 2; IV, XIV, 24; VI, X, 25. *Plaudo:* I, V, 10; I, XIII, 27; II, X, 18; II, XIII, 24; II, XIII, 25; II, XIV, 26; III, IV, 9; III, VII, 15; III, VII, 16; IV, II, 2; IV, XI, 12; IV, XVI, 30; IV, XVI, 33; V, XI, 24; VI, I, 1; VI, X, 27; *Plausus:* I, XI, 11; I, XIII, 27; II, XI, 20; II, XIII, 24; II, XIII, 25; II, XIV, 26; III, III, 5; III, III, 6; III, IV, 7; III, IV, 8; III, IV, 9; III, IV, 10; III, V, 11; III, V, 12; III, VII, 15; III, VIII, 18; IV, I, 1; IV, II, 2; IV, VII, 8; IV, XVII, 35; V, XI, 24; VI, X, 27; VI, XIV, 47. *Ictus:* I, IV, 9.

53 'Intende ergo et aurem in sonum, et in *plausum* oculos: non enim audiri, sed videri opus est plaudentem manum, et animadverti acriter quanta temporis mora in levatione, quanta in positione sit.' Augustine, *De musica*, II, XIII, 24; Taliaferro translation, p. 233.

54 'Vehementer admiror quomodo eo *percuti* potuerint illi pedes, quorum divisio simpli et dupli ratione constat.' *Ibid.*; my italics.

55 'M. Quantum ergo silendum est, dum repetitur? D. Unum tempus, quod est unius brevis syllabae spatium. M. Age, jam *percute* hoc metrum, non voce, sed *plausu*. D. Feci. M. *Percute* etiam hoc modo anapaestum. D. Et hoc feci.' Augustine, *De musica*, IV, I, 1; Taliaferro, p. 260.

56 Franco defines the perfect long as follows: '(6) Longa perfecta prima dicitur et principalis. (7) Nam in ea omnes aliae includuntur, ad eam etiam omnes aliae reducuntur. (8) *Perfecta dicitur eo quod tribus temporibus mensuratur*' (CSM 18, p. 29; my italics). His justification for this new concept of the long is: 'Est enim ternarius numerus inter numeros perfectissimus pro eo quod a summa trinitate, quae vera est et pura perfectio, nomen sumpsit' (CSM

with mid-thirteenth-century Parisian intellectual life with whom Franco may have had contact: Roger Bacon and John of Garland.[57] In his *Opus majus* and *Opus tertium*, both apparently completed in 1267,[58] Bacon exhorts his colleagues to the study of the liberal arts with the aim of 'reforming the teaching of Christian wisdom', as Etienne Gilson puts it.[59] As one might expect of Bacon, his primary focus is upon the mathematical arts, including music. But whereas Boethius is his prime authority for arithmetic, his chief witness for music is not Boethius, but rather Augustine.[60] Accordingly, Bacon spends much of his time discussing metrics, drawing a large portion of his discussion in the *Opus tertium* directly from Augustine, specifically from the second book. At the end of this section, just before turning to a defence of mathematics in general, he states that

18, pp. 29–30; my italics). I would posit that the source of this justification was Augustine. Cf. Augustine's statement on the perfection of the number three in I, XII, 20 of *De musica*: 'Quare in *ternario numero* quamdam esse *perfectionem* vides, quia totus est: habet enim principium, medium et finem' (Finaert and Thonnard, p. 70; my italics).

[57] On Bacon, see A. B. Emden, 'Bacon', *A Biographical Register of the University of Oxford to A.D. 1500*, I (Oxford, 1957), pp. 87–8. The principal source of biographical material for Emden's article is S. C. Easton, *Roger Bacon and his Search for a Universal Science* (New York, 1952). See also J. S. Brewer, ed., *Fr. Rogeri Bacon opera quaedam hactenus inedita*, Rerum Britannicarum Medii Aevi Scriptores (Rolls Series) 15 (London, 1859; repr. Frankfurt, 1964), Preface, and R. B. Burke, trans., *The Opus majus of Roger Bacon* (New York, 1928; repr. 1962), Introduction. For the place of Bacon's work within the intellectual life of the thirteenth century, see P. Kibre, 'The *Quadrivium* in the Thirteenth Century Universities', *Arts libéraux et philosophie au moyen âge: Actes du quatrième congrès international de philosophie médiévale*, 1967 (Montreal, 1969), pp. 175–91, and L. Ellinwood, 'Ars musica', *Speculum*, 20 (1945), pp. 290–9. The starting-point for any study of John of Garland must be L. J. Paetow, *The Morale Scolarium of John of Garland, with an Introduction to his Life and Works*, Memoirs of the University of California, IV/2 (Berkeley, 1927). See also Paetow's *The Arts Course at Medieval Universities, with Special Reference to Grammar and Rhetoric*, The University of Illinois: The University Studies, III/7 (Urbana-Champaign, 1910), and T. Lawler, *The Parisiana Poetria of John of Garland*, Yale Studies in the History of English 182 (New Haven, 1974), Introduction.

[58] *Opus majus*, ed. J. H. Bridges, *The 'Opus majus' of Roger Bacon* (London, 1900; repr. Frankfurt, 1964); *Opus tertium*, ed. Brewer, *Fr. Rogeri Bacon opera quaedam hactenus inedita*, pp. 1–310. According to Easton, *Roger Bacon*, p. 153, the two works were composed in the same year. Bacon's own remarks in the *Opus tertium* (e.g. 'Nam secundum quod exposui in Opere Majori . . .', Brewer, *Opus tertium*, p. 228) make it clear that the *Opus majus* was the earlier of the two works.

[59] E. Gilson, *History of Christian Philosophy in the Middle Ages* (New York, 1955), p. 294. This remark was made specifically with regard to the *Opus majus*, but certainly pertains to its companion work as well. On the relationship of these two works to each other and to Bacon's *Opus minus*, see Easton, *Roger Bacon*, pp. 144–66.

[60] Cf. Waite, *The Rhythm of Twelfth-Century Polyphony*, p. 36. The fact that Boethius plays such an important role in Bacon's discussion of arithmetic, but a distinctly secondary role in his discussion of music, is not mentioned by Waite, but it further buttresses his own case for the influence of Augustine on the development of the system of the rhythmic modes (*ibid.*, pp. 29–39).

motions of various kinds – gesticulation, exultation, leaping, clapping, singing, and all the movements of the body – are an important component of music. He continues: 'This indeed is a necessary part of music, just as Augustine teaches in the second book of his *Musica*, saying that *plausus* is necessary, because delight is necessary not only for the hearing but for the eye' – a direct reference to book II, chapter 13 quoted above.[61]

That the theory and practice of *percutio* were known not just to students of theology, but to poets and musicians as well, is suggested finally by the use of the term in a work by John of Garland – a man himself mentioned favourably by Roger Bacon in 1272,[62] and one whose putative connections with music are well known.[63] In his *Parisiana poetria de arte prosaica, metrica, et rithmica*, written in the first half of the thirteenth century, John provides a rather full discussion of poetic metres in his chapters on *Rithmica*.[64] As the following excerpt will show, this discussion makes extensive use of the concept of *percussio*, beginning with discussion of the simplest type of rhythmic poetry, the iambic dimeter:

A simpliciori igitur erit inchoandum, scilicet a rithmo qui constat ex duabus *percussionibus*, quia, cum rithmus imitetur metrum in aliquo, illud metrum quod est breuius constat ex duabus *percussionibus*, sicut iambicum dimetrum, quod constat ex duobus metris, et metrum ex duabus *percussionibus* . . . Rithmus dispondaicus continet quattuor *percussiones*, que sunt ex quattuor dictionibus uel partibus earundem dictionum. (Lawler, *Parisiana poetria*, p. 160; my italics.)

---

[61] 'Illa enim est pars necessaria musicae, sicut *Augustinus docet secundo Musicae*, dicens quod *plausus* necessarius est, quia non solum est delectatio auditus necessaria, sed visus.' Bacon, *Opus tertium*, cap. LXIV, ed. Brewer, *Opus tertium*, pp. 267–8 (my italics). Cf. the passage quoted from Augustine, II, XIII, 24, cited in n. 53 above.

[62] Cf. Paetow, *Morale scolarium*, pp. 95–6. See also Lawler, *Parisiana poetria*, p. xi.

[63] Among the many works attempting to answer this question, see in particular A. Machabey, 'Jean de Garlande, compositeur', *Revue Musicale*, no. 221 (1953), pp. 20–2; W. Waite, 'Johannes de Garlandia: Poet and Musician', *Speculum*, 35 (1960), pp. 179–95; R. A. Rasch, *Iohannes de Garlandia en de ontwikkeling van de voor-Franconische notatie*, Musicological Studies 20 (Brooklyn, 1969), and most recently Reimer, *Johannes de Garlandia*, I, pp. 1–17. Reimer feels that John of Garland the poet and Johannes de Garlandia the author of *De mensurabili musica* are not the same person.

[64] Ed. Lawler, *Parisiana poetria*. For a study of the relationship of John's *Parisiana poetria* to the contemporaneous Parisian sequence and, in turn, to the theory and practice of rhythm in the late twelfth and thirteenth centuries, see M. Fassler, 'The Role of the Parisian Sequence in the Evolution of Notre-Dame Polyphony', *Speculum*, 62 (1987), pp. 345–74. Like the present author, Fassler underscores the importance of the beat or *ictus*, which John of Garland describes with the term *percussio* (see in particular pp. 358–61 of Fassler's study).

('We should begin with what is simplest, namely with a rhymed poem whose line consists of two stresses, for rhymed poetry imitates quantitative poetry in various ways, and the shortest quantitative measure consists of two stresses; iambic dimeter, for instance, has two measures, and each measure has two stresses ... A dispondaic couplet has four stresses, whether in four separate words or as parts of the same words.' *Ibid.*, p. 161)

Clearly, the concept of *percussio* as a rhythmic beat or stress was current in mid-thirteenth-century Paris. That it had also penetrated into musical theory by the late thirteenth century is demonstrated by its use in the music treatise of Johannes de Grocheio. In his description of the ductia, we find the following words: 'A ductia is an untexted musical piece [*sonus*] measured with an appropriate beat [*percussio*]. I say ... "with a proper beat" because strokes [*ictus*] measure it and the motion of the person performing it, and they impel one's spirit to ornate movement according to the art that they call dancing, and they measure its motion in *ductiae* and *choreii*.'[65] Later he makes the statement: 'To compose a ductia or stantipes is to demarcate the piece via puncta and proper *percussiones* [beats].'[66]

I believe that we have now heard enough testimony to suggest a new reading for *percuti* in Franco's seventh sentence. But what to make of *floratura*? This word is so rare that there is only one witness to it in the entire card file of the *Mittellateinisches Wörterbuch* in Munich, not to mention any other of the medieval Latin dictionaries or glossaries I have consulted.[67] That single reference is the one found

---

[65] 'Est autem ductia sonus illitteratus, cum decenti percussione mensuratus. Dico ... *cum recta percussione*, eo quod ictus eam mensurant et motum facientis et excitant animum hominis ad ornate movendum secundum artem, quam ballare vocant, et eius motum mensurant in ductiis et choreiis.' Johannes de Grocheio, [*De musica*], ed. E. Rohloff, *Der Musiktraktat des Johannes de Grocheo*, Media Latinitas Musica 2 (Leipzig, 1943), p. 52, lines 38–44, and Rohloff, ed., *Die Quellenhandschriften zum Musiktraktat des Johannes de Grocheio* (Leipzig, n.d.), p. 136, lines 13–20.

[66] 'Componere ductiam et stantipedem est sonum per puncta et rectas *percussiones* in ductia et stantipede determinare.' Rohloff, *Der Musiktraktat*, p. 53, lines 23–4; *Die Quellenhandschriften*, p. 136, lines 147–8.

[67] The lexica and glossaries consulted include the following: F. Arnaldi, *Latinitatis italicae medii aevi ... lexicon imperfectum* (Brussels, 1939); A. Bartal, *Glossarium mediae et infimae latinitatis regni hungariae* (Leipzig, 1901; repr. Hildesheim, 1970); J. H. Baxter and C. Johnson, *Medieval Latin Word List from British and Irish Sources* (Oxford, 1934); A. Blaise, *Lexicon latinitatis medii aevi*, Corpus Christianorum, Continuatio Medievalis (Turnhout, 1975); A. Castro, *Glosarios latino-españoles de la edad media* (Madrid, 1936); L. Diefenbach, *Glossarium latino-germanicum mediae et infimae aetatis* (Frankfurt, 1857); C. Du Cange, *Glossarium mediae et infimae latinitatis* (Niort, 1883–7; repr. Graz, 1954); A. Forcellini, *Totius latinitatis lexicon* (Padua, 1864–98); *Glossarium mediae latinitatis sueciae* (Stockholm, 1968); R. E. Latham, *Revised Medieval Latin Word List from British and Irish Sources* (Oxford, 1965); *Lexicon mediae et infimae latinitatis polonorum* (Wrocław, Warsaw, Kraków and Gdańsk,

in Franco. There is, however, at least one other appearance of the word that may finally solve the puzzle of *percuti* and *floratura*.

In the seventh book of his *Speculum musicae*, Jacques de Liège, a great admirer and ardent glossator of Franco's treatise, makes the following statement in his chapter 'Quid sit cantus mensurabilis':

Haec et alia multa ars requirit mensurabilis . . . et propterea cantus hic dicitur quia in eo distinctae voces simul sub aliqua temporis morula certa vel incerta proferuntur. Dico autem 'incerta' propter organum duplum quod ubique non est certa temporis mensura mensuratum ut, in *floraturis*, in penultimis ubi supra vocem unam tenoris in discantu multae sonantur voces.[68]

'The art of mensurable [music] requires these and many other things . . . and for that reason [this type of] cantus is discussed at this point, because in it diverse pitches are performed under some determinate or indeterminate sustaining of the time. I say "indeterminate", moreover, on account of organum duplum, which is not measured everywhere in a fixed measure of time, as for example in *floraturae* on penultimates [notes or syllables] where many pitches are sounded in the discant over one pitch of the tenor' (my italics).

Jacques's use and description of *floratura* forges a direct terminological and conceptual link with Franco. The problematic final

---

1975); W.-H. Maigne d'Arnis, *Lexicon manuale ad scriptores mediae et infimae latinitatis* (Paris, 1866); J. F. Niermeyer, *Mediae latinitatis lexicon minus* (Leiden, 1976); A. Souter, *A Glossary of Later Latin to 600 A.D.* (Oxford, 1949); *Thesavrvs lingvae latinae* (Leipzig, 1940–).

[68] Jacques de Liège, *Speculum musicae*, ed. R. Bragard, *Jacobi Leodiensis Specvlvm mvsicae*, CSM 3 (1973), bk VII, cap. II, pp. 7–8. The edition reads 'fioraturis' instead of 'floraturis'. For the passage in question, however, both of the manuscripts containing it (Florence, Biblioteca Medicea-Laurenziana, Plut. 29.16, fol. 122ᵛ, and Paris, Bibliothèque Nationale, fonds lat. 7207, fol. 275ᵛ) have 'floraturis', with 'l', not 'i', in the first syllable. I wish to thank Dr Anna Lenzuni, of the Biblioteca Medicea-Laurenziana, and Dr François Avril, of the Bibliothèque Nationale, for their assistance in confirming these readings.

I should also like to thank Professor Peter Lefferts for informing me (in a letter of 30 November 1988) of two further references to *floritura/floratura*. The first is in maxim 11 of rubric XIII of Robertus de Handlo's *Regule*, in which Handlo gives examples of the types of music exhibiting the fifth of Franco's rhythmic modes, consisting of breves and semibreves (I quote from the draft text of Professor Lefferts's forthcoming edition of the treatise): 'Ab hoc siquidem modo proveniunt hoketi omnes, rundelli, ballade, coree, cantifractus, estampete, floriture, . . .' (cf. *CS* I, p. 402b). The second reference occurs in both versions of the *quartum principale* of the *Quatuor principalia* (*CS* III, p. 354b=*CS* IV, p. 278a): 'Discantus enim sic dividitur . . . alius est copulatus qui dicitur copula, id est floritura.' As Lefferts points out, this passage is a gloss on Franco's initial mention of *copula* as a type of discant in chapter 2 of the *Ars cantus mensurabilis* (CSM 18, p. 26). As both of these references would suggest, the relationship between *copula* and *floritura* is one that deserves a thoroughgoing treatment. (I should note here that the *quartum principale*, glossing the first sentence of Franco's chapter on organum purum, says 'organum proprie sumptum mensuram non retinet' [*CS* III, p. 363b=*CS* IV, p. 297a], but does not mention *floratura* in this context; indeed, it does not treat of sentence 7 of the chapter at all.)

sentence (sentence 7, Excerpt 6 above) of Franco's discussion of organum purum can now be read as follows: 'It should be noted that whenever in organum purum several *figurae* come together over a single pitch [in the tenor], only the first should be beaten in fixed rhythm; all the rest should be taken in *floratura* [that is, performed in a rhythmically free fashion].'

The formal picture one gets from this passage in Franco and its parallel in Jacques de Liège is one in which a section of organum begins over a penultimate in the tenor with the duplum in fixed rhythm, the rhythm of discant, but which ends in non-fixed rhythm. It is thus reminiscent of a passage in the de la Fage Anonymous, in which the author states that if one wants to make discant more beautiful and elegant, one can place a section of organum at the end, 'on either the ultimate or penultimate syllable of the text'.[69] This is of course a technique found rather frequently in the polyphony of both St Martial and Notre Dame. It is also a technique documented by Franco himself. In chapter XI of his work, as mentioned earlier, Franco had stated that discant should continue in its measured rhythm 'as far as the *penultimate*, where such measure is not attendant, there being rather a *point of organum in that place*'.[70]

Following Franco's and Jacques's descriptions, then, one would progress from a section of discant to a section of organum on the penultimate note or syllable in the tenor. The performer would then be expected to take the first ligature of the duplum in the organum section in measured rhythm; the remainder would then be in unmeasured rhythm. (I would posit that it may have been this division into measured and unmeasured parts that Franco alludes to when he says that 'organum is a kind of music not measured in its every part'.)[71]

---

[69] 'Sed si forte in fine clausulae in *ultima* aut in *penultima dictionis sillaba*, ut discantus pulchrior et facetior habeatur et ab auscultantibus libentius audiatur, aliquos *organi modulos* volueris admiscere licet facere.' A. Seay, ed., 'An Anonymous Treatise from St. Martial', *Annales Musicologiques*, 5 (1957), pp. 7–42; passage quoted from p. 33 (my italics).

[70] CSM 18, p. 75 (my italics); cf. n. 12 above.

[71] Cf. n. 22 above. There is yet a further interpretation of Franco's statement that should at least be mentioned here as a hypothesis. As discussed earlier in this paper, some parts of organum purum seem in Franco's view to involve a duplum whose notation is rhythmically fixed – 'rhythmisch streng festgelegt', in Reckow's words. It may be no accident that the musical example manifesting this conception is the opening section or 'pars' of *Iudea et Iherusalem*, which in both the practical sources and the manuscripts of Franco's treatise is written in a clear first-mode pattern. It was this example and the 'rules of consonance' connected with it that led Reckow to hypothesise that Franco might have been working

In addition to their witness to certain structural features of organum, Franco's remarks also tell us something important about the performance of this genre. Specifically, they allow us to confirm for at least some parts of organum purum a performance style that is relatively free and unfettered from a rhythmic point of view.[72] The de la Fage Anonymous had described this style as being 'joined with its cantus not note against note, but with an unlimited multiplicity and a kind of wondrous flexibility'. 'It ought to begin', he says, 'with one of the consonances or together with the chant, and from there, in a modulating or frolicking fashion, as it seems appropriate and as the organisator wishes, it ought to ascend above or descend below and finally place a terminus at the octave or together with the chant.'[73] Later on, the same author says that the ascent and descent, 'in a modulating or frolicking fashion', should take place 'cito' (quickly).[74] Johannes de Garlandia's remarks about the rhythmic freedom of organum *in speciali* are well known, thanks to Professor Roesner's work, as are the views of the author of the *Discantus positio vulgaris* (thanks to Professor Knapp). The *Discantus positio* states that

with settings of organum written in modal notation or perhaps even rewritten in mensural notation. Evidence that would support this view has been offered by Roesner, who points out ('Johannes de Garlandia on *organum in speciali*', p. 159 n. 85) that in the manuscript Berlin, Staatsbibliothek der Stiftung Preussischer Kulturbesitz, lat. 4° 523, material notated in *modus non rectus* in other sources has been re-notated mensurally. Reckow's hypothesis thus seems quite plausible. Under such circumstances it could well be that the one 'part' of organum purum still being performed in its original manner in Franco's time was that 'on penultimates', which – even if notated in *figurae* suggesting fixed rhythmic values – was to be performed in a rhythmically free fashion.

[72] With this point in mind, one contemplating an edition of this music would be well advised to read the remarks by F. Zaminer, *Der vatikanische Organum-Traktat (Ottob. lat. 3025): Organum-Praxis der frühen Notre Dame-Schule und ihrer Vorstufen*, Münchner Veröffentlichungen zur Musikgeschichte 2 (Tutzing, 1959), pp. 99–100, and H. H. Eggebrecht, 'Organum purum', *Musikalische Edition im Wandel des historischen Bewußtseins*, ed. T. Georgiades (Kassel, 1971), pp. 93–112, esp. pp. 110–12. See also J. Yudkin, 'The Rhythm of Organum Purum', especially pp. 374–6.

[73] 'Organum autem non aequalitate punctorum sed infinita multiplicitate ac mira quadam flexibilitate cantui suo concordat in aliqua, ut dictum est, consonantiarum, aut cum cantu debet incipere et inde modulando vel lasciviendo, prout oportuerit et organizator voluerit, vel ascendere superius vel inferius descendere, tandem vero in diapason aut cum cantu terminum ponere' (Seay, 'An Anonymous Treatise', p. 35, sent. 11). On the treatise itself, and specifically on this passage and its significance, see H. H. Eggebrecht, 'Die Mehrstimmigkeitslehre von ihren Anfängen bis zum 12. Jahrhundert', *Die mittelalterliche Lehre von der Mehrstimmigkeit*, Geschichte der Musiktheorie 5 (Darmstadt, 1984), pp. 9–87, esp. pp. 59–66. Eggebrecht points out that the edition by Seay needs to be revised to incorporate readings from Barcelona, Biblioteca Central, MS 883, and Parma, Biblioteca Palatina, MS parm. 1158. My translation is a modified version of that by E. Sanders ('Consonance and Rhythm', p. 265).

[74] Seay, 'An Anonymous Treatise', p. 35, sent. 13.

ligatures of more than four notes 'are not, as it were, subject to rule, but are executed at pleasure [*ad placitum*]. These are associated particularly with the organum and the conductus.'[75] Finally, the phrase applied to organum by the *Discantus positio* is echoed by the author of a supplement to Robert Kilwardby's *De ortu scientiarum*, written shortly before 1250.[76]

The anonymous author of this work provides stylistic descriptions of discant, of cantilena 'quam Gallici "motez" vocant', of conductus, and finally of the type of music 'qui proprie "organum" appellatur, quod solum a duobus diversis poterit modulari'. Of this genre 'which is properly called organum', he goes on to say that 'while the lower voice is held in a rather long and protracted fashion, the upper voice scampers about *ad placitum*' ('dum inferior vox longius protrahendo tenetur, superior *ad placitum* discurrit' – my italics).[77]

As the testimony of the 'Kilwardby Anonymous' and other authors makes clear, a free style of performance – 'ad placitum' – was held to be a central feature of organum purum in the thirteenth century. By taking a fresh look at Franco and the terms he uses to describe organum purum we may now be able to say that despite his attempt to bring as much polyphonic music as possible under rational, mensural control – an understandable Scholastic position[78] – Franco is not quite the 'compleat mensuralist' that he has been thought to be. Instead, even he is forced to admit that parts of organum purum must be performed in a rhythmically free fashion –

---

[75] 'Quodsi plures quam quatuor fuerint, tunc quasi regulis non subjacent, sed *ad placitum* proferuntur. Quae etiam ad organum et conductum pertinent singulariter' (Cserba, *Hieronymus de Moravia*, p. 190; my italics). Translation by Janet Knapp ('Two XIII-Century Treatises', p. 203).

[76] On Kilwardby, who taught in Paris *c.* 1240, see pp. xi–xvii of the Introduction to the edition of *De ortu scientiarum* by A. G. Judy O.P., Auctores Britannici Medii Aevi 4 (Oxford and Toronto, 1976) and M. Haas, 'Studien zur mittelalterlichen Musiklehre I: Eine Übersicht über die Musiklehre im Kontext der Philosophie des 13. und frühen 14. Jahrhunderts', *Forum Musicologicum*, 3 (Winterthur, 1982), pp. 323–456, esp. pp. 403–8. According to Judy (*op. cit.*, pp. xvii–xxxi), the supplement is contained in the manuscripts Munich, Bayerische Staatsbibliothek, clm 28186, fols. 258r–259ᵛ; Florence, Biblioteca Medicea-Laurenziana, Plut. XXVII, dext., cod. 9, fol. 143ᵛ–145ʳ; and Kraków, Biblioteka Jagiellońska 754, fols. 42, 43ᵛ, 44ʳ. It has been discussed briefly by F. Reckow on p. 283 of his '"Ratio potest esse, quia . . .": Über die Nachdenklichkeit mittelalterlicher Musik-theorie', *Die Musikforschung*, 37 (1984), pp. 281–8. I am very grateful to Professor Reckow for information about the treatise and the forthcoming edition of its text.

[77] The quotations are from the draft text of the edition of the 'Kilwardby Anonymous' now being prepared by Dr Ulrike Hascher-Burger. I am most grateful to Dr Hascher-Burger for allowing me to quote from her text before its publication.

[78] Cf. n. 11 of this study.

in *floratura*. He thus takes a logical place within the tradition of thirteenth-century writing about music, and our picture of both that music and its theory is richer and more consistent than ever before.

The Ohio State University

Early Music History (1989) Volume 9

TIM CARTER

MUSIC-PRINTING IN LATE
SIXTEENTH- AND EARLY
SEVENTEENTH-CENTURY
FLORENCE: GIORGIO MARESCOTTI,
CRISTOFANO MARESCOTTI AND
ZANOBI PIGNONI*

A number of scholars have begun to explore the activities of music-printers in sixteenth-century Italy. The first music-print produced by movable type was issued by Ottaviano Petrucci in 1501, and by the 1540s improvements in printing techniques, and particularly the introduction of single-impression printing, had set music-printing on a firm commercial footing, first and foremost in Venice, the centre of the printing trade on the peninsula. The two chief Venetian music-printers in the mid-century, Antonio Gardano and Girolamo Scotto, headed commercial enterprises the organisation of which merits close study by economic historians. But the activities of these and other music-printers must also be examined for their effect on contemporary musical culture. Through their editorial policies and commercial strategies, printers such as Gardano and Scotto had an undeniable influence on the composition and dissemination of music in this period, creating and defining a market or markets for their

*The research for this study was done under the auspices of the Harvard University Center for Italian Renaissance Studies, Villa I Tatti, Florence, and the Newberry Library, Chicago, whose support I gratefully acknowledge. A preliminary report on this material was presented in my 'The Music Trade in Late Sixteenth-Century Florence' at the Fourteenth Annual Convention of the International Musicological Society, Bologna, 1987; and a companion-piece, 'Music-Selling in Late Sixteenth-Century Florence: The Bookshop of Piero di Giuliano Morosi', appeared in *Music & Letters*, 70 (1989), pp. 483–504. I thank the staff of the Archivio di Stato, the Biblioteca Nazionale Centrale, and the Biblioteca Marucelliana, Florence, for their unfailing courtesy and assistance, and also Jane Bernstein, Iain Fenlon and Nigel Fortune for their comments on earlier drafts.

wares which increasingly directed the activities of contemporary composers.

However, any study of the organisation of music-presses in Venice in the sixteenth century is hampered by an apparent scarcity of archival documents – account books, contracts, business letters – detailing the activities of individual printers. Scholars have been left with two broad options: first, to extrapolate information from music-prints themselves, and second, to comb the archives of the various civic administrative offices that dealt with printers in the city. The first option, as seen, for example, in the recent work by Mary S. Lewis on the Gardano press,[1] produces studies that focus inevitably on typographical processes (from which some of the operating principles of contemporary music-printers can be more or less accurately deduced) and on the transmission of particular repertories (which may or may not have a bearing on editorial policies and marketing strategies). However, such studies are necessarily limited by our lack of information on even the most fundamental issues of the printing trade, including its financial organisation (for example, how much was paid by whom for a given music-print?) and other aspects of the process of printing and selling music (what were the standard print-runs of contemporary music-prints and how were they distributed across the peninsula?). The second option – using civic administrative archives – has been adopted by Richard J. Agee in his work on the privileges and licences that protected and monitored printers in Venice.[2] But the protection and control of the printing trade by a particular civic office indicates only indirectly the commercial operation of that trade, and is even less revealing in the case of music-printing, which seems to have existed on the periphery of the printing trade as a whole, which did not always make consistent and extensive use of the privilege system,

---

[1]   M. S. Lewis, 'Antonio Gardane and his Publications of Sacred Music, 1538–55' (Ph.D. dissertation, Brandeis University, 1979). For a parallel example dealing with Rome, see S. Cusick, *Valerio Dorico: Music Printer in Sixteenth-Century Rome* (Ann Arbor, 1981). Would that commercial records for Italian printers had survived to the same extent as for the Plantin-Moretus press in Antwerp, see L. Voet, *The Golden Compasses: A History and Evaluation of the Printing and Publishing Activities of the Officina Plantiniana at Antwerp*, 2 vols. (Amsterdam, 1969–72).

[2]   R. J. Agee, 'The Privilege and Venetian Music Printing in the Sixteenth Century' (Ph.D. dissertation, Princeton University, 1982); *idem*, 'The Venetian Privilege and Music-Printing in the Sixteenth Century', *Early Music History*, 3 (1983), pp. 1–42; *idem*, 'A Venetian Music-Printing Contract and Edition Size in the Sixteenth Century', *Studi Musicali*, 15 (1986), pp. 59–65.

and which posed few problems or threats for church and state censors.

If our understanding of the activities of Venetian music-printers is limited by a lack of appropriate archival sources, we might perhaps look elsewhere to establish paradigms for the effective organisation and operation of a music-press. Venice was certainly the major centre for music-printing in sixteenth- and early seventeenth-century Italy, and indeed it may have been one of the very few cities, if not the only one, where commercial music-printing was securely established. But music-presses also operated to various extents and at various times elsewhere in Italy, including Rome, Milan, Naples, Ferrara and Florence. Of course, it is unlikely that more regionally oriented presses will provide a direct model for the larger-scale operations of, say, Gardano and Scotto: for example, in smaller centres music-printers are more likely to have offered just a service for local composers and/or their patrons wanting (and willing to pay for) their work to appear in print to satisfy perhaps somewhat circumscribed personal and professional ambitions. Also, these printers are less likely to have devoted their capital and labour solely, or even primarily, to music. But the activities of small-scale regional presses are not without interest for historians of printing. Moreover, any account of how music-printing seems to have operated differently outside Venice will likely demonstrate the commercial advantages apparently enjoyed by printers in the republic. Finally, if regional music-printers did primarily offer a service to local musicians, the interaction between printers, composers, patrons and specific markets may be more effectively revealed.

Florence was one such regional centre of music-printing in late sixteenth- and early seventeenth-century Italy.[3] Despite the city's

---

[3] Some brief general comments on music-printing in Florence over the 1600s are made in P. Fabbri, A. Pompilio and A. Vassalli, 'Frescobaldi e le raccolte con composizioni a voce sola del primo Seicento', *Girolamo Frescobaldi nel iv centenario della nascita*, ed. S. Durante and D. Fabris (Florence, 1986), pp. 233–60. The following abbreviations are used here to identify *fondi* in the Archivio di Stato, Florence: Aud. Rif., Auditore delle Riformagioni; Dep. Gen., Depositeria Generale; GCS, Guicciardini–Corsi–Salviati; LC, Libri di Commercio; Mag. Pup., Magistrato de' Pupilli; Mag. Sup., Magistrato Supremo; MdP, Mediceo del Principato; Med. Spez., Arte dei Medici e Speziali; Misc. Med., Miscellanea Medicea; Prat. Seg., Pratica Segreta; PdB, Provvisioni della Balìa; Reg. Dir., Regio Diritto; S. M. Nuova, Santa Maria Nuova; Trib. Mer., Tribunale di Mercanzia; Urb.,

apparent importance as the source of a number of musical genres and styles taken up with some enthusiasm by composers in the early Baroque period (opera, the solo madrigal, the solo aria), there was only one major firm printing music, headed successively by Giorgio Marescotti (d. 1602), his son Cristofano (d. 1611), and Zanobi Pignoni (*fl.* 1607–41). Other printers turned occasionally to music, particularly from the 1620s onwards, but only the Marescotti–Pignoni press issued music on anything like a regular basis. Even so, its output was sporadic and apparently highly selective, as the checklist of editions containing music printed in Florence given in the Appendix reveals. In terms of quantity, this output bears no comparison with that of the Venetian presses – when working at peak capacity Antonio Gardano was able to produce $1\frac{1}{2}$–2 editions of music per month[4] – and indeed it scarcely matches the activity of printers in Rome and Milan. Moreover, music formed only a small part of the printing activities of the firm (see Table 1): between 1563 and 1613, the Marescotti press produced well over three hundred titles (excluding legislative broadsheets and pamphlets), but only twenty concerned with music survive (seventeen music-prints and three treatises). However, the Marescotti, and later Pignoni, issued some significant first editions, including early operas by Giulio Caccini, Jacopo Peri and Marco da Gagliano, Caccini's important *Le nuove musiche* of 1602, and other collections by the leading monody-composers in Florence. Clearly, the Marescotti–Pignoni press was of some significance for music-making in the city.

The fact that the Marescotti–Pignoni press did not devote itself exclusively to music emphasises the fact that music-printing in Florence can be understood only in the context of the Florentine printing trade as a whole. Indeed, as we shall see, its mixed fortunes were inextricably linked to larger-scale problems facing Florentine

Urbino. Petitions and memoranda are often undated, or bear a date only in the *rescritto*, an official annotation indicating action to be followed. This *rescritto* could be added anything from a few days to several months after the original submission. Documents which can be dated only in this manner are so indicated. The Florentine year began on 25 March; where necessary, *stile fiorentino* and *stile comune* datings are combined in a single formula, e.g. 23 February 1562/3. The monetary units adopted here are, in order of increasing value, denari, soldi (1 soldo=12 denari), lire (1 lira=20 soldi), scudi (in general, 1 scudo=7 lire). Lire, soldi and denari may be expressed in a single formula, e.g. L. 3.12. 8. Quotations follow the source, with expanded abbreviations and contractions indicated by italics. All translations are my own.

4 Lewis, 'Antonio Gardane and his Publications of Sacred Music', p. 160.

printers and caused in part by the particular economic policies of the Medici grand dukes and the commercial disadvantages that hindered the city's trade. Thus one must start with some general comments on printing in Florence in the first half of the sixteenth century.

The chief presses in the city were run by members of the Giunti and Sermartelli families, although a number of other printers (such as Antonfrancesco Doni in 1545–7) also worked in the city at various times.[5] The printing trade survived the political uncertainties of pro- and anti-Medici faction in the first three decades of the century and the eventual transition from republic to *principato*. However, the return of the Medici in 1530 to become Dukes (later, Grand Dukes) of Florence brought inevitable changes. By the 1540s, Duke Cosimo I de' Medici was increasingly manipulating the arts and letters in Florence, in part to foster political stability and his personal prestige. In 1541, Cosimo formalised the statutes of the Accademia Fiorentina, and in 1543 he encouraged the reorganisation of the university at Pisa. By 1546, if not before, he had turned his attentions to printing. His apparent aim was to support the activities of the Accademia and the university by founding a ducal press, which would also be responsible for publishing editions of the principal manuscripts of the Medici library housed in San Lorenzo. It is not known whether he also hoped that such a move would limit the potential dangers of a free press in the city.

Cosimo looked outside Tuscany for a suitable printer to head the new press. It may seem surprising that he ignored more obvious

[5] See F. Ascarelli, *La tipografia cinquecentina italiana* (Florence, 1953), pp. 133–46; C. Bareggi, 'Giunta, Doni, Torrentino: tre tipografie fiorentine fra repubblica e principato', *Nuova Rivista Storica*, 58 (1974), pp. 318–48; B. Maracchi Biagiarelli, 'Il privilegio di stampatore ducale nella Firenze medicea', *Archivio Storico Italiano*, 123 (1965), pp. 304–70; L. Perini, 'Editoria e società', *Firenze e la Toscana dei Medici nell'Europa del Cinquecento: la corte il mare i mercanti; la rinascita della scienza; editoria e società; astrologia, magia e alchimia*, ed. L. Perini (Florence, 1980), pp. 245–308. On the Giunti, see D. Decia, R. Delfiol and L. S. Camerini, *I Giunti tipografi editori di Firenze, 1497–1570: annali* (Florence, 1978); L. S. Camerini, *I Giunti tipografi editori di Firenze, 1571–1620: annali* (Florence, 1979); W. A. Pettas, *The Giunti of Florence: Merchant Publishers of the Sixteenth Century* (San Francisco, 1980). According to Ascarelli, the Sermartelli firm did not begin its activities until 1554, but the family can be traced back to the fifteenth-century Florentine printer Bartolomeo di Francesco 'detto de' Libri', see B. Maracchi Biagiarelli, 'I Sermartelli, discendenti di Bartolomeo de' Libri', *La Bibliofilia*, 63 (1961), pp. 281–8. From 1519 to 1524, Bartolomeo's son, Michelangelo, operated a press in Siena before returning to Florence. On the press run by Antonfrancesco Doni, see C. Ricottini Marsili-Libelli, *Anton Francesco Doni scrittore e stampatore: bibliografia delle opere e della critica e annali tipografi* (Florence, 1960).

local candidates such as Doni or the Giunti, although it was not unusual to bring craftsmen from the north to Florence: witness Cosimo's slightly earlier negotiations to attract Flemish tapestry-weavers to the city.[6] By 1547, he had settled on a Flemish printer and bookseller currently working in Bologna, Lorenzo Torrentino. Torrentino was said to have greater expertise, more qualified staff and better equipment than his closest Florentine rivals, the Giunti.[7] However, Cosimo may simply have felt safer with an outsider untainted by memories of the republic. He offered Torrentino a number of incentives to move to Florence as the 'stampatore ducale', including an annual salary of 100 scudi, tax exemptions, exclusive rights to the printing of state legislation, a universal privilege of 'copyright' on all works printed, and a monopoly on the sale of books (except legal texts) imported from France and Germany. These concessions gave Torrentino a considerable advantage over his competitors.

At first the venture went well and Torrentino issued a series of fine editions, but by the late 1550s his firm was in severe financial difficulties. The printer blamed the worsening economic situation in Florence and the political uncertainties caused by the threat of the pro-republican exiles. However, Torrentino was later described as a 'thoughtless man dedicated to his own pleasures'.[8] It seems that

---

[6] C. Adelson, 'Documents for the Foundation of Tapestry Weaving under Cosimo I de' Medici', *Renaissance Studies in Honor of Craig Hugh Smyth*, ed. A. Morrogh, F. Superbi Gioffredi, P. Morselli and E. Borsook, 2 vols. (Florence, 1985), II, pp. 3–21. The parallels between the tapestry workshop and the ducal press were noted in a decision of the Pratica Segreta on the renewal of Lorenzo Torrentino's privileges taken on 15 July 1560: 'li pare si possa aiutare con darli una stanza per sua habitatione, et per la stamperia, come Vostra Eccellenza da alli Maestri Tappezzierj' (Prat. Seg. 5, ins. 69, given in Maracchi Biagiarelli, 'Il privilegio di stampatore ducale', pp. 338–9; another copy in Aud. Rif. 3, fol. 518ʳ, given, with an incorrect reference, in Bareggi, 'Giunta, Doni, Torrentino', p. 347).

[7] See the letter from Lelio Torelli to Lorenzo Pagni, 8 January 1546/7, given in D. Moreni, *Annali della tipografia fiorentina di Lorenzo Torrentino impressore ducale* (2nd edn, Florence, 1819), p. xxv: 'si potrebbe concludere seco, o con li Giunti chi più a Sua Eccellenza piacesse; et quella risponse al [Cosimo] Lattino, che più li piacea questo Messer Lorenzo, come nel vero, et di comodità di pratiche di fuori, et di correttori, et di lettere, et di diligentia è più da piacere'. On Torrentino, see also G. Hoogewerff, 'L'editore del Vasari: Lorenzo Torrentino', *Studi vasariani: atti del convegno internazionale per il IV centenario della prima edizione delle 'Vite' del Vasari* (Florence, 1952), pp. 93–104.

[8] 'homo spensierato et dedito à sua piaceri', in a memorandum from Paolo Vinta to Grand Duke Francesco I, 15 April 1577, Aud. Rif. 12, fol. 209ʳ, given (with some inaccuracies) in Maracchi Biagiarelli, 'Il privilegio di stampatore ducale', pp. 352–3. Torrentino's own complaints about Florence are in a petition for the renewal of his privileges in 1560, summarised in Prat. Seg. 5, ins. 69 (original in Misc. Med. 314, ins. 3, no. 1), given in Maracchi Biagiarelli, *op. cit.*, pp. 338–9. Dissatisfaction with Florence is also suggested by the fact that in the early 1560s, Torrentino established a press in Mondovì.

Cosimo had cause to regret his initial enthusiasm for a ducal press. When Torrentino's concessions came up for renewal in 1559–60, they were drastically reduced. He died in February 1563 owing some 2000 scudi to the duke, and Torrentino's sons failed to maintain the firm to any significant extent after the mid-1560s.[9]

Torrentino was not alone in facing financial problems, as a number of petitions to the court by Florentine printers reveal. These problems were caused both by the type of book generally printed in Florence and by particular weaknesses in the Florentine economy. The Giunti compared the output of the Florentine presses with that of other printers in Italy, noting in particular the legal texts published in large numbers in Turin (and, they might have added, by the branch of the Giunti firm in Venice):

However, the books which are printed in Florence are not of this type, so they cannot compete with them in terms of price, but they are books of greater exquisiteness and honour, and less practical. [They cannot compete] because of the effort and great expense in producing them owing to the wide variety of typefaces required by one such book, where there may be texts in Greek, Latin and in translation, with paraphrases, annotations and glosses, each of which requires different fonts. Moreover, we have to transcribe material in the library of San Lorenzo, which costs many dozens of scudi, and twice as much again is spent on the proof-readers and workers of the press, far more than is spent on the ordinary works in current circulation.[10]

Florentine printers concentrated on texts in the humanities, producing luxury editions distinguished by their careful editing and fine presentation. In contrast, a number of printing firms in northern

---

[9] Torrentino's sons petitioned for the maintenance of their father's privileges on 16 February 1562/3, see Aud. Rif. 8, fol. 692^r. They were granted, but were not renewed in 1566, see Aud. Rif. 9, no. 174. The sons formed partnerships with Bernardo Fabroni and Carlo Pettinari (the latter petitioned for a monopoly on the printing of state legislation on 30 January 1567/8, see Aud. Rif. 10, no. 117, but it was denied). The partnership with Pettinari lapsed in 1570, and there are no further records of the activities of Torrentino's heirs in Florence. For other documents on the parlous financial state of the firm after Lorenzo Torrentino's death, see Reg. Dir. 6025, fol. 378^r; 6029, fol 55^r.

[10] An undated petition (but after 1563) by Filippo and Jacopo Giunti for concessions and the title of 'stampatore ducale', Misc. Med. 314, ins. 3, no. 3, fol. [1]^r: 'Ma li libri che si hanno da stampare in Fiorenza, non sono di questa carattata, che non si potrebbe competere con loro ne prezzi, ma sono libri piu squesitj e di piu honore e manco vtile, rispetto alla fatica e spesa grande al condurlj, per tante sorte di caratterj che uà in vno di questi librj, doue sia piu Testj Grecj latinj e tradottj, con parafrase Annotatione e comentj, che hanno a esser tuttj caratterj variatj, e in oltre si ha da fare trascriuere le copie della libreria di san lorenzo, doue si spende molte dozzine di scudj, e nej corettorj e lauorantj della stampa, si spende doppiamente, piu che non si fa nelle opere ordinarie e corrente . . .'.

Table 1 *Comparison of the output of the Giunti (Florence), Torrentino, Marescotti, and Giunti (Venice) presses*

	Giunti (Florence) (1530–1610)	Torrentino (1547–63)	Marescotti (1563–1613)	Giunti (Venice) (1530–1610)
(a) by subject				
Classics	55 (9%)	36 (14%)	2 (1%)	75 (6%)
History, Politics, Geography	88 (14%)	49 (19%)	20 (6%)	46 (3%)
Language and Literature	286 (47%)	87 (34%)	131 (41%)	14 (1%)
Law	45 (7%)	24 (9%)	25 (8%)	430 (32%)
Medicine	9 (1%)	9 (4%)	6 (2%)	191 (14%)
Music	—	—	20 (6%)	—
Philosophy	23 (4%)	21 (8%)	15 (5%)	109 (8%)
Religion (incl. Liturgical texts)	93 (15%)	28 (11%)	73 (23%)	478 (35%)
Other	15 (2%)	2 (1%)	30 (9%)	20 (1%)
Total	614	256	322	1363
(b) by language				
Latin	141 (23%)	93 (36%)	73 (23%)	1257 (92%)
Greek	22 (4%)	1	—	7
Vernacular	451 (73%)	162 (63%)	248 (77%)	99 (7%)

Sources: Giunti (Florence), Torrentino, Giunti (Venice), after the tables in Perini, 'Editoria e società', pp. 279, 290, 292; Marescotti, compiled from the checklist of prints in Delfiol, 'I Marescotti', pp. 183–204 (excludes state laws, edicts, etc.).

Italy, and particularly Venice, tended to rely upon more marketable, and therefore more profitable, editions of legal and liturgical texts (see Table 1). For this and other reasons, Florentine printers faced specific difficulties, as Filippo and Jacopo Giunti explained to a court official in early 1563:

For until now, when we have had to print a book of importance and requiring expense, and have been able to persuade the authors of books [to do so], we have had them printed in Venice for the following reasons, as Your Lordship will readily understand. First, since taxes here are great and numerous, and [since] everything to do with this business [is] very expensive, one cannot print large, important books without some support, unless by one who wishes to run the risk of patent losses, as experience up to now will have shown many. Second, given the competition with Venice, France and Germany, where many presses flourish, where there are men very skilled at this [trade], and where everything is cheaper, one cannot print large and, as has been said, important books without support and assistance unless one is to make large losses.

As well as the aforesaid taxes and expenses, also to be considered is the fact that whoever prints in Florence similarly spends much on transport, since one is necessarily required to export books to various places so as to sell them, and most especially to Venice, where many foreigners go to buy [them], for in that city there is the opportunity to make a selection of books, and [there are] many bookshops. As I say, one must sell abroad, for it is indeed true that for every book printed in Florence, however good, twenty-five, thirty, forty or some such number is enough for the whole state, and the normal practice is to print 1000 copies of every book. Thus all the other main printing centres do not have these expenses, or at least not as great in terms of transport, whereas we are forced to export to other countries at infinite cost. [This is] not to mention the many dangers which affect our profession, [such as] whether the book turns out badly, or whether it is reprinted in a lesser format with a smaller typeface, or whether, finally, it is printed by others with additions, glosses or tables and other such things, as one sees happen daily much to the damage of he who first printed the book in its plain version. And particularly for the aforesaid reasons, when this occurs in Florence the books remain stockpiled in shops and after a while become wrapping for grocers' wares, as daily experience shows.[11]

[11] A petition of 13 March 1562/3 for concessions and the title of 'stampatore ducale', Reg. Dir. 6029, fols. 122^r–122^v: 'Che quando fino ahora hauemo hauto a stampare qualche libro d'importanza e di grande spesa, e potuto disporre a cio fare gl'Autori delle opere, noi gli hauiamo fattj stampare, come puo *Vostra Signoria* ageuolmente sapere, in Vinezia *per* queste cagionj, Prima *perche* essendo qua grandj e molte le gabelle et in gran prezzo tutte le cose attenentj a questo esercitio, non si puo senza qualche aiuto stampare librj grandj e d'importanza, se non da chj vuole mettersj a rischio dj manifesto danno, come la sperienza può gia hauer a moltj insino a hoggi dimostrato. Secondariamente *per* questo, *che* hauendosi a concorrer con Vinezia francia & Alemagna, doue le stampe fioriscono in gran copia, e sono gl'huominj a ciò molto attj, e tutte le cose a miglior mercato, *non* si puo qui senza qualche aiuto e habilità stampare, ne senza perderuj grossamente libri grandj come si è detto, e d'importanza.

Oltre alle dette gabelle e spese è da considerar' ancora che chi stampa in Fiorenza spende assaj similmente nelle vetture, bisognando necessariamente mandar' fuorj e in diuersj luoghj i libri *per* smaltirgli, et a Vinetia massimamente, doue concorrono moltj forestierj a comp*r*are, *per* esser in *q*uella citta com*m*odo dj fare assortimento di librj, e molte Botteghe di librarj, bisogna dico smaltirglj fuora, essendo questo verissimo, che d'ogni libro c*h*e si stampa in fiorenza quantunque buono 25, 30, o, 40, o, vn cosi fatto numero condisce tutto lo stato, e l'ordinario è stampar' d'ognj libro mille, la doue tuttj gl'altri principali luoghj di stampe no*n* hanno queste spese, o, al meno cosj grande di vetture a vn pezzo, doue noj siamo forzatj condurglj in altrj paesi co*n* infinite spese, *per* tacere i moltj pericolj aj qualj sottogiace quest'arte, o *perche* riesca cattiuo il libro, o, *perche* sia ristampato in minor volume e minorj caratterj, o, *perche* finalmente è mandato fuorj da altrj con nuoue additionj postille tauole e altre cosi fatte cose c*he* si veggono ognj giorno fare co*n* gran danno di chi ha da prima stampato il libro semplicemente, e particularmente *per* le dette cagionj in fiorenza doue quando ciò auiene, rimangono i librj a far la guardia aj magazzinj e doppo qualc*he* [fol. 122^v] tempo inuolture delle mercanzie de pizzicagnolj, si come la sperienza giornalmente ne dimostra.' This petition and its supporting documents are also transcribed (with some inaccuracies) in Maracchi Biagiarelli, 'Il privilegio di stampatore ducale', pp. 347–51.

Such complaints will be familiar to economic historians of late sixteenth-century Florence, for a number of the city's industries faced similar problems. To give just one obvious example, woollen cloth manufacture was also suffering from its traditional concentration on luxury goods, from increased competition from the north, and from counterfeit products.

The Giunti's complaints may be exaggerated: for example, according to one official estimate, the Giunti might be expected to pay some 400 lire each year in taxes on paper and books, which is not an unduly high sum.[12] However, their comments do merit consideration. They felt that several issues prevented Florentine printers from competing on equal terms with their counterparts in other cities, and particularly Venice. In addition to the expense of producing luxury editions, labour costs were high, paper and other printing materials were expensive, and taxes on imports and exports were burdensome. The Florentines were further disadvantaged by the city's geographical position, inland and away from the major trade routes. This led to high transportation costs for export, even though exportation was essential given the limited market for luxury editions in Tuscany. These editions were also easily pirated, with obvious loss to the original printer. Finally, there was the problem of a slow turnover, with its resulting effect on cash-flow. Printers and booksellers regularly complained that they could not sell their wares: 'this book business is different from others, and from what is often assumed, for not all books are always sold, and they tend to fill up rooms and shelves'.[13] Similarly, 'printing books and other works demands considerable expense and much time in selling them'.[14] Florentine printers envied the commercial advantages of Venice: indeed, in 1546 Giovan Maria Giunti resisted Duke Cosimo's

---

[12] An estimate prepared by Lelio Torelli in response to the Giunti's petition of 13 March 1562/3 (see n. 11), Reg. Dir. 6029, fol. 123ʳ; see also Maracchi Biagiarelli, 'Il privilegio di stampatore ducale', pp. 349–50. Imported books seem to have been taxed at 12.5% of their value, exported books at 8.3%, and imported paper at L. 1.19. 0 per 100 Florentine lbs. (1 Florentine lb. equals approximately 12 English ounces). On this and other matters of taxation and costs, see also Pettas, *The Giunti of Florence*, pp. 124–52.

[13] Misc. Med. 314, ins. 3, no. 3 (see n. 10), fol. [1]ᵛ: 'questa mercantia di librj, è diuersa dal altre, e secondo che è stimata, per che e librj non si uendon tuttj, e si attende a empier delle stanze, e scanzie . . .'.

[14] A petition (*rescritto* dated 23 February 1624/5) by Salvestro Marchetti and Carlo Massini for a five-year privilege on all their new prints, Aud. Rif. 34, fol. 253ʳ: 'nello stampare libri et altre opere ui ua qualche spesa, e longhezza di tempo nello smaltirle'.

attempts to have him remove his press from Venice to Florence precisely because 'this business cannot be undertaken in any city better than in this one'.[15] According to Filippo and Jacopo Giunti, the only answer was for the duke to grant protective measures of the type awarded to Torrentino in 1547. Only then would they be able to 'avoid these dangers, carry out enough work, compete with other cities, sell goods at a cheaper price, and thus act for the honour and profit of merchants and for the use and benefit of the university'.[16]

Cosimo did offer some protection to Florentine printers as a whole. He delayed enforcing the *Index librorum prohibitorum*, which he deemed an unreasonable intrusion into affairs of state.[17] He also became more selective in awarding privileges to authors or printers limiting the reprinting, and sometimes sale, of individual titles: these privileges were increasingly restricted to editions printed in Florence so as to benefit local craftsmen and to protect the state's revenues from taxes on imported paper and exported books. However, the duke would go little further. For example, Cosimo and his successors remained reluctant to issue Florentine printers with a universal privilege covering all their titles. This again protected state revenue: each privilege issued brought 1 scudo into the treasury. More

[15] Giovan Maria Giunti to Duke Cosimo, Venice, 11 September 1546, given in P. Camerini, *Annali dei Giunti*, I: *Venezia*, 2 vols. (Florence, 1962–3), I, p. 304: 'perché tale exercitio in altra città d'Italia non si può fare meglio che in questa'. On the attractions of Venice for the printing trade, see also P. Manzi, 'Editori tipografi e librai napoletani a Venezia nel secolo XVI', *La Bibliofilia*, 76 (1974), pp. 35–138; P. F. Grendler, *The Roman Inquisition and the Venetian Press, 1540–1605* (Princeton, 1977), pp. 3–24, 225–33; T. Pesenti, 'Stampatori e letterati nell'industria editoriale a Venezia e in terraferma', *Storia della cultura veneta*, IV: *Il Seicento*, I, ed. G. Arnaldi and M. Pastore Stocchi (Vicenza, 1983), pp. 93–129. On the similar attractions of Antwerp, see Christopher Plantin's remarks quoted in K. K. Forney, 'Tielman Susato, Sixteenth-Century Music Printer: An Archival and Typographical Investigation' (Ph.D. dissertation, University of Kentucky, 1978), p. 6.

[16] Reg. Dir. 6029, fol. 122ᵛ (continuation of the passage in n. 11): 'Le quali tutte cose apertamente dimostrano per lo contrario che con qualche esentione et habilità si possono fuggir questj pericolj, lauorar assaj cose, concorrer con le altre città, dar l'opere a miglior mercato, e cosj exercitarsi con honore e vtile de mercantj e commodo e beneficio dell'Vniversita.'

[17] A. Panella, 'L'introduzione a Firenze dell'Indice di Paolo IV', *Rivista Storica degli Archivi Toscani*, 1 (1929), pp. 11–25; Pettas, *The Giunti of Florence*, pp. 162–8. In late 1562, Duke Cosimo urged his agent at the Council of Trent, the Archbishop of Ragusa, to seek moderation in the application of the Index, see the letters in Reg. Dir. 6028, fols. 398–9. Relations between the civil and ecclesiastical censors in Florence remained tense, see Aud. Rif. 20, fols. 193ʳ, 352–3, 391–4 (and the comments of the Venice branch of the Giunti firm given in P. Camerini, *Annali dei Giunti*, I: *Venezia*, II, p. 16), and also A. Panella, 'La censura sulla stampa e una questione giurisdizionale fra Stato e Chiesa in Firenze alla fine del secolo XVI', *Archivio Storico Italiano*, 5th series, 43 (1909), pp. 140–51.

Tim Carter

important, it also maintained some control over printers' outputs, whether to guarantee quality or to monitor books for their political content.[18]

On the whole, Florentine printers were left to stand or fall in a free market. The Medici paid little heed to repeated requests from individual printers for more specific protection. Filippo and Jacopo Giunti's comments of 1563 given above prefaced an appeal for some of Torrentino's original concessions, including exemption from import and export taxes and a universal privilege for all their titles. In return, they offered to increase their capacity, to present a complimentary copy of each of their editions to the duke, and to print free of charge 100 copies of each state law or edict.[19] The petition was denied, mainly, it seems, because of the loss of tax revenue that would result. The Giunti continued to submit similar petitions, as did most other Florentine printers, whether for tax concessions, exclusive rights, or simply the title of Ducal/Grand-Ducal Printer. Nearly all such requests were refused. Perhaps the Medici were disillusioned with the printing trade after Torrentino's collapse. It is also possible that with their political position secure they now had less interest in a state printing-house. However, when a reason was given for refusing such requests, it was the need to maintain tax revenues, to safeguard free enterprise and to prevent monopolies.

[18] Paolo Vinta argued for restricting privileges in early 1573 (Aud. Rif. 11, no. 115); thereafter they were awarded to editions printed outside Tuscany only if these were sufficiently prestigious or supported by a prominent patron. He then objected to universal privileges (the Giunti appear to have had an unused one between 1560 and 1573, see Aud. Rif. 7, no. 27[bis]; 11, no. 199) on the grounds that individual privileges avoided favouring one printer over another, allowed the grand duke to display repeatedly his benevolence, and maintained a check on output and quality (Aud. Rif. 11, no. 118). On the cost of printing and other privileges (including 100 scudi for the title of Marchese), see Aud. Rif. 4, fols. 551–2; the Giunti sometimes attempted to circumvent this charge through multiple applications (Aud. Rif. 22, fols. 94–5). Civil censorship in Florence merits a detailed study. Unlike Venice, no formal system seems to have operated regularly, but books had to be approved variously by members of the Accademia Fiorentina (1585, Aud. Rif. 15, no. 24), by the court *auditore* (1591, Aud. Rif. 18, no. 134, Prat. Seg. 95, fol. 72ᵛ; 1618, Reg. Dir. 19, fol. 422ʳ), and by an academic at the University (1598, Aud. Rif. 23, fol. 73ʳ), while in December 1602, the Giunti requested a clarification of procedure (Reg. Dir. 10, fol. 21ʳ). Censors monitored quality (Reg. Dir. 9, fol. 326ʳ), political content (for Scipione Ammirato, see Aud. Rif. 20, fols. 137–40), and undesirable references to internal and foreign affairs (Reg. Dir. 13, fol. 247ʳ; 16, fol. 899ʳ; 19, fol. 422ʳ). Privileges could also be used to encourage particular types of publication: in May 1616, Antonio Guiducci was granted one for a book on 'la uita, estasi, e reuelationi di Suor Giovanna della Croce' with the revealing suggestion that it might 'dar' animo alli stampatori che piu volentieri imprendino simili imprese' (Reg. Dir. 18, fol. 697ʳ).

[19] Reg. Dir. 6029, fols. 121–33, also given in Maracchi Biagiarelli, 'Il privilegio di stampatore ducale', pp. 347–51 (see above, n. 11).

38

The Medici's laissez-faire attitude to the Florentine printing trade surely caused it to suffer, if only by discouraging innovative and thus financially hazardous activities. In October 1571, Jacopo and Bernardo Giunti made one request to the court that is particularly relevant to this study:

Jacopo and Bernardo Giunti, booksellers, seeking to introduce the printing of musical works to the city of Florence, petition that Your Highness grant them a privilege for such time as seems appropriate to you, that no-one shall print such works in your most felicitous states, or sell such works printed by them without their permission, even if they print works already printed elsewhere, and moreover that no-one may import works printed in Venice or elsewhere that the Giunti shall print in Florence.[20]

This was not the first attempt to introduce music-printing to Florence. On 8 February 1515, Giovanni Bernardo di Salvestro, a priest, and Giovanni Battista di Cristoforo, a brass-worker, had received a ten-year privilege for music-printing in the city: 'wanting to do something praiseworthy for the liberal art of Music, they have found a way to print it just as other books made up of letters are produced, something which no-one else has succeeded in doing in Florence'.[21] However, they seem not to have acted on this privilege. Similarly, in the mid-1540s, Antonfrancesco Doni had employed a press-worker with musical skills, who, he claimed, was poached by the Giunti. He too seems to have planned to establish a music-press in the city, although these plans were curtailed by his departure from Florence in 1547.[22] The Giunti had also demonstrated some interest

---

[20] A memorandum by Paolo Vinta, 8 October 1571, Aud. Rif. 11, no. 41: 'Jacopo et Bernardo Giunti librari desiderando d'intromettere nella Città di Firenze la stampa dell'opere musicali, supplicano Vostra Altezza li conceda un' Privilegio per quel tempo che à lei parrà, che nissuno possa ne' suoi felicissimi stati stampare simili opere ò, stampato dalli supplicanti uendere senza loro consenso, quantunche stampassino cose altra uolta stampate, et inoltre che nissuno possa condurre opere stampate in Venetia, ò, in altre bande ogni uolta, che da Giunti sarà stampato in Fiorenza'. Jacopo Giunti seems to have separated from his brother, who raised objections to this request so as to guarantee his own privileges.

[21] PdB, 8 February 1514/5: 'volendo essi fare qualche opera lodevole circa l'arte liberale della Musica avean trovata moda di stamparla come si fanno gli altri libri di lettera cosa non riuscita ad alcuno in Firenze'. I am most grateful to Professor Timothy McGee for communicating this source and a transcription to me.

[22] J. Haar, 'A Gift of Madrigals to Cosimo I: the Ms. Florence, Bibl. Naz. Centrale, Magl. XIX, 130', *Rivista Italiana di Musicologia*, 1 (1966), pp. 167–89. For Doni's complaints about the Giunti luring staff away from his press, including, as well as a German apprentice from Nuremberg and a Flemish type-founder, 'un altro . . . che compone musica, un altro che scrive al greco, uno che intaglia nel legno et al torchio un francese', see his letter given in Bareggi, 'Giunta, Doni, Torrentino', pp. 327–8.

in music in 1563, when the heirs of Bernardo Giunti commissioned the Venetian printer, Francesco Rampazetto, to print Serafino Razzi's *Libro primo delle laudi spirituali* on their behalf. However, by the early 1570s members of the firm were clearly contemplating a more serious investment. Perhaps they were encouraged by the evident success of music-printers in Venice, and also by the activities of two leading composers working in Florence, Francesco Corteccia and Alessandro Striggio, both of whom had been taken up with some enthusiasm by the Gardano and Scotto presses. But Jacopo and Bernardo Giunti wanted guarantees to protect their new venture. They sought exclusive rights in Tuscany both to music-printing and to the sale of Giunti music-prints, and an embargo on the importation of music printed elsewhere which they might choose to reprint in Florence.

Paolo Vinta, the court *auditore* who relayed the Giunti petition to the grand duke, noted the implications of their request for tax revenues and offered the usual warnings about monopolies. He also revealed that there was most concern at the potential restriction on music-selling in the city:

I have heard the opinion of the other booksellers in Florence, and although all are content that the supplicants should obtain a privilege only for the new things which they print, yet each of them says in his own interest that it is not appropriate that they should receive a privilege for old works already printed, especially if they [the booksellers] are prohibited from importing them from abroad, given that the Giunti would quickly reprint all the finest [editions], and in the end would have everything to do with music in their shop. Thus the others would be deprived of them and would also be forced to regard those books which they already have in their shops as lost, without any hope of selling them. Moreover, it does not seem reasonable to me to prohibit the importation of works and books printed elsewhere, even if the Giunti should reprint them here, not only because it would prejudice Florentine [revenues from] taxes but also because it would create a monopoly, and out of abundance there would be a shortage.[23]

---

[23]   Aud. Rif. 11, no. 41 (see n. 20): 'Ho inteso l'opinione delli altri librari di Fiorenza, et sicome tutti si contentano che li supplicanti ottenghino dà quella il Priuilegio circa le cose nuoue solamente, cosi ciascuno di loro per il suo interesse dicè non essere conueniente, che l'impetrino quanto alle opere antiche, e di gia stampate, Maxime quando fussino impediti di non poter condurne di fuore, atteso che li Giunti ristamperebbono con prestezza tutte le più belle, et ridurrebbono in somma nella bottega loro tutte le cose di Musica, et li altri nè sarebbono priui, et anco sarieno forzati tenere quei libri, che hauessino in bottega persi, senza speranza di poterli uendere, [*sic*] Inoltre à me non pare ragioneuole il prohibire, che non si possi condurre dell'opere et libri stampati altroue, ancorche li Giunti li ristampas-

The request was denied: 'His Highness does not wish to restrict the printing of music to them [the Giunti] alone, nor to prevent imports of it'.[24] The Giunti renewed their petition in 1573 as part of an application for the title of Grand-Ducal Printer.[25] This time they sought only exclusive rights to music-printing and implied that if the title were granted they would establish a music-press. Once again they were refused. In the absence of such protection, the Giunti laid aside their plans. Their only subsequent publication concerning music was an edition of Vincenzo Galilei's *Dialogo della musica antica e moderna* issued in 1602. Here the Giunti simply printed new first and last pages: the rest was made up of left-over copies of the first edition issued by Giorgio Marescotti in 1581.[26]

Giorgio Marescotti had arrived in Florence from France in the mid-1550s – in May 1570 he was said to have been in the city for sixteen years[27] – and he matriculated in the Arte dei Medici e Speziali on 7 April 1558.[28] By 1558 he rented a *bottega* from the Badia; in 1562 he appealed for special permission to sell 'engravings

> sino qui, non solo perche si preiudicherebbe alle gabelle di Fiorenza, mà ancora perche instituirebbono un' Monopolio, et dell'abundantia, si faria carestia.'

[24] Aud. Rif. 11, no. 41 (see n. 20), unsigned and undated annotation (but in the hand of Lelio Torelli): '*Sua* Altezza *non* uuole ristringner' *in* loro soli lo sta*mpar*' le Musiche ne inpeder' *che non* sen' u*en*ghono'.

[25] See the memorandum by Paolo Vinta, 9 June 1573, Aud. Rif. 11, no. 199, also given (with some inaccuracies) in Pettas, *The Giunti of Florence*, pp. 328–9.

[26] It is not clear whether the Giunti obtained copies of the first edition of the *Dialogo* from the Marescotti shop (which still had two bundles containing two loose reams, some twenty-four copies, of the treatise in 1603, see n. 35), or from Galilei or some other source. The practice of reissuing old prints with new title-pages was by no means uncommon – it was one solution to the problem of slow turnover – and was even officially sanctioned: for example, in November 1565 Duke Cosimo gave the Giunti official permission to print new title-pages (dated 1565) for a number of old books recently purchased from the estate of Lorenzo Pasquali (Mag. Sup. 1139, no. 53; and see I. del Badia, 'Libri con falsa data di stampa', *Miscellanea Fiorentina di Erudizione e Storia*, 1 (1886), p. 15; Pettas, *The Giunti of Florence*, pp. 180–1, 323).

[27] See the memorandum by Francesco Vinta, 6 May 1570, Aud. Rif. 10, no. 453: 'Giorgio Mareschot Franzese libraro, et accasato già xvj anni nella Città di Fio*ren*za desidera co*n* il fauore di V*ostra* Alt*ezza* stampare, et fare stampare alla giornata libri latinj, et Volgari, in lingua Thoscana, o, altra lingua scritti Et per cio sup*pli*ca quella le faccia gratia dun' priuilegio p*er* xx annj . . .'. The privilege was denied. On Marescotti, see T. De Marinis, 'Nota sul tipografo Giorgio Marescotti', *La Bibliofilia*, 71 (1969), pp. 179–80; R. Delfiol, 'I Marescotti, librai, stampatori ed editori a Firenze tra Cinque e Seicento', *Studi Secenteschi*, 18 (1977), pp. 146–204 (including a checklist of Marescotti prints).

[28] The matriculation entry for 'Giorgio d*e* xpofori [Cristofori] de' malischottis gallus terra di*c*ta Constanzo *partium* gallia librarius in garbo' is in Med. Spez. 12, fol. 116ʳ. Marescotti's origins in France are unclear, although one Nicolas Malescot was a bookseller in Paris in 1542–3, see P. Renouard, *Répertoire des imprimeurs Parisiens*, ed. J. Veyrin-Fourer and B. Moreau (Paris, 1965), p. 291, and see below, n. 39.

and designs pertaining to painters, sculptors, historians and other professions' after mass on feast days;[29] by 1563 he was having works printed at the Sermartelli and Torrentino presses; and in 1564 or 1565 editions bearing his own imprint began to appear. He may have been apprenticed to, or employed by, Lorenzo Torrentino, and he acquired Torrentino's press at some time after his death:

In years past, the aforesaid Giunti purchased the books and printing shop of Torrentino, and one of them wished to continue the business and then to ask Their Highnesses for the privileges [held by] the aforesaid Torrentino. However, out of rivalry, the sale was disrupted, and [instead] it [the printing shop] was bought by Giorgio Marescotti. Since this is the established site of the ducal press, they [the Giunti] desire to obtain it because it is more appropriate and convenient, better lit for work, and it holds many men. They offer to give the aforesaid Giorgio another site where the Caccini used to be, and if he cannot [move] at present, they will wait six months, a year, or eighteen months until he is accommodated, even though the aforesaid Giorgio has another shop and rents out many rooms to others because there are too many for his needs.[30]

As well as taking over the Torrentino press, Marescotti also purchased the bulk of his stock of books. He regarded himself as *de facto* the official Grand-Ducal Printer, even though the title was never officially granted.

Like his competitors, Giorgio Marescotti repeatedly petitioned the court for trading concessions. In one such petition of mid-1585, he claimed:

Giorgio Marescotti humbly informs Your Most Serene Highness that his inclination has always been, and is now more than ever, to use his labour

[29] See the memorandum by the consuls of the Arte dei Medici e Speziali, 29 May 1562, S. M. Nuova 193, no. 189: 'Giorgio marescottj franzese libraro *in* firenze chomanda *per* le sue precj di poter smaltir' diuerse sorte di disegni di pittura, attene*nt*j à pittorj, scultorj, et storiografi, et altre professionj, *con* poterli uender' in giornj festiui et distenderli *in* pubblico doppo le messe d*e*lle feste, accioche trouandosj egli hauerli condottj *in* q*ue*st*a* Citta, habbino exito piu facilme*nt*e'. Such petitions were becoming increasingly common as the authorities began to clamp down on trading on Sundays and feasts.

[30] Misc. Med. 314, ins. 3, no. 3 (see n. 10), fol. [2]ʳ: 'Li detti Giuntj allj annj passatj comperorno li librj e la stamp*er*ia del Torrentino, e voleuon vn di loro seguire la d*et*ta stampa, e domandarne poj a lor altezze li pr*i*uilegij del d*et*to Torrentino ma *per* inuidia fu rotto loro la vendita, e fu compera da giorgio Mariscotti. e *per* esser quello el sito solito della stamperia ducale, dessiderano ottener quello *per* esser piu a *pro*posito, e comodo e lucido *per* lauorare, e tener moltj huominj, e offeriscono al detto Giorgio di darlj un altro sito di bottega doue stauono e Caccinj, e non possendo di presente, lo aspetteranno 6 mesi vn a*nn*o o 18 mesi tanto ch*e* si accomodj, ancor ch*e* d*et*to Giorgio habbi vn altra bottegha, et appiogiaua molte stanze ad altri *per* essere a luj troppo.' For Marescotti's taking over Torrentino's plant and stock, see also the petition by Modesto Giunti to Cammillo Guidi, June 1605, Misc. Med. 314, ins. 3, no. 7.

and industry to live and to support his family, to plan for the future and to
make his profession flourish in this your delightful city of Florence. He has
done so well enough and with honour for the thirty years in which he has
lived here, not only by importing from far afield many fine books on all
subjects and in various languages, plus designs, astrological charts and
other goods appropriate to his profession. He has also enlarged his press
with various fonts, with which he daily prints books and other things.
Furthermore, he has obtained punches and matrices to print music and has
already printed some partbooks, and he is the first to have done so in this
your aforesaid city of Florence and in your most fortunate states, but not
without difficulty and great expense. However, often when he believes
himself to be making a profit, he makes a large loss, as he did not too many
months ago when pirates robbed him of a number of bales of books from
France, part of which he recovered through the good services and assistance
of Your Most Serene Highness. Moreover, there are those who reprint his
titles, in particular those of greater value, often contrary to the originals and
to the dissatisfaction of whoever commissioned the printing. This is
particularly the case with Edicts, Orders, Decrees, Laws and Provisions,
and other similar things of the Magistrates of Your Most Serene Highness,
which the aforesaid supplicant has sought to print in their entirety (those
which he could secure) for the benefit and assistance of the Ministers and
subjects of Your Most Serene Highness.[31]

[31] An undated petition by Marescotti to the grand duke (sent to the court *auditore* on 2
October 1585), Aud. Rif. 15, no. 54: 'Giorgio Marescotti, umilmente spone a V*ostra* A*ltezza*
S*erenissi*ma come l'animo suo, è stato sempre et è piu che maj, che con le sue fatiche, et
industria, possa uiuere, sustentar, et la sua famiglia, con giouare ancora al prossimo, et
fare fiorire l'arte sua, in questa sua inclita cita di Firenza, sicome ha fatto assaj bene, et
honoratamente, in trenta anni ch'egli ui sta: non solamente, a condurre dj paesi lontanj,
molti belli librj, et d'ognj professione, et di diuersi linguagij, figure dj disegnj, cosmografie,
et altre mercantie appartenantj a detta sua arte, ma ha ancora arrichitto la sua stamparia,
dj uarie sorte dj carratterj, de quali giornamente, ne stampa librj, et altre cose, et dj piu ha
condotto, Ponzonj, madre, per stampare Musica, che gia ne ha stampato alcune mute, et è
il primo che la messa in questa sua detta cita di Firenze, et ne i suoj felicissimj stati, ma non
gia senza difficulta, et spese grande Et perche spese uolte, quando egli si crede
guadagnare, perde in digrosso, come fece non troppo mesi sono, che li corsarj li tolsano
alquante balle di librj di Francia, che per il buon mezo, et soccorso di V*ostra* A*ltezza*
S*erenissi*ma ne riscalo una parte, Poj uj sono alcunj li quali uanno ristampando le sue cose,
pero quelle che hanno piu credito, spesse uolte in contrario delli originali, et con male
satisfattione di chi fa stampare, et in particolare li Bandj, Ordinj, Decreti, Legge,
Prouisionj, et altre cose similj de Magistrati dj V*ostra* A*ltezza* S*erenissi*ma Li quali il detto
supplicante si e studiato dj stamparli tuttj, (pero quegli che ha potuto hauere) per
benefizio, et consolattionj, de Ministrj, et sudittj di V*ostra* A*ltezza* S*erenissi*ma Et acioche
egli possa in parte riparare à sj grandi dannj, et male fattj, egli umilmente, et dj cuore
supplica V*ostra* A*ltezza* S*erenissi*ma che per sua benignita, li conceda grazia, che nissuno
possa ristampare, nellj suoj felicissimj stati, dettj Bandj, Ordinj, Decretj, Legge, Prouisionj, et altre cose similj appartenantj a dettj magistratj, non piu stampati se non da luj,
tempo sei mesi dal dj che saranno finitj dj stampare, et annj dodecj per i librj et altre cose
nuoue ch'egli alla giornata stampara, et altroue stampate, condurre in dettj suoj felicissimj
statj. sotto le solite pene, et preiudizij, del che gliene restara obligatissimo, con tutta la sua
famiglia . . .'.

To 'recover from such great losses and bad practices', Marescotti sought a six-month privilege on state legislation printed by him, and a twelve-year privilege in the case of books. Given the difficulties facing the Florentine book trade, the printing of state legislation had the merit of guaranteeing a regular income. Marescotti's arguments for such legislation being a special case – accuracy was important – were also justified. The six-month privilege on state documents printed by Marescotti was granted, although the twelve-year privilege on books was denied as usual, and specifically on the grounds that the system of applying for privileges for single titles allowed the state to maintain some control over the Florentine presses.

Two years later, Marescotti unsuccessfully petitioned for the title of Grand-Ducal Printer 'so that he can advance his business, wherein he has introduced music-printing, which was not here before, and can maintain his disordered family'.[32] From both these petitions, it seems clear that, like the Giunti, Marescotti felt that the introduction of music-printing was a matter of some prestige that merited special consideration. His involvement with music seems to date from the early 1580s. In 1580 or 1581, Marescotti printed Francesco Bocchi's *Discorso . . . sopra la musica* (the dedication is dated 15 October 1580, and the title-page, 1581). His first volume to contain printed music, Galilei's *Dialogo . . . della musica antica, et della moderna*, appeared in mid-1581 (the dedication is dated 1 June), although the author would have preferred to see it issued in Venice (see below, p. 65). Marescotti then printed an anthology of three-part madrigals 'by the most excellent composers of our times' in 1582, Galilei's *Contrapunti a due voci* in 1584, and an edition of Arcadelt's *Il primo libro de madrigali a quattro voci* in 1585.

It is not clear why Marescotti should have established a music-press. His evident links with Vincenzo Galilei and later Giulio Caccini suggest some association with the 'camerata' sponsored by Giovanni de' Bardi and active in Florence in the 1570s and 1580s. Bardi and his colleagues may well have offered Marescotti encouragement, if not financial support, for his new venture. Furthermore, music may have represented an attempt by Marescotti to diversify

---

[32] An undated petition by Marescotti (sent to the court *auditore* on 6 November 1587), Aud. Rif. 16, no. 40: 'acciòche egli possa tirare innanzi il suo esercitio nel quale ha introdotto di stampare in musica che non ci era, e mantener la sua sconcia famiglia'.

his activities so as to ensure survival in difficult economic times. It seems that by the last two decades of the century, Florentine printers were facing even more severe pressures than before: in 1596 Filippo Giunti complained to Belisario Vinta, a court secretary, that 'between hunger and the Index, this business is indeed going to ground'.[33] They reacted by concentrating on material that was safe from Inquisitorial intervention and was generally of more local interest. Both the Giunti and Marescotti increasingly focused on devotional works, academic treatises, and occasional publications containing laudatory verse, funeral orations and descriptions of court festivities. Music was similarly 'safe' and allowed Marescotti to exploit a market not covered by his competitors.

We do not know when and from where Marescotti obtained his music font, although shortly after his death in 1602 the press had at least two, a so-called 'musica di Parigi' and a 'musica fatta in Firenze' (see below, p. 49). Perhaps the rather squat font (staff height, 10 mm; minim height, 8 mm) that appears in all of Giorgio Marescotti's music editions is the 'musica di Parigi' (Figure 1). He may have brought it with him from France in the 1550s. However, given that the font does not seem to have been used before 1581, it is more likely that Marescotti acquired it in the late 1570s, or even immediately before the appearance of Galilei's *Dialogo*. The fact that Cristofano Malvezzi had his *Il primo libro de ricercari à quattro voci* of 1577 printed in Perugia by Pietro Giacomo Petrucci supports, although by no means confirms, the view that there were no facilities for printing music in Florence in that year. Moreover, the poor quality of the music examples in the *Dialogo* suggests that Marescotti lacked experience in handling the font and even that it remained as yet incomplete.

Giorgio Marescotti does not seem to have been entirely committed to music-printing, even if for a time he may have felt that there were rewards to be gained from it. Although the costs of his two Galilei editions were perhaps paid in the main, if not entirely, by the author and/or his dedicatees, the three-voice anthology and the Arcadelt edition were presumably self-financed ventures issued for commercial gain. The anthology plunders three Venetian prints stretch-

---

[33] Filippo Giunti to Belisario Vinta, 26 September 1596, MdP 873, fol. 403ʳ, given in L. S. Camerini, *I Giunti tipografi editori di Firenze, 1571–1620*, p. 25: 'perché tra la fame e l'Indice questo mestieri va in terra a fatto'.

Figure 1   Jacopo Peri, *Le musiche . . . sopra l'Euridice* (Florence, Giorgio Marescotti, 1600), p. [2] (detail). Reproduced by permission of the British Library.

ing back at least some twenty years: four pieces from the *Madrigali a tre voci de diversi* (Venice, Gardano, 1551[10], also reprinted in 1555, 1561 and twice in 1569), eight from *Il primo libro delle muse, a tre voci* (Venice, Scotto, 1562[8]), and four from Andrea Gabrieli's *Libro primo de madrigali a tre voci* (Venice, 'appresso li figliuoli di Antonio Gardano', 1575, reprinted in 1582). In addition, there are six presumably new madrigals by Alamanne de Layolle, an organist who had arrived in Florence in 1565. Layolle may have acted as the editor of the collection and indeed may have been something approaching a music adviser to Giorgio Marescotti (especially as both had come from France), for he was involved in legal disputes with both the Giunti and the Marescotti presses in the 1570s and 1580s.[34] Both the anthology and the Arcadelt reprint, which had an obvious appeal, were potentially popular items that might attract the more conservative music-lover of limited abilities (Galilei's *Contrapunti a due voci* also seems to cater for this market). But these apparently self-financed ventures seem to have had only mixed success – in 1603, the Marescotti shop still stocked some 120 copies of the 'Madrigali a 3 diuersi' (see below) – and to judge by Marescotti's later music-prints he seems to have returned just to printing on commission. His next publication to do with music after 1585 was Galilei's *Discorso . . . intorno all'opere di messer Gioseffo Zarlino* (1589), a rather shabby octavo edition with no music examples, and he printed no music between 1585 and 1596/7, when Stefano Venturi del Nibbio's *Il terzo libro de madrigali a cinque* appeared.

It seems likely that for Giorgio Marescotti music-printing turned out to be commercially unviable. He had introduced music-printing 'not without difficulty and great expense', as he said in 1585, and this, coupled with his failure to secure the title of Grand-Ducal Printer, may have limited his output. No doubt music also suffered as much as books from the more general problems of the Florentine book trade discussed above. For example, music seems to have sold no less slowly than the other luxury items identified by Filippo and Jacopo Giunti in 1563: in 1603 the Marescotti shop still stocked two bundles of 'dialogi d*el* Galileo' (printed in 1581, some 24 copies, and a number may already have been passed over to the Giunti), two bundles of 'Madrigali a 3 diuersi' (1582, some 120 copies), two bundles of 'Contra Punti a 2' (1584, some 190 copies), two bundles of the 'discorso d*el* Galileo' (1589, some 112 copies), two bundles of 'Musiche d*el* Venturi' (1596/7, some 75 copies), and one bundle of 'Intauolature diuersi'.[35] Moreover, in the 1590s Marescotti seems not to have been a popular choice for Florentine composers seeking a

---

[34] For Layolle, see F. A. D'Accone, 'The Intavolatura di M. Alamanno Aiolli', *Musica Disciplina*, 20 (1966), pp. 151–74. These disputes, and others involving Florentine printers, are noted in the records of the Accademia Fiorentina in Florence, Biblioteca Marucelliana, MS B. III. 53–4. I am most grateful to Professor D'Accone for directing me to this source.

[35] See the inventories and accounts of Giorgio Marescotti's estate in Mag. Pup. 692, fols. 96–127 (dated 14/15 February 1602/3), and Mag. Pup. 695, fols. 448–533 (dated 11 November 1603). The most detailed lists of printing equipment and stock are in Mag. Pup. 695, and the bundles and bales of unbound treatises and music are listed on fols. 465ʳ, 470ʳ, 471ʳ, 511ʳ. I have estimated the number of copies from the size of the bundles (given in reams). In addition, listed on fol. 469ᵛ is '1 Mazo di Madrigali del Caualiere R*i*sma una

printer for their music. These issues will be discussed further below. Thus he was left to print only specialised items of limited appeal, probably with only a small print-run and involving little or no capital investment on his part. Certainly Giulio Caccini's *L'Euridice composta in musica*, Jacopo Peri's *Le musiche . . . sopra l'Euridice* and Caccini's *Le nuove musiche* would seem to fall into this category.

Giorgio Marescotti died in early April 1602, causing delays in the appearance of *Le nuove musiche*. His heirs managed to produce Giovanni del Turco's *Il primo libro de madrigali a cinque* in mid-1602 (the dedication is dated 1 July), but by December they were embroiled in an extensive controversy over the estate. Marescotti left a wife, Agnoletta di Benedetto Bati (they had married in 1565), at least three daughters, Vincenzia, Margherita (aged 18) and Maria (16), and two sons, Cristofano (32) and Pietropagolo (16). The two younger daughters and Pietropagolo were declared wards of the Magistrato de' Pupilli, while Agnoletta Bati and Cristofano Marescotti fought for control of the firm. Cristofano's case was not helped by the fact that according to other members of the family he was 'not suitable to act [as guardian], for in the past, while the aforesaid Giorgio was alive, he lived licentiously and scarcely to the satisfaction of his father, and they fear that he will do the same to the detriment of his brother, of minority age, and of the two sisters'.[36]

The litigation is well documented in the files of the Magistrato de' Pupilli.[37] Moreover, the magistrates also commissioned a series of

---

quinterni 10' (presumably some 27 copies of Giovanni del Turco's *Il primo libro de madrigali a cinque* printed in mid-1602). Other unbound prints in the listing include 'Madrigali Ian gero quinterni 8' and 'Madrigali dorlando [di Lasso] quinterni 14': they are entered separately from the other music-prints stored in the shop, but it is unlikely that they are now lost editions by Marescotti himself. No volume of lute intabulations printed by Marescotti survives, although he did own a font for lute tablature, see nn. 38, 41.

[36] A memorandum by the Magistrato de' Pupilli, 26 November 1602, Mag. Pup. 2285, no. 210: 'ser Gherardo di Gismondo Gherardini, et maestro Dario d'Andrea Grazzi generi di detta madama Agnoletta, et cognati del detto Christofano chiamati d'ordine nostro per dire quanto occhore loro in benefitio de pupilli, fanno instantia, che tal tutela come à noi deferita s'accetti asserendo, che detto Christofano non è habile à esercitarla essendo uissuto per il passato mentre era uiuo detto Giorgio licentiosamente, et con poca satisfatione del padre, et dubitano che sia per fare il medesimo in danno del fratello d'età minore et delle due sorelle'. Cristofano Marescotti had matriculated in the Arte dei Medici e Speziali on 21 May 1602, Med. Spez. 14, fol. 108^r.

[37] See the minutes of the Magistrato de' Pupilli, Mag. Pup. 31, fols. 143^r, 174^r, 216^v–217^r, 229^v–230^r, 245^v; 32, fols. 49^v–50^r, 170^r, 206^r, 237^v; 33, fols. 80^v–81^v, 84^v; 34, fols. 10^v, 82^v. Supporting documents are in Mag. Pup. 692, fols. 96–127, 575–80; 694, fols. 468, 630, 701; 695, fols. 218, 448–533, 602, 689, 692; 699, fols. 722–3; 715, fols. 214–19, 256–65, 303–8, 742, 921, 1037; 2657, fols. 743–52.

Table 2 *Marescotti assets and debts, 30 October 1603*
(values to the nearest scudo)

Assets		Debts	
Books, engravings, etc.	3385	Dowries	2310
Printing equipment (presses, type, etc.)	680	Salary owed to Tommaso Rognoni	300
Type-founding equipment (moulds, punches, etc.)	280	Outstanding debts	1234
Woodblocks	20		3844
Household furnishings, etc.	200		
Outstanding credits with customers, exports, etc.	1921		
Other	35		
	6521		

Source: Mag. Pup. 695, fols. 532ʳ–533ʳ.

inventories and valuations of the estate prior to effecting an equitable division of property. These give details of the printing equipment, stock and financial affairs of the firm. There were three printing-presses, plus another for engravings. Among the numerous fonts were the 'musica di Parigi' and the 'musica fatta in Firenze', one for lute tablature and another for printing plainchant.[38] The extensive stocklist of books includes many music editions as well as bundles of unbound prints issued by the Marescotti press. But although the final balance-sheet of the firm seems sound enough, closer examination reveals a number of problems (see Table 2). A large part of the firm's debts was made up of dowries due to the two daughters and other relations which had to be paid or repaid before the estate could be partitioned. On the other hand, the assets were largely in printing equipment, stock and money owed by customers (whether individuals or other booksellers) who had bought on credit. Although the firm was not running at a loss, it was faced with precisely those severe cash-flow problems that were, it seems, endemic to the Florentine book trade. Moreover, although an impeded cash-flow might do little harm in prosperous times – indeed, it made good sense to have as much capital as possible tied

---

[38] The music and tablature fonts are listed in an undated (but 1603?) inventory in Mag. Pup. 2657, fols. 743–52, see fols. 746ʳ–746ᵛ. Twenty-one 'punsonj di Canto Fermo' were sold by July 1608, Mag. Pup. 715, fol. 1037ᵛ (see n. 41).

up in one's business – it was potentially disastrous when a firm was on the verge of collapse. The result was inevitable: for the Marescotti firm to meet its current debts, plant and stock would have to be liquidated.

This is precisely what occurred. The estate owed 2310 scudi in dowries to Giorgio's wife, his brothers-in-law, his daughters, and to Cristofano's wife, Margherita Pugliani, plus 300 scudi in back-pay to a French employee, Tommaso Rognoni (Thomas Roigny), and some 1200 scudi in other debts.[39] The dowries were recovered either by the direct transfer of plant and stock or in cash. Thus Giovanni Battista Boschetti, who married Cristofano's sister, Margherita, in 1603, took part of his 600 scudi in printing equipment and moved to Pisa to establish a press near the university (he employed one Giovanni Fontani as a general manager because he himself knew nothing of the printing trade).[40] Other members of the family owed dowries took away equipment, books and furnishings. To meet these and other debts, efforts were also made to sell much of the rest of the firm's plant and stock. There were no Florentine buyers, and Margherita Pugliani's brother, Pietropagolo Bizzari, was asked to sell a chest of fonts in Venice, which he did after some delay in 1606 to the Venice branch of the Giunti firm. This chest included at least one of the two music fonts, plus those for lute tablature and plainchant.[41]

[39] It is not known whether Thomas Roigny is related to Jean de Roigny, a Parisian printer and bookseller also associated with Robert Estienne, see Renouard, *Répertoire des imprimeurs Parisiens*, pp. 379–80; E. Armstrong, *Robert Estienne, Royal Printer: An Historical Study of the Elder Stephanus* (Cambridge, 1954), p. 18. See also Delfiol, 'I Marescotti', p. 152, n. 18.

[40] For various attempts to establish a press at Pisa in the early 1600s, see Reg. Dir. 8, fols. 125–8 (June 1600, by one Giorgio in the employ of Don Antonio de' Medici); 10, fol. 573^r (June 1603, by Volcmar Timan); 11, fol. 247 (early 1604, by the Giunti). Boschetti negotiated loans, concessions and exemptions to move to Pisa in mid- to late 1604, Aud. Rif. 25, fol. 321^r; Reg. Dir. 11, fols. 416^r–417^r (also given in Maracchi Biagiarelli, 'Il privilegio di stampatore ducale', pp. 355–6). He was still active there in 1613, Reg. Dir. 17, fol. 142^r.

[41] Details of the sale, which followed unsuccessful attempts to sell the fonts in Florence, are given in Mag. Pup. 715, fols. 214–19, 256–65, 303–8. *Ibid.*, fol. 1037, is a list of the fonts sold, dated 11 July 1608, including '118 punsonj di Musjcha in vna scatola / 50 punsonj dj detta In vna altra scatola / . . . / 25[?] Madre della Musjcha dj piu sorte / . . . / [?] punsonj dj Musjcha per in Tauolatura / . . . / 26 Madre della Musjcha / 10 Madre della In Tauolatura dj leuto / . . . / 12 Madre della Musjca / . . . / 21 punsonj di Canto Fermo / . . .'. There seems to have been a dispute about the price received (80 ducats): it was not as high as had been hoped, even though 'nella Città di Venetia, è Carestia di Madre, punzoni, tasselli, et altri strumenti, da formare lettere, et stamperia, et perciò à chi ne cavassi, di detta Città, et ne portassi altroue, ui è il pregiuditio della Galera, et perdita delle robe, et altri pregiuditij, et perciò chi vene portasse, ò facessi

Giorgio Marescotti's competitors were quick to act on the apparent collapse of the firm after his death. Both the Giunti and Michelangelo Sermartelli renewed their attempts to gain the title of Grand-Ducal Printer, universal privileges and rights to the printing of state legislation.[42] Cosimo Giunti offered to establish a press in Pisa in return for these concessions. Somewhat later, in June 1605, Modesto Giunti also urged the grand duke to act speedily, especially over the question of printing state legislation, 'for it will soon be necessary to act to secure this business, since the aforesaid Marescotti heirs are unable to continue it for many reasons, and in particular because they have already lost the greater part of their press, part sold to make money and part given to relations in lieu of dowries'.[43] He also noted the Giunti's large stock and its distinguished customers, including the Duke of Urbino, the Prince of Massa 'and an infinite number of other literati, [who] when they want an exquisite book come first to us, as happens continually on the part of those who have seen the recently printed catalogue of all our books'.[44] Similarly, Modesto Giunti claimed that the title of Grand-Ducal Printer would enable his press 'to maintain, continue and increase as never before this great selection of books from Germany, Flanders, Spain, England, and all parts of the world, as has always

condurre, da altre Bande, per uenderle ne cauerebbe prezzo grande, come sarebbe, se in quel luogho doue l'hauessi fussero stimate, è valessero scudi cento in venetia ne cauerebbe scudi 150. ò piu . . .' (Mag. Pup. 715, fol. 215^r–215^v). Other Florentine printers (including Michelangelo Sermartelli, Cosimo Giunti, Francesco Tosi and Antonio Guiducci) were also called upon to testify to the quality and value of Giorgio Marescotti's fonts.

[42]   See the petitions in Misc. Med. 314, ins. 3, nos. 4–7; Reg. Dir. 11, fols. 247–55; Maracchi Biagiarelli, 'Il privilegio di stampatore ducale', pp. 356–8.

[43]   Misc. Med. 314, ins. 3, no. 7 (see n. 30), fol. [1]^r: 'che in breue sarà forza pigliar prouedimento a questo negozio per esser detti eredi del Mariscotti inabili a poterlo continuare per molte cause, è in particolare per hauer già dato esito alla maggior parte della stamperia, parte uenduta per toccar danarj, e' parte data a' cognati in conto di Dote'.

[44]   Ibid., fol. [1]^v: 'infiniti altri signori litterati, quando uoglion qualche libro squisito, subito fanno far capo a noj, come uien fatto continuamente da quelli che anno uisto il catalogo stampato li giorni passati, di tutti e' nostri libri'. The Catalogus librorum qui in Iunctarum Bibliotheca Philippi haeredum Florentiae prostant (Florence, 1604 [?stile fiorentino]) probably appeared in early 1605, see the documents in L. S. Camerini, I Giunti tipografi editori di Firenze, 1571–1620, p. 27, and a copy was sent to the Duke of Urbino on 12 March 1604/5, Urb. Classa I^a, Div. G, 237, fol. 264. Its appearance should probably be linked directly to the Giunti's attempts to gain concessions, exemptions and privileges on Giorgio Marescotti's death. The extensive list of music is transcribed in P. Kast, 'Die Musikdrucke des Kataloges Giunta von 1604', Analecta Musicologica, 2 (1965), pp. 41–71, and in O. Mischiati, Indici, cataloghi e avvisi degli editori e librai musicali italiani dal 1591 al 1798 (Florence, 1984), pp. 110–34.

been our plan'.[45] In return, Sermartelli vaunted his Greek and Latin fonts, the fact that he employed a type-founder, that he had two well-stocked bookshops in the city, and that he had connections with the book trade throughout Italy, France, Spain and Germany.[46]

The Marescotti heirs attempted to staunch rumours of their firm's demise. They submitted a counter-claim against the Giunti and Sermartelli, seeking to maintain their privileges on the grounds that Giorgio Marescotti had loyally served the Medici continuously for thirty-three years until his death.[47] The six-month privilege on state legislation was renewed, mainly, it seems, because of the support of Grand Duchess Christine of Lorraine, who had some sympathy for her French compatriots.[48] However, the effects of the litigation were quickly felt in the firm's output: five titles survive from 1602, none from 1603, five from 1604, two from 1605, one from 1606, and one from 1607. Those from 1602–4 bear the imprint 'appresso gl'heredi del Marescotti', while Cristofano Marescotti's name appears alone on Marescotti prints from late 1604 onwards.

The litigation on the death of Giorgio Marescotti and the partial liquidation of the firm were scarcely conducive to successful business, and Cristofano Marescotti had a long fight to gain control of the firm: indeed, for a time he was forbidden to go within 100 yards of the printing shop, and he spent one day imprisoned in the Bargello for failing to present documents to the magistrates.[49] Not until 1607–8 did things set back on an even keel. Cristofano Marescotti found himself at the head of a much reduced press. Of the twenty-five fonts known to have been owned by his father, at least seventeen were sold in whole or in part in Venice, and others must have gone to Pisa with Boschetti. It seems that the firm no longer had the facilities to print

---

[45] Misc. Med. 314, ins. 3, no. 7, fol. [1]^v: 'Il che sarà un darci animo a mantenere, continuare è crescer piu che maj, questo grand' assortimento di libri di Germania, Fiandra, Francia, Spagna, Inghilterra, è d'ogni parte del mondo, com'è stato sempre nostro proposito'.

[46] Sermartelli's undated (but late 1603?) petition survives in Reg. Dir. 11, fols. 248^r–248^v (also Misc. Med. 314, ins. 3, no. 6).

[47] The Marescotti heirs' undated (but late 1603?) petition survives in Reg. Dir. 11, fols. 249^r–249^v (also Misc. Med. 314, ins. 3, no. 8), given in Maracchi Biagiarelli, 'Il privilegio di stampatore ducale', pp. 356–7.

[48] Christine's support is reported in a memorandum from Belisario Vinta to Giovanni Battista Concini, 15 January 1603/4, Reg. Dir. 11, fol. 251 (given in Maracchi Biagiarelli, 'Il privilegio di stampatore ducale', pp. 357–8); on his death Giorgio Marescotti owed her 100 scudi, Mag. Pup. 692, fol. 112^r. Belisario Vinta himself was reluctant to become involved in the arguments because he was godfather to members of both the Giunti and the Marescotti families.

[49] Mag. Pup. 31, fol. 216^v (9 September 1603); 32, fol. 49^v (14 June 1604).

on a large scale. The last known major edition by the Marescotti press is Arcangelo Giani's *Della historia del B. Filippo Benizzi* (some 490 pp.) of 1604. Thereafter, extant non-music publications bearing the Marescotti imprint are all small-scale occasional items (no more than 22 pp.). Instead, Cristofano Marescotti turned to the one field where, it seems, he did still have the necessary equipment and materials: in 1606, 1607, 1610 and 1611, nothing but music is known to have appeared from his press.

At least one of the Marescotti music fonts was sold in Venice. This was probably the one (the 'musica di Parigi'?) which Giorgio Marescotti had used in all his editions containing music from 1581 to 1602. The font then disappears from Marescotti prints, although it was used for the music examples in Antonio Brunelli's *Regole utilissime*, a treatise issued in 1606 by Volcmar Timan, a German printer working in Florence. Giorgio Marescotti frequently rented out his punches to other Florentine printers,[50] and Timan may have procured the type necessary for his examples either from Giorgio or from the estate. However, when Cristofano Marescotti began printing music, he used a new font (staff height, 11 mm; minim height, 12 mm), perhaps the 'musica fatta in Firenze'. This font has longer note-stems and wider staves (Figure 2). Its appearance marked the beginning of a series of workmanlike editions of the new music of Florentine composers, including Piero Benedetti, Severo Bonini, Marco da Gagliano, Jacopo Peri and Raffaello Rontani. The preface to Peri's *Le varie musiche* of 1609 and the dedication of Francesco Rasi's *Madrigali* of 1610 are signed by the printer himself, although it is not clear whether this is because Cristofano Marescotti had a financial interest in the editions or because of the reticence of a 'noble' composer. All these editions filled a niche not yet fully exploited by the Venetian presses, which seem to have been cautious over issuing music in more modern secular styles.

Cristofano Marescotti died in early September 1611. His heirs managed to see Piero Benedetti's *Musiche* through the press, but then financial problems again hit the firm. His widow, Margherita Pugliani, attempted to continue the business, and she retained the Marescotti copyright on state legislation for two further two-year periods so that she could secure a dowry for her daughter,

---

[50] This is clear from the testimonies of Florentine printers on the quality and value of Giorgio Marescotti's fonts (see n. 41) in Mag. Pup. 715, fols. 256–65.

Figure 2   Severo Bonini, *Madrigali, e canzonette spirituali . . . per cantare a una voce sola* (Florence, Cristofano Marescotti, 1607), p. 6 (detail). Reproduced by permission of the British Library.

Caterina.[51] By 1613 the firm was actually run by Caterina and her husband, Domenico Magliani. However, Magliani murdered one of his apprentices, injured another and went into exile. Also in the firm, whether before or as a result of the Magliani scandal, was Zanobi di Francesco Pignoni. At some stage, Pignoni formed a partnership with Margherita Pugliani and became the effective head of the Marescotti press. However, apparently by mid-1614 the partnership was dissolved, and Margherita left the premises to establish a new

[51]   Reg. Dir. 15, fols. 642ʳ–647ʳ (containing Margherita's petition, sent to the court *auditore* on 21 September 1611, comments by other printers and a memorandum); 16, fol. 930ʳ (the renewal on 7 July 1613); S. M. Nuova 199, no. 14.

shop directly opposite. Presumably Pignoni bought her out, for he seems to have retained much of the Marescotti printing equipment, including the music font.[52]

Pignoni made an impressive debut as a music-printer in 1614–15 with no fewer than six editions, three of which seem to have appeared in the space of one month (the dedication of del Turco's *Il secondo libro de madrigali a cinque voci* is dated 1 August 1614; of Caccini's *Nuove musiche e nuova maniera di scriverle*, 18 August 1614; of Brunelli's *Varii esercitii*, 6 September 1614). Domenico Visconti's *Il primo libro de madrigali a cinque voci* appeared in very early 1615 (the dedication is dated 6 January 1615, which is most probably *stile comune*), and Pignoni's other two editions of 1614 (by Raffaello Rontani and Marco da Gagliano) do not have dated dedications. Clearly, Pignoni could work quickly. Significantly, he was also a musician, calling himself 'Musico di Cappella di V*ostra* A*ltezza* S*erenissima*' in a petition to the grand duke of 1615.[53] But the most likely reason for Pignoni's turning to music with such apparent enthusiasm lies in a contract dated 18 July 1614 registered in the records of the Tribunale di Mercanzia:

The Most Magnificent Signor Cavalier Giovanni di Antonio del Turco on his own behalf, Signor Lodovico di Francesco Arrighetti on behalf of his company registered under the name of Francesco Arrighetti & Co., Bankers, and Signor Giovanni Battista di Zanobi da Gagliano on his own behalf, have given and do give in *accomandita* to Zanobi di Francesco Pignoni, bookseller in the city of Florence, present and acknowledging the provenance and receipt in *accomandita* from the aforementioned the sum and amount of 300 scudi of 7 lire per scudo, with 100 scudi from each of the aforementioned Signor Cavalier, Signor Lodovico and Signor Giovanni Battista da Gagliano, and thus in total the aforesaid sum of 300 scudi, to invest in the business of bookselling and printing in the city of Florence under the name of the aforesaid Zanobi Pignoni & Co., Booksellers of

---

[52] See the memoranda of August 1615 and November 1616 in Reg. Dir. 18, fols. 478ʳ (where Pignoni petitions for the privileges previously awarded to Margherita), 790ʳ–791ʳ. Domenico Magliani may have been related to one Salvestro Magliani who was employed in the Giunti press in 1589, see LC 554, fol. 19ᵛ. In October 1614 Pignoni is included in a list of Florentine printers and booksellers as 'stampatore et libraio alla condotta', i.e. on the Via della Condotta, where the Marescotti had their shop, and separately from the 'Heredi di Cristofano Marescotti' (i.e. Margherita), Reg. Dir. 18, fols. 64ʳ–65ᵛ. He had matriculated in the Arte dei Medici e Speziali on 15 November 1607, see Med. Spez. 14, fol. 190ʳ.

[53] Reg. Dir. 18, fol. 478ʳ (*rescritto* dated 8 August 1615). In another petition (*ibid.*, fol. 479ʳ) Pignoni styles himself 'uno de' Cantori di Cappella di V*ostra* A*ltezza* S*erenissima*'.

Florence, for the time and period of the forthcoming three years, having begun on the 9th day of June past . . .[54]

The contract continues with the usual conditions attached to *accomandita* (in effect, limited-liability) business investments.

The three investors in Pignoni's company were all important figures in Florentine musical life. Giovanni del Turco was a nobleman and sometime composer: the Marescotti press had issued his *Il primo libro de madrigali a cinque* in 1602. Lodovico Arrighetti was a patron and dilettante: he was the dedicatee of Marco da Gagliano's *Il quinto libro de madrigali a cinque voci* (Venice, 1608), and two pieces by him were included in subsequent publications by the composer.[55] Giovanni Battista da Gagliano, Marco da Gagliano's brother, was a performing musician and composer. However, it seems that Giovanni Battista da Gagliano was actually acting on behalf of another Florentine patron, Cosimo del Sera, the dedicatee of Marco da Gagliano's *Il sesto libro de madrigali a cinque voci* (Venice, 1617). Marco da Gagliano, the grand duke's *maestro di cappella* and perhaps the leading musician in Florence, does not figure in the arrangement, although it seems likely that he had a hand in the proceedings. Indeed, it may be possible to link this new venture in music-printing with the activities of Gagliano's Accademia degli Elevati or some successor to this group.[56]

We do not know what requirements Pignoni had to meet in return

---

[54] Trib. Mer. 10838, fol. 126ʳ: 'Addi 18 di luglio 1614 / Il Molto Magnifico Signor Caualiere Giouanni di Antonio del Turco in nome proprio, il Signor Lodovico de Francesco Arrighetti in nome della sua compagnia cantante sotto nome di Francesco Arrighetti e [Compagni] di Banco, et il Signor Giouanni battista di Zanobi da Gagliano in suo nome proprio hanno dato, et danno in accomandita a Zanobi di Francesco Pignoni libraio nella citta di Firenze, presente, et confessante hauere hauuto et riceuuto in acomandita da li prenominati la somma, et quantità di scudi trecento di lire 7. per scudo, con scudi cento da ciascuno delli predetti Signor Caualiere, Signor Lodovico et Signor Giovanni battista da Gagliano et cosi in tutto la detta somma di scudi 300, per esercitarli nell'esercitio del libraio et stamperia nella citta di Firenze sotto nome di detto Zanobi pignoni e [Compagni] librai in Firenze per tempo et termine di Anni tre prossimi futuri, et già cominciati il il [*sic*] di 9 di giugno prossimo passato . . .'. Another copy, with minor variants, is in Trib. Mer. 10837, fols. 125ᵛ–126ʳ. I am most grateful to Professor Edmond Strainchamps and Dr David Butchart for sharing with me their own information on this company.

[55] 'Pur venisti cor mio' (*a* 2) in M. da Gagliano, *Musiche a una dua e tre voci* (Venice, 1615); 'Movetevi a pietà del mio tormento' (*a* 5) in idem, *Il sesto libro de madrigali a cinque voci* (Venice, 1617).

[56] E. Strainchamps, 'New Light on the Accademia degli Elevati of Florence', *The Musical Quarterly*, 62 (1976), pp. 507–35. In April 1609 the Elevati had plans to issue an anthology of madrigals by their members, but this seems to have come to nothing, see *ibid.*, pp. 523–4.

for this investment in his business. However, it can hardly be coincidence that in the same year as Pignoni received 300 scudi from three Florentine music patrons he should also have issued such a large number of music-prints. It seems more than likely that these prints were encouraged, if not directly funded, by the del Turco–Arrighetti–da Gagliano partnership, with or without further payments from individual composers or their patrons. It is not clear whether the partners viewed their investment as a profit-making proposition – the firm does seem to have made a profit in its brief life – or simply as a means of enlightened patronage. However, in view of the apparently uncommercial nature of music-printing in Florence it is significant that this major initiative should have been the result of a special partnership between patrons, composers and a printer.

The imprints of the del Turco, Caccini, Brunelli and Visconti editions mention the company, as required by the *accomandita* contract, while those of the Rontani and Gagliano volumes list the printer alone. If this is not an oversight, it is possible either that they appeared in the first half of 1614 before the company came into effect, or that they were private initiatives somehow kept distinct from the activities of the *accomandita* partnership. If either or both appeared in early 1614, this may have encouraged del Turco and his colleagues to invest in the firm. Whatever the case, Pignoni and his financiers perhaps felt that they were giving a new impetus to Florentine music-printing. Certainly the unusual breadth of repertory issued in this year – polyphonic madrigals, sacred music, and chamber songs (including another collection of 'nuove musiche' by Caccini) – suggests an attempt to establish a Florentine music-press on a hitherto unprecedented scale. They may also have sought to take advantage of the gradual but noticeable decline in the activities of the Venetian presses in this decade. Other regional printers (such as Giovanni Battista Robletti in Rome) were to embark upon similar initiatives, and arguably with some success. But Pignoni's company was short-lived; it was dissolved a year after its foundation, on 15 June 1615.[57] On 14 June 1615, the printer had entered into a new *accomandita* arrangement with his uncle, the bookseller Pasquale d'Antonio Pignoni, whose initial investment of 440 scudi seems to have been in the form of stock and printing

---

[57]   Trib. Mer. 10838, fol. 132^r.

equipment.[58] The arrangement lasted until 1 December 1621, by which time Pasquale Pignoni's investment had increased to some 2000 scudi. However, with the del Turco–Arrighetti–da Gagliano partnership dissolved, the impetus for printing music seems to have been lost: Marco da Gagliano published his *Musiche a una dua e tre voci* and Visconti his *Il primo libro de arie a una e due voci* in Venice in 1615 and 1616 respectively. One suspects that Pignoni's first initiative for music-printing failed, whether because of the increasingly unhealthy economic climate in northern Italy, the ever present limitations of the Florentine book trade, or simply the lack of composers of stature in (or attracted to) Florence who might have supported a more commercially oriented press. Pignoni concentrated instead on other material, including poetry, entertainment texts and *descrizioni*.[59]

Pignoni did return to music-printing in mid-1617, issuing three editions by Benedetti, Filippo Vitali and Giovanni Battista Bartoli. One by Francesca Caccini appeared in 1618, and two, by Andrea Falconieri and Jacopo Peri, in 1619. (Again, the dedication of Peri's *Le varie musiche . . . con aggiunta d'arie nuove* is signed by the printer, although Pignoni's motives for doing so are unclear.) The first of this series, Benedetti's *Musiche . . . libro quarto* (the dedication is dated 16 September 1617), is dedicated to Alessandro Covoni, who is said to have established a 'camerata' in the city, presumably for musical discussion and performance.[60] Once again, there seems to be a link between music-printing and a Florentine patron and dilettante. However, we do not know the exact relationship between Covoni and Pignoni, nor whether the other composers printed by Pignoni in 1617–19 were associated with this patron. But the presence of Benedetti and Peri here does emphasise the connections between Pignoni and the Marescotti press. Benedetti's first book of *Musiche*

[58] Trib. Mer. 10838, fols. 137ʳ, 179ᵛ–180ʳ; 10839, fol. 8ʳ. For a time, Pignoni held the company in partnership with one Giovanni di Romolo Benucci. Pasquale d'Antonio Pignoni had matriculated in the Arte dei Medici e Speziali on 3 January 1586/7, Med. Spez. 13, fol. 231ʳ, and in 1588 he was associated with a bookshop owned by the heirs of Giovanni Passignani, GCS Libro 408, opening 102.

[59] In August 1615, Pignoni sought a privilege for his self-financed editions of Gabriello Chiabrera's *Firenze, poema eroico* and Andrea Salvadori's *Lettere eroiche*, Reg. Dir. 18, fol. 479ʳ.

[60] Covoni, a 'paggio nero di *Sua Altezza Serenissima*', composed a madrigal for the court in May 1616, see A. Solerti, *Musica, ballo e drammatica alla corte medicea dal 1600 al 1637: notizie tratte da un diario con appendice di testi inediti e rari* (Florence, 1905; repr. New York, 1968), p. 131.

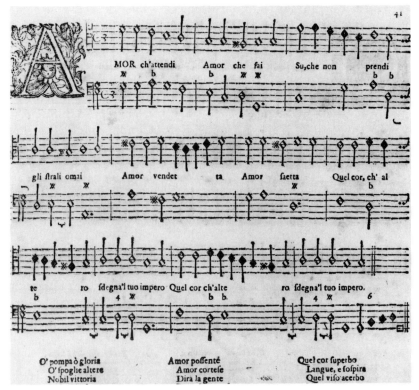

Figure 3   Giulio Caccini, *Nuove musiche e nuova maniera di scriverle* (Florence, Zanobi Pignoni, 1614), p. 41 (detail). Reproduced by permission of the British Library.

was printed by Cristofano Marescotti's heirs in 1611, and Pignoni's print of Peri's *Le varie musiche* is an enlarged second edition of a volume issued by Cristofano Marescotti in 1609. Pignoni's music font is the same as that used by Cristofano Marescotti, they share the same series of engraved capitals (compare Figures 2 and 3), and in some Pignoni prints (for example, the Falconieri and Peri editions of 1619) the Marescotti mark (a ship in a shield) appears.

Pignoni's apparent interest in music lapsed once more after 1619, whether because of a lack of investment by Florentine composers or patrons, or of financial difficulties in the economic crisis of the late 1610s.[61] His next music-print was an opera performed at the

---

[61]   R. Romano, 'Tra xvi e xvii secolo. Una crisi economica: 1619–1622', *Rivista Storica Italiana*, 74 (1962), pp. 480–531; translated as 'Between the Sixteenth and Seventeenth Centuries: The Economic Crisis of 1619–22', *The General Crisis of the Seventeenth Century*, ed. G. Parker

festivities celebrating the wedding of Odoardo Farnese and Margherita de' Medici in 1628, Marco da Gagliano's *La Flora*. This is a rather ugly volume in which the font appears increasingly worn. It compares unfavourably with the elegant editions of Pietro Cecconcelli, another printer who had established himself in Florence by the 1620s and who issued two volumes of music by Vitali in 1623 and one by Francesca Caccini in 1625.[62] Cecconcelli's prints present a new music font (Figure 4: staff height 12 mm; minim height, 11.5 mm) that was eventually taken over by Giovanni Battista Landini, who issued four music-prints between 1630 and 1635. Pignoni further issued music in 1631, 1637 and 1641, either printing undistinguished material by local composers – Gregorio Veneri and Bartolomeo Spighi were *maestri di cappella* at the cathedrals of Prato and Livorno respectively, and Antonio Guelfi was a pupil of Giovanni Battista da Gagliano – or attempting to capture a popular market, as with Giovanni Battista Abatessa's *Cespuglio di varii fiori*. We have no record of Pignoni printing music after 1641, although the Marescotti–Pignoni font appears again in Vitali's *Musiche a tre voci . . . libro quinto* (Florence, 1647), printed by Lando Landi and Giovanni Antonio Bonardi.[63]

It is clear that music-printing in Florence operated very differently from the great music-presses in Venice. No Florentine printer devoted himself exclusively to music, and only Pignoni seems to have had professional interests or abilities in the field. No printer (after Giorgio Marescotti in the early 1580s) produced potentially profit-making anthologies or raided popular prints issued elsewhere in Italy. Each concentrated on local repertories, and these repertories and the printing-format (often folio) associated with them have all the hallmarks of a 'luxury' item designed for limited consumption: Florentine printers largely ignored what was apparently the staple fare of more commercially oriented music-presses at the turn of the century, polyphonic madrigals and sacred music (the latter was

and L. M. Smith (London, 1978), pp. 165–225. For the effects of this crisis on music-printing, see the comments in A. Pompilio, 'Editoria musicale a Napoli e in Italia nel Cinque-Seicento', *Musica e cultura a Napoli dal xv al xix secolo*, ed. L. Bianconi and R. Bossa (Florence, 1983), pp. 79–102.

62 Cecconcelli seems to be first mentioned in official records to do with the book trade in December 1618, Aud. Rif. 31, fols. 453–4.

63 One Giovanni Landi was a *fattore* in the Marescotti press in 1612, see Delfiol, 'I Marescotti', p. 178. He may have been an older relative of Lando Landi.

Figure 4   Francesca Caccini, *La liberazione di Ruggiero dall'isola d'Alcina* (Florence, Pietro Cecconcelli, 1625), p. 3. Reproduced by permission of the British Library.

coming to dominate the output of Venetian music-printers).[64] Moreover, Florentine printers did not reprint their editions (with the exception of Peri's *Le varie musiche*). Few Florentine music-prints seem to have involved a significant capital investment on the part of the printer. Although Giorgio Marescotti, at least, may have retained bulk copies of some of his editions for sale in addition to receiving (or in part-payment of) his printing costs (see above, p. 47), only his 1582 anthology and his 1585 Arcadelt edition appear to have been entirely self-financed. (Although Cristofano Marescotti's editions of Peri's *Le varie musiche* (1609) and Rasi's *Madrigali* (1610), and Pignoni's second edition of Peri's collection (1619), may have been initiatives on the part of the printer, the evidence is doubtful.) All this suggests that Florentine music-printers came to cater largely for a 'vanity press', working mainly on commission with most if not all expenses being borne by the composer and/or his patron(s).

The operation of a 'vanity press' in sixteenth-century music-printing – clearly it was not limited to Florence – is a phenomenon that has not yet been fully explored. No doubt sixteenth-century Italian music-printers did issue volumes on their own initiative and for profit – as with some anthologies and reprints or the music of well-established composers – perhaps paying composers lump sums for their manuscripts, entering into profit-sharing agreements, or even paying royalties on copies sold.[65] Nevertheless, a significant proportion of music-prints were undoubtedly 'vanity' publications, with composers or their patrons paying all costs. But even if Florentine printers did cater largely for 'vanity' editions, they still suffered disadvantages when compared with their Venetian counterparts. It is significant that a number of Florentine composers continued to have their music printed in Venice even after Giorgio Marescotti had established a music-press in Florence. Cristofano Malvezzi, Luca Bati and Marco da Gagliano all issued their five- or six-part madrigals there, and Carlo Berti (in charge of the music at Ss Annunziata) his psalms, magnificats and motets. Indeed, during the period of the Marescotti firm's activities in music-printing

---

[64] T. Carter, 'Music Publishing in Italy, c.1580–c.1625: Some Preliminary Observations', *Royal Musical Association Research Chronicle*, 20 (1986–7), pp. 19–37.

[65] For a document outlining these various methods of payment from a printer to an author, although not in connection with a music-print, see T. Carter, 'Another Promoter of the 1582 "Rassettatura" of the *Decameron*', *The Modern Language Review*, 81 (1986), pp. 893–9.

(1581–1611), well over twice as many new editions by Florentine composers appeared in Venice as in Florence.

This apparent preference for Venice was not necessarily to do with quality or speed of production: the best prints issued by the Marescotti–Pignoni press are by no means slapdash, and both Giorgio Marescotti and Zanobi Pignoni could work quickly when required (witness the appearance of Caccini's *L'Euridice composta in musica* and Peri's *Le musiche . . . sopra l'Euridice* apparently six weeks apart in 1600–1, and Pignoni's six prints of 1614–15). But the Giunti's petition to the court of 1563 (see above, pp. 34–5) makes clear the advantages of Venice that might have led some Florentine composers to reject the idea of having their music printed closer to home. Venice offered a choice of printers if not with greater expertise at least with a larger capacity: Filippo and Jacopo Giunti complained that they had just one printing-press, and that operating only 'a mezzo torculo', while Venetian and northern printers normally had more (they said that Girolamo Scotto had two working presses, and Christopher Plantin in Antwerp, three).[66] Venice allowed Florentine composers to take advantage of the larger distribution networks apparently established by Venetian printers (should they have wished to do so). Finally, it seems clear that these printers enjoyed lower production costs, whether because of their larger capacity or of cheaper materials and labour, and lower overheads.

On the question of production costs, some useful evidence is provided by the litigation over Giorgio Marescotti's estate in 1602. Giulio Caccini claimed that he was owed L. 52. 6. 8, in part on account of a number of unbound copies of his *L'Euridice composta in musica* and *Le nuove musiche* which he had asked the Marescotti shop to sell on his behalf (a clear indication that these were 'vanity' editions).[67] The submitted accounts reveal that sixteen copies of

---

[66] Misc. Med. 314, ins. 3, no. 3 (see n. 10). The term 'a mezzo torculo' refers to the operation of a press by one worker instead of the normal two, see Voet, *The Golden Compasses*, II, p. 318. The Giunti claimed that with two working presses they could print 6000–7000 (presumably single-sided) sheets per day, which is somewhat more than modern estimates (Voet suggests 1250 double-sided sheets per press per day, *op. cit.*, II, p. 20).

[67] Mag. Pup. 31, fols. 216ᵛ–217ʳ (7 October 1603). An account sheet submitted by Caccini, similarly dated 7 October 1603, is preserved in Mag. Pup. 695, interleaved sideways between fols. 108–9 and 116–17. Caccini deposited in total twenty-six copies of *L'Euridice composta in musica* and forty-six of *Le nuove musiche* in the Marescotti shop, for which he was owed 127 lire. However, he himself owed the Marescotti L. 74.13. 4 for copies of these two

L'Euridice were valued at L. 32 (L. 2 per copy), and fifteen copies of *Le nuove musiche*, L. 25 (L. 1.13. 4 per copy). No doubt the shop would have sold these copies at a higher price; a 10% mark-up seems to have been common in such circumstances. The specified values of the Caccini volumes compare unfavourably with those of Venetian music-prints. The price per sheet of *L'Euridice* (in folio, 56 pp., i.e. 14 sheets at 4 pp. per sheet) is some 34 denari, and of *Le nuove musiche* (in folio, 52 pp., i.e. 13 sheets), some 30 denari. In 1596, the Scotto firm in Venice advertised their (unbound) quarto partbooks at a price equivalent to 12 denari per sheet (L. 1 for five partbooks comprising a total of 20 sheets at 8 pp. per sheet).[68] This seems to have been a standard price for printed music in quarto format. Even such a complex volume as Vincenzo Galilei's *Fronimo: dialogo . . . sopra l'arte del bene intavolare*, with text, mensural notation and lute tablature, of which the Scotto firm printed a second edition in 1584 (in folio, 192 pp., i.e. 48 sheets), is advertised at only L. 3.10. 0, i.e. 17.5 denari per sheet. It seems possible that printing costs in Florence could easily have been double or more those in Venice.

If it was a question of making money from printing one's own music, then Venice clearly had distinct advantages. Severo Bonini wished (according to the preface to his *Il secondo libro de madrigali, e mottetti a una voce sola*, printed by Cristofano Marescotti in 1609) that the good fortune of his first book of chamber songs would also be that of his second, 'for scarcely was it printed in Florence than it was reprinted in Venice, and through its good fortune it was so esteemed that all at once was it snatched from the presses'.[69] A number of

prints which he had re-purchased from the shop (one for presentation to the court on 18 November 1602, presumably in connection with the performance of *Euridice* on 5 December), for various binding expenses (including 1 lira for the 'Legatura dj vno petrarcha'), and also for '1 Canzonette dj Giuljo romano', costing L. 1.13. 4. This is kept distinct from *Le nuove musiche*, and it would be intriguing if Caccini had indeed published a volume of canzonets which is now lost. However, the term is inappropriate for the now convincingly disputed *Fuggilotio musicale* by 'D. Giulio Romano', a second edition of which was printed by Giacomo Vincenti in Venice in 1613, see H. W. Hitchcock, 'Depriving Caccini of a Musical Pastime', *Journal of the American Musicological Society*, 25 (1972), pp. 58–78. The magistrates adjudicated that the sum owed Caccini should be paid in equal parts by the heirs.

68 Mischiati, *Indici, cataloghi e avvisi*, pp. 99–106. The Scotto prices are comparable with those in the Vincenti catalogue of 1591 given in *ibid.*, pp. 92–8. It seems clear that, in general, the cost of printed music was *pro rata* the number of sheets in the print, see I. Fenlon, 'Il foglio volante editoriale dei Tini, circa il 1596', *Rivista Italiana di Musicologia*, 12 (1977), pp. 231–51, see p. 242.

69 '. . . che appena stampato in Firenze si ristampò in Venetia, et hebbe per sua buona ventura tanto di credito, che in un tratto fu levato via di su le Stamperie'. Bonini's

Florentine authors preferred to print in Venice because it allowed them greater profits and more convenience.[70] So too, it seems, did a number of Florentine composers.

But Bonini's hopes for his edition also suggest another concern. Even without the financial and commercial attractions of the Venetian presses, it seems clear that it was almost *de rigueur* for composers above or aspiring to a certain rank to have their music printed there, if only for the sake of professional esteem. Cristofano Malvezzi, Luca Bati and Marco da Gagliano were all in charge of the music at the Duomo and San Giovanni Battista and canons of San Lorenzo and thus effectively occupied the position of *maestro di cappella* to the grand duke. They were anxious, and for more than just personal reasons, to proclaim abroad the glories of Florentine music-making.[71] Indeed, during the period in which Giorgio and Cristofano Marescotti printed music, those Florentines who generally chose not to have their music printed in Florence can all be included in the category of professional or 'establishment' composers in the city, and the music that they printed in Venice largely involved genres that scarcely figure in the output of the Marescotti presses, polyphonic madrigals and sacred music. Significantly, Vincenzo Galilei, who merits at least partial inclusion among the 'professionals', initially planned to have his *Dialogo . . . della musica antica, et della moderna* printed in Venice (according to his dedication). However, the manuscript sent there was 'lost' – Galilei suspected foul play by Gioseffo Zarlino – and so some two-thirds of the treatise was hastily reassembled and issued in Florence. Similarly, although Giorgio Marescotti then printed Galilei's *Contrapunti a due voci*, the

Madrigali, e canzonette spirituali . . . per cantare a una voce sola (Florence, Cristofano Marescotti, 1607) was reprinted in Venice by Alessandro Raverii in 1608.

70   See the petition by Giulio Cesare Giusti, August 1577, for a privilege for 'vn libro intitolato Le Battaglie à difesa della lingua italica' by his father, Mutio, Aud. Rif. 12, no. 262. Although Giusti was planning to dedicate it to Grand Duke Francesco I, he wanted to have it printed in Venice 'perche li nè cauera maggior frutto, et harò piu commodità di stampatori'. The privilege was granted, but on condition that the book be printed in Florence.

71   D. S. Butchart, 'The Madrigal in Florence, 1560–1630' (D.Phil. dissertation, University of Oxford, 1980), pp. 34–5, 44, discusses such advertising, and particularly in Luca Bati's dedication to Jacopo Corsi of his *Il primo libro de madrigali a cinque voci* (Venice, Angelo Gardano, 1594). It is also significant that Cristofano Malvezzi should have decided to issue the *Intermedii et concerti, fatti per la commedia rappresentata in Firenze nelle nozze del Serenissimo Don Ferdinando Medici, e Madama Christiana di Loreno, Gran Duchi di Toscana* in Venice (Giacomo Vincenti, 1591), whether or not this decision was prompted by any lack of capacity in the Marescotti press in Florence.

composer turned to Angelo Gardano in Venice for his *Il secondo libro de madrigali a quattro et a cinque voci* (1587; the Gardano press had printed his *Il primo libro* in 1574). On the other hand, musicians who printed in Florence were largely *dilettanti* (for example, Giovanni del Turco), composers of limited status (Severo Bonini, Piero Benedetti), or professional singers (Giulio Caccini, Jacopo Peri, Francesco Rasi). Moreover, prints issued in Florence often seem to contain music of somewhat specialised interest perhaps intended for selective circulation, and where cost may have been no objection or where a small print-run would have made it less worthwhile to approach the Venetian presses. It seems clear that most Florentine musicians deliberately chose a particular printer or place of publication depending on their financial interests in, and their personal ambitions for, their music.

Another indication of the selective nature of many Florentine music-prints is their apparently close links with particular Florentine patrons or musical salons. We have already seen the possible connections between Giorgio Marescotti's first music editions and the 'camerata' centring on Giovanni de' Bardi, and the importance for Zanobi Pignoni's entrance into music-printing of the group of patrons who helped finance his company. There is another patron associated with at least three of Pignoni's prints of 1614–15. Raffaello Rontani dedicated his *Le varie musiche . . . libro primo* to Don Antonio de' Medici, Domenico Visconti's *Il primo libro de madrigali a cinque voci* has a dedication to Don Antonio signed by Artemisia Torri, the prince's mistress, and Artemisia Torri is herself the dedicatee of Antonio Brunelli's *Varii esercitii*. According to Brunelli's dedication, the composer was then staying in Don Antonio's palace, the *casino* behind San Marco.[72] The world of Florentine music-making was indeed small, suggesting a provincialism and insularity that are perhaps typical of much Florentine art and thought in this period.

But insularity was by no means inimical to artistic innovation, as Florentine music-prints of the first decade of the seventeenth century

[72] For Don Antonio as a patron, see Solerti, *Musica, ballo e drammatica*, pp. 25, 28, 29, 30, 31, 34, 36, 45, 58 and 62, and for his support of the castrato Giovanni Gualberto Magli (whom he sent for two years' further training in Naples in October 1611), see Dep. Gen. 389, appendix no. 1064; Dep. Gen. 1520, opening 114. The prince appears to have maintained a significant musical establishment, see the dedication of Rontani's *Le varie musiche . . . a una due e tre voci . . . libro primo* (Florence, Zanobi Pignoni, 1614).

reveal. Even if Giorgio and Cristofano Marescotti's editions contained specialised material deemed inappropriate for Venice, for whatever reason, these editions nevertheless have a distinction that sets them apart, at least in modern eyes, from the more routine output of the Venetian presses. The opera scores of Peri, Caccini and Marco da Gagliano, or Caccini's *Le nuove musiche*, are by no means insignificant publications. However, such distinction appears lacking from many Florentine music-prints of the 1610s, in large part because Florence was no longer in the vanguard of contemporary trends. Books of chamber songs printed there tend to be weighty in terms of both literary content and musical style, with a greater emphasis on madrigals than on strophic arias. In the first decade of the century this music may not have been appropriate for Venice because of its apparent progressiveness. By the second decade, however, it was probably too conservative. The Venetian presses instead seem to have preferred the more overtly popular of the new genres (witness Antonio Brunelli's three books of *scherzi*, arias, canzonets and madrigals issued by Giacomo Vincenti in 1613–16). Even outsiders seem to have had a clear perception of the now conservative orientation of Florentine musical tastes. Andrea Falconieri, a Neapolitan pursuing a roving career in northern Italy, issued two books of chamber songs in 1619, one in Florence (his *Il quinto libro delle musiche*, printed by Pignoni) and the other in Venice (*Musiche . . . libro sexto*, printed by Bartolomeo Magni). The former has fourteen madrigals and six arias, and the latter four madrigals and fifteen arias (plus letter-tablature for a guitar accompaniment, an increasingly popular addition to Venetian songbooks).

Each attempt by a Florentine printer to create a well-established music-press in the city appears to have foundered for a complex web of reasons: the laissez-faire policies of the grand duke, the apparent inability of the Florentine presses to compete on equal terms with their colleagues in Venice and the north, the financial problems and family misfortunes of particular printing firms, and the increasingly restricted vision of Florentine composers and their patrons. Florentine music-printing, like Florentine printing in general, faced too many disadvantages to be able to operate on a sound commercial and competitive basis. But to the historian, failure is no less revealing than success. This study has raised many issues relevant both to a more general study of music in Florence over the 1600s and to a broader economic history of printing in Italy. Moreover, we have seen something of the fragile networks involving printers, composers and patrons upon which the success or failure of a music-press could depend. Exploring these networks remains a major task for historians of music-printing in the late sixteenth and early seventeenth centuries.

Royal Holloway and Bedford New College,
University of London

APPENDIX

Florentine editions with printed music, 1581–1641

This checklist gives details of editions of music and treatises with music examples printed in Florence during the period of the Marescotti and Pignoni presses.

1581   [1]   Vincenzo Galilei, *Dialogo . . . della musica antica, et della moderna*, Giorgio Marescotti, 1581, 1 vol. Ded. to Giovanni de' Bardi, Florence, 1 June 1581.

1582   [2]   *Della scelta di madrigali de piu eccellenti autori de' nostri tempi a tre voci, libro primo*, Giorgio Marescotti, 1582, 3 partbooks.

1584   [3]   Vincenzo Galilei, *Contrapunti a due voci*, Giorgio Marescotti, 1584, 2 partbooks. Ded. by Michelangelo Galilei (Vincenzo Galilei's son) to Federigo Tedaldi, Florence, 31 August 1584.

1585   [4]   Jacques Arcadelt, *Il primo libro de madrigali a quattro voci nuovamente con ogni diligenza ristampato*, Giorgio Marescotti, 1585, 4 partbooks.

1596/7 [5]   Stefano Venturi del Nibbio, *Il terzo libro de madrigali a cinque*, Giorgio Marescotti, 1596, 5 partbooks. Ded. to Cosimo Ridolfi, Florence, 20 February 1596 (=1597?).

1600   [6]   Giulio Caccini, *L'Euridice composta in musica in stile rappresentativo*, Giorgio Marescotti, 1600, 1 vol. Ded. to Giovanni de' Bardi, Florence, 20 December 1600. Note: copies survive with two different title-pages.

1600/1 [7]   Jacopo Peri, *Le musiche . . . sopra l'Euridice*, Giorgio Marescotti, 1600, 1 vol. Ded. to Maria de' Medici, 6 February 1600/1.

1601/2 [8]   Giulio Caccini, *Le nuove musiche*, 'appresso I Marescotti', 1601 (colophon: 'Appresso li Heredi di Giorgio

Marescotti', 1602), 1 vol. Ded. to Lorenzo Salviati, Florence, 1 February 1601/2. The imprimaturs are dated 30 June and 1 July 1602. A note by Cristofano Marescotti explains that the delay in appearance was due to the death of his father. Note: copies survive with two different title-pages.

1602 [9] Giovanni del Turco, *Il primo libro de madrigali a cinque*, the heirs of Giorgio Marescotti, 1602, 5 partbooks. Ded. to Alfonso Fontanelli, Florence, 1 July 1602.

[10] Vincenzo Galilei, *Dialogo della musica antica e moderna . . . in sua difesa contro Ioseffo Zerlino*, Filippo Giunti, 1602, 1 vol. Ded. to Giovanni de' Bardi, Florence, 1 June 1581. New first and last pages added to copies of 1581 edition [1].

1606 [11] Antonio Brunelli, *Regole utilissime per li scolari che desiderano imparare a cantare, sopra la pratica della musica*, Volcmar Timan, 1606, 1 vol. Ded. to Valerio Ansaldo. Uses same font as found in Giorgio Marescotti music-prints.[73]

[12] Girolamo Montesardo, *Nuova inventione d'intavolatura per sonare i balletti sopra la chitarra spagnuola, senza numeri e note*, Cristofano Marescotti, 1606, 1 vol. Ded. to Francesco Buontalenti.

1607 [13] Severo Bonini, *Madrigali, e canzonette spirituali . . . per cantare a una voce sola*, Cristofano Marescotti, 1607, 1 vol. Ded. to Don Simone Finardi, Badia di Ripoli, 1 May 1607.

1608 [14] Marco da Gagliano, *La Dafne . . . rappresentata in Mantova*, Cristofano Marescotti, 1608, 1 vol. Ded. to Vincenzo Gonzaga, Florence, 20 October 1608.

1609 [15] Severo Bonini, *Il secondo libro de madrigali, e mottetti a una voce sola*, Cristofano Marescotti, 1609, 1 vol. Ded. to Angelo Minerbetti, Santa Trinità (Florence), 29 November 1609.

[16] Jacopo Peri, *Le varie musiche : . . a una due, e tre voci*, Cristofano Marescotti, 1609, 1 vol.

1610 [17] Antonio Brunelli, *Regole e dichiarationi di alcuni contrappunti doppii*, Cristofano Marescotti, 1610, 1 vol.[74]

[18] Francesco Rasi, *Madrigali di diversi autori*, Cristofano

---

[73] F.-J. Fétis, *Biographie universelle des musiciens et bibliographie générale de la musique*, 8 vols. (2nd edn, Brussels, 1860–5), II, p. 97, reports a copy of Brunelli's 'Esercisi ad una e due voci' published in Florence in 1605. No details of the printer are given, and the volume now appears lost.

[74] Fétis, *Biographie universelle des musiciens*, II, p. 97, reports copies of Brunelli's 'Motetti a due voci, lib. 1°' (Florence, 1607), 'Motetti a due voci, lib. 2°' (Florence, 1608), 'L'Affettuoso invaghito, canzonette a tre voci' (Florence, 1608). Again, no details of the printer(s) are given, and the volumes now appear lost.

Marescotti, 1610, 1 vol. Ded. by Cristofano Marescotti to Giorgio Scali, Florence, 20 February 1609/10.

[19] Raffaello Rontani, *Gl'Affettuosi: il primo libro de madrigali a tre voci* . . . *per concertare nel chitarrone, ò semplicemente cantati*, Cristofano Marescotti, 1610, 3(?) partbooks. Ded. to Filippo Salviati, Florence, 15 December 1610.

1611 [20] Piero Benedetti, *Musiche*, the heirs of Cristofano Marescotti, 1611, 1 vol. Ded. to Cosimo della Gherardesca, Florence, 12 December 1611.

1614 [21] Antonio Brunelli, *Varii esercitii* . . . *per una, e due voci*, Zanobi Pignoni & Co., 1614, 1 vol. Ded. to Artemisia Torri, Florence, 6 September 1614.

[22] Giulio Caccini, *Nuove musiche e nuova maniera di scriverle*, Zanobi Pignoni & Co., 1614, 1 vol. Ded. to Piero Falconieri, 18 August 1614.

[23] Marco da Gagliano, *Missae, et sacrarum cantionum, sex decantandarum vocibus*, Zanobi Pignoni, 1614, 7 partbooks.

[24] Giovanni del Turco, *Il secondo libro de madrigali a cinque voci*, Zanobi Pignoni & Co., 1614, 5 partbooks. Ded. to Cosimo II de' Medici, Florence, 1 August 1614.

[25] Raffaello Rontani, *Le varie musiche* . . . *a una due e tre voci* . . . *libro primo*, Zanobi Pignoni, 1614, 1 vol. Ded. to Don Antonio de' Medici.

1615 [26] Domenico Visconti, *Il primo libro de madrigali a cinque voci*, Zanobi Pignoni & Co., 1615, 5 partbooks. Ded. by Artemisia Torri to Don Antonio de' Medici, Florence, 6 January 1615 (most probably *stile comune*).

1617 [27] Giovanni Battista Bartoli, *Il primo libro de madrigali a cinque voci*, Zanobi Pignoni, 1617, 5 partbooks. Ded. to Lorenzo Bonsi, Florence, 22 December 1617.

[28] Piero Benedetti, *Musiche* . . . *a una, e dua voci* . . . *libro quarto*, Zanobi Pignoni, 1617, 1 vol. Ded. to Alessandro Covoni, Florence, 16 September 1617.

[29] Filippo Vitali, *Musiche* . . . *a due tre, e sei voci libro primo*, Zanobi Pignoni, 1617, 1 vol. Ded. to Giovanni Corsi, Florence, 15 October 1617.

1618 [30] Francesca Caccini, *Il primo libro delle musiche a una, e due voci*, Zanobi Pignoni, 1618, 1 vol. Ded. to Cardinal [Carlo] de' Medici, Florence, 16 August 1618.

1619 [31] Andrea Falconieri, *Il quinto libro delle musiche a una, due, e tre voci*, Zanobi Pignoni, 1619, 1 vol. Ded. to Niccolo Berardi.

[32] Jacopo Peri, *Le varie musiche a una, due, e tre voci . . . con aggiunta d'arie nuove*, Zanobi Pignoni, 1619, 1 vol. Ded. by Zanobi Pignoni to Ferdinando Saracinelli. Enlarged second edition of 1609 print [16].

1623 [33] Filippo Vitali, *Il secondo libro de madrigali a cinque voci*, Pietro Cecconcelli, 1623, 5(?) partbooks. Ded. to Cardinal [Carlo] de' Medici, Florence, April 1623, and to Roberto Capponi.

[34] Filippo Vitali, *Intermedi . . . fatti per la commedia degl'Accademici Inconstanti recitata nel palazzo del Casino dell'ill.mo rev.mo S. Cardinale de Med.ci*, Pietro Cecconcelli, 1623, 1 vol. Ded. to Roberto Capponi, Florence, 29 May 1623.

1625 [35] Francesca Caccini, *La liberazione di Ruggiero dall'isola d'Alcina*, Pietro Cecconcelli, 1625, 1 vol. Ded. to Archduchess Maria Magdalena, Florence, 4 February 1625 (*stile comune*).

1628 [36] Marco da Gagliano, *La Flora del Sig. Andrea Salvadori*, Zanobi Pignoni, 1628, 1 vol. Ded. to Duke [Odoardo Farnese] of Parma and Piacenza.

1630 [37] Girolamo Frescobaldi, *Primo libro d'arie musicali . . . a una, a dua, e a tre voci*, Giovanni Battista Landini, 1630, 1 vol. Ded. to Ferdinando II de' Medici. Imprimaturs dated 25, 27 September 1630.

[38] Girolamo Frescobaldi, *Secondo libro d'arie musicali . . . a una, a dua, e a tre voci*, Giovanni Battista Landini, 1630, 1 vol. Ded. to Roberto Obizi. Imprimaturs dated 25, 29 September 1630.

1631 [39] Antonio Guelfi, *Madrigali da concertarsi con cinque voci et il basso continuo*, Zanobi Pignoni, 1631, 6(?) partbooks. Ded. to Alessandro Buondelmonti, Florence, 28 September 1631.

[40] Gregorio Veneri, *Madrigale a cinque: canone*, Zanobi Pignoni, 1631, broadsheet. Ded. to Enea Bizochi, Prato, 12 November 1631.

1635 [41] Domenico Anglesi, *Libro primo d'arie musicali . . . a voce sola*, Giovanni Battista Landini, 1635, 1 vol. Ded. to Duke Salviati, Florence, 18 September 1635.

[42] Antonio Gardane, *Libro primo a due voci*, Giovanni Battista Landini, 1635, 2 partbooks.

1637 [43] Giovanni Battista Abatessa, *Cespuglio di varii fiori, ovvero intavolatura de chitarra spagnola*, Zanobi Pignoni, 1637, 1 vol. New edition of volume printed in Orvieto by Giovanni Battista Robletti, 1635.

1640   [44]   Antonio Carbonchi, *Sonate di chitarra spagnola con intavolatura franzese*, Amadore Massi and Lorenzo Landi, 1640, 1 vol.

1641   [45]   Bartolomeo Spighi, *Musical concerto d'arie, e canzonette a una, dua, e tre voci*, Zanobi Pignoni, 1641, 1 vol. Ded. to Lodovico da Verrazzano, Livorno, 16 November 1641.[75]

---

[75] One further study of some relevance appeared while this essay was in press: N. Guidobaldi, 'Music Publishing in Sixteenth- and Seventeenth-Century Umbria', *Early Music History*, 8 (1988), pp. 1–36.

Early Music History (1989) Volume 9

CRAIG MONSON

ELENA MALVEZZI'S KEYBOARD MANUSCRIPT: A NEW SIXTEENTH-CENTURY SOURCE*

It is safe to say that the collections of the Museo Comunale Bardini, situated in Piazza dei Mozzi on the oltrarno in Florence, remain comparatively little known. The museum's vast store of paintings, sculpture, architectural ornament, rugs and tapestries, armour, bronzes, furniture and musical instruments all belonged to Stefano Bardini, the nineteenth- and early twentieth-century collector and art dealer.[1] Born in 1836 in the province of Arezzo, Bardini came to Florence to study painting at the Accademia delle Belle Arti. After the political turbulence of the 1860s, when Bardini fought with the Garibaldini, the young painter turned to restoration, connoisseurship and art dealing. By the age of forty-five he had established his reputation and an extraordinary personal collection. At the height of his career his patrons included the Rothschilds, the Vanderbilts, Isabella Gardiner and J. Pierpont Morgan. Many objects now in some of the world's best-known public collections passed through his hands.

In 1881 Bardini determined to build a museum for his personal

---

*Shorter versions of this paper were read at the Sixteenth Annual Conference on Medieval and Renaissance Music in Edinburgh in August 1988 and at the Annual Meeting of the American Musicological Society in Baltimore in November 1988. In addition to those singled out in specific contexts below, I should like to thank Jeffrey Kurtzman, John Nádas, Oliver Neighbour, Dolores Pesce, Joshua Rifkin and Jerome Roche for their help and advice. I am also grateful to the staff of the Museo Bardini in Florence and to the staffs of the following Bolognese institutions for their assistance: the Archivio Arcivescovile, the Archivio di San Domenico, the Archivio di Stato (abbreviated ASB below), the Biblioteca Communale (BCB) and the Museo Civico Medioevale.

[1] The most recent discussions of Bardini and his collection are F. Scalia, *Il Museo Bardini* (Milan, 1984), and F. Scalia, *Museo Bardini le armi* (Florence, 1984), which form the basis for this description.

collection by transforming the Florentine church of San Giorgio della Pace and the adjoining monastery into a palace in antique style. No fewer than three other museums were required, however, to house his huge and diverse holdings. The palace in Piazza dei Mozzi and its contents passed to the city of Florence at Bardini's death in September 1922.

Room 19 of the Museo Bardini, devoted to musical instruments, also contains a single music manuscript catalogued as MS 967. Nothing is known about how and when it fell into Bardini's hands. The records of the Museo Bardini contain nothing at all about its date, provenance or contents. The manuscript had been in storage for decades before it was finally put on display by the present director of the city museums, Fiorenza Scalia, on 18 November 1977, when the museum reopened after a rearrangement of the collection that had taken three years.[2] Since then no visitor to the museum had asked to examine it until the summer of 1987.

This large manuscript, 23.5×16.7 cm in oblong format and 4.8 cm thick, containing intabulations for keyboard of eighty-two madrigals, motets and chansons (counting their parts 1 and 2 separately), turns out to be the largest single Italian Renaissance collection of such keyboard intabulations to have come to light. It consists of 165 unnumbered ruled folios in twenty-one gatherings of eight folios each.[3] A single unruled guard sheet of a different paper appears at the beginning and end.

On each page two systems of two-staff keyboard notation were drawn with a rastrum, with six lines on the upper staff and eight on the lower (see Figure 1). The music, apparently copied by a single scribe, fills the manuscript almost completely. The scribe must have conceived the succession of pieces largely as bound, for in most instances, especially after gathering 2, works span the end of one fascicle and the beginning of the next. (The contents of fascicles are indicated by braces in the left margin of the inventory of the manuscript in Appendix 1.) And although fascicles 7 and 12 begin with new works, they are linked to the preceding fascicles by similar

---

[2] I should like to thank Dr Scalia for permitting me extended access to the Bardini music manuscript in the summer of 1987 and for her many other kindnesses.

[3] The first folio of gathering 19 has been removed; a stub remains. The original folios 4 and 5 at the centre of that gathering have also been removed, leaving a tiny fragment in the crease, and resulting in the loss of the end of the seventy-third piece, *Alcun non è*, and the beginning of the seventy-fourth piece.

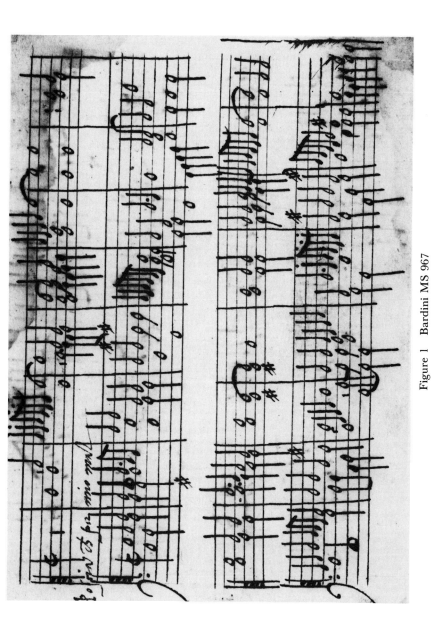

Figure 1   Bardini MS 967

repertory.[4] Fascicles 1 and 2, which contain a number of blank folios at their beginnings and/or ends, offer the prime exception to this pattern.[5] The colour of the ink used for titles sometimes contrasts with that of the music, suggesting that titles were not copied concurrently with the notes. Titles have been omitted from a few pieces, and no composers' names are given anywhere in the manuscript.

All the paper apart from the guard sheets betrays the same watermark, which appears at the edge of the page, cut in half, and consists of a simple encircled anchor. It does not correspond precisely to the recorded types of this very common design, but it most nearly resembles Mošin's type It. II. 1.a. numbers 346–435, dated 1479–1578, of Venetian provenance.[6]

It may well have been the lavishly decorated brown leather binding (see Figure 2) that prompted Stefano Bardini's purchase of the keyboard score.[7] The Bardini manuscript is one of only three Italian keyboard manuscripts from before 1700, and the only one from the sixteenth century, with this sort of elaborate binding.[8] The layout of the decoration and the tools involved clearly reflect the forms Tammaro De Marinis has identified as typical of Bolognese binding. The ornamented 'heart-shaped' tool employed in the frame, for example, is illustrated in various forms on Bolognese bindings that De Marinis has catalogued: no. 1287 (plate CCXXII), no. 1289 (plate CCXXIII), no. 1308 (plate CCXXV), and no. 1311 (plate CCXXVI). The first three of these also employ similar devices within the corners of their frames. The rich foliage that largely fills the

---

[4] Fascicle 6 ends and fascicle 7 begins with chansons published by Moderne; fascicle 11 ends with Rore's *Hellas comment*, part 2 of *En vos adieux*, while fascicle 12 begins with *En vos adieux*: the scribe apparently managed to copy the two parts of the chanson in reverse order.

[5] Fol. 8^r of fascicle 1 is largely blank; fol. 8^v of fascicle 1 and fols. 1–4^r of fascicle 2, and fol. 8^r of fascicle 2 and fols. 1–3^r of fascicle 3, are also blank. In fascicle 19 fol. 1 has been removed and fol. 2^r (counting the missing folio as 1) is blank. At the end of the manuscript, fols. 5^v– 8^v of fascicle 21 are blank.

[6] V. Mošin, *Anchor Watermarks*, Monumenta Chartae Papyraceae Historiam Illustrantia 13 (Amsterdam, 1973), pp. 17–18. The Bardini watermark is closest to nos. 383–4 (Fabriano, 1502), 387 (Zagorja, 1500–10) and 403 (Pozega, 1524). It is unlike any of the encircled anchors in C. M. Briquet, *Les filigranes* (2nd edn, Leipzig, 1923), I, nos. 464–72.

[7] The Museo Bardini contains a number of other volumes whose bindings are quite elaborate, but whose contents are of lesser interest.

[8] A. Silbiger, *Italian Manuscript Sources of 17th Century Keyboard Music* (Ann Arbor, 1980), p. 17, points out that of known keyboard manuscripts only the late manuscripts, Florence, Biblioteca del Conservatorio di Musica Luigi Cherubini, MS D.2358, and London, British Library, MS Add. 40080, have elegant bindings.

Figure 2   The cover of Bardini MS 967

interior of the Bardini binding, on the other hand, reappears in De Marinis's examples no. 1315 (plate CCXXIV), 1311 (plate CCXXVI), 1320 (plate CCXXVII), 1330 (plate CCXXVIII) and 1337 (plate CCXXIX). Of this style, which De Marinis suggests may have been established by the Bolognese scholar Achille Bocchi for the bindings of his own works, the author writes, 'The model of rich foliage having been found . . . it was widely adopted, so as to make immediately recognisable as Bolognese every binding similarly decorated.'[9]

The coat-of-arms on the front cover of the Bardini manuscript most closely resembles that of the prominent Malvezzi family of Bologna, 'recorded among the principal [families] of Italy for its illustrious origins, for its honoured men and for their most noble deeds at various times past', according to the seventeenth-century Bolognese historian, Pompeo Dolfi,[10] who reproduces the usual version of the Malvezzi coat-of-arms (see Figure 3). The coat-of-arms on the Bardini manuscript notably lacks the label (Italian: 'lambello') above the three lilies. Although the label is a characteristic feature of the Malvezzi coat-of-arms, it may occasionally be omitted.[11]

Exactly the same coat-of-arms, with three lilies and no label, reappears, however, on the first page of an early fifteenth-century manuscript of the life of the Blessed Diana d'Andolò, founder of the Dominican convent of Sant'Agnese in Bologna. This manuscript, now in the Biblioteca Comunale of Bologna with the signature MS B2019, must be the same 'Life of the Blessed Diana' that the religious historian Giovambattista Melloni saw in the archive of the convent in 1773, for his detailed description of the contents of the

---

[9] 'Inventato poi il modello dei ricchi fogliami . . . esso fu ampiamente adottato, così da far subito riconoscere come bolognese ogni rilegatura similmente ornata.' T. De Marinis, *La legatura artistica in italia nei secoli xv e xvi*, II (Florence, 1960), p. 9.

[10] 'ricordata frà le principali d'Italia, per sangue illustre, per Huomini honorati, e per nobilissimi fatti in diversi tempi vsciti da loro', *Cronologia delle famiglie nobili di Bologna* (Bologna, 1670), p. 490.

[11] A version without lilies and label appeared on the bell dated 1484 of the public oratorio at Bell'Aria, near the villa of the Marchesi Malvezzi-Campeggi (see ASB, Archivio Malvezzi De Medici, libro 8). The same form of the coat-of-arms has also been inserted in the margin on fol. 103 of the copy of Francesco Sansovino's *Delle origine et de fatti delle famiglie illustri d'Italia* (Venice, 1609) at the Kunsthistorisches Institut in Florence (catalogued 'Q1326'), beside the entry 'Signori Malvezzi'. A version of the coat-of-arms with lilies but without the label appears in a large printed table of 'Nomi, e Cognomi de' SENATORI BOLOGNESI, con il tempo de' loro possessi nel Senato', for 'Pirriteo Malvezzi Marchese, e Caval. di S. Stef. Adi 1603' (ASB, Archivio Malvezzi De Medici, Libro 1). The same print appears as a fold-out at the back of Dolfi, *Cronologia*.

MALVEZZI.

Figure 3   The Malvezzi coats-of-arms

Sant'Agnese chronicle exactly corresponds to that of MS в2019.[12]

The coat-of-arms on the Bardini manuscript, then, would appear to relate both to the Malvezzi of Bologna and to the convent of Sant'Agnese in that city. An inscription on the back cover of the Bardini manuscript, '.S. / .LENA. / MALVE / CI / A.', provides a link between the two. The Fondo Sant'Agnese, currently housed in the Archivio di Stato of Bologna, includes a number of references to a 'Soror Helena de Malvitijs'. These occur in notarial acts on behalf of the monastery prepared in the parlatorio of the convent, with the nuns assembled before the grating. In such cases it was customary to copy into the documents the names of the nuns, ordered according to the date of their profession. The name of Elena Malvezzi appears in thirteen such lists from the Fondo Sant'Agnese between 1528 and

---

[12] *Atti, o memorie degli uomini illustri in santità nati, o morti in Bologna*, classe II, vol. I (Bologna, 1773), p. 194. The coat-of-arms on the first page of BCB MS в2019 does not correspond to the seal of the convent, however. Only one example of the seal of the prioress of Sant'Agnese survives, on a document dated 1399 in the Fondo Sant'Agnese (Demaniale 12/5602). It shows a figure in flowing garb, apparently holding an animal in its arms, presumably a lamb: a typical representation of St Agnes.

1551.[13] Her name does not appear in the next earlier list of nuns, from March 1523. No similar documents survive at Sant'Agnese between 1551 and 1569, by which time Suor Elena's name has disappeared.[14]

A search beyond the Fondo Sant'Agnese reveals Elena's name in another similar document dated 1558 from the Archivio Arcivescovile of Bologna.[15] By a lucky chance, a further listing turns up in the rough draft of a document dated 25 May 1526 from the *notarili* of Alessandro Stiatici senior, a notary who occasionally served various Dominican orders in Bologna.[16] In this instance, 'S. helena di Malvizi' is the final name on the list. She must therefore have made her profession at Sant'Agnese between March 1523 and May 1526, most probably towards the end of that period.[17]

Additional details of the life of Suor Elena can be gleaned only from eighteenth- and nineteenth-century transcripts of original documents no longer known. An eighteenth-century obituario from Sant'Agnese preserved in the Archivio di San Domenico in Bologna (v. 7020) records the death of 'M[ad]re S[uor] Elena' on 11 October 1563. The designation 'Madre' indicates that Elena was among the most reverend members of the order at the time of her death.[18] A similar entry reappears in the 'Necrologia delle suore di S. Agnese' transcribed by the eighteenth- and nineteenth-century Bolognese archivist and historian Baldassare Antonio Maria Carrati, with the additional note 'Priora una volta'.[19]

[13] ASB, Demaniale 25/5615, AA1286; Demaniale 26/5616, BB1315, BB1331, BB1345; Demaniale 27/5617, CC1354, CC1361, CC1366, CC1382, CC1384, CC1397; Demaniale 28/5618, DD1403, DD1405, DD1420.

[14] ASB, Demaniale 25/5615, AA1273 (dated 6 March 1523); Demaniale 29/5619, EE1496 (dated 20 December 1569). Another list dated 4 December 1557 (EE1455) lists only the prioress, sub-prioress and seven members of the order.

[15] Ricuperi beneficiari, fasc. 8. The same fascicle also contains another document from 1531 listing Suor Elena as well.

[16] ASB, Notarili, Stiatici Alessandro seniore, filza 10 (1525–7). One further appearance of Suor Elena's name occurs in ASB, Notarili, Notaio Bartolomeo Algardi, filza 11 (1542–3), no. 25, a document dated 27 November 1542. I should like to thank Oscar Mischiati for bringing this to my attention.

[17] The additions to the lists of nuns in the notarial acts suggest that one or two girls joined the order every year. Had Elena Malvezzi made her profession much before 1526 there would probably have been other names below hers on the list from May 1526.

[18] According to the standard history of the monastery of Sant'Agnese, M. G. Cambria, *Il monastero domenicano di S. Agnese in Bologna* (Bologna, 1973), p. 34, the term 'Madre' was reserved for members of the council of the convent. I should like to thank M. Giovanna Cambria for making a copy of her book available to me and for answering several questions about the history of her order.

[19] BCB MS B921, p. 133. Cambria was not aware of Carrati's transcripts, which very usefully complement her history of the convent of Sant'Agnese.

It is also only thanks to another of Carrati's transcripts that the names of the prioresses of Sant'Agnese from 1497 to 1787 and the dates of their election are known today.[20] Suor Elena appears on p. 150 of his list. The exact entry reads: '1559 [crossed out] 1561. 30. ott[obr]ᵉ P[rior]a S[uor]ᵃ Febronia Bianchini e sotto P[rior]ᵃ S[uora] Elena Malvezzi'. The altered year, 1561, cannot be correct, however, because both the San Domenico necrology and Carrati list Febronia Bianchini's death in late October 1561 (San Domenico gives the date as 24 October, Carrati as 29 October), before the emended date. A comparison of the necrologies and Carrati's list of prioresses suggests the following scenario:

3 April 1559: Diana Dulcini elected prioress

28 October 1559: Diana Dulcini dies[21]

30 October 1559: Febronia Bianchini elected prioress, Elena Malvezzi sub-prioress

24/29 October 1561: Febronia Bianchini dies. Elena Malvezzi succeeds her?

11 October 1563: Elena Malvezzi dies

14 October 1563: Leona Vittori elected prioress

Even though no specific record of Elena's election as prioress survives, the fact that Carrati's necrology describes her as 'priora una volta' and that the next election was held three days after her death suggests that Suor Elena served not only as sotto-priora, but may also have served a two-year term as prioress between October 1561 and October 1563.

Although it is thus possible to establish with reasonable certainty the period of Suor Elena Malvezzi's affiliation with Sant'Agnese, her relationship to her own family is less clear. No reference to her has come to light in the archives of the various branches of the Malvezzi family. This is perhaps not surprising since she was not only a daughter rather than a son, but also a daughter who ended up as the bride of Christ, not the bride of some prominent and influential Bolognese. In 1927, however, Giuseppe Fornasini, who chronicled the history of the Malvezzi for a fashionable family wedding in that year, observed her name in the notes of Baldassare Carrati, who had listed her among the children of Lorenzo di Battista Malvezzi.[22]

[20] *Ibid.*, pp. 149–56.

[21] The San Domenico necrology lists 'Mʳᵉ S. Diana Felcini', an obvious error, because there was no member of the order by that name.

[22] G. Fornasini, *Breve cenno storico genealogico intorno alla famiglia Malvezzi* (Bologna, 1927),

Lorenzo di Battista (1467–1529), a Malvezzi of considerable, if at times dubious, distinction, was ultimately responsible for the branch of the family known as Malvezzi De Medici.

Suor Elena's place among Lorenzo's offspring is anything but clear. Fornasini had based his work on Carrati, who in turn had relied on the seventeenth-century *erudito* Giovanni Nicolò Pasquale Alidosi. Alidosi's work can still be consulted in the Archivio di Stato of Bologna, where one finds the following list of Lorenzo Malvezzi's progeny:[23]

Test[ament]o di Lorenzo di Batt[ist]ª Malvezzi

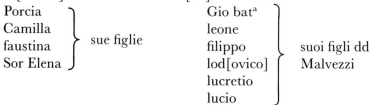

Porcia
Camilla
faustina   sue figlie
Sor Elena

Gio batª
leone
filippo   suoi figli dd
lod[ovico]   Malvezzi
lucretio
lucio

No true copy of Lorenzo's will survives in the Archivio Malvezzi De Medici. Of the two later summaries of the will found there, one, misdated 1628, mentions none of his daughters by name. The other, reproducing the original date of 9 March 1528, indicates that 'due Donzelle' had already married with surprisingly meagre dowries of 50 scudi, and provides dowries of 600 scudi for 'Porcia, Camilla e faustina sue figle' if they should become nuns.[24]

The baptismal registers of Bologna, in addition to recording the births of the three daughters listed by name in the summary of Lorenzo's will – Portia (b. 1517), Camilla (b. 1525) and Faustina (b. 1526) – include two others: another Camilla, born 1 June 1511, and Adola, born 18 March 1515.[25] Could either of these have been

p. 87. Although this work is indispensable for a study of the Malvezzi family, Fornasini relies heavily upon a manuscript family history preserved in ASB, Archivio Malvezzi-Campeggi, serie 2a, busta 27/264, that contains numerous inaccuracies. A great many printing errors also crept into Fornasini's genealogical tables. Fornasini also mistakes the date of Elena Malvezzi's election as sub-prioress for her death date.

23 ASB, Studio Alidosi, no. 26, vacchetino no. 293, p. 14. A similar list also appears in Studio Alidosi, pezzo 'Famiglie M', fascicolo 'Malvezzi'.

24 ASB, Archivio Malvezzi De Medici, Busta 123F, fasc. F31. Unfortunately, no original copy of Lorenzo's will is to be found among the surviving documents of the notary Bartolomeo Scudieri, who had initially drafted it, though Alidosi reports having seen one in the seventeenth century. A document drafted the day after Lorenzo's will, 10 March 1528, still survives, in addition to a number of other Malvezzi documents. See ASB, Notarili, Scudieri Bartolomeo, pezzi 2–3.

25 Archivio Arcivescovile, Reg. Batt., vol. 1516–19, fol. 156; vol. 1524–8, fols. 3ᵛ and 226ᵛ; vol. 1510–15, fols. 86 and 459ᵛ, respectively. The names of all the sons can also be found in the

Suor Elena? She had made her profession at Sant'Agnese by May of 1526. Although in the post-Tridentine period, at least, no girl was to profess before the end of her sixteenth year,[26] the earlier sixteenth century witnessed considerable latitude and laxity regarding the acceptance of postulants and their professions. Adola would have been much too young even to approach the post-Tridentine criterion. The absence of any reference to her in the Malvezzi archives suggests that perhaps she did not survive. This leaves the elder Camilla as the only other known possibility. Assuming she had lived to adolescence, Camilla would have been almost fifteen by May 1526.[27] Suor Elena's distant cousin, Cleofe di Tiberio Malvezzi, had joined Sant'Agnese in 1509 at the age of fifteen.[28] It is therefore not impossible that Camilla was the daughter of Lorenzo who entered Sant'Agnese around 1526, at which time she would have taken the name Elena. It is also possible, however, that Elena had been born before 1506, during her father's exile in Rome in the aftermath of the Malvezzi's abortive plot to assassinate Giovanni II Bentivoglio in 1488.[29] In that case her name would not appear in the baptismal registers of Bologna. Or could she perhaps have been illegitimate? Although she consistently appears as 'S. Elena Malvezzi' in the notarial acts of Sant'Agnese, both the San Domenico necrology and Carrati's transcript cited above list her simply as 'Madre Suor Elena . . .'. The dots in place of the family name might have been used because the previous decedent in the lists had also been a Malvezzi. But perhaps they might indicate that Suor Elena was not a legitimate member of the family.

When and by whom might the Bardini manuscript have been

baptismal records. All entries are cited, more or less complete, in Fornasini, *Breve cenno storico*. It is an interesting coincidence that in October 1523 Lorenzo's youngest son, Lucio Cornelio, was held for baptism by 'S^r ercule gunzaga da . . . Mantua' (Reg. Batt. vol. 1523–4, fol. 134). The eighteen-year-old Bishop of Mantua, at the time enrolled at the *studium* in Bologna, was to become a major figure in musical patronage in Mantua. See I. Fenlon, *Music and Patronage in Sixteenth-Century Mantua*, I (Cambridge, 1980), pp. 47–78.

[26] Cambria, *Il monastero domenicano*, p. 32.

[27] In *Breve cenno storico* Fornasini, presumably following the MS family genealogy (Archivio Malvezzi-Campeggi, serie 2a, 27/264, p. 49) incorrectly claims that the elder Camilla married Alessandro Crescenzi in 1530 (p. 87). The younger Camilla married Crescenzi in 1543. See Archivio Malvezzi De Medici, Libro 124G, fasc. G37 for her dowry contract, dated 20 November 1543.

[28] A notice of her dowry contract dated 18 May 1509 appears in a list of *istrumenti* in Archivio Malvezzi-Campeggi, libro 3. According to Fornasini, *Breve cenno storico*, p. 67, she had been born on 11 August 1494.

[29] For a detailed discussion of the plot, see Fornasini, *Breve cenno storico*, pp. 17–20.

copied? The presence of the Malvezzi coat-of-arms and Suor Elena's name probably indicates no more than that it was her personal property. But the inclusion in several chant manuscripts from Sant'Agnese of the names and coats-of-arms of the nuns who had copied or commissioned them[30] raises the possibility that the Bardini manuscript could have been commissioned or even copied by Elena Malvezzi. The latest concordances for pieces in the manuscript had first appeared in print in 1559. This suggests that the manuscript may have been copied during the last years of Elena's life, when she held the office of sotto-priora and possibly prioress of Sant'Agnese. The volume might have been prepared and bound as a gift to the prioress. Or if she copied it herself it could have been sent out for binding, as was the practice with chant manuscripts from the monastery.[31]

The manuscript offers an interesting and rather varied sampling of the vocal music that must have been current in Bologna around 1560. As mentioned above, none of the pieces in the source includes an attribution. Of the fifty settings of Italian texts, thirty-nine have so far been identified from printed sources.[32] Fourteen of the twenty-one Latin motets and all eight of the French or Spanish pieces have also been identified in this fashion. Thirteen of the eighty-two works have neither title nor attribution, but most have turned out to be subsequent sections of titled works. Three pieces have so far eluded any sort of identification, though their character suggests that they, too, derive from vocal originals. Incipits of the unidentified works appear in Appendix 2.

The published versions had appeared in print between 1542 and 1559, though it would be difficult to confirm that the prints themselves served as the direct source of the transcriptions. The very first

---

[30] Bologna, Museo Civico Medioevale, MS 638, bears two coats-of-arms, one of which can be identified with Franceschina Conforti, who had commissioned the manuscript, which was completed on 8 April 1400. Museo Civico MS 592 incorporates five different coats-of-arms within various illuminated initials, one pertaining to the prioress, Caterina Caccianemici, and another to Pompilia Bargellini, 'the best and most exquisite singer', who together had commissioned the work. Museo Civico MSS 583 and 589 were copied by Bernardina Isolani of Sant'Agnese in 1508, and both include her coat-of-arms. Another manuscript in Isolani's hand and bearing her coat-of-arms, but not previously identified with Sant'Agnese, also survives in the Biblioteca Estense in Modena (MS α.Q.1.8).

[31] Records of payment for the binding of choirbooks from Sant'Agnese exist for 1479 and 1482. See ASB, Demaniale 107/6772 (Sant'Agnese), account book, 1477–88, fols. 29ᵛ and 81ᵛ [82ᵛ].

[32] I am indebted to James Haar for the identification of Corteccia's *Foll'è pur il desio*.

pieces in the manuscript, *Ogni loco mi porge doglia* (i) / *Poscia che per mio mal* (ii) by the young Palestrina, represent the most recently printed, for they had seen the light only in Gardano's *Il secondo libro de le muse a cinque voci* (Venice, 1559). The fact that the Bardini transcription omits a two-breve repetition of the words 'così sovente' near the beginning of part 2 might indicate that the keyboard version did not come directly from *Il secondo libro de le muse*, though such brief omissions are not unusual in sixteenth-century intabulations.

One can occasionally establish with greater certainty, on the other hand, the most probable printed source for a piece on the basis of variants among the printed versions themselves. Clemens's *Tristitia et anxietas/Sed tu Domine* (nos. 8–9), for example, appear to derive not from Susato's *Liber primus ecclesiasticarum cantionum* of 1553, but from the version printed in Scotto's *Motetti del laberinto* of 1554, which reveals the same melodic variants, brief omissions and considerably shorter conclusion as found in the Bardini transcription.

The Bardini version of Janequin's *L'alouette* (no. 24) includes an alto part printed only in Moderne's *Le difficile des chansons*, I.[33] No. 55, Janequin's *Guillot ung jour*, also appears in *Le difficile*, I, while no. 23 *S'il est ainsi*, no. 25 *Háganle todos el buz*,[34] no. 31 *Ung laboureur* and no. 56 *Robin dormant* all turn up in Moderne's *Le difficile des chansons*, II (1544). *S'il est ainsi* and *Robin dormant* survive in print only in Moderne's collection.[35] Thanks to the Bardini manuscript it would now be possible to reconstruct their bass parts, missing from the incomplete original prints. Despite the fact that the Bardini version omits Moderne's repetition of the final section of *Robin dormant*, and with it the brief coda, all the other evidence suggests that the scribe of the Bardini manuscript had copies of *Le difficile* at hand, which could have provided all but two French works for the manuscript, the others being by Cipriano de Rore.

Cipriano de Rore is by far the most prominent composer in the

---

[33] See S. F. Pogue, *Jacques Moderne, Lyons Music Printer of the Sixteenth Century* (Geneva, 1969), pp. 163–5. There is nothing about the transcription to confirm Pogue's hypothesis that this version might be *a 7*. A. Tillman Merritt, 'Janequin: Reworkings of Some Early Chansons', *Aspects of Medieval and Renaissance Music: A Birthday Offering to Gustave Reese*, ed. J. LaRue (New York, 1966), p. 606, points out that the alto part also appears in the Bourdeney–Pasche manuscript (Paris, Bibliothèque Nationale, MS Rés. Vm^a 851).

[34] *Háganle todos el buz* is in fact the section of Flecha's *La Batailla en Spagnol* beginning 'Venga al gran sennor': the Bardini scribe had presumably copied the opening line from the relevant section of the tenor or bassus book, which begin with the second line of text.

[35] Pogue, *Jacques Moderne*, pp. 181–2, lists no concordances for these works.

source, accounting for eighteen madrigals, motets and chansons. All eleven madrigals *a* 4 appear in blocks (nos. 37–44 and 51–3). Most of the readings reveal no appreciable differences from those in his *Primo libro a 4* (1550 and 1551).[36] Rore's two five-part Italian works in the Bardini manuscript had not appeared together in a single printed collection. The choice of the five-part *Da quei bei lumi* may have been governed by its use of *misura comune*, like all Rore's four-part madrigals in the manuscript. *Da quei bei lumi* is one of only two pieces from Scotto's 1542 *Di Cipriano Rore i madrigali a cinque voci* in that mensuration, and the only one from Gardane's 1544 *Di Cipriano il primo libro de madregali cromatici a cinque voci*. *Padre del ciel* also employs *misura comune*, but in this case the scribe's choice of Petrarch's Good Friday sonnet – though here with the more feminist title *Madre del ciel* and without its second part – fits well with the origins of the manuscript at Sant'Agnese. In the Bardini manuscript *Padre del ciel* is copied beside Berchem's *Lasso, che desiando vo*, its neighbour in printed collections, which suggests that both might have derived from Rore's *Secondo libro de madrigale a cinque* (Venice: Gardane, 1544).[37]

[36] Bar 82 of *Carità di signore* is omitted (an easy slip since the lower three parts are largely repetitive and the cantus rests); in *Non vide il mondo* bar 17 is omitted and bar 18 copied twice. More noticeable is the altered opening imitation of *Un lauro mi difese* (see below). The Bardini manuscript's more leisurely and repetitious beginning lacks the effect of the 1550 printed stretto of tenor and cantus. The scribe may simply have transcribed the left hand of bar 2 twice and made the cantus fit accordingly.

Rore, *Un lauro mi difese*

Bardini version

1551 printed version

[37] By the same token, the fact that the variously attributed no. 35 *Novo piacer* and no. 36 *Non ved'hoggi 'l mio sole* had both appeared in *Il primo libro di madrigali de diversi eccellentissimi autori a misura di breve* (Venice: Gardane, 1542) suggests that both might have come from that collection.

In other cases the number of madrigals that reappear in certain prints and the placement of the works in the Bardini manuscript point still more strongly to the scribe's reliance on specific printed collections. Of the twelve Ruffo madrigals in Bardini, eleven had been published in his *Primo libro de madrigale a cinque* (Venice, 1553).[38] Nine of those appear in close proximity on pages 17–28 of the print, including seven that occur one right after the other. The Bardini transcriptions, which appear in blocks but not necessarily always in the same order, show no significant variants from the print. Interestingly enough, Ruffo's *Secondo libro di madrigale a cinque* (1553), the probable printed source for the only other Ruffo madrigal transcription (no. 21, *Chiuso gran tempo*), also contains Nasco's *Tempus erat* (i)/ *Ante meos oculos* (ii) (nos. 79–80) and Perissone Cambio's *Ditemi, o diva mia* (no. 75). Ruffo's *Primo* and *Secondo libro* were thus probably the sources on which the scribe relied for some fifteen works.

Where all the Rore madrigals had employed *misura comune*, eight of the twelve Ruffo madrigals had been printed with a C mensuration. Of the eleven Italian works that have so far eluded identification, only two use ¢. Eight of the unidentified works form a substantial block (nos. 66–73) towards the end of the manuscript and share numerous features in common. All of these use the time-signature C and five of them (nos. 68–72) are very brief (only twelve to twenty-two breves long). Many move consistently in black notes, with lively and off-beat patterns. They create the impression that they may well have been copied from a single unknown, rather uniform, and possibly unpublished, source. Thus, the Bardini manuscript further substantiates our changing view of the relationship between manuscripts and prints of the madrigal repertory, a view largely articulated by James Haar and Iain Fenlon,[39] which clarifies the importance of manuscript sources and their frequent independence from prints. For although many of the Bardini madrigals probably derive from printed sources, about 20% appear to have remained unpublished and perhaps were not intended for publication.

The Bardini manuscript is likely to prove particularly helpful for the study of various performance practices. It promises, for example,

---

[38] I should like to thank Maureen Buja for making her transcriptions of Ruffo madrigals available to me.

[39] See, for example, 'A Source for the Early Madrigal', *Journal of the American Musicological Society* [hereafter *JAMS*], 33 (1980), pp. 164–5.

Example 1. Ruffo, *Deh porgi la mano*. (Bracketed sharps and dots inserted in the vocal version are from the Bardini manuscript. Those on the staves appear in the printed version.)

to be of interest to those dealing with issues of accidentals and *musica ficta*. The manuscript continues the earlier keyboard tradition of the *Frottole intabulate* (1517), Cavazzoni's *Recerchari, mottetti, canzoni* (1523), Attaingnant's keyboard intabulations of 1530, and of other sixteenth-century manuscript sources, in most commonly using dots to indicate accidentals.[40] As in the earlier sources no distinction is made between the raising and lowering of the pitch, which obviously can cause considerable ambiguity. To complicate matters further, in transcriptions with a key-signature of one flat, individual dots are added to various B's, as if to 'confirm' the key-signature. In many cases the absence of a dot in such works seems intentional – the scribe wanted B♮. In several other instances the absence of the dot could be an oversight. Not infrequently, a dot and a flat are used simultaneously for a single pitch, which at least makes those points unambiguous.

---

[40] See Silbiger, *Italian Manuscript Sources*, p. 24, for an enumeration of some of the manuscript sources.

Example 1 – *continued*

In many instances added accidentals and/or dots would bolster commonsense decisions about *musica ficta* – for example, at cadences. But it is reassuring to have the guidance of a scribe from *c.* 1560, not only for individual pieces, but also for this relatively large repertory. Thus, while many might sharpen the first as well as the second cantus *c″* in bar 3 of Ruffo's *Deh porgi la mano* (see Example 1), fewer might think to sharpen the quick quintus *f″*'s of bar 5 as the Bardini scribe does, to initiate the subsequent series of major harmonies, a type of alteration which recurs several times in the manuscript. And these F♯'s are perhaps less surprising than the one the Bardini scribe adds to the very first *f′* of the piece.

The Bardini intabulation of the opening of the second section of Corteccia's *Foll'è pur il desio* (see Example 2), on the other hand, introduces F♯'s, C♯'s and a G♯ on a scale that might surprise many modern editors. The only sharp from the Corteccia passage actually included in the original print of 1547 had appeared in the cantus at bar 20. Interestingly enough, Frank D'Accone, in his modern edition of the work, has interpreted the original sharp as a 'cautionary sign',

Example 2. Corteccia, *Foll'è pur il desio*. (Bracketed sharps and dots inserted in the vocal version are from the Bardini manuscript. Those on the staves appear in the printed version. The sharp with an asterisk is transcribed as a natural by D'Accone.)

i.e. as signalling F♮.[41] The vexed problem of cautionary signs was the subject of some debate a few years ago.[42] The Bardini manuscript illustrates how one sixteenth-century musician responded to a number of musical passages whose problematic accidentals have been interpreted as cautionary signs. Predictably enough, the Bardini scribe's readings of these passages are hardly unambiguous, and suggest the danger of seeking cut-and-dried solutions to the

[41] For a discussion of Corteccia's – or his printer's – use of such signs see F. D'Accone, ed., *Music of the Florentine Renaissance*, x: *Francesco Corteccia: Collected Secular Works: The First Book of Madrigals for Five and Six Voices*, Corpus Mensurabilis Musicae [hereafter CMM] 32/x (Stuttgart, 1981), pp. xii–xiii; see also *ibid.*, vol. vii: *Matteo Rampollini: Il primo libro de la musica* (n.p., 1974), pp. xv–xvi; also D'Accone, 'Matteo Rampollini and his Petrarchan Canzone Cycles', *Musica Disciplina*, 27 (1973), pp. 83–6.

[42] See D. Harrán, 'New Evidence for Musica Ficta: The Cautionary Sign', *JAMS*, 29 (1976), pp. 77–98, and 'More Evidence for Cautionary Signs', *JAMS*, 31 (1978), pp. 490–4. For a response to Harrán's first article, see I. Godt's letter to the editor, *JAMS*, 31 (1978), pp. 385–95, which includes Harrán's answering arguments.

Example 2 – *continued*

problem. The fact that in the keyboard manuscript the most frequently used sign, the dot, can represent either a sharp or a flat further clouds the issue. One might even go so far as to claim that all the dots in the previous example are themselves 'cautionary', and therefore indicate that the notes should all be left unaltered. While that obviously represents an extreme position, the dot on the tenor *c'* in bar 22, at least, might reasonably be considered 'cautionary' – or a scribal error.

The Bardini manuscript contains intabulations of at least two pieces that have been scrutinised by Don Harrán and Frank D'Accone for cautionary signs, no. 28 *Foll'è pur il desio* by Corteccia and no. 35 *Novo piacer* ascribed to both Arcadelt and Rampollini. Bars 58–60 of *Novo piacer* (see Example 3) had served Don Harrán as an illustration of the use of cautionary signs to prevent harmonic dissonances that might arise through *musica ficta* – here the augmented fifth (bar 59).[43] The Bardini transcription is down a fourth. The manuscript version of bar 56 appears to confirm Harrán's reading of Rampollini's sharp for the cantus note as a natural to avoid an

43 Harrán, 'New Evidence for Musica Ficta', p. 83.

Example 3. Arcadelt/Rampollini, *Novo piacer*

augmented fifth, *bb* -*f♯'* (in Bardini, transposed *f*-*c♯'*). The transposed *f'* in the top part at the beginning of bar 59 of the Bardini intabulation also seems to confirm Harrán's reading of the accidental on the corresponding note in Rampollini's print as cautionary. But the transposed *b♮* in the tenor of the Bardini manuscript at the same point contradicts Harrán's suggested *ficta* on the corresponding note of the print (tenor *eb'*) – which had provided Harrán's reason for interpreting the cantus sharp as a cautionary sign in the first place. In his version of bar 58 the Bardini scribe also apparently felt no necessity to sharpen the alto *c'*, rising to *d'*, Harrán's suggested *ficta* (*f♯'* to *g'*).

Comparable ambiguities appear in bars 35–42 of *Foll'è pur il desio* (see Example 4), which contains several problematic accidentals which Frank D'Accone has interpreted as cautionary in his edition. The Bardini version contains no dots or sharps for the quintus *f*'s in bar 36 (unless the anomalous dot adjacent to the right-hand *d'* was intended for the left-hand *f*'s), and none for the tenor *B* in bar 37, appearing to confirm the 'cautionary' nature of the sharps affixed to these notes in the original print. But in bars 40–1 the scribe

Example 4. Corteccia, *Foll'è pur il desio*

Example 4 – *continued*

specifically sharpens the cantus *g''*'s and altus *c''*'s (and dots a
subsequent *f'* (bar 41) and two *c''*'s (bar 42) as well), thus contradict-
ing an interpretation of the cantus and altus sharps as 'cautionary'.
Such chromaticism transforms the passage into a series of major
harmonies (E-A-D-G) similar to the one in the example from Ruffo's
Deh porgi la mano (Example 1) – a type of alteration which recurs
several times in the Bardini manuscript.

In the original printed version of the previous passage sharps had
been placed between the repeated G's and C's. Although the
placement of the sharps is a bit ambiguous in the Bardini keyboard
version, the accidentals appear to refer to both repeated notes. A
comparison of a number of other printed and manuscript madrigals
suggests that sharps printed between repeated notes could be
interpreted to apply to both. Several examples appear in Ruffo's
Occhi leggiadri (see Example 5), which, as mentioned earlier, may
have been copied into the manuscript from the print of 1553. The
printed version inserts a sharp between the two *c''*'s in the cantus in

Example 5. (a) Ruffo, *Occhi leggiadri*

bar 5, while the Bardini scribe clearly applies the accidental to the first *c''*. In bar 19 a similar shift of the sharp appears in the tenor. At bar 33 the sharp has been shifted from between the two alto *f'*'s. At bar 44 the sharp on the cadential tenor *c'* has been extended back to the previous ornamental *c'* (no surprise), while in bar 45 both quintus *f'*'s have apparently been raised by a single sharp between them. Elsewhere the apparent rising chromatic figures near the conclusion to Ruffo's *L'aquila è gita al ciel* (Example 5b) become less unorthodox at the hands of the Bardini scribe, who seems to apply a single sharp to both of the repeated notes.[44]

In at least one instance, however, the scribe of the Bardini manuscript seems to take too literally his rule of applying a single accidental 'backwards' to both notes of a repeated pair. Example 6

[44] For some other examples of sharps printed between repeated notes in Ruffo prints, see *Occhi vaghi amorosi, O fortunato e aventuroso lago, Pace non trovo* and Nasco's *Non ha donna* from Ruffo's *Secondo libro di madrigali a cinque voci* (Venice, 1553).

Example 5. (b) Ruffo, *L'aquila è gita al ciel* (bracketed dots, accidentals or omissions are indicated in Bardini)

presents the Bardini version of the chromatic conclusion to Rore's *Hellas comment voules vous*, a moment which commentators from Zarlino to Einstein, Meier and Lowinsky have singled out for its expressive setting.[45] In the Bardini version of 'les yeulx en pleurs' the cantus and bassus do not fall F-E-Eb-D, but F-Eb-Eb-D, trading the more extreme melodic chromaticism for a suspended augmented fourth, Eb-A, in the harmony. Perhaps the scribe had doubts about this result, for evasive action is taken to avoid suspending the diminished fifth version two bars later.

The Bardini scribe's treatment of pitch inflection on repeated notes might seem self-evident. But the fact that some modern editions restrict such accidentals to the second note, especially if

[45] *Gioseffe Zarlino: The Art of Counterpoint*, trans. G. A. Marco and C. V. Palisca (New Haven, 1968), p. 48. A. Einstein, *The Italian Madrigal*, trans. A. H. Krappe, R. H. Sessions and O. Strunk, I (Princeton, 1949), p. 392. B. Meier, 'Staats-kompositionen von Cyprien de Rore', *Tijdschrift van de Vereniging voor Nederlandse Muziekgeschiedenis*, 21 (1969), p. 90. E. Lowinsky, *Cipriano de Rore's Venus Motet* ([Provo, Utah] 1986), p. 38.

Example 5(b) – *continued*

ornamental pitches intrude between the repeated notes, suggests that not all editors would agree. Two short examples from works that occur both in modern editions and in the Bardini manuscript illustrate the point. In the suspensions concluding parts 1 and 2 of Clemens's *Peccantem me/Deus in nomine* a sharp appears only on the last note of the F-E-F resolution in the original print. Bernet Kempers's edition of the motet[46] takes the print literally, though when the same figure occurs in other motets, but without any original accidentals, the editor inflects both of the repeated notes with editorial accidentals. The Bardini version of *Peccantem me/Deus in nomine* (which is transposed down a fifth) raises both of the repeated pitches. The situation at bar 22 of Cipriano de Rore's *Da quei bei lumi*, on the other hand, is more problematic. Bernhard Meier reproduces the cantus part as it appears in the original print: a'-g'-a'-$g\sharp'$ (see Example 7).[47] The Bardini scribe adds a dot to the first g',

---

[46]   *Jacobus Clemens non Papa opera omnia*, CMM 4/ix (n.p., 1960), pp. 42 and 47.
[47]   *Cipriani Rore: opera omnia*, CMM 14/ii (n.p., 1963), p. 100.

Example 6. Rore, *Hellas comment*, 'les yeulx en pleurs' (accidentals in brackets implied by Bardini)

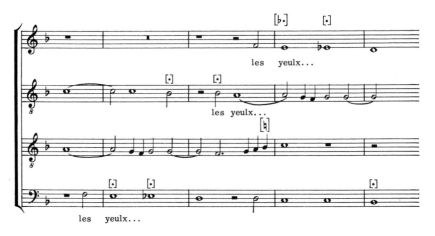

and both a dot and a sharp to the second. Did the scribe intend both to be inflected, or could the dot alone on the first *g'* perhaps have been intended in this case to serve as a cautionary sign?

Few will be surprised that in matters of *musica ficta* the Bardini manuscript provides no easy answers. In the matter of cautionary signs it is useful, at least, to observe one contemporary scribe interpreting – and perhaps struggling with – problematic passages. It is also enlightening to observe the Bardini scribe's attitude towards the inflection of repeated pitches, his varied approach (many modern editors would probably say 'inconsistent approach') to similar situations that reappear across this repertory of more than eighty pieces, and to discover the general tendency to add accidentals more lavishly than many modern editors would be inclined to do, judging at least by editions of the Bardini madrigals and motets in various volumes of Corpus Mensurabilis Musicae.

Example 7. Rore, *Da quei bei lumi*

The Bardini manuscript was most probably intended for solo keyboard performance. As solo arrangements, however, the Bardini intabulations fall uniformly into the least adventurous sort of transcription. The amount of figuration added to the models is relatively restrained and limited to stereotypical ornaments at cadences, occasional filling-in with passing notes, and, more rarely, scalar passages on held chords. Examples of such straightforward intabulations are hardly uncommon in other sources, of course, but frequently rub shoulders either with more idiomatic ricercari such as those by Veggio in one of the Castell'Arquato keyboard manuscripts, or with arrangements of vocal models that add *passaggi* more lavishly and uniformly, as in Florence, Biblioteca Medicea Laurenziana, MS Acquisti e Doni 641, Alamanne de Layolle's keyboard tablature, for example.[48] Such elaborate settings find no place in the Bardini manuscript, which consistently reveals only the simpler variety.

The Bardini intabulations also stand somewhat apart from many other keyboard collections in their very systematic use of transposi-

---

[48] See H. C. Slim, 'Keyboard Music at Castell'Arquato by an Early Madrigalist', *JAMS*, 15 (1962), pp. 35–47; F. D'Accone, 'The Intavolatura di M. Alamanno Aiolli', *Musica Disciplina*, 20 (1966), pp. 151–74.

tion throughout the repertory according to the *chiavette*. As the table in Appendix 3 shows, pieces which employ *chiavi naturali* in their sixteenth-century published versions have invariably been entered in the manuscript at the original notated pitch. Those employing *chiavette* are almost always transposed down a fourth or a fifth. The choice between a fourth and a fifth appears to have had to do with the scribe's desire to avoid unusual accidentals. The choice almost invariably also prevented the bass from falling below *F*. In only a few cases where the total vocal ranges are unusually wide does this procedure land the scribe in difficulties.[49]

Such a consistent and regular use of transposition according to the 'clef code' raises the possibility, at least, that the Bardini manuscript may have been used not only for solo keyboard performance, but perhaps also for vocal accompaniment. Other keyboard sources presumably intended for solo instrumental performance tend to ignore the possibility of transposition. Of the twenty-six intabulations in Antico's *Frottole intabulate de sonare* (1517), Jeppesen notes that five are transposed up a fourth or fifth.[50] Munich, Bayerische Staatsbibliothek MS 9437, a mid-sixteenth-century Italian source that mingles vocal intabulations with ricercars and similar instrumental works, transposes only the first of its intabulated madrigals.[51] Two of the works from Attaingnant's three keyboard prints of chanson transcriptions (1530) were transposed, but their

---

[49] In Gombert's *O adorandum/Quod transiturus* (nos. 29–30), for example, which employs the *chiavette*, the more wide-ranging bass (which falls to *A* in the original) forces the scribe below *F* to two low *E*'s. Ruffo's *Deh porgi* (no. 20) is even more extreme, with the cantus climbing to *g″* in the course of the piece and bass dropping to *A* for its final note, which might have forced the scribe to low *D*. The obvious expedient of putting the note up an octave avoided the problem. Very few pieces ignore the system. One might expect Ruffo's *Occhi vaghi/Occhi leggiadri* (nos. 4–5), combining treble clef in the cantus with tenor in the bassus and with an overall range of *c* to *g″*, to have been transposed down; the pieces appear in the manuscript at pitch, however. It might be significant that they are the first pieces in the manuscript to employ the *chiavette* and are followed by the first blank folios. The piece in the same clefs that had followed them in Ruffo's print, *Viverò dunque*, occurs only towards the end of the manuscript – where it is in fact transposed down a fifth. The only other exception, no. 21, *Chiuso gran tempo*, also by Ruffo, employs treble and baritone clefs in the original print, but has been entered at pitch in the manuscript. In these cases where the pieces appear at published pitch, the scribe avoided leger lines by introducing a treble clef on the right-hand staff and a baritone clef on the bass staff.

[50] K. Jeppesen, *Die italienische Orgelmusik am Anfang des Cinquecento* (2nd edn, Copenhagen, 1960), I, pp. 58 and 21*–23*.

[51] The source has been edited in M. L. Martinez-Göllner, *Eine neue Quelle zur italienischen Orgelmusik des '500*, Münchner Editionen zur Musikgeschichte 3 (Tutzing, 1982). I should like to thank Oscar Mischiati for bringing this manuscript to my attention.

vocal models had been in natural clefs.[52] None of the nine from Munich MS 2987 (*c.* 1550) was transposed.[53]

The great majority of the vocal originals for these transcriptions had used natural clefs, of course, so one would not expect to find them transposed. Only two of the Attaingnant chansons had used *chiavette*,[54] but both were transcribed for keyboard at original pitch. Four of the Munich 2987 chansons had also employed *chiavette*, but none of them has been transposed either. Ten works in Munich 9437 had employed transposing clefs; only the first appears transposed. Andrea Gabrieli's lavishly decorated setting of *Io mi son giovinetta*,[55] which shows *chiavette* in the original version, adopts the original pitch level for the intabulation. The version of this popular Ferrabosco madrigal entered in fascicle III of the keyboard manuscripts at Castell'Arquato, where it occurs with dances that were obviously conceived for keyboard, also appears at the original pitch,[56] as does the more elaborate keyboard arrangement in London, British Library, Add. MS 30491 and in Mayone's 1609 keyboard collection.[57] I have as yet been unable to examine the clefs of the several transposed originals from Antico's 1517 collection. It may be significant, however, that the copy in Rome, Biblioteca Polesina, contains the manuscript note 'Questo libro si e de canto d'organo.'[58]

Examples of keyboard works of somewhat later date associated either specifically or indirectly with vocal performance, on the other hand, do survive in transposed versions. The 1593 print of the Gabrieli's *intonazioni* includes versions transposed by a fourth or a fifth as well as those at original pitch, since they presumably were intended to provide the pitch for the choir.[59] The scribe who transcribed several madrigals, motets, a hymn and a Magnificat in

[52] See Sermisy, *Secourez moy* (+4) from *Vingt et cinq chansons musicales* and Claudin, *Dont vien cela* (−4) from *Vingt et six chansons musicales* in A. Seay, ed., *Pierre Attaingnant: Transcriptions of Chansons for Keyboard*, CMM 20 (n.p., 1961).

[53] See J. Bonfils, ed., *Chansons françaises pour orgue*, Le Pupitre 5 (Paris, 1968).

[54] Claudin, *Hau, hau, hau le boys* from *Dixneuf chansons musicales* and Claudin, *Changeons propos* from *Vingt et cinq chansons musicales*, edited in A. Seay, *Pierre Attaingnant*, pp. 24–7 and 116–18, respectively.

[55] See P. Pidoux, ed., *Andrea Gabrieli: Intonationen für Orgel* (Kassel, 1941), pp. 32–5.

[56] See H. C. Slim, ed., *Keyboard Music at Castell'Arquato*, I: *Dances and Dance Songs*, Corpus of Early Keyboard Music [hereafter CEKM] 37/I (n.p., 1975), p. 20.

[57] See R. Jackson, ed., *Neapolitan Keyboard Composers*, CEKM 24 (n.p., 1967), pp. 27–32.

[58] H. M. Brown, *Instrumental Music Printed Before 1600: A Bibliography* (2nd edn, Cambridge, MA, 1967), p. 23n.

[59] O. Kinkeldey, *Orgel und Klavier in der Musik des 16. Jahrhunderts* (Leipzig, 1910), p. 132.

fascicles II, IV and VI of the Castell'Arquato keyboard sources transposes the two whose known vocal models had used *chiavette*.[60] More akin to what we find in the Bardini manuscript, however, are those collections of works for three and four voices with keyboard and lute accompaniment published by Simone Verovio in Rome between 1586 and 1596. Of the accompaniments for some fifty-one works in *chiavette*, all but ten are transposed down a fourth or fifth.[61] The character of these accompaniments – their relationship to the vocal originals and the extent and nature of their additional embellishments – is very like that of the Bardini manuscript.

Transposition, of course, is not uncommon in similar lute intabulations of comparable vocal repertories intended strictly for instrumental use, which might call into question any suggested accompanimental use of the Bardini keyboard intabulations. Examination of a small sample[62] suggests that vocal models orig-

---

[60] The final twenty-two breves of Ferrabosco's *Io mi son giovinetta* and the even verses of a Lassus *Magnificat primi toni*. An anonymous, untitled transcription of a vocal work on fol. 10ᵛ of fascicle IVA may be a piece originally in *chiavette* which the scribe failed to transpose, however. All the Castell'Arquato vocal intabulations are discussed in H. C. Slim, 'Some Puzzling Intabulations of Vocal Music for Keyboard C. 1600, at Castell'Arquato', *Five Centuries of Choral Music: Essays in honor of Howard Swan*, ed. G. Paine (New York, forthcoming). The music will appear shortly in H. C. Slim, ed., *Keyboard Music at Castell'Arquato*, II: *Masses, Magnificat, Liturgical Works, Dances and Madrigals*, CEKM, 37/II (forthcoming). I should like to thank Prof. Slim for kindly allowing me to examine the article and edition in proof.

[61] The accompaniment to *Donna se'l cor legas* from *Ghirlanda di Fioretti* (1589) is also transposed, despite the use of soprano clef in the cantus, presumably because the part extends from *c'* to *g''*. The reason for the failure to transpose the ten works in *chiavette* is not immediately apparent. The same clef combinations and ranges reappear among the transposed works. Two examples of Verovio pieces with transposed accompaniments are printed in Kinkeldey, *Orgel und Klavier*, pp. 280–2. Another is reproduced in facsimile in T. Bridges, 'Verovio, Simone', *The New Grove Dictionary of Music and Musicians*, ed. S. Sadie, 20 vols. (London, 1980), XIX, p. 677.

[62] The following pieces were examined in modern edition and compared with their original vocal models (chiav=*chiavette*, nat=*chiavi naturali*, P=at pitch, −M2=transposed down a major second, +4=up a perfect fourth, etc.): *Tout ce qu'on peut* (chiav, −4) by Rore, *Soupirs ardans* (chiav, −4), *Les yeux qui me sceurent prendre* (nat, −M2), *L'yver sera* (chiav, −4), *Au temps heureux* (nat, +M2) by Arcadelt, *M'amie un jour* (chiav, −4) by Certon from J. Vaccaro, ed., *Oeuvres d'Adrian Le Roy: Sixiesme livre de luth (1559)* (Paris, 1978); *Las je me plains* (nat, P), *Pourtant si je suis brunette* (nat, P), *Martin menoit* (chiav, −M2), *Vignon vignetta* (nat, P) by Sermisy, *Pater noster* (nat, P), *Stabat mater* (chiav, −M2) by Josquin, *La guerre* (nat, P, +M2), *Martin menoit* (chiav, −M2), *Le chant des oyseaux* (chiav, −M2) by Janequin, *O bone Jesu* (nat, P) by Compère, *Reveilley moy* (nat, −M2) by Garnier, *Pour avoir paix* (chiav, −M2) by Layolle, *Hors envieulx retires vous* (nat, +m3) by Gombert, *Fortune alors* (nat, P) by Certon, *De mon triste desplaisir* (nat, P) by Richafort, *Quanta beltà* (nat, P), *Quand'io penso al martir* (nat, P) by Arcadelt from A. Ness, ed., *The Lute Music of Francesco Canova da Milano*, Harvard Publications in Music 3–4 (Cambridge, MA, 1970); *Vestiva i colli* (chiav, −5), *Se tra quest'herbe e fiore* (chiav, −M2), *Io son ferito* (chiav, −M2), *Il dolce sono* (chiav, −M2) by

inally employing *chiavette* are also regularly transposed down for the lute. The intervals of transposition include not only the fourth and fifth, however, but also the whole tone. Both Adrian Le Roy's *Sixiesme livre de luth* (1559) and Francesco da Milano's *Intabolatura da leuto* in its various editions are consistent about their interval of transposition for works originally in *chiavette* (down a fourth and a whole tone respectively). Vincenzo Galilei, on the other hand, introduces all three of these intervals of transposition for various works in *Il Fronimo* (1584). Less consistency is apparent in lute transcriptions of vocal models in natural clefs. Although intabulations at the original pitch predominate in this case, instances of transposition up or down a whole tone, up a minor third or up a fourth also occur, often within a single collection. Some of this variety, compared to keyboard intabulations, must represent attempts to compensate for the limitations of the lute.

The insertion of words for a few of the Bardini intabulations also raises again the possibility of the manuscript's use for some sort of

Palestrina, *Io mi son giovinetta* (chiav, −4) by Ferrabosco, *Chi salira per me* (chiav, −M2), *A casa un giorno* (nat, P) by Wert, *Come havran fin* (nat, +m3), *Quando lieta sperai* (nat, P) by Rore, *Qual'anima ignorante* (nat, P) by Willaert, *Deh porgi la mano* (chiav, −5) by Ruffo, *In qual parte del cielo* (nat, P) by Monte, *Nasce la pena mia* (nat, P) by Striggio, *La notte che segui* (chiav, −4), *In dubio di mio stato* (chiav, −4), *In dubio di mio stato* (another setting, nat, P) by Lassus, *O del mio navigar* (nat, P) by Porta from C. MacClintock, trans. and ed., *Vincenzo Galilei: Fronimo (1584)*, Musicological Studies and Documents 39 (Neuhausen-Stuttgart, 1985); *Adiuva me Domine* (nat, P), *Pater peccavi* (nat, −M2) by Consilium, *Si bona suscepimus* (nat, P) by Sermisy, *Praeter rerum seriem* (nat, P), *Benedicta es caelorum regina* (nat, P) by Josquin, *Noe noe psallite* (chiav, −5) by Mouton, *Je suis déshéritée* (chiav, −5) by Lupus/ Cadéac, *D'un seul soleil* (nat, P), *L'aveugle dieu* (nat, P) by Janequin, *Il se treuve en amytie* (nat, P), *Mons & vaulx* (nat, P), *Quel bien parler* (nat, P), *Voulant honneur* (nat, P) by Sandrin from J. Vaccaro, ed., *Oeuvres d'Albert de Rippe*, ii (Paris, 1974) (a number of other works in this collection are listed as transposed in the introduction, but I have been unable to examine their models); *Dignare me laudare* (chiav, −5), *Praeparate corda vestra Domino* (chiav, −5) by Maillard, *Je n'ay point plus d'affection* (nat, P) by Sermisy, *Voulant honneur* (nat, P) by Sandrin from A. Souris and R. de Morcourt, eds., *Adrian Le Roy: Premier livre de tabulature de luth (1551)* (Paris, 1960); *Qui souhaittez* (nat, P), *Voulant honneur* (nat, P) by Sandrin, *De mes ennuys* (nat, P) by Arcadelt, *D'amour me plains* (nat, +M2) by Rogier Pathie, *Elle voyant* (nat, +M2) by Certon from M. Renault, ed., *Oeuvres de Julien Belin* (Paris, 1976); *Jesu nomen* (nat, P), *Erravi sicut* (nat, P), *Circumdederunt me* (nat, P) by Clemens, *Cantibus organis* (nat, P), *Domine si tu es* (nat, P), *Venite filii* (nat, P) by Gombert, *Qui habitat in adiutorio* (nat, P), *Faulte d'argent* (nat, P) by Josquin from I. Homolya and D. Benkő, eds., *Valentini Bakfark opera omnia*, ii (Budapest, 1979); *Amy souffres* (nat, P) by Moulu, *De retourner* (nat, P), *Languir me fais* (nat, P), *Vivray je tousjours* (nat, P), *J'atens secours* (nat, P), *Secourez moys* (nat, P), *Il me suffit* (nat, P), *Tant que vivray* (nat, P), *D'ou vient cela* (nat, P), *Jouissance* (nat, −M2), *Si j'ay pour vous* (nat, −M2), *Elle s'en va* (nat, −M2) by Sermisy, the anonymous *J'ay trop aime* (nat, P), *Ces fascheux sotz* (nat, P), *Dolent depart* (nat, P), *Je demeure seule esgaree* (nat, P), *Amour vault trop* (nat, P), *Une bergerote* (nat, P), *Le jaulne et blanc* (nat, P), *De toy me plains* (nat, P), *Puis que deux cueurs* (nat, −4) from D. Heartz, ed., *Preludes, Chansons and Dances for Lute, Published by Pierre Attaingnant* (Neuilly-sur-Seine, 1964).

vocal accompaniment, however. Words are connected with only
three pieces, and in only one case is the original text complete. This
complete text is provided for part 1 of *O adorandum sacramentum* by
Gombert (no. 29). Although the words had to be squeezed in
between the staves and above the right-hand part, the placement is
usually quite precisely related to the underlay of the cantus part from
the sixteenth-century printed source. Words appear for only the first
three pages of Phinot's *Domine nonne bonum* (no. 62). Again, despite
the difficulties of finding space for the words, their placement
corresponds quite closely to the underlay of the original cantus part.
But the rather abrupt abandonment of the attempt gives an
experimental air to the enterprise.[63]

The third texted piece offers puzzles and surprises of a different
sort. Where the placement of the text in the two motets revealed
some attempt to follow the printed cantus part, in Ruffo's *L'aquila è
gita al ciel* the text is entered haphazardly in the space between staves
and also below each system (see Figure 4). And the text copied with
the music bears scant relationship to the original – unless 'l'aquila'
shared a secondary ribald meaning similar to that of 'uccello' and
hence inspired the re-texting. For although the new text may be
rendered appropriate to the convent by its talk of cassocks and
cloaks, the 'little thing' being adored here is considerably removed
from the object of veneration in the texted *O adorandum sacramentum*,
as shown below:

Bardini manuscript text:

> Vu ch'ave quella cosetta
> Che dilletta e piase tanto
> Ah! lasse che una man ve metta
> Sotto la sottana e[']l vostro manto.
> Perdone se mi de botto
> Anca senza alcun rettegno
> De toccarve non me sdegno
> La cossetta zo de sotto.

Ruffo's original text:

> L'aquila è gita al ciel ne piange amore
> Amor casto e la madre sua pudica

---

[63] It is interesting to note that the scribe has copied only the portion of Phinot's text that has a
liturgical use (an antiphon at the Benedictus at lauds for the fifth Sunday after Epiphany)
but abandons it just two words short of its conclusion ('Hoc fecit [inimicus homo]').

Figure 4   Bardini MS 967, Ruffo, *L'aquila è gita al ciel*

105

Par ch'ogni gratia sospirando dica
L'aquila al ciel sen porta il nostr'honore.
Mostra l'alma natura alto dolore
Che vede l'empia universal nemica
Mandar tant'honorata sua fatica
Così rapidamente a l'ultim'hore.

Apart from the common use of eight lines divided into four-line groups, there is little formal relationship between Ruffo's original text and the manuscript poem. Their disagreement about the number of syllables per line would hamper any attempt to fit the new text to the old music. And the fact that the Bardini text is copied only under the first half of the piece further complicates matters. Yet despite the haphazard manner of entering the words, the new text is not totally divorced from the music. The text happens to break off around the strongest cadence on the final, halfway through the music, which had also marked the completion of the first stanza of Ruffo's text. The conclusion to the first four lines of the manuscript text also corresponds quite closely to the marked cadence on the fifth degree and the change of texture after the first couplet of Ruffo's original. The repetition of 'a-a-a' and 'o-o-o' with 'expressive' intent also suggests some sort of intended performance for the Bardini re-texting. Exactly how it worked in practice remains elusive, however.[64]

So if *L'aquila è gita al ciel* raises more questions than it answers, it may reveal that within the cloistered halls of the sacred virgins at Sant'Agnese thoughts might turn from spiritual exercises to more earthly – or earthy – preoccupations. Modest erotic allusions within the cloisters are occasionally revealed in the *commedie* written and performed by nuns. But the graphic erotic character of this *L'aquila è gita al ciel* is more overt and particularised than, for example, the 'bird' that flies out of the basket of flowers in which the naked Florido has hidden to startle an imprisoned lady in the *Amor di virtù* by Suor

---

[64] The handwriting of the added text contrasts somewhat with that of the original title, raising the possibility that the text might have been a subsequent addition as a kind of joke at the nuns' expense. The colour of the ink at least closely matches that of the music, however – indeed, it matches the music ink more closely than Ruffo's original title. The hand itself is not unlike hands from the second half of the sixteenth century. Rebecca Edwards has observed very similar scribal characteristics in Venetian documents dated 1566 and 1584, for example. I should like to thank Ms Edwards for her observations in this matter.

Beatrice del Sera of San Niccolò in Prato.[65] So far, the only other comparably graphic musical works from a sixteenth-century nunnery I have found turn up in Suor Elena's own manuscript. Several of the French chansons apparently copied from Moderne's prints rival, indeed surpass, the Italian re-texting in earthiness.[66]

[23]   S'il est ainsi que cognee sans manche
       Ny sert de rien ny oustil sans poignee
       Affin que lung dedans lautre semmanche
       Prens que soys manche & tu seras cogne.

[31]   Ung laboureur sa journee commanssoit
       Assez matin entrevoit ung loup musse
       En ung buisson qui sa proye pelissoit
       Mays quand le jour fut ung petit haulse
       Ce loup estoit ung cordelier trousse
       Voyre sans faulte robe & jacquette
       Qui sur la crette dung beau fosse
       Pelissonoit une jeune fillette.

[55]   Guillot ung jour estoit avec Barbeau
       Et luy monstroit son gran dyable de chose
       Laquelle aussy descouvrir son bas beau
       Estant plus rouge et plus vermeil que rose
       'Lors luy dist belle ou m'amour est enclose
       Je le feray tant que l'ons s'en rira.
       Avant amy trop lengtemps on repose
       N'espargnons point la chair qui pourira.'

[56]   Robin dormant Perrichon le sveilla
       D'un coup de pied jecte parmy sa cuisse
       Dont Robinet assez se merveilla
       Luy demandant est il chose que puysse.
       Metz ton bourdon au lieu par ou je pisse
       Dist Alison Robinet fi la cole
       Dist Alison [in 1 partbook: Perichon] luy rifusant la lisse
       Il est trop gros, Robinet, tu m'affolle.

If, as suggested, the Bardini manuscript might have been intended at least partly for vocal accompaniment, what sort of performance might have been envisioned? In discussing six vocal

---

[65] See E. Weaver, 'Spiritual Fun: A Study of Sixteenth-Century Tuscan Convent Theatre', *Women in the Middle Ages and the Renaissance* (Syracuse, 1986), p. 204 n. 54.
[66] The Bardini keyboard manuscript, of course, contains only their titles, and not the full texts, which have been recovered from Moderne.

intabulations from Castell'Arquato keyboard fascicles ivb and vi, which likewise include such textual insertions, Colin Slim has suggested that the keyboard musician may have sung the cantus parts of these works himself, and that he may have known the texts of the popular madrigals he had intabulated so well that no underlay was necessary for them.[67] Perhaps Suor Elena accompanied herself in similar fashion. The similarity of the Bardini intabulations to the keyboard parts Verovio published to accompany small vocal ensembles suggests, on the other hand, that Suor Elena's manuscript might have been used to accompany a group of nuns singing at least the soprano and alto parts. Such a practice would represent a precursor of the situation described by Ludovico Viadana in 1602: 'I saw that singers wishing to sing to the organ, either with three voices, or two, or to a single one by itself, were sometimes forced by the lack of compositions suitable to their purpose to take one, two, or three parts from motets in five, six, seven, or even eight.'[68] If that was the case, the nuns at Sant'Agnese would also have needed access to vocal partbooks. It is probably unreasonable to assume that the nuns owned the twenty or so prints concordant with the keyboard score. Perhaps a set of manuscript partbooks once accompanied the Bardini manuscript.

It might come as something of a surprise that such a manuscript, which is predominantly secular – indeed, in the case of a few pieces, downright bawdy – should be associated with a nun, one who appears to have been a highly respected, and possibly the leading, member of her order at the time it was compiled. But music in its various facets could be a common aspect of life in sixteenth-century nunneries, for convents represented a prime place of musical activity for women during the sixteenth and seventeenth centuries.[69] A closer look at musical life in the cloisters of Bologna suggests that the Bardini manuscript would not have been out of place at Sant' Agnese, though guardians of the nuns' spiritual welfare would have deplored its presence there.

We can only speculate about Elena's musical background and

---

[67] 'Some Puzzling Intabulations'.

[68] *Cento concerti ecclesiastici* (1602), quoted in O. Strunk, *Source Readings in Music History* (New York, 1950), p. 419.

[69] The most detailed discussion of music in Italian nunneries appears in J. Bowers, 'The Emergence of Women Composers in Italy, 1566–1700', *Women Making Music*, ed. J. Bowers and J. Tick (Urbana and Chicago, 1986), pp. 116–67.

that of the other nuns, and about the place of Elena's music manuscript in the monastery of Sant'Agnese. One suspects that she and her fellow nuns would have had upbringings comparable to those of other members of the Bolognese nobility. Of the eighty-three professing nuns at Sant'Agnese around the time the Bardini manuscript was compiled, at least sixty were members of Bologna's leading noble families or related to them by marriage.[70] According to a note in the Malvezzi family archive, the accomplishments of Elena's sister, the younger Camilla, included, for example, 'piety, and religion, honesty and kindness, needlework, singing and playing, letters, both Greek and Latin'.[71] Elena herself may have enjoyed similar talents. Had she been destined for the convent from an early age music might well have been emphasised in her studies.[72]

Just as there is no concrete information about Elena Malvezzi's own musical interests, hardly anything has come to light in the Fondo Sant'Agnese about music in the convent itself. The monastery has a venerable and modestly illustrious history, for it represents the oldest of the seven Dominican convents in Bologna, founded in 1223 by Giordano di Sassonia according to the wishes of San Domenico himself, to support a group of pious women led by the Blessed Diana of the noble Andalò family of Bologna.[73] Some fifteen years after Diana's death in 1236 the order had moved from outside the walls of Bologna to a site just within the south wall of the city, near the Porta San Mamolo (see Figure 5). During Suor Elena's lifetime, when no fewer than 2000 nuns lived in thirty-four convents in Bologna, and the nunneries and monasteries occupied one-sixth of the total area of the city, about a hundred sisters resided within the walls of Sant'Agnese. By July 1798, six months before the convent was suppressed by Napoleon, the number of sisters had dwindled to twenty-two.

The entire Fondo Sant'Agnese has yielded only four possible

---

[70] Of the eighty-three nuns listed in the notarial document of 1558 in Bologna, Archivio Arcivescovile, Ricuperi beneficiari, fascicolo 8, forty-six come from the 100 noble families described in Dolfi, *Cronologia*, while another fourteen bear family names mentioned by Dolfi as having married members of the 'first families'.

[71] 'la pietà, e religione, honesta et bontà . . . l'ago, la musica, il suono, le lettere, tanto greche, quanto latine'; ASB, Archivio Malvezzi-Campeggi, serie 2a, 27/264, a loose sheet among 'Allegati alla qui unita Istoria Malvezzi'.

[72] In 'The Emergence of Women Composers', p. 132, Jane Bowers points out that the study of music was considered appropriate for girls intended for the religious life.

[73] On the history of Sant'Agnese, see Cambria, *Il monastero domenicano*, on which I have relied for the following details.

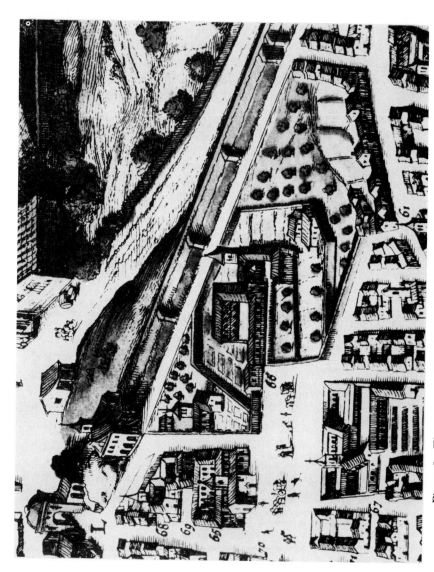

Figure 5   The convent of Sant'Agnese, Bologna, c 1650 (no. 66); from J. Bleau, *Theatrum civitatum et admirandorum Italiae* (Amsterdam, 1663)

references to music. These date from the 1470s and 1480s, and two are concerned with the binding of choirbooks. The fourth is hardly more promising, for it reveals that in January 1479 Sant'Agnese did not even have a working organ of its own: 'To Mr Biaggio Mastellazo, on the 18th of the said [January], one soldo to pay for transporting the organ for the Feast of Sant'Agnese from San Sebastiano to the monastery.'[74] From 1602 onwards, on the other hand, it is possible to trace a string of nun organists at Sant'Agnese down to the suppression of the convent in 1799. The list begins, interestingly enough, with one 'Leonora Florida Ferrabosco', certainly a relative of the composer Alfonso Ferrabosco the elder, and possibly his daughter.[75]

Various chronicles and *avvisi* from outside the archive of the nunnery also record a number of elaborate musical services at the convent in 1673, 1703, 1705, 1713 and 1724. The service in 1703 drew such a large and boisterous crowd that Archbishop Giacomo Boncompagni subsequently forbade the use of polyphony to all the nunneries of Bologna. On 30 July 1704 the archbishop wrote to the Sacred Congregation in Rome:

I [was] considering the scandals to be inevitable when music went on there [in convent churches], for which reason the gathering of the people was copious . . . In the church of the nuns of Sant'Agnese subject to the government of the Dominican Fathers, not only did they follow the usual immodesties there, but also second Vespers could not be completed because the high altar was occupied by the people; during the singing of the Magnificat it was impossible for the priest, bedecked in his cope, and for the

[74] 'A m^r Biazzo mastellazo ad xviij d[el] dto [soldo] uno p[er] pagare lo portadore d[el] l'organo p[er] la festa di S. Agnese da S. Sebastiã al mon.' ASB, Demaniale 107/6772 (Sant'Agnese), account book, 1477–88, fol. 26^v.

[75] According to Baldassare Carrati (BCB, MS в921, p. 127) a Suora Leonora Florida Ferraboschi had professed at Sant'Agnese on 7 March 1602. In a notarial document dated 14 October 1601 (ASB, Notarili, Cavazza Ercole Prot° ii, fol. 182^r–184^v) Susanna Ferrabosco, wife of Alfonso Ferrabosco, and Carlo Emanuele, his son, agreed to sell a piece of property partly to provide £1000 towards the nun's dowry of Catherina, Susanna's daughter and Carlo Emanuele's sister ('Et quas pecunias diceru[n]t mille [?] errogare in monacaz^ne Dna Catherina eos filia et sorore.'). A thousand lire would represent a plausible dowry for a nun organist around 1600. A very rough draft of another document dated 20 November 1602 (ASB, Notarili, Maladrati Francesco, Filza 1 [1583–1602], fol. 171) – several months after the apparent profession of Leonora Florida Ferrabosco – still speaks of providing £1000 for the marriage or nun's dowry of Catherina, however. None of the other members of the Ferrabosco family whose names appear in the records of Bolognese nunneries seems to correspond more closely to Catherina, the daughter of Alfonso Ferrabosco, however. Leonora Florida Ferrabosco also served as sotto-priora of Sant'Agnese from 2 May 1639 until 13 April 1643 (BCB, MS в921, p. 152).

other two assistants to proceed to cense the altar, and it was necessary for them to move to the sacristy; the musicians [were] also leaving since they could not perform the music because of all the noise that prevented their hearing the voices.[76]

Thus, despite the paucity of musical evidence in the convent archive, the nuns of Sant'Agnese clearly practised elaborate music in the seventeenth and eighteenth centuries, and may also have employed polyphony during the sixteenth century, as other Bolognese convents unquestionably did around Suor Elena's time. An exhortation in Giovanni Boccadiferro's manuscript 'Discorso sopra il Governo delle Monache', dedicated to Giovanni Campeggi, Bishop of Bologna from 1553 to 1563 (precisely the period when the Bardini manuscript was compiled), and directed at the nuns in the bishop's charge, stated: 'It is again necessary that you resolve to put aside all these pernicious customs that until now have caused your ruin. Leave off, therefore, your *canto figurato*, which, although becoming to other male religious orders, for you – or a goodly part of you – has been the cause of great harm.'[77] A more specific proscription regarding elaborate music was officially published for all the Dominican convents in Bologna on 20 July 1582: 'that polyphony not be sung in the choir and also not to the organ, except on the most solemn occasions'.[78]

Elaborate music must have remained common, however, for in 1593 Alfonso Paleotti, the future Archbishop of Bologna, wrote to Cardinal Alessandrino:

Because in our city it is fashionable for the nuns to perform these solemn

---

[76] 'Considerando Io essere inevitabili gli scandali, quando vi si continuasse la Musica, per la quale essendo copioso il Concorso del Popolo . . . nella Chiesa delle Monache di S. Agnese soggette al governo de P. P. Domenicani non solo vi seguirono le solite immodestie ma altresi nel secondo Vespro non puote terminarsi, poiche occupato sino lo stesso Altar Maggiore dalla gente, nell' atto di cantarsi il Magnificat, non fu possibile al Sacerdote parato col Piviale, et alli due Assistenti andar ad incensare l'Altare, e gli convenne portarsene in Sacristia, partendo li Musici ancora, che non puotero proseguire la Musica a cagione del gran rumore, che impediva loro di sentire le voci.' ASB, Demaniale 48/2909 (Santa Christina).

[77] 'Fa anchor bisogno che vi disponiate . . . a por da banda tutti quei perniciosi costumi che sin hora hanno causato la ruina vostra. Lasciate dunque il canto figurato, quale anchora che alli altri religiosi sia dicevole, a voi o gran parte di voi è stato causa di gran danno.' BCB, MS ʙ778, p. 195, quoted in M. Fanti, *Abiti e lavori delle monache di Bologna* (Bologna, 1972), pp. 26–7.

[78] 'quod non cantetur in cantu figurato in choro, nec in organo, nisi in maximis solemnitatibus'; Cambria, *Il monastero domenicano*, p. 112, quoting from *In monasterium bononiensibus (20 julii) ordinationes*.

sorts of music, which are the cause of many scandalous disturbances such as we experience daily, therefore I request you, most illustrious Sir, to speak of it in the most illustrious Congregation, which judging it may send me orders to prohibit the said solemn music, which will be a most godly act.[79]

A few years later the by then Archbishop Alfonso Paleotti published a collection of his own decrees for the good government of Bolognese nunneries. The particulars of his more detailed prohibitions about music suggest the sorts of music-making that must have gone on in the convents during earlier decades:

There should not be any [nun] who dares to sing or play at the grates or at the doorways, in the presence of any man or woman . . . It is also forbidden to admit any sort of *maestri* to teach in their monasteries, and especially musicians, and further to rehearse any of their music either on the organ or in song. [We are] notifying them that from the publication of the present order all previous licences conceded to them for any reason or in any manner are considered revoked and cancelled. [We are] advising all the nuns that they cannot sing vernacular pieces, but Latin, ecclesiastical and religious ones, whether in the choir, on the organ, as well as in their cells, under penalty of being forbidden ever to sing and play in future.[80]

Paleotti's prohibition of vernacular music indicates that secular collections such as Elena Malvezzi's may not have been uncommon before that time, and may have been employed not only in the privacy of the nuns' cells, but also for more public performances at the grates or doorways of the parlatorios. The denial of admission to

---

[79] 'Perché nella nostra città s'usa di far queste musiche solenni dalle suore, quali son cagione di molti scandalosi disordini come giornalmente proviamo, perciò supplico vostra signoria illustrissima di farne parola nell'illustrissima Congregazione che parendoli mi mandino ordini di prohibir dette musiche solenni, che sarà opera santissima'; quoted in G. L. Masetti Zannini, 'Espressioni musicali in monasteri femminili del primo Seicento a Bologna', *Strenna Storica Bolognese*, 35 (1985), p. 197.

[80] 'Non vi sia alcuna, che ardisca di ca[n]tare, o suonare alle Grate, ne alle Porte alla presenza d'alcun' huomo, o donna . . . Se le prohibisce ancora . . . l'admettere qual si voglia sorte de Maestri ad insegnare alli loro Monasterij, e specialmente Musici, ancora che per provare qualche loro Musica, si nell'Organo, comme nel Canto. Notificandole, che dalla publicatione del presente ordine s'intendeno rivocate, & annullate tutte le licenze fin qui, per qual si voglia causa, & in qual si voglia modo concesse. Auvertendo le Monache tutte, si in Choro, e sul'Organo, come nelle loro Camere, che non cantino cose volgari, ma latine, Ecclesiastiche, e religiose, sotto pene d'esser prive di piu cantare, e suonare per l'auvenire.' *Compendio d'ordini rinovati, et stabiliti per il buon governo delli monasterij di monache dall'Illmo et R^mo Mons^re Alfonso Paleotti* (Bologna, 1598), pp. 7–8, preserved in BCB, MS Gozz. 405 and headed in ink 'Ordine del Monast° delle Suore di Sta Elena'. The portion after the first sentence has been scratched through several times in ink. Similar prohibitions reappear again and again in about a dozen decrees preserved in archives of Bolognese nunneries during the period from 1600 to 1675. On similar decrees in other cities, especially Milan, see Bowers, 'The Emergence of Women Composers'.

outside musicians also suggests a possible avenue for the acquisition of music from outside the monastery: outsiders could easily have brought music into the convent to teach and rehearse.

Other evidence from the convents of SS. Gervasio e Protasio, Santa Margarita, San Giovanni Battista, Santa Catterina, San Guglielmo and San Agostino attests to the presence of harpsichords, lutes, guitars, chittaroni, clavichords, violins, several trombones and even small organs, privately owned, particularly before 1620.[81] Documents from Santa Margarita, San Gervasio and San Guglielmo also bear witness to the private ownership of books of music 'to sing and to play', ranging in number from seven to 'a trunkful'.[82] But the Bardini manuscript is the only such music book to have come to light.

Indeed, it seems ironic that the most concrete evidence of the sorts of private music-making that went on in Bolognese convents should come from Sant'Agnese, for which such scanty archival records about music survive. The Bardini manuscript not only provides a very rare view of the secular music presumably performed within the sixteenth-century cloister, but also offers suggestions about how it may have been performed. And it allows us to retrieve a few previously incomplete works, including the ribald *S'il est ainsi* and *Robin dormant*, which until now languished without their bass parts. If the manuscript might have been used at least partly for vocal accompaniment, one may conclude with the engaging image of this Bolognese bride of Christ, Elena Malvezzi, perhaps joined by her fellow nuns, trilling her way through such dubious texts, possibly in even more dubious French. Clearly in Bologna, too, there was fuel for the refining fires of the Counter-Reformation.

Washington University

[81] ASB, Demaniale 32/6061 (SS. Gervasio e Protasio), Demaniale 51/3918 (Santa Margarita), Demaniale 95/4021 (Santa Catterina), Demaniale 80/814 (San Guglielmo), Demaniale 41/4884 (San Agostino). On the private ownership of an organ at San Agostino and the use of trombones at San Giovanni Battista, see G. L. Masetti Zannini, 'Espressioni musicali', pp. 203 and 200–1 respectively.

[82] Demaniale 51/3918 (Santa Margarita), inventory of Suor Emilia Arali: 'libri p[er] sonar e cantar n 7'; Demaniale 32/6061 (San Gervasio), a coverless *Libro di memorie*, fol. 97, records that the future organist, Verginia di Giulio Cesare dal Grosso, was to be furnished with 'tutti li instrumenti et libri quali esercita et si appartengono alle Sue Virtu'; Demaniale 80/814 (San Guglielmo), *Raccordi p[er] il monastero*, entry no. 21: 'una cassa de libri da cantare'.

APPENDIX 1

Contents of Museo Bardini, MS 967

	[No.]	Title	Composer	Folio	Print
1	1	Ogni loco mi porge doglia [i]	[Palestrina]	1	1559[16]
	2	Poscia ch[e] per mio mal [ii]	[Palestrina]	3	1559[16]
	3	La bella nimpha		4[v]	
	4	Occhij vaghi [i]	[Ruffo]	5[v]	1553 [R3071]
	5	Occhij leg[g]iadri [ii]	[Ruffo]	7	1553 [R3071]
		[fol. 8 three-quarters blank; fols. 8[v]–12 blank]			
2	6	L'aquila e gita al ciel [i (only)]	[Ruffo]	12[v]	1553 [R3071]
	7	Poi che quel cuor di giaccio [i (only)]	[Ruffo]	14[v]	1553 [R3071]
		[fol. 15[v] quarter blank; fols. 16–19 blank]			
3	8	Tristitia vïa [et anxietas] [i]	[Clemens non Papa]	19[v]	1553[8], 1554[14]
	9	Sed tu Domine [ii]	[Clemens non Papa]	22[v]	1553[8], 1554[14]
	10	Alla dolce ombra [i]	[Berchem]	24[v]	1554[22], 1555[25]
	11	No[n] vid j l mondo [ii]	[Berchem]	26	1544[22], 1555[25]
4	12	Un lauro mi difese [iii]	[Berchem]	27[v]	1554[22], 1555[25]
	13	Pero piu ferm' ogn hor [iv]	[Berchem]	29	1554[22], 1555[25]
	14	Selve sassi [v]	[Berchem]	30	1554[22], 1555[25]
	15	Tanto mi piacque [vi]	[Berchem]	31[v]	1554[22], 1555[25]
5	16	Magnus Sa[n]ctus Paulus [i]		34	
	17	A Christo de celo vocatus 2[a] pars		36	
	18	Cu[m] vocatus fueris ad nuptias		37[v]	
	19	Sdegno regge il timo[n] [ii – *sic*]	[Ruffo]	41	1553 [R3071]
6	20	Dhe porgi mano alla (i – *sic*]	[Ruffo]	42	1553 [R3071]
	21	Chiuso gra[n] tempo	[Ruffo]	43	1553 [R3071]
	22	In die tribulationis mee	[Rore]	44[v]	1544[6]
	23	S'il est ainsi	[Fresneau]	47[v]	1544[9]

APPENDIX 1 — *continued*

Contents of Museo Bardini, MS 967

	[No.]	Title	Composer	Folio	Print
7	24	La louete	[Janequin]	49	1544[9]
	25	Haganle todos el buz [Venga al gran sennor]	[Flecha]	52ᵛ	1544[9]
	26	Angustie mihi su[n]t undique [i]	[Rore]	56	1549[8]
	27	[Deus aeterne] 2ᵃ pars	[Rore]	57ᵛ	1549[8]
8	28	Folle e pur il pensiero [desio]	[Corteccia]	59	1547 [C4160]
	29	O adorandu[m] sacrame[n]tu[m] [i]	[Gombert]	61	1541 [G2984]
	30	Quod transiturus de hoc mundo [ii]	[Gombert]	64	1541 [G2984]
9	31	Ung labourr	[Fresneau]	67	1544[9]
	32	P[ate]r N[oste]r qui est in celis		68ᵛ	
	33	Ave maria		71ᵛ	
	34	Cu[m] foderet ferro		74ᵛ	
10	35	Novo piacer	[Arcadelt?/ Rampollini?]	77	1542[17]
	36	No[n] vedd' oggi el sole	[Corteccia]	78ᵛ	1545 [R215]
	37	[Qual'è più grand'o amore]	[Rore]	80	1542[17]
11	38	Ala dolce ombra [i]	[Rore]	81ᵛ	1550 [R2500], 1551 [R2501]
	39	[Non vide'l mondo] [ii]	[Rore]	82ᵛ	1550 [R2500], 1551 [R2501]
	40	[Un lauro mi difese] [iii]	[Rore]	84	1550 [R2500], 1551 [R2501]
	41	[Però più ferm'ogn'hor] [iv]	[Rore]	85	1550 [R2500], 1551 [R2501]
	42	Selve [sassi] [v]	[Rore]	86	1550 [R2500], 1551 [R2501]
	43	Hellas come[n]t [voules vous] [ii – *sic*]	[Rore]	87ᵛ	1550 [R2500], 1551 [R2502]

APPENDIX 1 — *continued*

Contents of Museo Bardini, MS 967

	[No.]	Title	Composer	Folio	Print
	44	En vox a dieux [i – *sic*]	[Rore]	89	1550 [R2500], 1551 [R2501]
12	45	[Peccantem me quotidie]	[Clemens non Papa]	90v	1547[6]
	46	[Deus in nomine tuo] [ii]	[Clemens non Papa]	92v	1547[6]
13	47	Usquequo D[omi]ne [i]	[Rore]	95v	1545 [R2474]
	48	[Illumina oculos meos] [ii]	[Rore]	97v	1545 [R2474]
	49	Quis te victore[m] dicat [i]	[Clemens non Papa]	100	1555[8]
	50	[Non te hostis vincet] 2ª pars	[Clemens non Papa]	102v	1555[8]
	51	Carita de Signore [ii (only)]	[Rore]	105	1550 [R2500], 1551 [R2501]
14	52	La giustitia im[m]ortale	[Rore]	106	1550 [R2500], 1551 [R2501]
	53	Amor ben mi credevo	[Rore]	108	1550 [R2500], 1551 [R2501], 1550 [R2500]
15	54	L[']empia dureza	[Janequin]	110	1544[9]
	55	Guillot ung iour	[Bon Voisin]	112	1544[9]
	56	Robin dormant		113	
	57	Se vã occhij lucẽti		115	
	58	[untitled]		116v	
	59	[untitled]		118	
16	60	Madre [Padre!] del ciel [i (only)]	[Rore]	120v	1554 [New Vogel 2391]
	61	Lasso ch[e] desiando vo	[Berchem]	122v	1544 [New Vogel 2391]
17	62	D[omi]ne no[n]ne bonu[m] seme[n]	[Phinot]	126	1555[14]
	63	Che sej tu senza fiam[m]e [ii (only)]	[Animuccia]	129	1554 [A1243]
	64	O, lumẽ [lumine?]		131v	

APPENDIX 1 — *continued*

Contents of Museo Bardini, MS 967

	[No.]	Title	Composer	Folio	Print
	65	Da quei bei lumi	[Rore]	134	1542 [R2479], 1544 [R2480]
	66	Vie pur [più?] ch̄l loco, e, in pregio [pregione?]		137	
	67	Qui pur credea haver tranquillo porto		139	
18	68	Ite felici		140ᵛ	
	69	Ardo de un si soave, e, dolce focho		141ᵛ	
	70	Qua[n]to piu don'a miri		142ᵛ	
	71	No[n] voria ch̄l mirar		143	
	72	Vagi felici e fortunati		144	
	73	Alcu[n] no[n] è ch̄ vinte [?] piu di me		145ᵛ	
		[folio cut out, with end of preceding piece]			
19	74	[continuation of piece, missing its opening]		147ᵛ	
	75	Ditemi, o diva mia	[Perissone Cambio]	148ᵛ	1553 [R3074]
	76	Vivero donque	[Ruffo]	150	1553 [R3071]
	77	O fortunato [e aventuroso] [i]	[Ruffo]	152	1553 [R3071]
20	78	[Aure fresch'e soave] [ii]	[Ruffo]	153	1553 [R3071]
	79	Tempus erat [i]	[Nasco]	154	1553 [R3074]
	80	Ante meos oculos [ii]	[Nasco]	155ᵛ	1553 [R3074]
	81	O camaretta [che già fosti] [i (only)]	[Ruffo]	157	1553 [R3071]
21	82	Pace no[n] trovo	[Ruffo]	158ᵛ	1553 [R3071]
		[fols. 162ᵛ–165ᵛ blank, but ruled]			

APPENDIX 2

Incipits of unidentified works in Museo Bardini, MS 967

3. La bella nimpha

16. Magnus Sanctus Paulus [i]

17. A Christo de celo vocatus ii

18. Cum vocatus fueris ad nuptias

32. Pater Noster qui est in celis

33. Ave Maria

34. Cum foderet ferro

54. L'empia dureza

57. Se vã occhij lucēti

58. [Untitled]

59. [Untitled]

64. O, lumē

66. Vie pur cĥl loco, e, in pregio

67. Qui pur credea haver tranquillo porto

68. Ite felici

69. Ardo de un si soave, e, dolce focho

70. Quãto piu don'a miri

71. nõ voria cħl mirar

72. Vagi felici e fortunati

73. Alcũ nõ e cħ vinte piu di me

74. [Incomplete piece, missing opening]

[conclusion to incomplete piece]

APPENDIX 3

Transpositions in Museo Bardini, MS 967

No. Title	Original final	Transposition
1–2. Ogni loco/Poscia che	e	P[a]
4–5. Occhij vaghi/Occhij legiadri	d	P
6. L'aquila e gita al ciel	g	-4^b
7. Poi che quel cuor	C	-5^c
8–9. Tristitia vīa/Sed tu	g	P
10–15. Alla dolce ombra	C	-5
19–20. Sdegno regge/Dhe porgi	d	-5
21. Chiuso gran tempo	g	P

124

No. Title	Original final	Transposition
22. In die tribulationis	F	P
23. S'il est ainsi	C	−5
24. La louete	F	P
25. Venga al gran sennor	F	−4
26–7. Angustie mihi sunt/Deus aeterne	F	P
28. Folle è pur il pensiero	d	P
29–30. O adorandum/Quod transiturus	F	−4
31. Ung labouur	g	P
35. Novo piacer	g	−4
36. Non vedd' oggi	d	P

125

No. Title	Original final	Transposition
37. Qual'è più grand'	F	P
38.–42. Ala dolce ombra	G	−5
43–4. Hellas coment/En vox a dieux	F	P
45–6. Peccantem me/Deus in nomine tuo	d	−5
47–8. Usquequo Domine/Illumina	F	−4
49–50. Quis te victorem/Non te hostis	F	−4
51. Carita de Signore	G	P
52. La giustitia immortale	d	P
53. Amor ben mi credevo	e	P

No. Title	Original final	Transposition
55. Guillot ung iour	g	−4

| 56. Robin dormant | F | P |

| 60. Madre del ciel | g | −4 |

| 62. Domine nonne bonum semen | d | P |

| 63. Che sej tu senza fiamma | d | P |

| 65. Da quei bei lumi | e | P |

| 75. Ditemi, o diva mia | a | P |

| 76. Vivero donque | a | −5 |

| 77–8. O fortunato/Aure fresch' | a | −5 |

No. Title	Original final	Transposition
81. O camaretta	F	P

82. Pace non trovo	g	P

Notes

[a]P — at original pitch.
[b]−4 — transposed down a fourth.
[c]−5 — transposed down a fifth.

Early Music History (1989) Volume 9

ANDREW WATHEY

THE PEACE OF 1360–1369 AND ANGLO-FRENCH MUSICAL RELATIONS*

The Treaty of Brétigny, concluded in May 1360, inaugurated the longest period of peace between England and France that the century had yet seen.[1] Although the English success in this agreement later turned out to be less than complete, the king and higher nobility in England could now look to the consolidation of their position in the overseas dependencies of Brittany, Gascony and Ponthieu, to the enjoyment of their new-found wealth at home, and

*This article originated as a paper read in different forms at Princeton University and to a meeting of the Royal Musical Association in London in February 1989. For their help and comments I am very grateful to Margaret Bent, Edward Powell and Simon Walker; my thanks also to Roger Bowers, who kindly made available the text of his paper 'Fixed Points in the Chronology of English Fourteenth-Century Polyphony' in advance of its publication. The archival work underlying this study was undertaken with the help of support from Downing College, Cambridge, and a grant from the Research Fund of the University of Lancaster. Unpublished documents are in the Public Record Office, London, unless otherwise stated. Crown-Copyright material is here reproduced by permission of the Controller of H.M. Stationery Office.

The following abbreviations are used:

BPR	*Register of Edward the Black Prince*, 4 vols. (London, 1930–3)
CPL	*Calendar of Entries in the Papal Registers relating to Great Britain and Ireland: Papal Letters*, IV
CPL: Petitions	*Calendar of Entries . . .: Petitions to the Pope*
CPR	*Calendar of Patent Rolls*
Urbain: LC	*Urbain* V *(1362–1370): Lettres Communes*, ed. M. Hayez *et al.*, 11 vols., Bibliothèque des Écoles Françaises d'Athènes et de Rome, 3rd ser., 5bis (Paris and Rome, 1954–86)

[1] For what follows see G. L. Harriss, *King, Parliament and Public Finance in Medieval England to 1369* (Oxford, 1975), pp. 466–508; J. Le Patourel, 'The Treaty of Brétigny, 1360', *Transactions of the Royal Historical Society*, 5th ser., 10 (1960), pp. 19–39. Among the numerous political narratives of this period see A. Tuck, *Crown and Nobility, 1272–1461: Political Conflict in Late Medieval England* (London, 1985), pp. 135–9, 158–65; C. Allmand, *The Hundred Years War: England and France at War, c. 1300–c. 1450* (Cambridge, 1988), pp. 17–22; T. F. Tout, *Chapters in the Administrative History of Medieval England: the Wardrobe, the Chamber and the Small Seals*, 6 vols. (Manchester, 1920–33), III, pp. 231–65; R. Delachenal, *Histoire de Charles* V, 5 vols. (Paris, 1909–31), II, pp. 193–265.

129

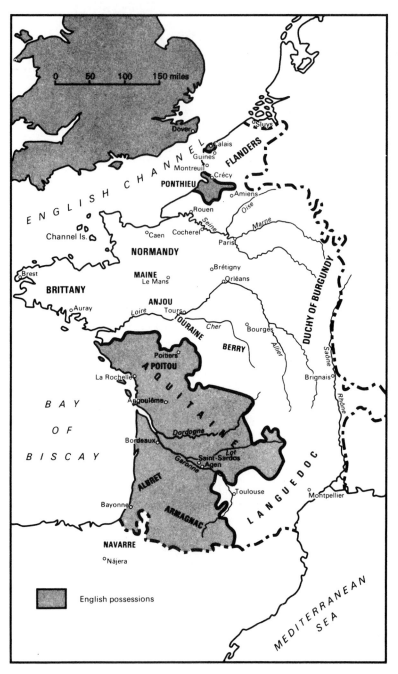

Figure 1 English possessions in France after the Treaty of Brétigny 1360 (from C. Allmand, *The Hundred Years War* (Cambridge, 1988), p. xii)

130

to a superficially more amicable relationship with French magnates. External relations were thus transformed, and the period between 1360 and 1369 also saw a fundamental change in the accessibility in England of French musical culture and in the opportunities for contacts with French musicians.

Yet although the Bishop of Winchester, addressing the 1363 parliament as Chancellor, could describe the king 'dwelling in his own land in the seat of peace, desiring above all the quiet and tranquillity of nobles, lords and commons',[2] the peace with France throughout this period was far from stable or secure. On a number of fronts hostilities might well have reopened at any time; following the accession of Charles v and the French victory over Charles, King of Navarre, at Cocherel in 1364, a new war became inevitable. In this year a spy of the Black Prince reported the new French king's determination to string Edward iii along until the hostages were recovered and his own domestic scores settled, then to secure alliances with Edward's enemies, re-conquer Aquitaine and finally attack and destroy England.[3] Here as in other respects the years between 1360 and 1369 share much with the other periods of peace punctuating the fourteenth-century conflict between England and France. From its very inception the peace of the 1360s was essentially diplomatic rather than political in expression, and this feature characterises also the most important facets of its later course. The contrasts between such a peace, even without political guarantees, and the periods of open conflict were of course enormous. The nobles and commons were relieved of the burden of war taxation, and the national revenue was spared that of military action. Diplomatic dealings with other rulers were sharply reoriented to accommodate the changed formal relationship with the Valois succession. Most important, the diplomatic activity of these years, broadly defined, gave rise to numerous special situations; it was these – rather than the mere fact of the peace itself – that served as the cradles of opportunity where contacts and access between musical cultures were concerned.

It will be as well to begin with some of the conditions whose effects on Anglo-French musical relations were felt throughout the period of the Hundred Years War, and with their impact on those groups

---

[2] *Rotuli Parliamentorum*, 7 vols. (London, 1783–1832), ii, p. 283.
[3] See Delachenal, *Histoire de Charles v*, iii, pp. 551–4.

where musical skills were concentrated. In the main, the presence abroad of English magnates' chapels was limited to the occasions where the representation of the kingship was at stake.[4] This is nowhere more clearly demonstrated than in the context of the English presence in Normandy between 1417 and 1449. Probably the only large and regularly constituted body of English singers was the household chapel of the regent and – after 1435 – that of the governor general or royal lieutenant. These men were uniquely placed in that they shouldered the weight of the English kingship in France with its attendant ceremonial needs. English magnates were in general cautious about taking their domestic establishments to France, and the costs of garrisoning a large retinue in a secure location or of maintaining it on a permanent war-footing could be enormous. In the earlier phases of the conflict, where the financial resources of the realm were more completely mobilised for war and where the king in person was more often the principal protagonist, expeditions made abroad by the royal chapel were probably more frequent. We possess lists of the chaplains who accompanied Edward III to the Netherlands in 1338, to Brittany in 1342, to France in 1346 and for the expedition to Rheims and the Ile-de-France in 1359–60.[5] Yet after this year royal absences from the realm declined sharply – there was none longer than two months until the fifteenth century – and with it the royal chapel's opportunities for foreign travel.[6] In the years that followed the Treaty of Brétigny, the most sustained opportunities for contacts with French musical cultures on French soil that were enjoyed by the clerks of English chapels arose from the grant of Aquitaine to Edward the Black Prince in 1362. Here too the presence of a household chapel can be linked with the

---

[4] For what follows see A. Wathey, 'Dunstable in France', *Music & Letters*, 67 (1986), pp. 3–4; A. Wathey, *Music in the Royal and Noble Households in Late Medieval England: Studies of Sources and Patronage* (New York and London, 1989), pp. 53, 56–7.

[5] See for the 1338 expedition c 81/1743/65; *The Wardrobe Book of William de Norwell, 12 July 1338–27 May 1340*, ed. B. Lyon *et al.*, Académie Royale de Belgique: Commission Royale d'Histoire (Brussels, 1983), pp. 352–3, 391–2, 303–5; for the Brittany expedition see E 36/204, fol. 108. For chaplains and clerks with the 1346 expedition see E 101/391/9, fols. 4^{r-v} and, for wages paid in arrears after the expedition, E 101/390/12 *passim*; extracts are printed in G. Wrottesley, *Crécy and Calais, from the Original Records in the Public Record Office* (London, 1898), pp. 212–14, 215; A protection for Queen Philippa's chaplains for this expedition is c 81/1746/115. For the expedition of 1359–60 see E 101/393/11, fols. 76^v, 88–90^v.

[6] See *Handbook of British Chronology*, 3rd edn, ed. E. B. Fryde, D. E. Greenway, S. Porter and I. Roy, Royal Historical Society Guides and Handbooks 2 (London, 1986) [hereafter *HBC*], p. 39.

exercise of regalian rights and duties and the ceremonial that these entailed.[7] As royal lieutenant in Gascony from 1355 the prince had made striking use of solemn entries and other ceremonies, but with this grant the scope for ritual manifestations of his standing in the duchy was now much enhanced. In some measure this ceremonial can be held accountable for contemporaries' comments about the brilliant court that the prince kept at Bordeaux.[8] A recently discovered list of the entourage that accompanied the prince nonetheless does not include all those who are known as chaplains and clerks of the chapel in these years.[9] A similar role in facilitating access to French musical cultures, although perhaps with greater potential for sustained contacts, can be attributed to the household chapels of John II in England, 1357–60 and 1363–4, and possibly to those of the dukes of Anjou, Bourbon and Berry.

By contrast the minstrels of the king and higher nobility enjoyed a much greater freedom of movement. Their use for diplomatic errands, to carry news, letters and sometimes precious objects, was the main source of this mobility, and for these purposes they are almost indistinguishable from heralds, pursuivants and other messengers. The minstrel schools have therefore as much diplomatic as musical significance, and the English administration was fully aware of the potential threat that minstrels serving alien masters might

---

[7] See R. Barber, *Edward Prince of Wales and Aquitaine: A Biography of the Black Prince* (London, 1978), pp. 177–81, 184; G. E. Cokayne, *The Complete Peerage of England Scotland Ireland Great Britain and the United Kingdom Extant Extinct or Dormant*, 12 vols. (London, 1910–56), III, pp. 435–7. See also Tout, *Chapters*, v, pp. 291–2. For an account of the entry made by the prince into the Abbey of St Seurin, Bordeaux, on 16 September 1355, 'cum magno exercitu comitum et baronum Anglie', see J.-A. Brutails, *Cartulaire de l'église collégiale Saint-Seurin de Bordeaux* (Bordeaux, 1897), pp. 4–5; see also H. J. Hewitt, *The Black Prince's Expedition of 1355–1357* (Manchester, 1958), pp. 43–4, 140, Appendix 2 below *sub* William Oxwick, and H. Mullot and J. Poux, 'Nouvelles recherches sur l'itinéraire du Prince Noir à travers les pays de l'Aude', *Annales du Midi*, 21 (1909), pp. 298–311. For later ceremonial see among much else Y. Renouard, *Bordeaux sous les rois d'Angleterre*, Histoire de Bordeaux 3 (Bordeaux, 1965), pp. 386, 388.

[8] For example the remarks, made in the context of the prince's attempts in 1368 to levy the *fouage* in Aquitaine, in *Chroniques de J. Froissart*, ed. S. Luce *et al.*, Société de l'Histoire de France (Paris, 1869–), VII, p. 66. See also *La vie du Prince Noir by Chandos Herald*, ed. D. B. Tyson, Beihefte zur Zeitschrift für romanische Philologie 147 (Tübingen, 1976), pp. 91–2.

[9] London, British Library, MS Cotton Julius C. IV, fols. 288–91 (Appendix 1, Document 1). See also *CPL: Petitions*, I, pp. 454–6; *Urbain: LC*, I, pp. 478–9 (4239–50). Warrants for protections for clerks joining this expedition are C 81/1713/19 and C 81/1713/76. For other clerics with the prince as administrators in Aquitaine in these years see P. Chaplais, 'The Chancery of Guyenne, 1289–1453', *Studies Presented to Sir Hilary Jenkinson*, ed. J. Conway Davies (Oxford, 1957), pp. 85–9; Tout, *Chapters*, v, pp. 289–400 *passim*.

Table 1 *Safe-conducts and protections for minstrels, 1360–1400*

Date	Beneficiary	From	To
18 Feb 1360	Sauxonetus le Menestrier, minstrel of the King of France (*Foedera*,[a] III/1, p. 470)		France
4 Feb 1361	Pierre de Vannes, Gylet de Uscy, Colyn Prodhome and Philipot de Vannes, minstrels of the Duke of Orléans, six horses worth under 40s. and two valets (*Foedera*, III/2, p. 599)	France England	England France
4 Feb 1361	Boteoun le Taborier, Guilmyn le Mestre and Baudet de Seint Omer, minstrels of the Duke of Berry (*Foedera*, III/2, p. 599)	France England	England France
15 March 1368	Janyn Pountoyse, Petre Man, Poul and Henselyn Tabourner, minstrels of Sir John Chandos, two valets, their belongings, four horses worth under 40s., 200 marks in bills of exchange and 20s. each for expenses (c 81/915/19)	Dover	Gascony
12 May 1368	Thomas de Balsham and Edward Paule, minstrels of Edward Prince of Wales and Aquitaine, four garceons, six horses, £6 in bills of exchange and 20s. each for expenses (c 81/908/37)	Southampton, Weymouth or Plymouth	to the prince in Aquitaine
8 July 1368	Myttok 'Roi des menestralx de Brabant', Guynaud la Voegle, Swankyn and Rolether, minstrels, six horses which they brought with them, a horse worth under six marks, another worth under 40s., their valets, Chynkes and Wauter, 40s. in bills of exchange and 20s. each for expenses (c 81/918/2)	Dover	Calais
8 Feb 1372	Martyn Wenger, minstrel, with his belongings and 40s. for expenses (c 81/942/16)	London	Holland
17 Jan [1379]	Four minstrels of the Duke of Lancaster, with seven		Calais

	horses and three servants, 'sont a aler as escoles es parties doutre mer' (c 81/1730/59)		
10 June 1379[b]	Copin de Holland, piper in the company of William de Ermyn, treasurer of Calais, to go to Calais for one year 'ibidem in municione eiusdem ville moratur' (c 81/988/52)		Calais
1 March 1385[b]	Hugh Huwane, minstrel and archer, in the company of Ferdinand, master of the Order of St James in Portugal, for one year (c 81/1024/4)		Portugal
25 April 1386[b]	John Wilton, King's Minstrel, serving with John [Duke of Lancaster], King of Castile and León in Spain, for one year (c 81/1036/39)		Spain
14 July 1389	Henry Mareschall and Henry Windesore, King's Minstrels, with two servants, four horses, their belongings, and reasonable expenses (c 81/506/5339)	Dover or Sandwich	
14 Feb 1390	Gautier le Hoy, mestre Johan his son and Wauterlet his brother, minstrels of the Duke of Bourbon, a servant, four horses, their belongings and reasonable expenses (c 81/513/6040)	Dover	Picardy
13 April 1390	Rappelin and Hartof, minstrels of the Duke of Bavaria, their valets, horses, belongings and reasonable expenses 'pur passer la meer ver le dit duc en quelconque port que lour plerra' (c 81/515/6256)		
1 Feb 1397[b]	Lawrence Lutour, minstrel in the company of Thomas Earl of Nottingham, Captain of Calais, to go to Calais, 'ibidem in municione eiusdem ville moratur', for one year (c 81/1076/10)		Calais

[a] See note 20.
[b] Denotes warrants for protections; all others are for safe-conducts.

pose to national security.[10] In periods when peace appeared imminent and diplomatic activity was high, the travels of minstrels as emissaries and bearers of news increased in volume; it is worth noting that the only securely documented occasions when minstrel schools were held in England – in February 1385 and October 1390 – fell during periods of truce.[11] In the years between 1360 and 1369, English minstrels appear frequently as messengers between London and the Black Prince in Gascony and Spain. From details of fees paid to the royal minstrels in these years it is clear that they too spent much of their time *extra curiam* on foreign business.[12] Finally, the minstrels of the dukes of Orléans and Berry, and the other captives, can be found travelling between England and France – on numerous occasions – on business connected with the administration of their masters' estates.[13] The question nonetheless remains to what extent the high-class polyphonic cultures were absorbed by the musical practices of minstrels of this type. And it could also be questioned how effectively they were able to transmit what they did absorb to corresponding high-class cultures elsewhere. Minstrels could no doubt adapt polyphonic compositions for instrumental performance; it is more questionable whether these compositions could

[10] On minstrel schools see G. Greene, 'The Schools of Minstrelsy and the Choir School Tradition', *Studies in Music from the University of Western Ontario*, 2 (1977), pp. 31–40; L. Gushee, 'Minstrel', *The New Grove Dictionary of Music and Musicians*, ed. S. Sadie, 20 vols. (London, 1980) [hereafter *NG*], XII, p. 350; C. Wright, *Music at the Court of Burgundy, 1364–1419: A Documentary History*, Musicological Studies 28 (Henryville, Ottawa and Binningen, 1979), pp. 32–4. A number of references are collected in N. Wilkins, *Music in the Age of Chaucer*, Chaucer Studies 1 (Woodbridge, 1979), pp. 134–5. For other details of minstrel schools see c 81/1730/59 (cf. Table 1); Brussels, Archives Générales du Royaume, Chambre des Comptes [hereafter AGR, CC] 2702 (Receiver of the Count of Flanders, 1374), fol. 19; H. Izarn, *Le compte des recettes et dépenses du roi de Navarre en France et en Normandie de 1367 à 1370* (Paris, 1885), p. 348, and below n. 52. See also B. Schofield, 'The Adventures of an English Minstrel and his Varlet', *The Musical Quarterly*, 35 (1949), pp. 361–76; M. C. Gómez, 'La musique à la maison royale de Navarre à la fin du Moyen-Age et le chantre Johan Robert', *Musica Disciplina*, 41 (1987), pp. 113–15.

[11] For the 1385 gathering see c 81/1355/35, a protection of 23 February 1385 for two minstrels of Anne of Bohemia 'daler a lescole en diverses parties de nostre roialme'. For that of 1390 see Paris, Bibliothèque Nationale [hereafter BN], MS fonds fr. 26954 (p.o. 470), dossier 'Bourgeois' (10443), no. 1, a warrant of Louis Duke of Touraine of 5 October 1390 for the expenses of his minstrels 'et pour les aider a abiller et mettre en bon estat pour aler en Engleterre a la feste'; see also MS fonds fr. 28636 (p.o. 2152), dossier 'Orléans' (48873), no. 66.

[12] See Table 1. For Massyet le Harper, bringing news to Queen Philippa from the Black Prince in Spain, see E 403/433, m. 16 (2 December 1367); see also E 404/7/44/8. For the fees of royal minstrels in this period see E 403/401–E 403/438 *passim*.

[13] See Table 1, and T. Carte, *Catalogue des rolles gascons, normans et françois conservés dans les archives de la Tour de Londres*, 2 vols. (Paris, 1743), II, pp. 81ff.

subsequently be recovered. Their own repertories and practices, however, no doubt passed very readily from one group of noble's minstrels to another.

The conditions of the 1360s undoubtedly made incidental travel to France simpler and more frequent for a variety of purposes. The largely unremarkable bands of pilgrims travelling to Rome are found in greater numbers; the same is true for the representatives of Norman and Picard religious houses – the Carthusians in St Omer, the abbeys of Beaubec, Lyre, St Wast and of St Stephen, Caen – visiting their newly restored English possessions.[14] The files of warrants for safe-conducts also reveal numerous groups of foreign merchants and bankers. English attempts to stem the flow of funds to the papacy account for the existence of many of these documents, but it is also true that after the summer of 1369 the stream of travellers dries up almost completely.[15] Even so, freedom of movement cannot alone be held accountable for the increased opportunities for contacts between French and English musical cultures. Although the autonomous wanderings of individuals have frequently been invoked as a powerful stimulus – if not the necessary condition – for musical transmissions, it is doubtful whether this group played more than a marginal role. Musicians in royal and noble service predominate in this area if only because their masters enjoyed a monopoly of permanent long-distance communications. In so far as musicians' doings were tied to those of king and nobility, it is in the shape of this upper echelon's relations with its Continental counterparts that the origins of musical contacts must in the first instance be sought.

For the most part the transmission of musical culture between England and France has been studied from the standpoint of musical style.[16] For an older school of writers, influence formed the cornerstone in explaining contacts, transmissions and their effects, and was built to form a complete rationale for the growth of musical cultures

---

[14] See generally c 81/380–416, c 81/908–27, c 81/1334–6 and Carte, *Catalogue des rolles*, II, pp. 81–100. For monastic representatives see c 81/1335/52, 54, 57; c 81/1336/4, 13, 15.

[15] See J. J. N. Palmer and A. P. Wells, 'Ecclesiastical Reform and the Politics of the Hundred Years War during the Pontificate of Urban v (1362–70)', *War, Literature and Politics in the Late Middle Ages*, ed. C. T. Allmand (Liverpool, 1976), pp. 179ff.

[16] For parts of what follows see Wathey, *Music in the Royal and Noble Households*, pp. 2, 65–6; see also the cautionary remarks in D. Fallows, 'The Contenance angloise: English Influence on Continental Composers of the Fifteenth Century', *Renaissance Studies*, 1 (1987), pp. 189–208.

and their relationships with one another. The notion of centre and periphery bulked large in this system, cast in a fixed relationship as producer and consumer. Although it was allowed that insular cultures did not always follow the centre, and that minor shifts of emphasis were possible, few if any writers felt the need to question the nature of a periphery that was at once stagnant and yet supposedly innovative. Under the weight of an all-embracing theory of stylistic influence, the circumstances and contexts surrounding individual contacts disappeared from view. The focus of attention in the study of transmission thus became much narrower. The Continental receptions of English musical culture in the fifteenth century became simply the 'Contenance angloise' – Martin Le Franc's famous words taken out of context and grotesquely generalised – which was treated as though it were a coherent movement with a programme of stylistic reform. (A similar point can also be made about the historiography of isorhythm in fourteenth-century France.) In part this approach was a symptom of a wider subjection of writing on the music of this period to the survival patterns of musical sources. Periods in which few musical remains could be placed were held to mark a decline or stagnation in musical activity. Alternatively, they were seen as purely preparatory phases to periods of crowning achievement in which the most important remains were known to lie. For England, the early fifteenth century – the period of the Old Hall manuscript – was stressed at the expense of earlier and later periods, and the poorer survival of complete books used to confirm the subject status of its musical cultures.

In more recent years many of these generic assumptions have disappeared, particularly in studies devoted to music in the service of Europe's courts and major urban settlements. Yet even here, a purely positivistic assessment of the evidence for transmission – backed by speculative conceptions of individual mobility, of magnate–retainer relationships and of state consciousness – have limited the value of conclusions in this area. Above all, this work lacked a secure grasp of the bare conditions against which contacts could occur, and of the role of the political geography of western Europe, broadly defined: the numerous divides that characterised the allegiances and enmities of its rulers; the effects of feudal and familial ties, and the domestic consequences of foreign relations. The barest familiarity with the workings of medieval states should have suggested that their relations with their neighbours mattered not only in themselves but also for these states' own internal stability. In this respect England and its rulers in the late medieval and early modern periods must be considered as part of a wider European political community, and the effects for the transmission of musical culture of this shift in perspective traced accordingly.

Shortly after the opening of the Westminster parliament of January 1365, the Chancellor initiated a discussion in the Lords on the state of the royal finances.[17] The king's 'estate' had already been shown to a select band of peers, and the Chancellor now explained how all of the revenues of the crown sufficed to meet barely one half of the charges placed upon them. These remarks formed the basis of an appeal to parliament to consider some way in which the honour and estate of the king could be aided. In response, the Lords and Commons granted what was in effect a peacetime tax, restoring the wool subsidy to its pre-1360 levels from the following Michaelmas. In his speech, the Chancellor mentioned three areas of expenditure for which the tax was explicitly sought: (i) the support of the garrisons in Calais, Gascony, the Scottish border and Ireland; (ii) fees and annuities; (iii) the costs of gifts to foreign visitors and ambassadorial expenses. The first two items touched respectively on vital aspects of national security, and on the private interests of individuals present at the parliament, many of whom were crown annuitants. The presence here of the third item – the costs of diplomacy, in effect – reveals much about the importance it was accorded in these years. For the case made to the 1365 parliament, supported by written statements of national revenue and expenditure, reflects not only the priorities of the king and council in framing financial policy, and the Exchequer's capacity to analyse the scale of demands, but also what the Lords and Commons could be induced to accept as legitimate areas of heavy public expenditure.[18] The support given to this activity by the political

[17] *Rotuli Parliamentorum*, II, p. 285, 'Et en presence de lui estoit pleinement monstre son estat . . . et a quele somme les revenuz de sa terre se extendent; les fees et annuitees desqueux il estoit chargez; les grantz sommes de payementz q'il avoit fait pur l'establissement de Gascoigne, de Caleis, de diverses chastelx et villes devers le north; et pur les guerres de Irlande, et aillours; et les custages et dons faites as pluseurs estranges venantz devers lui pur divers causes'. For what follows see Harriss, *King, Parliament and Public Finance*, pp. 468–70, 478–9.

[18] Harriss, *King, Parliament and Public Finance*, pp. 471ff, for what follows.

community as a whole attests the absolute necessity of pursuing territorial gains by diplomatic means; it also documents the degree of public commitment behind an extensive programme of investment in this process that was already well under way.

Edward III's modern biographers have tended to view the 1360s as a period of stagnation in English public life, in which the vision and grasp of their subject began to decline.[19] Yet it is clear that English foreign policy in these years was anything but moribund, and this decade saw a heavy and systematic reinvestment of the profits of war in overseas schemes.[20] Immediately following the conclusion of the treaty at Brétigny, English envoys were set to work on a variety of projects. An early attempt to enlarge English dominance in Brittany by resolving the disputed succession to the duchy was launched in March–April 1361. Efforts were made to build a network of allegiances, hostile to the French crown, in Castile, Béarn, and elsewhere in the Languedoc. And substantial resources were devoted – with limited success as it turned out – to enlisting Charles, King of Navarre, whose fiefs and military installations in eastern Normandy, within striking distance of Paris, ranked him Charles V's most dangerous enemy. In general the years up to 1364 saw heavy spending on a variety of schemes designed to strengthen the English hand in France. The later years of the decade – from 1367 onwards – saw Edward more concerned to build up resources against a possible reopening of the conflict. There was one project, however, that preoccupied the machinery of English diplomacy throughout the middle years of the decade: the marriage planned between Edmund Earl of Cambridge and Margaret de Mâle, 'the richest heiress in Christendom', daughter of the Count of Flanders.[21] Had the mar-

[19] See for example M. Prestwich, *The Three Edwards: War and State in England 1272–1377* (London, 1980), pp. 276ff; see also Tout, *Chapters*, III, pp. 231ff.

[20] See for what follows M. Jones, *Ducal Brittany, 1364–1399: Relations with England and France during the Reign of Duke John IV* (Oxford, 1970), pp. 15–16; P. Tucoo-Chala, *Gaston Fébus et la Vicomté de Béarn (1343–1391)* (Bordeaux, 1959), pp. 93–9; P. Chaplais, *English Medieval Diplomatic Practice, Part 1: Documents and Interpretation*, 2 vols. (London, 1982), II, pp. 511–14. See also T. Rymer, *Foedera, Conventiones, Litterae etc . . .*, 4 vols. in 7, Record Commission (London, 1816–69), III/2, pp. 606, 637, 656, 671, 686.

[21] See J. J. N. Palmer, 'England, France, the Papacy and the Flemish Succession, 1361–9', *Journal of Medieval History*, 2 (1976), pp. 339–64; M. Ormrod, 'Edward III and his Family', *Journal of British Studies*, 26 (1987), pp. 412–14; F. Trautz, *Die Könige von England und das Reich, 1272–1377* (Heidelberg, 1961), pp. 394–7; Delachenal, *Histoire de Charles V*, I, pp. 499–510; F. Quicke, *Les Pays-Bas à la veille de la période bourguignonne, 1356–1384* (Brussels, 1947), pp. 76–83, 140–5. For other documents relating to the marriage see Chaplais, *English Medieval Diplomatic Practice*, II, pp. 514–15, 731–3.

riage gone ahead, a vast English-dominated fief would have been created on France's north-eastern borders, doubling the menace of Gascony in the event of renewed hostilities. Negotiations with the Count of Flanders were successful enough, and after some concessions a treaty was sealed at Dover in October 1364. The marriage partners were, however, within the forbidden degrees, and, under immense French pressure, Urban v was induced to refuse the necessary dispensation.[22] The pope's unwillingness to bend on this occasion can be held accountable not only for the ensuing diplomatic struggle between England and Avignon, the virtual extinction of papal authority in England, and the abduction and harsh treatment of papal collectors. It resulted also in the conclusion of a treaty with the Duke of Milan, Urban's worst enemy, for a marriage between his niece, Violante Visconti, and Lionel Duke of Clarence, the second son of Edward III. This went ahead with full solemnity at Milan in July 1368.[23] Finally, it is possible to see the struggle for the Flemish inheritance in a broader light. Taken in conjunction with the 1362 grant of Aquitaine to the Black Prince, and the marriages of Edward's other children into the Breton and Castilian successions, the Flanders project emerges as the lynch-pin of a scheme designed to create a confederation of Plantagenet states on France's borders, bound by feudal and family ties to the English crown. Edward's attempt to bequeath intact to his family his gains in France are reminiscent, in design at least, of the Angevin empire planned by Henry II for his offspring.[24] Here too the management of political and territorial designs in mainland Europe was geared to a domestic settlement of the royal patrimony.

It is possible also to see some aspects of the captivity of John II and the princes of the 'fleur de lys' in the light of this activity. As Edward

---

[22] See Palmer and Wells, 'Ecclesiastical Reform and the Politics of the Hundred Years War', pp. 169–89.
[23] See Trautz, *Die Könige von England und das Reich*, pp. 396–9; Palmer, 'England, France, the Papacy and the Flemish Succession', pp. 357–9. For the marriage treaty see *Foedera*, III/2, p. 827. The duke travelled to Milan via Paris, where he received an extended welcome from Charles v, the dukes of Berry and Burgundy and from Margaret, dowager Countess of Flanders; see F. Lehoux, *Jean de France, duc de Berri: sa vie, son action politique (1340–1416)*, 3 vols. (Paris, 1966–8), I, pp. 205–6. For protections and other documents connected with the journey see *Foedera*, III/2, p. 845; c 76/51, mm. 3, 5–9. The duke's chapel furnishings, including 'cynk peire de vestimentz pur la chapelle ove tout lapparaill . . . livres, croices, reliqs, ioialx et autres mesnues necessaires', were taken to Milan via Sluys by staff of the duke's wardrobe, who left London in March 1368; see c 81/915/22.
[24] Ormrod, 'Edward III and his Family', pp. 414–15.

quickly discovered, further political and territorial concessions could be extracted from direct negotiations with the hostages.[25] The agreements of 1362 with the dukes of Anjou, Bourbon, Berry and Orléans effectively bypassed Paris, providing England with a political role in France at local as well as national level. Diplomacy conducted in England in these years thus enabled Edward to threaten a division of interest between the French crown and its most important lieutenants; it was mainly this, rather than chivalric impulse, that prompted John II's return to England in 1363 after the escape of the Duke of Anjou.[26] Certainly the English hoped to gain from a generous treatment of the hostages, and spent heavily on entertainment, gifts and other rewards. The scale of this operation is made clear by a warning note in a statement of national revenue and expenditure drawn up in late 1363 to 'fait a remembrer des coustages et douns qe serront faitz par cause de la venue le Roi de France'. And on one occasion at least Edward found the opportunity to remind Charles V of the courtesy shown in England to his father and brothers.[27] Alongside the major feasts and state ceremonial, the hostages were treated to a continual round of lesser meetings, entertainments and other events more social than diplomatic in character.[28] In these day-to-day exchanges, contacts became more continuous, and here the other members of the king's family played a

[25] See Delachenal, *Histoire de Charles V*, II, pp. 54–9, 339–45; R. Cazelles, *Société politique, noblesse et couronne sous Jehan le Bon et Charles V*, Société de l'École des Chartes: Mémoires et Documents 28 (Geneva, 1982), pp. 428–32; Ormrod, *op. cit.*, p. 412. See also Lehoux, *Jean de France*, I, pp. 170–2.

[26] See P. Chaplais, 'Some Documents Regarding the Fulfilment and Interpretation of the Treaty of Brétigny (1361–1369)', *Camden Miscellany XIX*, Camden Third Series 80 (London, 1952), pp. 7–8; Delachenal, *op. cit.*, II, pp. 344–50. See also Chaplais, *English Medieval Diplomatic Practice*, II, pp. 704–5; Cazelles, *Société politique*, pp. 447–9.

[27] See Lehoux, *Jean de France*, I, p. 194, n. 4; a letter of John II written on his release in July 1360 was also made to echo this sentiment: 'notre frere le roy d'Angleterre et notre soeur la Reine nous ont grandement honorez' (BN, MS nouv. acq. fr. 7376, fols. 434^{r–v}). For the statement see Harriss, *King, Parliament and Public Finance*, p. 530. The spending of John II and the princes was also heavy during these years. See L. Douët-d'Arcq, *Comptes de l'argenterie des rois de France au XIVe siècle*, Société de l'Histoire de France (Paris, 1851), pp. 203–78; Chantilly, Musée Condé, Archives, ser. I, I/1, fols. 18–51 (printed with errors in H. Duc d'Aumale, *Notes et documents relatifs à Jean, roi de France et à sa captivité en Angleterre*, Miscellanies of the Philobiblon Society 2 (London, 1855–6), pp. 82–160); H. Moranvillé, 'Extraits de journaux du trésor (1345–1419)', *Bibliothèque de l'École des Chartes*, 49 (1888), p. 371. See also British Library, Add. Charter 3332 (a bond for goods supplied to the Duke of Anjou, 11 April 1361); Paris, Archives Nationales [hereafter AN], KK 13^c (Journal du Trésor, 1358–9); BN, MS fonds fr. 26003, no. 1036.

[28] See for example Lehoux, *Jean de France*, I, pp. 165–6; p. 163, n. 4. See also Douët-d'Arcq, *Comptes*, pp. 249, 270.

striking part. Queen Philippa in particular emerges as a central figure in the princes' life at the English court, acting as host and possibly as an intermediary in their dealings with the king. It was in this period that Froissart claimed to have enjoyed the queen's patronage.[29] Contemporary French writers were quick to note the frequency of her meetings with the Duke of Berry, but John II and the other dukes enjoyed hospitality on a similar scale. Her role in furthering diplomatic causes may well also account for something of the extravagance with which her entourage was periodically charged.

The internal domestic effects of English policy towards France in these years were varied.[30] The principal and the lesser retainers of the crown and higher nobility continued to gain at home from networks of patronage forged in service abroad. To the fruits of English colonisation in Gascony, Brittany and Ponthieu could be added considerable rewards in the shires that were the result of continued cooperation with former comrades-in-arms and continued membership of their military masters' affinities. The deepening rift in relations with the papacy served to unify clerical opinion behind the king; the growing imperialism among the ruling classes also made its effects felt at home. At a lower level these years also saw the absorption of a small but not negligible number of aliens into the royal and higher-noble affinities, occasionally from those of French magnates. This pattern embraces knights and esquires, whose chief qualification for service was access to local networks of patronage overseas; it also embraces clerks, administrators and more menial servants, such as the two henchmen, named 'Mustard' and 'Garlyk', taken over from the retinue of John II.[31] Their presence was designed

---

[29] See R. Barber, 'Jean Froissart and Edward the Black Prince', *Froissart: Historian*, ed. J. J. N. Palmer (Woodbridge, 1981), pp. 25–35. For Philippa's household see Tout, *Chapters*, v, pp. 250–9, and C. Given-Wilson, *The Royal Household and the King's Affinity: Service, Politics and Finance in England 1360–1413* (New Haven and London, 1986), pp. 92–3; Given-Wilson, 'The Merger of Edward III's and Queen Philippa's Households, 1360–9', *Bulletin of the Institute of Historical Research*, 51 (1978), pp. 183–7. Contemporary concern about the expenditure of Philippa's household was echoed by the eighteenth-century annotator of Manchester, John Rylands University Library, MS Latin 237 (an account of household debts), e.g. 'mirandum est quam vasta piscium consumpta fuit' (fol. 19), and 'excesiva provisionem quantitas pro pulletria Reginae Phillippae' (fol. 27).

[30] For what follows see Harriss, *King, Parliament and Public Finance*, pp. 476–7; Tuck, *Crown and Nobility*, pp. 143–4. See also S. K. Walker, 'John of Gaunt and his Retainers, 1361–1399' (D.Phil. dissertation, University of Oxford, 1986), pp. 65ff, 75–8.

[31] For example A. Goodman, 'John of Gaunt: Paradigm of the Late Fourteenth-Century

both to lend a cosmopolitan glamour to royal and magnate follow-
ings, and to advertise the European horizons of their masters'
political ambitions. In the case of the royal household, the presence
of these men can also be linked to Edward III's attempts to lay secure
foundations for the affinities of his children. Throughout the 1360s
there was considerable overlap between the royal following and
those of the Black Prince, Lionel Duke of Clarence and John of
Gaunt.[32] The servants of the king's sons were often granted fees and
annuities from the crown, in addition to those received from their
immediate masters; several of these grants were made on condition
that their recipients should continue in the service of their masters
after the king's death.[33] Much of the large and oft-remarked expansion of Edward III's household in the years after 1362 was made up of
those prepared to devote a lifetime of service to his children. Notably
it was among the younger men at the bottom, rather than among
those of higher rank, that the bulk of this expansion occurred to
reach a total of over 600 by Christmas 1368.[34] Where these men were
aliens, their presence can convincingly be linked to Edward's
territorial designs for his sons in Europe; by retaining these men,
Edward sought to ensure that his sons were bequeathed the core of
an affinity and administration fitting for their planned overseas
careers. Not all of the king's appointments of Frenchmen drew on the
retinues of the captives, of course. English interests in Brittany
provided a potent source of French in natural opposition to the
Valois monarchy, as did older feudal ties in Gascony.[35]

It is against this general background that the presence in England of
Matheus de Sancto Johanne can be placed. On 13 May 1368, a letter

Crisis', *Transactions of the Royal Historical Society*, 5th ser., 37 (1987), pp. 138–9; Hewitt, *The Black Prince's Expedition*, pp. 215–16. For Edward's henchmen see E 361/4, m. 4d.

[32] See Wathey, *Music in the Royal and Noble Households*, pp. 176–7; Walker, 'John of Gaunt and his Retainers', p. 25; Tout, *Chapters*, v, pp. 289–400.

[33] A similar practice in the indentures of John of Gaunt is described by Walker, 'John of Gaunt and his Retainers', p. 35.

[34] For household numbers at Christmas 1368, see E 101/395/10, E 101/395/2 *passim*, and in particular E 101/395/2 (214): 'Nous vous envoions close desouz nostre prive seal un roule . . . fesant mension de les persones de nous et de nostre treschere compaigne la roine et de sys centz et noef persones esceantz de la tenaill de nostre dit houstel'. The assessments of the size of the royal household in Given-Wilson, *The Royal Household*, pp. 39–41, 278, based solely on the account books of the Keeper and Controller of the Household Wardrobe, are misleading for this period.

[35] See for example Jones, *Ducal Brittany*, pp. 22–59.

was sent to the Chancery, under the privy seal, requesting letters of safe-conduct for one of the chaplains of the household chapel of Queen Philippa, John Louchevel, and two of the clerks, Matheu Seintjon and William Cog, to travel to France.[36] Accompanied by their valet, Philip de Parys, and two 'garceons', they were to leave the realm from Dover, where they would be permitted to pass with £20 in bills of exchange, their horses and 20s. each for their more pressing expenses. The letter inevitably reveals most about the immediate context of their departure from service in England. But we are relatively well informed about the household chapel of Queen Philippa, and from other sources it is possible to piece together something of the clerks' likely sphere of action. From very early in the reign of Edward III, Philippa's household included a chapel staffed by a combination of her own chaplains, those of the king and – for a time – some of the clerks in her domestic administration.[37] After the amalgamation of Edward's and Philippa's households in 1360 the chapels of the king and queen became less distinct.[38] Yet each retained something of its separate identity, if only because chaplains in royal service tended to be assigned duties with one or the other master. It is likely that a considerable amount of the French clerks' time was spent at the queen's manor at Sheen and at Eltham, but the strength of the links with the royal chapel was still such as to blur any useful distinction: a period of service in one chapel probably also meant work in the other.[39] Philippa granted annuities to the chaplains and clerks of the king; she also supported their attempts to secure ecclesiastical preferment at home, and on

---

[36] c 81/916/21; see Appendix 1, Document 2. It is, however, clear that letters of this type were themselves occasionally used as safe-conducts; see, for example, Paris, AN, p 1358[1], no. 498, a warrant to issue a safe-conduct for the return to France of two servants of the Duke of Bourbon. For protections and safe-conducts see, generally, Chaplais, *English Medieval Diplomatic Practice*, I, pp. 308–27; M. M. Crow and C. C. Olson, eds., *Chaucer Life Records* (Oxford, 1966), pp. 28–9, 64–6.

[37] Lists of the clerks of Philippa's chapel survive for 1330–1 (Manchester, John Rylands University Library, MS Latin 234, fols. 14ᵛ–15, 23–4) and 1344–5 (E 101/390/8, fols. 3, 7). See also London, Society of Antiquaries, MS 208, fol. 2ᵛ (1351–2); Rylands, MS Latin 235, fols. 7, 17–18ᵛ (1331–2); MS Latin 236, fol. 3ᵛ (1357–8). For Terrico de Hanonia, a clerk of the chapel, see sc 6/1091/4 (1340–1); see also R. Ellis, *Catalogue of Seals in the Public Record Office: Personal Seals*, 2 vols. (London, 1978–81), II, p. 22. For Philippa's chapel furnishings in 1330–1, including service books, see E 101/385/5, m. 2d.

[38] See Given-Wilson, 'The Merger of Edward III's and Queen Philippa's Households', pp. 183–7.

[39] For the building projects undertaken for Philippa at Sheen see H. M. Colvin, *The History of the King's Works*, 6 vols. (London, 1963–82), II, pp. 994–1002; for Eltham see p. 934.

one occasion sponsored the claims for advancement of two chaplains – John Aleyn and Ralph de Nottingham – at Avignon.[40] She also entrusted John Aleyn, commonly identified with the composer of the motet *Sub Arturo plebs*, with a mission from Windsor to look for one of her own clerks, Mag. William Holme, in Oxford.[41] A gradual increase in the size of Philippa's chapel can be traced from Christmas 1363, when there were four chaplains, to Christmas 1368, when there was a total of nine.[42] To this figure can be added three boys, one of whom was a John Francoys, and – since the sources for the numbers of chaplains and clerks do not attempt to provide complete lists – there may also have been other adults. The French chaplain and clerks are in fact absent from the surviving lists. Although it cannot be assumed that their period of service fell between Christmas 1366 and Christmas 1368 – the lists closest to the date of the letter – it is nonetheless worth remarking that the bulk of the expansion in the number of queen's chaplains (so far as this can be gauged) is found between these two dates.

The file in which the letter for the French clerks' safe-conduct survives contains some sixty similar documents all from May 1368. Among these are several issued to esquires, clerks and valets travelling to join the Duke of Clarence in Milan, at least one of whom, a John Burton, was also a valet in the household of Queen Philippa.[43] It is possible that this has some significance for the ultimate destination of the French clerks, even though 'France' and not 'Lombardy' or 'Milan' is clearly specified. More important is the timing of their departure. The privy seal letter and probably its administrative precursors were issued towards the end of the period in which the main political business of the 1368 Westminster parliament was transacted.[44] Here the Chancellor warned the Lords

---

[40] For example the grants of lands and annuities made to William de Ireland, variously described as a clerk in both chapels, in *CPR 1364–1367*, pp. 100, 396; see also *BPR*, IV, p. 478, for a gift from the Black Prince. For chaplains of the king and Lionel, Earl of Ulster and later Duke of Clarence, presented to benefices by Philippa, see *CPR 1367–1370*, p. 298; SC 1/40/30. For a gift made to a chaplain of Queen Philippa by the Countess of Ulster, see London, British Library, Add. MS 18632, fol. 101 (12 January 1358). For Aleyn and Nottingham see *CPL: Petitions*, I, p. 416; see also *Urbain: LC*, II, p. 366 (7706–7).

[41] E 101/396/2, fol. 35.

[42] For this and what follows see the sources cited in Table 2 as Lists e–i, and E 101/395/2 (202), (207).

[43] See C 81/916/1; for others see C 81/916/9, 23, 34.

[44] See *HBC*, p. 563. For what follows see *Rotuli Parliamentorum*, II, pp. 294–5; Harriss, *King, Parliament and Public Finance*, pp. 469–70.

and Commons in no uncertain terms of the possible reopening of the war with France, incorporating in his address a plea for the support of the garrisons in Calais, Guisnes, Ponthieu and other lands overseas. The substance if not the form of this business would have been widely known before the parliament, and it may be that for aliens menially placed in royal service, prudence now seemed to counsel departure. Be that as it may, most of this group of clerics and their servants are immediately lost from view after this date. Nothing more is heard of John Louchevel, Philippa's chaplain. A William Cog died as vicar of the church of St Audomer in St Omer in 1391;[45] if this is the same man as the clerk of Philippa's chapel, then this last preferment may possibly mark Cog's return to a native locality. He too, however, remains for the most part obscure.

For the composer Matheus de Sancto Johanne a reasonably full biography was constructed by Günther – albeit with too much reliance on papal sources – and is most recently and reliably summarised by Andrew Tomasello's book on music under the Avignon popes.[46] Matheus is found as a clerk in the household chapel of Louis Duke of Anjou, the younger brother of Charles v, in 1378, seeking a benefice from Gregory vii; the supplication states that he has already served the pope, although this might mean anything from a mere errand to an extended period of employment. He appears as a papal chaplain from 1382 to 1386. He held a prebend at Tournai, and reserved another at Cambrai which fell vacant only after his death, which can thus be dated on or before 12 July 1391. To this it can be added that the composer very likely

---

[45] See H. Nelis, *Documents relatifs au Grand Schisme, III: Suppliques et lettres de Clément VII*, Analecta Vaticano-Belgica 13 (Rome, 1934), p. 336, no. 1881.

[46] See U. Günther, 'Matheus de Sancto Johanne', *NG*, xi, p. 820, and 'Zur Biographie einiger Komponisten der Ars Subtilior', *Archiv für Musikwissenschaft*, 21 (1964), pp. 180–5; A. Tomasello, *Music and Ritual at Papal Avignon, 1309–1403*, UMI Studies in Musicology 75 (Ann Arbor, 1983), pp. 252–3. See also R. H. Hoppin and S. Clercx, 'Notes biographiques sur quelques musiciens français du xive siècle', *Les colloques de Wégimont II, l'Ars Nova: recueil d'études sur la musique du xiv^esiècle*, Bibliothèque de la Faculté de Philosophie et Lettres de l'Université de Liège 149 (Paris, 1959), p. 76. A number of the other chaplains and clerks mentioned in the supplication (K. Hanquet, *Documents relatifs au Grand Schisme, I: Suppliques de Clément VII (1378–1379)*, Analecta Vaticano-Belgica 8 (Rome, 1924), p. 109, no. 347) were serving in the duke's chapel by May 1377; of these at least one, Jehan Lenfant, also moved to the papal chapel following the duke's death in 1384 (Paris, BN, MS fonds fr. 27509 (p.o. 1025), dossier 'de Douxmesnil' (23456), no. 3; Tomasello, p. 244). The 'Mahiet' who was a clerk in the chapel of the duchess of Anjou from September 1370 (Paris, BN, MS fonds fr. 11863, fol. 26) cannot be identified with Matheus de Sancto Johanne; see Hanquet, *op. cit.*, p. 175.

joined the Duke of Anjou's expedition to Rodez and the Rouergue in 1377; he was probably also with the duke's chapel at Avignon in 1380.[47] It is doubtful whether the 'Mathieu de monastère Saint Jehan' who enjoyed preferments from Queen Joanna of Sicily in 1363 was, as Günther suggested, the same man.[48] Nor can much credence be placed in her suggestion that the composer was the 'Mathieu' who was a clerk in the chapel of the Duke of Orléans, since this rests on a confusion between Louis, duke 1391–1407, and his son Charles.[49] From the supplication of 1378, it emerges that Matheus's native diocese was Thérouanne, which encompassed the county of Ponthieu, and it may be that this provides some clue to the origins of his English involvements.[50] The English crown took its ecclesiastical rights in northern France seriously, making full use of its powers of presentation to churches at Abbeville and elsewhere;[51] possibly English princes were able to recruit the clergy of these and surrounding territories into their service. Finally, it is worth recording that in the early and mid-1370s some other musicians who had served with English masters in the preceding decade were engaged by the Duke of Anjou. One at least of three minstrels, formerly serving in England and Aquitaine with Sir John Chandos, appears in the duke's employ by 1374 and there is some evidence that others were similarly placed.[52]

[47] See BN, MS fonds fr. 27509 (p.o. 1025), dossier 'de Douxmesnil' (23456), nos. 3, 7, 8.

[48] 'Zur Biographie', pp. 183–4, citing M. Dubrulle, *Les registres d'Urbain v (1362–1363): recueil des Bulles de ce Pape* (Paris, 1926), p. 28, no. 290 (*Urbain: LC*, II, p. 421 (8179)), after Clercx and Hoppin, 'Notes biographiques', p. 76. For this Matheus, a Cistercian monk, who was successively Abbot of St John in Lamis, in the diocese of Sispontino, and of Casenove, in the diocese of Penne, see also *Urbain: LC*, III, p. 624 (12500), V, pp. 231 (17238), 377 (17816).

[49] 'Matheus de Sancto Johanne', p. 820; both this and G. Reaney, 'The Manuscript Chantilly, Musée Condé 1047', *Musica Disciplina*, 9 (1955), p. 72, follow the confused reading of L. de Laborde, *Les ducs de Bourgogne: études sur les lettres, les arts et l'industrie pendant la xvᵉ siècle . . .*, 3 vols. (Paris, 1849–52), III, pp. 46, 357, in A. Pagès, *La poésie française en Catalogne du xiiiᵉ siècle à la fin du xvᵉ*, Bibliothèque Méridionale 23 (Paris and Toulouse, 1936), p. 30, n. 3. Mathieu appears in the account of the argentier of Charles Duke of Orléans for 1455 (Paris, AN, KK 271, fol. 23ᵛ); the chapel expenses for 1389 are printed in Laborde (p. 46) from BN, MS fonds fr. 28636 (p.o. 2152), dossier 'Orleans', no. 45. Louis de France was Duke of Touraine in 1389.

[50] See Hanquet, *Documents relatifs au Grand Schisme*, I, p. 109, no. 347.

[51] See S. B. Storey-Challenger, *L'administration anglaise du Ponthieu après le traité de Brétigny, 1361–1369*, Études Picardes 4 (Abbeville, 1975), pp. 101–67; Carte, *Catalogue des rolles*, II, pp. 88, 95–9.

[52] See c 81/915/19 (Jehan de Pountoyse; cf. Table 1); Paris, BN, Collection Clairambault 215, no. 83, a warrant (Nîmes, 28 October 1374) to pay Jehan de Pontoize and two others for good service 'et aussi pour aler aux escolles et eulx sen retourner devers nous'. See also

It is time to look at the musical consequences of Matheus de Sancto Johanne's period of service in England. At the end of the Old Hall manuscript there are two substitutes for the *Deo gratias*, of which the first, *Are post libamina*, is ascribed to 'Mayshuet'.[53] These two pieces also appear (without attribution) in a book copied in part from the Old Hall manuscript, in all probability for the household chapel of Henry VI; it is likely that Old Hall itself had similar antecedents, prepared for the chapels of Henry IV, John of Gaunt and Richard II, in which the bulk of its older contents was first copied.[54] It was readily assumed by Günther and others that Matheus de Sancto Johanne and Mayshuet were the same man, and on the basis of the evidence produced – the mere similarity of names – this has been rightly questioned.[55] Against the background of an earlier English involvement, however, the case for this identification, and for adding *Are post libamina* to the list of Matheus de Sancto Johanne's works, becomes much stronger. The content of the texts of this piece also takes on added significance. At the end of the triplex I, the text relates how 'the active, distinguished Frenchman composed this song on French melodies, but after he had revised it with the Latin language it more often became sweet to the English, replacing *Deo gratias*'.[56] (The later copy of this piece, perhaps predictably, replaces 'angli' with 'angeli'.) If 'Mayshuet' can be identified with Matheus de Sancto Johanne, it may be that other elements in this circumstantial account of the genesis of the piece should also be given some credence; a past period of service in England may have been very useful if Matheus recast the piece with the English in mind. If the text betrays a transmission of the piece as we have it or

B. Prost, *Inventaires mobiliers et extraits des comptes des ducs de Bourgogne de la maison de Valois (1363–1477)*, 2 vols. (Paris, 1902–4), I, p. 241.

[53] A. Hughes and M. Bent, eds., *The Old Hall Manuscript*, 3 vols., Corpus Mensurabilis Musicae 46 (n.p., 1969–73), I/2, pp. 419–23; III, pp. 43–4.

[54] See M. Bent, 'The Progeny of Old Hall: More Leaves from a Royal English Choirbook', *Gordon Athol Anderson (1929–1981): In memoriam, von seinen Studenten, Freunden und Kollegen*, 2 vols., ed. L. Dittmer, Musicological Studies 39 (Henryville, Ottawa and Binningen, 1984), pp. 1–54, and for what follows pp. 7ff. See also R. Bowers, 'Some Observations on the Life and Career of Lionel Power', *Proceedings of the Royal Musical Association*, 102 (1975–6), pp. 109–10; A. Wathey, 'The Production of Books of Liturgical Polyphony', *Book Production and Publishing in Britain, 1375–1475*, ed. D. Pearsall and J. Griffiths (Cambridge, 1989), pp. 151–5.

[55] *NG*, XI, p. 820; Bent, 'The Progeny', p. 6.

[56] See Hughes and Bent, III, p. 44, 'Practicus insignis gallicus sub gallicis hemus hunc discantavit cantum, sed post reformavit latini lingua anglis sepius fit amena, reddendo deo gracias'.

another version, between England and France, it reveals nothing, however, of when this took place. A period of service in the late 1360s may have forged links that stimulated the copying of Matheus's works into English sources, or underwrote transmissions in a more general way (even if the late 1360s are not possible).

The period spent by Matheus de Sancto Johanne in the service of Queen Philippa and other contacts in these years gain added significance in the context of the celebrated musician motet *Sub Arturo plebs* and the route that this and perhaps other English pieces took to the repertories of Chantilly, Musée Condé, MS 564 (where the remaining attributed works of Matheus de Sancto Johanne all appear). The texts of *Sub Arturo*, naming the composer and several other musicians, enjoy a long historiography as literary curiosities, beginning with Coussemaker's edition of 1869.[57] The motet's fourteenth-century credentials were conclusively established by Brian Trowell; more recently, as a larger number of written trans-missions has come to light, it has been possible to see this piece in the broader context of England's relations with the French motet repertories of the mid- and late fourteenth century.[58] Its date none-theless remains problematic and requires some comment here. Trowell initially suggested that *Sub Arturo* had been written for the triumphal Garter celebrations immediately preceding the first Treaty of London in 1358.[59] Yet this is too early for the piece as we have it, and apart from the generalised Arthurian allusion – itself recently called into question[60] – there is little specific to connect it

---

[57] *Les harmonistes du XIVe siècle* (Lille, 1869), pp. 12ff.

[58] 'A Fourteenth-Century Ceremonial Motet and its Composer', *Acta Musicologica*, 29 (1957), pp. 65–75. For transmissions see M. Bent, 'The Transmission of English Music 1300–1500: Some Aspects of Repertory and Presentation', *Studien zur Tradition in der Musik: Kurt von Fischer zum 60. Geburtstag*, ed. H. H. Eggebrecht and M. Lütolf (Munich, 1973), pp. 70–2. Recent discoveries include London, British Library, MS Royal 7 A. VI, London, Public Record Office, E 163/22/1/24, and Yoxford, Cockfield Hall, MS s.s., which preserves the lower two parts of *Sub Arturo*. This source was discovered by Adrian Bassett and first described by P. Lefferts, *The Motet in England in the Fourteenth Century*, UMI Studies in Musicology 94 (Ann Arbor, 1986), pp. 300–1. For *Sub Arturo plebs* see also *ibid.*, pp. 300–1; M. C. Gómez, 'Une version à cinq voix du motet *Apollinis eclipsatur/Zodiacum signis* dans le manuscrit *E-Bcen 853*', *Musica Disciplina*, 39 (1985), pp. 15–19. For editions see M. Bent, ed., *Two Fourteenth-Century Motets* (Newton Abbot, 1977), pp. 1–7; U. Günther, ed., *The Motets of the Manuscripts Chantilly, Musée Condé, 564 (olim 1047) and Modena, Biblioteca Estense, α M. 5, 24 (olim lat. 568)*, Corpus Mensurabilis Musicae 39 (n.p., 1965), pp. 49ff; see also F. Ll. Harrison, ed., *Motets of French Provenance*, Polyphonic Music of the Fourteenth Century 5 (Paris and Monaco, 1968), pp. 172ff.

[59] 'A Fourteenth-Century Ceremonial Motet', pp. 67–8.

[60] For example by Bent, 'The Transmission of English Music', pp. 70–1.

with the 1358 celebrations. Opinion remains divided between a date in the early 1370s, shortly before the death of the John Aleyn who was a clerk of the chapel, and a much later date, *c.* 1390, which presumes that the motet was written by an Aleyn or Alanus as yet untraced. A full re-examination of the evidence used by Trowell has since led Roger Bowers to suggest that the motet was written *c.* 1380, although he too acknowledges the problems that this date presents for the identity of John Aleyn.[61]

Whatever the date of *Sub Arturo* as it survives, however, it is clear that the text of the triplum, listing musicians' names, has strong roots in the musical world of the 1360s and early 1370s. For even if it is possible to dismiss the identification of Alanus as the John Aleyn of the royal household chapel, on stylistic grounds, several of the musicians named are known only from this earlier period. They appear as chaplains and clerks in the household chapels of the Black Prince, and of Edward III and Queen Philippa. However brief Matheus de Sancto Johanne's period of service in the last of these establishments, he must have worked with – if not alongside – at least three of those whom Alanus's motet praises: William Mugge, John de Corby, and Edmund de Bury, *alias* Bokenham, a Benedictine monk who served with the staff of the chapel from the late 1350s until 1377. He may possibly also have worked with Nicholas Hungerford, a chaplain of the Black Prince in 1365. To the highly stylised accounts of the musical abilities of these men given in the motet can now be added some new evidence from administrative sources. This helps not only to reinforce the identifications made by Trowell and, more recently, Roger Bowers, but also to strengthen the musical credentials of some of those named, to emphasise their cohesion as a group, and to locate their activities more firmly in the context of service to the king and higher nobility.[62] William Mugge, dean of St George's Chapel, Windsor, is now known also to have participated in the services of the royal chapel in the mid-1360s, obtaining a dispensation from full residence at Windsor in 1363 and receiving robes 'in the suit of the chapel' at Christmas in the following year. Edmund de Bury, described in the text of the motet

---

[61] Fixed Points in the Chronology of English Fourteenth-Century Polyphony', *Music & Letters*, 71 (1990), forthcoming; this study includes the best available edition (incorporating the readings of the Yoxford source) of the texts of the motet.

[62] For details of what follows see Appendix 1, Documents 3–6, and Appendix 2, *passim*.

as 'the golden foundation of the tenor', was given the care of the boys of the royal chapel by 1368 with responsibility for their welfare; to judge from other posts of this type, it may be that he was also entrusted with their musical instruction. He can also be shown to have acted as the agent of William Tiddeswell, the 'G. de Fontis Horarum' of the motet, who died probably in early 1364, receiving instalments of wages on his colleague's behalf and assisting with the administration of his estate. It can also be shown that John de Corby, 'who shines out in an unblemished fashion', served over a longer period than was hitherto thought, appearing among the clerks of the chapel by winter 1360–1. Finally, it is possible to trace in the careers of this group patterns of recruitment found more widely among royal clerks active in the 1360s and 1370s. John de Corby, John Ipswich and William Tiddeswell all appear among a group of clerics ordained by the Bishop of Winchester in the chapel of his manor at Southwark – as appears to have been customary for those intending careers in royal service – in the late 1340s and early 1350s.[63] Many of those in this group were taken into the employ of the king and his sons following the conclusion of the Crécy–Calais campaign, including Tiddeswell, Ipswich and possibly Corby. The king's return from France in 1360 was responsible for the recruitment of another generation of clerks into royal service, and it may be that this marks the opening of John de Corby's career in the chapel. In general it is the later identifications of musicians named in the texts of *Sub Arturo* that emerge as the least secure.[64] No identity has been conclusively traced for 'Richard Blich', 'Adam Levita', 'G. Martini' and others. If these men were active in a later period, it may be necessary to shift the focus of inquiry away from the royal household chapel. Alternatively, it may be that they too can be found working in the chapels of the king, his sons and other English magnates in the 1360s and early 1370s.

In this context, the case of Nicholas Hungerford, the *flos Oxonie* of the motet, calls for more extended comment. Towards the end of 1365 the Black Prince sponsored a petition at the Holy See for the reinstatement of Hungerford as prior of the Augustinian Priory of St

[63] See S. F. Hockey, ed., *The Register of William Edington, Bishop of Winchester, 1346–1366*, 2 vols., Hampshire Record Series 7–8 (Southampton, 1986–7), II, pp. 105–209.
[64] See Trowell, 'A Fourteenth-Century Ceremonial Motet', pp. 69–71, and Bowers, 'Fixed Points'.

Frideswide, Oxford, describing the supplicant as his chaplain.[65] But in a hitherto unnoticed letter of Urban v, providing a successor to the priory in 1370 after Hungerford's death, omitted from the published *Calendar of Papal Letters*, a much clearer impression is given of the end of his career: here it emerges that Hungerford was living as a member of the *familia* of Simon Langham, Archbishop of Canterbury, cardinal priest of San Sixto, and that he ended his days 'apud sedem apostolicam'.[66] Hungerford had been abroad in 1367–8, quite possibly serving as his master's representative at the Holy See; he was thus very likely already present when Simon Langham, recently dispossessed as Archbishop of Canterbury, joined the *curia* at Montefiascone in May 1369.[67] From this date until his death, probably at Viterbo or Rome, after 24 September, he served within the household.[68] Here there is a further manifestation of the pattern of service to king and higher nobility found among those named in *Sub Arturo*; it may be that other musicians as yet unidentified could be traced among the chaplains serving in the archbishop's household. A number of these men appear in letters emanating from the papal chancery, although undoubtedly there were also others.[69]

---

[65] See *CPL: Petitions*, I, p. 509. Hungerford had suffered at the hands of John Dodeford, canon of Carlisle, with whom he had attempted to exchange his position for 'a certain vicarage'. It seems, however, that he retained possession of the priory; conclusive evidence of a vacancy emerges only after Hungerford's death, when Dodeford renewed his attempts to secure presentation. News of the vacancy appears in a brief notice in the register of John Buckingham, Bishop of Lincoln (Lincolnshire Archives Office, Episcopal Register XII, fol. 88), and in the royal licence of 23 January 1370 granted to the priory to elect a successor (*CPR 1367–1370*, p. 337). See also W. Page *et al.*, eds., *The Victoria County History of the Counties of England: Oxfordshire* (Oxford, 1907–) [hereafter *VCH, Oxon.*], II, pp. 98–9.

[66] Vatican City, Archivio Segreto Vaticano, Reg. Aven. 171, fol. 302 (Appendix 1, Document 7); see *Urbain: LC*, IX, p. 517, no. 27776.

[67] In November 1367 Hungerford nominated attorneys in England for two years while he remained overseas (*CPR 1367–1370*, p. 30); his dealings abroad incurred considerable expenses, for which he attempted to use the assets of the Priory of St Frideswide as security until prevented in May 1368 (*CPR 1367–1370*, p. 120, printed in full in *The Cartulary of the Monastery of St Frideswide at Oxford*, 2 vols., Oxford Historical Society 28, 31 (Oxford, 1895–6), II, pp. 373–4). For Langham see A. B. Emden, *A Biographical Register of the University of Oxford to A.D. 1500*, 3 vols. (Oxford, 1957–9), II, pp. 1095–7; B. Harvey, *Westminster Abbey and its Estates in the Middle Ages* (Oxford, 1977), pp. 42, 95ff.

[68] See *Urbain: LC*, VIII, p. 21 (no. 23121).

[69] Thomas de Aston, Richard Bannebury, Robert Coueley, Thomas Forester, John Gilleti, Richard Melford, John Morite, Thomas de Southam, Robert de Suardeby and John Walkelyn are described as Langham's chaplains (*Urbain: LC*, VIII, pp. 75, 89, 104, 465; IX, pp. 74, 468; *CPL*, IV, p. 194; C. Tihon, ed., *Lettres de Grégoire XI (1371–1378)*, 4 vols., Analecta Vaticano-Belgica 11, 20, 25, 28 (Rome, 1958–75), I, p. 89; II, p. 640). John Aspullis, Richard de Croxton, Thomas Blakelake and William de Humberston appear as Langham's clerks (*Urbain: LC*, IX, pp. 32, 71, 89, 92).

Throughout the period that Langham spent at the papal court, his chapel was staffed predominantly by English clerics, some of whom appear to have served over a long period. He also engaged at least one papal chaplain, Johannes Capel, a native of St Omer, as *magister capelle*, and a Jean Gilleti, of the diocese of Cambrai, both of whom are found in his following by 1371.[70] Langham's extended stay at the *curia*, as cardinal priest of San Sixto and later as cardinal Bishop of Palestrina, inevitably afforded extensive opportunities for contacts. Not only the musical cultures of the papal chapel under Urban v and Clement vii, populated largely by clerics from northern French and Low Countries dioceses, but also those of local churches in Avignon and Rome were no doubt readily accessible.

The court of the Black Prince in Bordeaux after 1363 has often been seen as the principal agent in the transmission of *Sub Arturo* to southern French repertories, and in the reception of French isorhythmic motets in English sources.[71] But there is also a further possible route, more favoured perhaps by the patterns of allegiances to the French cause as they developed after the resumption of hostilities, that has hitherto escaped attention. The career of Louis Duke of Anjou as the royal lieutenant in Languedoc between 1365 and 1380 brought him into regular contact with the Valois monarchy's southern French vassals and with the kingdom of Navarre and its satellites.[72] Chief among these was the comté of Foix-Béarn under Gaston Fébus between 1343 and 1391. After 1370 relations between Anjou and Fébus became increasingly close. The duke played a central role in effecting the assimilation of Fébus to the French cause, mediating in the celebrated Foix–Armagnac conflict, securing a tentative promise of allegiance in an agreement struck at Tarbes in 1377, and a definitive pact in 1379. Following a conflict over the succession to the lieutenancy in which Fébus was himself involved, dealings were frequent also with Anjou's successor, John

---

[70] See *Lettres de Grégoire xi* i, pp. 84, 89 (nos. 144, 157). For Capel, styled here 'familiario suo ac magistro capelle sue', see also Tomasello, *Music and Ritual*, p. 237.

[71] See for example the remarks in *The Motets of the Manuscripts Chantilly, Musée Condé, 564 (olim 1047) and Modena, Biblioteca Estense, α M. 5, 24 (olim lat. 568)*, d. Günther, p. lii; see also *Motets of French Provenance*, ed. Harrison, p. xv.

[72] For what follows see Tucoo-Chala, *Gaston Fébus*, pp. 302–16. See also N. Valois, 'Louis d'Anjou et le Grand Schisme d'Occident', *Revue des Questions Historiques*, 51 (1892), pp. 115–58; P. Contamine, *Guerre, état et société à la fin du moyen âge: Études sur les armées des rois de France, 1337–1494*, École Pratique des Hautes Études: Sorbonne vi^e Section, Civilisations et Sociétés 24 (Paris, 1972), pp. 151–78; Delachenal, *Histoire de Charles v*, iv, pp. 245–66.

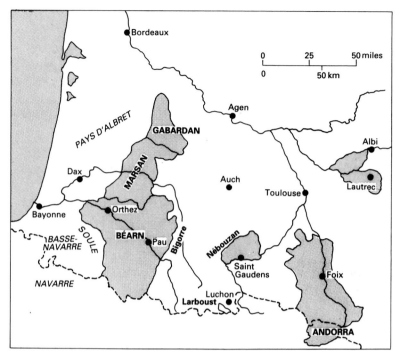

Figure 2 Foix – Béarn in the mid-fourteenth century (after P. Tucoo-Chala, *Histoire du Béarn* (Paris, 1962), p. 16)

Duke of Berry.[73] It has long been recognised that the origins of the repertories of Chantilly – even if not those of the book – lay within the circle of Gaston Fébus and the establishments that he maintained at the Château Moncade at Orthez and at Pau.[74] In addition to the several items in Chantilly whose texts mention Fébus, there is a ballade by Solage, *S'aincy estoit*, on the Duke of Berry, and the closely related fourteenth-century repertories of the Reina codex contain a further item, *Los pris honeur*, that celebrates Louis Duke of Anjou.[75]

---

[73] See Tucoo-Chala, *Gaston Fébus*, pp. 323–8; Lehoux, *Jean de France*, II, pp. 16–109.
[74] For the court of Fébus see Tucoo-Chala, pp. 277–81. For Chantilly, see G. Reaney, *Manuscripts of Polyphonic Music (c. 1320–1400)*, Répertoire International des Sources Musicales B IV² (Munich and Duisburg, 1969), pp. 128–60; 'Sources, MS', *NG*, XVII, p. 663.
[75] See W. Apel, ed., *French Secular Compositions of the Fourteenth Century*, 3 vols., Corpus Mensurabilis Musicae 53 (n.p., 1970–2), I, pp. 194–6, no. 100; II, pp. 74–5, no. 162. See also U. Günther, 'Eine Ballade auf Mathieu de Foix', *Musica Disciplina*, 19 (1965), pp. 69–81, especially pp. 71ff; H. M. Brown, 'A Ballade for Mathieu de Foix: Style and Structure in a Composition by Trebor', *Musica Disciplina*, 41 (1987), pp. 75–107. I am grateful to Christopher Page for the suggestion that the text of the ballade *Le mont Aön*, recently

During the Duke of Anjou's tours of duty in the Languedoc, his household chapel – numbering ten chaplains and four clerks by early 1378[76] – was based with the rest of the domestic establishment at Toulouse; it also spent some time with the duchess at Angers and Paris, and with the duke's entourage at Avignon and on military expeditions.[77] It is thus possible that Matheus de Sancto Johanne's move to the chapel of the Duke of Anjou provided a route for the transmission of his own and perhaps English works to southern French repertories, even if it is necessary to argue that these transmissions were not always close to his period of service in England. Other chaplains and clerks of the duke's chapel – again many were from Flemish and northern French dioceses – may of course also have helped to facilitate the movement of pieces. Even so, Gaston Fébus was not without English relations of his own. As a client of the King of Navarre he sent troops to join the English armies at the battle of Nájera in 1367; throughout the 1370s he made very effective use in his dealings with France of the threat of reconciliation with England, exchanging embassies with Edward III and Richard II and making loans to the Duke of Lancaster.[78]

Almost without exception, the presence of French composers in England in this period can be linked with diplomatic causes, broadly defined to include the management and aftermath of the French princes' captivity. It is well known that Pierre de Molins served as a

attributed to Solage (by P. M. Lefferts, 'Subtilitas in the Tonal Language of *Fumeux fume*', *Early Music*, 16 (1988), p. 179), refers to the Château Moncade. See also the remarks linking Ivrea, Biblioteca Capitolare, MS 115, to Fébus's court in U. Günther, 'Problems of Dating in Ars Nova and Ars Subtilior', *L'Ars nova italiana del trecento* IV, ed. A. Ziino (Certaldo, 1978), pp. 291–3.

[76] See MS fonds fr. 27509 (p.o. 1025), dossier 'de Douxmesnil' (23456), no. 4.

[77] See for example Delachenal, *Histoire de Charles V*, IV, pp. 246ff. See also Paris, BN, MS fonds fr. 26931 (p.o. 447), dossier 'Boulet' (10115), no. 3, a bill for the payment of chapel wages for January 1371 (Toulouse, 23 February 1371). Sizable groups of chaplains also accompanied the duke's expeditions to La Réole in 1374, to Avignon in 1375 and 1380, and to Rodez in 1377 (MS fonds fr. 28858 (p.o. 2374), dossier 'de Prechac' (53267), no. 2; MS fonds fr. 27509 (p.o. 1025), dossier 'de Douxmesnil', nos. 2, 3, 7, 8). Two payments to François de Furnes, styled 'maistre des orgues de nostre chapelle', were made in August 1370 and February 1371 at Cahors and Montauban (MS fonds fr. 27743 (p.o. 1259), dossier 'de Furnes' (28197), no. 5). For the duchess's household, see Paris, AN, KK 242, fols. 72^{r-v}, 93^v–96, 103^v–104^v. For the chaplains and clerks of the household chapel of Louis Duke of Anjou, see also Wright, *Music at the Court of Burgundy*, p. 55; BN, MS fonds fr. 26852 (p.o. 368), dossier 'Blez' (8037), no. 3; MS fonds fr. 29325 (p.o. 2841), dossier 'Thury' (63032), no. 2; MS fonds fr. 11863, fols. 25–9; MS fonds fr. 26014, no. 2075.

[78] See Tucoo-Chala, *Gaston Fébus*, pp. 305–6, 311, 336, 353. See also S. Armitage-Smith, ed., *John of Gaunt's Register*, 2 vols., Camden Third Series 20–1 (London, 1911), II, pp. 264–5, 307; for gifts to made by Gaunt to Fébus see II, p. 278.

clerk in the chapel of John II in London from 1357 until July 1359, when a large part of the French king's following was expelled on the advice of the privy council; he may also have joined the larger entourage resident in England with John II in 1363–4.[79] During these years the chapel had an organ, and on numerous occasions was supplemented by local clergy for important feasts. With the moves towards peace in 1360 several of John's servants rejoined their master and it is clear that this group included the clerks of the chapel. On his return from Brétigny, Edward III made generous payments by way of reward to the French king's clerks and minstrels; more gifts followed when the treaty was ratified at Calais in the following October.[80] The release of John from captivity in July 1360 served as the pretext for further celebrations, and these were the occasion of Edward's well-known gift to the French king, made among many others, of the 'instrument appelle leschequier'.[81] It may also be that the identity of the Johannes de Muris who accompanied the Bishop of Lectoure to England in the first diplomatic attempt, in 1357–8, to secure the French king's release should be given some thought.[82] More important is the visit made to England by Louis de Mâle, Count of Flanders, in 1364 to finalise the treaty for the marriage of his daughter and Edmund Earl of Cambridge.[83] The count travelled to Dover in late September accompanied by a large retinue almost all of whom were lavishly rewarded by Edward III with gifts of money and plate. In total over £630 – a huge sum by any

---

[79]   See Wright, *Music at the Court of Burgundy*, pp. 12–17; *Foedera*, III/1, p. 436; Douët-d'Arcq, *Comptes*, pp. 222, 259–60, 265. See also Cazelles, *Société politique*, pp. 366–9, 447–9.

[80]   See E 403/401, m. 16 (*sub* 3 July 1360), '*Clerici et ministralli Regis Francie*. Tribus ministrallis Regis Francie, in denariis eis liberatis per manus Johannis Says, militis, de dono regis per breve de privato sigillo inter mandata de hoc termino, xx li. Potage et sociis suis clericis de capella Regis Francie et cuidam Regi haraldorum de Francia, in denariis eis liberatis de dono regis per breve de privato sigillo inter mandata de hoc termino, x li'. For the later gift see E 403/403, m. 38 (*sub* 8 March 1361), '*Ministralli Regis Francie*. In denariis solutis apud Cales' diversis armigeris valletis et ministrallis Johannis Regis Francie de dono Regis, videlicet . . . diversis ministrallis Regis Francie, xxl li. . . . Potage clerico capelle, lxvi s. viii d. . . . iiii[or] ministrallis Ducis de Berry et Dauvergen' in precio xl regalis, . . . vi li. xiii s. iiii d. . . . tribus ministrallis in precio x regalis, . . . xxxiij s. iiii d'; see also the warrant, E 404/7/43/18 (Calais, 29 October 1360) '. . . A Potage clerc de la chapelle meisme nostre frere, vint escuz'. Potage returned to England in the spring of 1360 (Douët-d'Arcq, *Comptes*, pp. 240, 245, 248). An Henri Potage was the senior clerk of the chapel of Louis de Mâle, Count of Flanders, by 1374, and a clerk of the Duke of Burgundy, 1384–91 (Brussels, AGR, CC 2702, fol. 18; Wright, *op. cit.*, pp. 21, 56–7, 66, 72, 212–18). For further gifts made at Calais see Chaplais, *English Medieval Diplomatic Practice*, II, p. 825.

[81]   Douët-d'Arcq, *Comptes*, p. 273 (*sub* 4 July 1360).

[82]   See *Foedera*, III/1, p. 358.   [83]   For the treaty see *Foedera*, III/2, pp. 750–1.

standards – was paid out by the English exchequer to meet the costs of this largesse, and this does not take account of presents made by the king from other sources.[84] The cash gifts went for the most part to the count's domestic servants, who included seven minstrels and the six clerks of the chapel; one of these clerks was Egidius de Terwane, *alias* Egidius de Morino, who in the following year was styled variously 'chaplain' and 'cantor'.[85] It is likely that the household chapel of Edward III was also present for the mass that followed the affixing of seals to the treaty at Dover Castle on 19 October. There had probably also been other occasions in the period of the negotiations when Edward's chaplains and those of the Count of Flanders had come into contact. Again, some of those named in *Sub Arturo* were among the English present. Egidius de Morino himself appears in texts of two further musician motets: *Apollinis eclipsatur* and *Musicalis scientia*.[86] These and like compositions – including *Sub Arturo* – have long attracted attention for their generic connections. It may now be time to attempt a broader contextual explanation of their genesis and function, in which the political relations between rulers in fourteenth-century Europe and their neighbours also play a part.

By no means all aspects of Anglo-French relations in the period following the peace of Brétigny have been covered here, and it should also be emphasised that it is contacts – rather than transmissions – for which in the first instance documentation has here been sought. Nor, as was said at the outset, can these contacts be presented in isolation from those in the years before 1360 and after 1369. Even so, the release of England's foreign relations from the straitjacket of open war with France placed English activity on a new footing in spheres of action beyond French borders. Relations with Flanders, Navarre, Aragon, Castile and Milan suddenly take on a

---

[84] See for the gifts E 403/422, m. 22 (*sub* 21 June 1365); E 403/421, m. 6 (*sub* 31 October 1364) 'In denariis solutis apud Dovorr' officiariabus Comitis Flandrie de dono Regis videlicet sex clericis de capella ipsius Comitis, xx li. . . . ministrallis domini Lodevici, v marcarum; iiij[or] regibus haraldorum, xx marcarum'. The count's *clerici* and *cantores*, together with an unnamed papal chaplain, also received substantial gifts of plate from the Duke of Brabant at Brussels early in 1364 (AGR, CC 2350, p. 136).

[85] See AGR, CC 2351, fol. 71, 'Item domino Egidio de Teruwane cantori comitis Flandrie venienti Brux' pro curialitate xx[m] ln' Junii, vi mot.'; see also A. Pinchart, 'La cour de Jeanne et Wenceslas et les arts en Brabant pendant la seconde moitié du xive siècle', *Revue Trimestrielle*, 6 (1855), p. 27.

[86] *Motets of French Provenance*, ed. Harrison, pp. 50–61, 181–4 (nos. 9, 9a, 33). See also Gómez, 'Une version', pp. 14–29; a further, English, source of *Apollinis*, not noted by Gómez, is Public Record Office, E 163/22/1/24, fol. 2.

new aspect, and it follows that the task of tracing the proximities of English and Continental musical cultures similarly widens in scope. Two features nonetheless transcend the boundaries of this period. First, that the political geography of western Europe, with its periodic shifts and high degree of complexity in the localities, must be counted a major factor in shaping those musical cultures connected with the king and nobility. The conditions against which transmissions in this period took place are more coherently explained in these terms than by merely presuming the autonomous and unfettered movement of music and musicians. Second, is that England and its rulers must be counted part of a wider European political community. This is not to indulge in the fantasy of single national traditions, neatly arranged into a 'centre' and 'periphery'. Nonetheless, rulers looked beyond their own boundaries for sources of internal stability and opportunity, and foreign relations had a domestic impact on the cultural, as well as political and economic, life of communities with which kings and nobles were connected. It is these points, in the final analysis, to which any study of musical transmissions must be susceptible.

Royal Holloway and Bedford New College,
University of London

APPENDIX 1 — Documents

Document 1: Muster Roll for the expedition of Edward the Black Prince to Gascony, June 1363[1] (London, British Library, MS Cotton Julius c. IV, fols. 288–91 (see Figure 3))

[fol. 288]
La retenue vers Aquitaine lan xxxvij   [Summa?]Dviij

[fol. 291]
Clercs
Maistre Johan Assheton
Sire Robert de Walsham   +   *   H
Sire Hugh de Berton   +
Sire Johan de Stene   +

---

[1] For the date of this expedition, usually given as February 1363, see R. Barber, 'Jean Froissart and Edward the Black Prince', *Froissart: Historian*, ed. J. J. N. Palmer (Woodbridge, 1981), pp. 29–30.

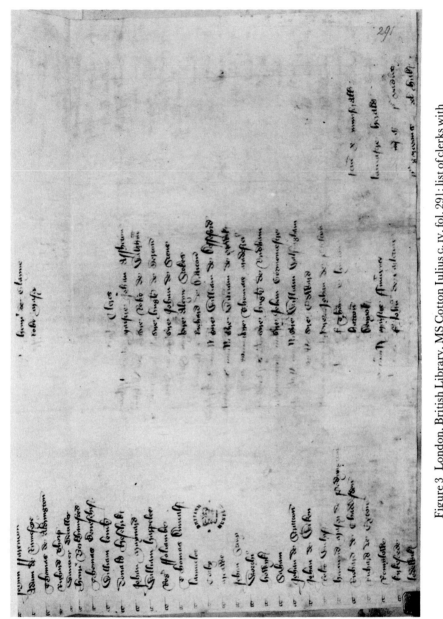

Figure 3 London, British Library, MS Cotton Julius c. rv, fol. 291; list of clerks with the Black Prince's expedition to Gascony, 1363 (Appendix 1, Document 1)

Sire Aleyn Stokes	+		H
Richard de Draiton	+		H
Sire William de Desseford			
Sire William de Oxewik	+	*	
Sire Thomas Madefrei	+	*	H
Sire Hugh de Bridham	+	*	H
Sire Johan Gormoncestre	+	*	H [almoner]
Sire William Walsingham		*	H
Sire Edward [Sotheward?]	[+]	*	
Sire Johan de Preston	+		H
Sire Thomas de Lyncon			
[Sire Thomas de] Horton	+	*	H
Donyok			
Maistre Framoryce			
Sire Johan de Carleton	+		

Item x ministralles
Lancastre herald

+ denotes those included in the Black Prince's roll of petitions for benefices submitted to the pope; see *CPL: Petitions*, I, p. 454 (from which square-bracketed material is supplied), and *Urbain: LC*, I, pp. 478–9 (4239–50).
* denotes those traceable from other sources as chaplains and clerks of the Black Prince's household chapel; H denotes those who appear in the Journal of John Henxtworth (London, Duchy of Cornwall Office, MS Accounts 1355), detailing expenses for the Black Prince's expedition to France of 1355–7.

Document 2: Privy seal bill, of 18 May 1368, authorising the issue of safe-conducts to John Louchevel, Matheu Seintjon and others to travel to France (c81/916/21)

Depar le Roi

Soient faitz briefs desouz nostre grant seal en due forme pur Johan Louchevel chapellein, Matheu Seintjon et William Cog, clercs de la chapelle nostre treschere compaigne la Roine de passer vers les parties de France ove un Philip de Parys leur vallet deux garceons trois hakeneys dix livres par eschange et pur chescun des ditz Johan, Matheu et William vint soldz pur leur despenses a Dovorr. Don' souz nostre prive seal a Westm' le xiii iour de May lan de nostre regne quarante second.

Andrew Wathey

Document 3: Exchequer issue roll entry, *sub* 16 December 1363, recording payments to Edmund monk of Bury, acting for William de Tyddeswell (E 403/417, m.26)

Willelmus de Tyddeswell. Willelmo de Tyddeswell clerico capelle Regis per manus Edmundi monachi de Bury. In denariis sibi liberatis per manus Magistri Johannis de Wormenhale[2] in partem solucionis xxvij li. ix s. ix d. sibi debito in garderoba domini regis de vadiis suis guerre robis restauro et repassagio equorum suorum ut patet per billam Willelmi de Farle[3] nuper custode garderobe predicte indors' de summa subscripta per breve de privato sigillo inter mandata de hoc termino necnon per breve de magno sigillo ut supra quoad huius solucionem faciendum ipsum custode inde non onerando, x li.

Document 4: Exchequer issue roll entries, *sub* 17 July 1364, recording payments to Edmund monk of Bury, acting for the executors of William de Tyddeswell (E 403/418, m. 18)

Executores testamenti Willelmi de Tyddeswell. Executoribus testamenti Willelmi de Tyddeswell per manus Edmundi monachi de Bury in persolucionem xxvij li. ix s. vij d. sibi debito in garderoba domini regis de vadiis suis guerre robis et repassagio equorum suorum ut patet per billam Willelmi de Farle nuper custode garderobe predicte dampnum in hanaperio de hoc termino per breve de privato sigillo termino Michaelis proxime preterito necnon per breve de magno sigillo inter mandata de termino Pasche anno xxxvj[4] quoad huius solucionem faciendum ipsum custode inde non onerando, xvij li. ix s. ix d. [*sic*]

Eisdem executoribus per manus eiusdem Edmundi in persolucionem lv s. v d. sibi debito in garderoba predicta de vadiis et robis suis ut patet per billam Henrici de Walton[5] nuper custode garderobe predicte dampnum in hanaperio de hoc termino per breve de privato sigillo inter mandata de hoc termino necnon per breve de magno sigillo termino Pasche anno xxxiiij[6] quoad huius solucionem faciendum ipsum custodem inde non onerando. De quibus quidem duabus billis superscriptis iidem executores remiserunt domino regis x li. v s. ij d.} lv s. v d.

---

2 For whom see A. B. Emden, *A Biographical Register of the University of Cambridge to 1500* (Cambridge, 1963), pp. 650–1.
3 Keeper of the Wardrobe, 3 November 1359–26 May 1360 (*HBC*, p. 80).
4 Easter Term 1362. |
5 Keeper of the Wardrobe, 16 December 1358–3 November 1359 (*HBC*, p. 80).
6 Easter Term 1360.

Document 5: Privy seal writ close, of 16 April 1365, addressed to Henry Snayth, Keeper of the Great Wardrobe, authorising the issue of robes to William Mugge for Christmas 1364 (E 101/395/2 (26))

Edward par la grace de dieu roi Dengleterre seignur Dirlande et Daquitaigne. A nostre ame clerc Henri de Snayth Gardein de nostre grande garderobe, saluz. Nous vous mandons qe a nostre ame clerc William Mugge facez liverer drap pur sa robe ovesque les furures de la suite des clercs de nostre chapelle et par manere come ils preignent pur la feste de Noel darein passee.[7] Et volons qe par cestes et vous eveiez due allouance en vostre aconte. Don' souz nostre prive seal a nostre Chastel de Wyndesore le xvi iour daverill, lan de nostre regne trente noefisme.

Document 6: Privy seal writ close, of 11 January 1369, addressed to Henry Snayth, Keeper of the Great Wardrobe, authorising the issue to John Sutton, a boy of the chapel under the care of Edmund monk of Bury, of robes for Christmas 1368 (E 101/395/2 (182))

Edward par la grace de dieu roi Dengleterre seignur Dirlande et Daquitaigne. A nostre ame clerc Henri de Snayth Gardein de nostre grande garderobe, saluz. Nous vous mandons qe a un petit clerc de nostre chapelle Johan de Sutton qest demorant devers nostre bian ame danz Esmon moigne de Bury facez liverer drap pur sa robe ovesque la furrure pur la feste de Noel darein passe par manere come ad este liverez par semblable cause a autres petitz clercs de nostre dite chapelle demorantz devers le dit Esmon avant ces heures. Et volons qe par cestes vous eveiez due allouance en vostre aconte. Don' souz nostre prive seal a Westm' le xj iour de Janver, lan de nostre regne quarante second.

⟨liberantur⟩

Document 7: Registered copy of a letter of Urban V (St Peter's, Rome, 20 November 1369) providing John Dodeford to the Priory of St Frideswide, Oxford, vacant *post mortem* Nicholas Hungerford (Vatican City, Archivio Segreto Vaticano, Reg. Aven., 171, fol. 302^{r-v})[8]

Dilecto filio Johanni de Dodeford priori prioratus conventualis Sancte Frideswyde ⟨ordinis⟩ Sancti Augustini Lincolnensis diocesis, Bacalari in Decretis, Salutem et cetera. Religionis ⟨zelus⟩ litterarum scientiam vite ac morum honestas aliaque probitatis et laudabilia merita super quibus apud nos fidedignorum commendaris testimonio nos inducunt ut tibi reddamur ad gratiam liberales. Dudum siquidem omnis prioratus dignitates per-

---

[7] Christmas 1364; see also E 361/4, m. 13.
[8] See *Urbain: LC*, IX, p. 517.

sonatus et officia ceteraque beneficia ecclesiastica secularia et regularia cum cura et sine cura tunc apud sedem apostolicam vacantia et inantea vaca' collacionem et disponi iuratum reservantes decrevimus [fol. 302^v] ex tunc irritum et inane si secus super hoc a quoquam quavis auctoritate scienter vel ignoranter contingeret attemptari. Cum itaque postmodum prioratus conventualis Sancte Frideswyde ordinis sancti Augustini Lincolniensis diocesis quem quondam Nicolaus de Hunggerford eiusdem prioratus prior dum viveret obtinebat per eiusdem Nicolai obitum qui dilecti filii nostri Symonis tituli Sancti Sixti presbiteri Cardinalis familiaris existens apud dictarum sedem diem clausit extremum apud sedem ipsam vacaverit et vacet ad presens nullus que preter nos hac vice de ipso prioratu disponere potuerit neque possit reservatione et decrev' obsistent' supradictis nos vocatos tibi in presbiteratus ordine constituto qui ut asseritur in dicto prioratu dictum ordinem expresse professus fuisti premissorum meritorum tuorum intuitu necnon consideratione dicti Cardinalis pro te dilecto suo nobis super hoc humiliter supplicantis gratiam facere specialem dictam prioratum qui ut asseritur a nullo monasterio dependet et nullos fructus vel proventus discretos a bonis dilectorum filiorum conventus eiusdem prioratus habet et ad quem quis consuevit per electionem assumi etiam si idem prioratus curatus sit et eius collacione disponi apostolice vel reservata existat sic vacantem cum omnibus iuri et pertinenti si apostolica tibi auctoritate conferimus et de illo eciam providemus decernentes prout est irritum et inane si secus super hoc a quoquam quavis auctoritate scienter vel ignoranter attemptatum forsan est hactenus vel contigerit imposterum attemptari. Non obstantibus quibuscumque constitutibus apostolicis necnon statutis et consuetudinibus prioratus et ordinis predictorum contrariis iuramento confirmatione apostolica vel quacumque firmitate alia roboratis seu si aliqui super provisionibus sibi faciendis de prioribus dignitatibus personatibus vel officiis aut aliis beneficiis ecclesiasticis in illis partibus speciales vel generales dicte sedis vel legatorum eius litteras impetrarint etiam si per eas ad inhibitionem reservationem et decretum vel quolibet sit processum quibus omnibus in assecutione dicti prioratus te volumus anteferri sed nullum per hoc eis quo ad assecutionem prioratuum dignitatem personatuum vel officiorum ac beneficiorum aliorum preiudicium generari. Seu si venerabili fratri nostro Episcopo Lincolnien' et dilectis filiis conventui dicti prioratus vel quibusvis aliis communiter vel divisim ab eadem sit sede indultum quod ad receptionem vel provisionem alicuius minime teneantur et ad id compelli non possint quodque de prioratibus dignitatibus personatibus vel officiis aut aliis beneficiis ecclesiasticis ad eorum collacionem provisionem presentationem seu quamvis aliam dispositionem coniunctim vel separatim spectantibus nulli valeat provideri per litteras apostolicas non facientes plenam et expressam ac de verbo ad verbum de indulto huiusmodi mentionem. Et qualibet alia dicte sedis indulgentia generali vel speciali cuiuscumque tenoris existat per quam presentibus non expressam vel totaliter non insertam effectus huiusmodi ⟨nostre⟩ gratie impediri valeat quomodolibet vel differri et de qua cuiusque totis tenoribus habendam sit in nostris litteris mentio specialis. Seu quod perpetuam vicariam de Wytengham per canonicos ecclesie Karleolen' cuius canonicatus existis teneri consuetam obtines et super perpetua vicaria de Hesill ecclesiarum parochialium Dunelmen' et Eboracen' diocesium te assecutis litigare. Volumus autem quia quamprimum vigore priori dictum prioratum fueris pacifice assecutus de Wytengham quam ut profertur obtines et deseres Hesill si eam interim evincas vicarias predictas quas extunc vacare decernimus omnino dimittem alioquis omni iuri tibi in eadem vicaria ecclesie de Hesill seu ad eam quomodolibet competenti prout etiam ad hoc te sponte obtulisti cedem tenearis. Nulli ergo, et cetera, nostre collationis provisionis constitutionis et voluntatis infringere, et cetera. Datum Rome apud Sanctum Petrum xij Kalendas Decembris Anno viij^{mo}. In eodem modo venerabilis fratribus Wyntoniensis et Wigorniensis Episcopis ac dilecto filio Archidiacono Oxonie in ecclesia Lincolnien'. Salutem, et cetera. Religionis, et cetera, usque teneatur. Quocirca discretioni vestre per apostolica scripta mandamus quatinus vos vel duo aut unus vestrum per vos vel alium seu alios eundem Johannem vel procuratorem suum eius nomine in corporalem possessionem dicti prioratus iuratumque [?] et pertinenciorum predictorum inducatis auctoritate nostra et defendatis inductum a moto exinde quolibet detenore facientes ipsum vel dictum procuratorem pro eo ad huius prioratum ut est moris admitti sibique de ipsius prioratus fructibus redditibus proventibus iuribus et obventibus universis integre respondere. Non obstantibus omnibus supradictis seu si eisdem Episcopo et conventui vel quibusvis aliis communiter vel divisim a prefata sede indultum existat quod interdici suspendi vel excommunicari non possint per litteras apostolicas non facientes plenam et expressam ac de verbo ad verbum de indulto huiusmodi mentionem. Contradictores auctoritate nostra, et cetera. Datum ut supra.

APPENDIX 2

This appendix includes the musicians named in the texts of *Sub Arturo plebs* for whom careers can be traced with some certainty in the 1360s and early 1370s. For the most part it is the later identifications of those named in the motet that are the least secure; for 'J. de Altobosco', 'G. Martini', 'Ricardus Blich', 'Johannes de Exonia' and 'Adam Levita' no firm identities have

Table 2

All of the following documents list those to whom robes were issued, with the exception of j, which is a list of prests made shortly after the renewal of hostilities with France in late summer 1369. The dates in the second column are those covered by the issues of robes, which are often but not invariably the periods covered by the documents. 'Winter' and 'summer' appear to correspond respectively with the exchequer's Michaelmas and Hilary, and Easter and Trinity, terms; they cannot, however, be identified with the feasts of Christmas, Easter or Whitsun. See generally for these records Wathey, *Music in the Royal and Noble Households*, pp. 98ff.

a	winter 1341–2; winter 1343–4	E 36/204, fol. 86 (Household Wardrobe Account, Controller's Book)
b	summer 1353; winter 1353–4	E 101/392/12, fols. 40^{r-v} (Household Wardrobe Account, Keeper's Book)
c	winter 1359–60; summer 1360	E 101/393/11, fol. 76^v (Household Wardrobe Account, Keeper's Book)
d	Christmas 1362	E 361/4, m. 8 (Great Wardrobe Enrolled Account)
e	Christmas 1363	E 101/395/2 (260) (Warrant to the Keeper of the Great Wardrobe) E 101/394/16, m. 9 (Great Wardrobe Roll of Particulars) E 361/4,\m. 12d,(Great Wardrobe Enrolled Account)
f	summer 1366	E 101/396/2, fol. 56 (Household Wardrobe Account, Keeper's Book)
g	Christmas 1366	E 101/395/9 (2) (Warrant to the Keeper of the Great Wardrobe)
h	Christmas 1368	E 101/395/2; E 101/395/10 (Warrants and schedule sent to the Great Wardrobe). See Wathey, p. 104.
i	summer 1369	E 101/396/11, fols. 16^v–17 (Household Wardrobe Account, Controller's Book)
j	late summer 1369	E 361/4, mm. 21d–22 (Prests; Household Wardrobe Enrolled Account)
k	funeral of Queen Philippa (Sept 1369)	E 101/395/2 (236) (Warrant to the Keeper of the Great Wardrobe)
l	winter 1371–2; summer 1372	E 101/397/5, fol. 43 (Household Wardrobe Account, Keeper's Book)
m	winter 1372–3; summer 1373	E 101/397/5, fol. 82 (Household Wardrobe Account, Keeper's Book)
n	winter 1376–7; summer 1377	E 101/398/9, fol. 31 (Household Wardrobe Account, Keeper's Book)
o	funeral of Edward III (July 1377)	E 101/397/20, m. 30 (Great Wardrobe Roll of Particulars)
p	24 June 1380	E 159/158, *brevia directa baronibus*, Trinity rot. 6 (Warrant to Exchequer)
q	2 Feb 1381	E 159/158, *brevia directa baronibus*, Trinity rot. 8 (Warrant to Exchequer)
r	24 June 1382	E 159/162, *brevia directa baronibus*, Trinity rot. 8 (Warrant to Exchequer)
s	winter 1383–4; summer 1384	E 101/401/2, fol. 42 (Household Wardrobe Account, Keeper's Book)

emerged beyond those tentatively advanced in Trowell, 'A Fourteenth-Century Ceremonial Motet', pp. 68–73, and Bowers, 'Fixed Points'.

The following additional abbreviations are used:

CCR	*Calendar of Close Rolls*
Fasti	J. M. Horn *et al.*, *John Le Neve: Fasti Ecclesie Anglicanae, 1300–1541*, 12 vols. (London, 1963–7)
Ollard	S. L. Ollard, *Fasti Wyndesorienses: The Deans and Canons of Windsor* (Windsor, 1950)
Reg. Brantingham	*The Register of Thomas de Brantingham, Bishop of Exeter (A.D. 1370–1394)*, ed. F. C. Hingeston-Randolph, 2 vols. (London and Exeter, 1901–6)
Reg. Buckingham	Lincoln, Lincolnshire Archives Office, Episcopal Register x
Reg. Courtenay	London, Lambeth Palace, Reg. Courtenay
Reg. Edington	*The Register of William Edington, Bishop of Winchester, 1346–1366*, ed. S. F. Hockey, Hampshire Record Series 7–8 (Southampton, 1986–7).
Reg. Gynwell	Lincolnshire Archives Office, Episcopal Register ix
Reg. Langham	*Registrum Simonis de Langham, Cantuariensis archiepiscopi*, ed. A. C. Wood, Canterbury and York Society 53 (Oxford, 1956)
Reg. Stretton	*The Registers or Act Books of the Bishops of Coventry and Lichfield . . .: Bishop Robert de Stretton, 1358–1385 . . .*, ed. R. A. Wilson, Collections for a History of Staffordshire, new ser. 10/ii (London, 1907)
Reg. Sudbury	*Registrum Simonis de Sudburia, Diocesis Londoniensis A.D. 1362–1375*, ed. R. C. Fowler and C. Jenkins, 2 vols., Canterbury and York Society 34–5 (Oxford, 1937–8)
Reg. Wykeham	*Wykeham's Register*, ed. T. F. Kirby, 2 vols., Hampshire Record Society (Winchester, 1896–9)

John Aleyn (J. Alanus)
Clerk of the royal household chapel, 1362–73 (lists d–f, h, i, k–m); probably from Patteshull, Northamptonshire. Died between Michaelmas and 7 December 1373 (*Fasti*, x, p. 38; *CPR 1370–1374*, p. 369). Sent on 4 May 1366 to Oxford from Windsor by Queen Philippa to find her clerk Mag. William Holme (E 101/396/2, fol. 35). Received 8d. on 20 October 1367, to pay for transporting the king's money from London to Westminster (E 403/429, m. 8). Receiver of loans from religious houses in Kent, 1370 (*The Issue Roll of Thomas de Brantingham, 1370*, ed. F. Devon (London, 1835), pp. 111, 471).

Bequeathed 'unus rotulus de cantu musicali' to St George's Chapel, Windsor (A. Wathey, 'Lost Books of Polyphony in England: A List to 1500', *Research Chronicle: Royal Musical Association*, 21 (1988), p. 13 (no. 133)).

Rector of Clee, prov. 29 April 1361; exch. with John Penreth for St Olave Southwark, 28 August 1363; still on 27 June 1373 (*CPL: Petitions*, I, pp. 321, 365; Reg. Buckingham, fols. 2ʳ⁻ᵛ; *CPR 1370–1374*, p. 277). Held a chantry in the church of St James, Garlickhithe, London, by 29 April 1361 (*CPL: Petitions*, I, p. 365). Rector of Chelmington, Norwich diocese, vac. by 26 March 1362 (*CPR 1361–1364*, p. 178). Canon of St George's Chapel, Windsor, pres. to 2nd stall 25 September 1362; res. on grant of 10th stall, 15 October 1368, held until death (*CPR 1361–1364*, p. 248; *CPR 1367–1370*, pp. 151–2; *CPR 1370–1374*, p. 369; Ollard, pp. 65, 136). Canon of St Paul's, London, pres. 18 December 1361; exch. with William Wynel for the Free Chapel of St Laurence, Halling, Kent, 19 February 1363; vac. by 9 November 1369 (*Reg. Wykeham*, I, p. 26; *Fasti*, v, pp. 47–8). Prebendary of the Royal Free Chapel in Exeter Castle by 22 April 1363; still in October 1366 and vac. by 1 November 1370. Prov. to a canonry at London with the expectation of a prebend, at the petition of Queen Philippa, on condition that he resign his Exeter prebend (*CPL: Petitions*, I, p. 416; *Urbain: LC*, II, p. 366 (7707); *Reg. Sudbury*, II, p. 152; *Reg. Brantingham*, I, p. 12). Rector of Brasted, Rochester diocese, by 22 April 1363 (*CPL: Petitions*, I, p. 416); exch. with Richard de Haukedon for the church of Nailstone, Lincoln diocese, 7 April 1365; vac. by 14 October 1366 (Reg. Buckingham, fols. 234ᵛ, 236ᵛ; *CPR 1364–1367*, p. 102). Rector of Shalden; exch. with John de Maydeford for the church of Preston Candover, Hants, 26 December 1366 (*Reg. Langham*, pp. 250–1). Rector of Shoreham, Kent, pres. 30 April 1366 (*CPR 1364–1367*, p. 232). Granted a prebend at Wells, 20 September 1367, *vice* Robert de Midelond (*CPR 1367–1370*, p. 6; *Fasti*, VIII, p. 82). Rector of Otford, Rochester diocese, vac. 20 January 1368 (*Urbain: LC*, VII, pp. 92 (21234), 131 (21522), 137 (21545); *CPL*, IV, p. 71). Archdeacon of Suffolk, prov. 20 January 1368, on condition that he resign Otford and his canonry of St George's, Windsor; until death (*Fasti*, IV, p. 33). Canon of Exeter Cathedral, pres. 15 February 1370, until death (*Fasti*, x, p. 38). To be distinguished from the John Aleyn of Huntingdon, pres. to the church of Wauton, 15 February 1365 (*CPR 1364–1367*, p. 82). See Trowell, pp. 68–9.

Edmund de Bury (Edmundus de Buria)

Alias Bokenham, a monk of Bury in royal service attached to the chapel from the mid-1350s until *c.* 1377 (lists e, g, h, k, o). Paid 13s. 4d. on 21 March 1351, owing on 23 July 1349 from the treasurership of Thomas Clopton (24 November 1347–4 July 1349) (E 404/489/138). Excused liability, 7 February 1361, for receipts of a pension previously granted on an unnamed manor (E 404/6/40/33). Granted £30 p.a. at the exchequer, 4 October 1361, assigned on the issues of the alien priory of Toft (Norfolk), a cell of the Benedictine Abbey of St Pierre, Préaux (*CPR 1361–1364*, pp. 80–1; for payments of this annuity see E 403/409 *et seq.*, E 404/620/89, E 404/7/43/44, E 404/7/45/12). Robes for Bury, 'et duobus sociis suis', for the feasts of Christmas 1362–4, for Bury at Christmas 1368, and for the funeral of Queen Philippa allowed in the Great Wardrobe account (E 361/4, mm. 9, 12, 13; E 101/395/2 (205); E 101/395/2 (236)). Given the custody of John Sutton, a boy of the chapel, by Christmas 1368, and others before this date (E 101/395/2 (182); Appendix 1, Document 6). Receiver of sums due to William Tiddeswell, 16 December 1363 and 17 July 1364; see Appendix 1, Documents 3–4.

Rural dean of Bocking, Essex, app. 24 October 1366; still in October 1367; vac. by 11 July 1381 (Canterbury, Cathedral Archives, Priory Register G, fols. 145ᵛ, 230ᵛ; *Reg. Langham*, pp. 146, 112). Petitioner for the pardon of John de Redgrave, indicted of murder, 26 April 1359 (*CPR 1359–1361*, p. 196). Urged, with several others, by Gregory IX to engage the king's help in freeing the pope's brother, Roger de Belloforti, imprisoned by Jean de Grailly, the Captal de Buch, 23 September 1371 (*CPL*, IV, p. 96). Granted a house called 'Fouleysmir', part of the Great Wardrobe estate, free of charge by the king, 26 December 1371 (E 101/397/4 (38)). See Trowell, p. 72.

Simon Clement (Symonis Clemens)
Possibly a clerk of the household chapel of the Black Prince, by 31 August 1363; styled 'chaplain' of the Prince, 29 January 1366 (*CPL: Petitions*, I, pp. 455, 517). Clerk of the royal household chapel 1376–winter 1383–4, probably until death (lists n–s). Died between 5 October 1383 and 1 April 1384 (*CPR 1381–1385*, pp. 313, 387).

Rector of Pimperne, Salisbury diocese, by 31 August 1363; still on 1 February 1366. Prov. to a canonry at York with the expectation of a prebend, notwithstanding his canonry and prebend at Salisbury, about which he was litigating in the papal court, 31 August 1363 (*Urbain: LC*, I, p. 479 (4242); *CPL: Petitions*, I, pp. 455, 517). Archdeacon of Worcester, notified by a mandate to the official of the Bishop of Angoulême, pres. 1 February 1366; vac. 4 May 1371 on exchange for the church of Allington, Wilts. (*Urbain: LC*, V, p. 173 (16921); *CPL: Petitions*, I, pp. 517; *Fasti*, IV, p. 62). Nominated by the king for the first vacant prebend in the collegiate church of South Malling, Kent, 23 February 1379 (*CPR 1377–1381*, p. 329). Granted a tenement in the parish of St Michael Paternosterchirche, London, 14 March 1381 (*CPR 1377–1381*, p. 608). See Trowell, p. 73.

John de Corby (J. de Corbe)
Clerk of the royal household chapel by winter 1360–1; until Christmas 1366 or after. Paid 40s. on 27 November 1363, owing on 1 August 1362 from the treasurership of William de Ferriby (26 May 1360–14 November 1361), for the cost of robes (lists d–g; E 403/417, m. 21; E 404/492/431). Paid 40s. in instalments on 12 February 1364 and 28 October 1364, owing on 13 November 1362 from William de Manton's treasurership (14 November 1361–31 January 1366) for robes for winter 1361–2 and summer 1362 (E 403/417, m. 31; E 403/421, m. 3; E 404/497/102). Given a complete vestment in 1362/3, probably for summer 1363 (E 361/4, m. 9).

Ord. deacon at Southwark by the Bishop of Winchester, 24 February 1347 (*Reg. Edington*, II, p. 117). Rector of Pickworth by Folkingham, Lincoln diocese, pres. 18 January 1358; vac. before 2 October 1369, when vac. by another incumbent (*CPR 1354–1358*, p. 646; Reg. Buckingham, fol. 33ᵛ). Canon of St Stephen's Church, Westminster, pres. 10 May 1363 and again on 19 June (*CPR 1361–1364*, pp. 338, 354); vac. by exchange with John Capel for the Rectory of Flamstede, Lincoln diocese, 26 February 1381, but Corby may not have taken possession since Capel resigned Flamstede again in 1391 (*CPR 1377–1381*, p. 605; Lincolnshire Archives Office, Episcopal Register XI (John Buckingham), fol. 265). Rector of Worfield, Coventry and Lichfield diocese, pres. 10 November 1363; vac. by 14 October 1366 (*ibid.*, p. 422; *Reg. Stretton*, p. 220). Prebend of Undredon in the Royal Free Chapel at Bridgnorth, pres. 9 March 1365 (*CPR 1364–1367*, p. 97). Rector of Esthurst, Chichester diocese, by 1366 (*Reg. Sudbury*, II, p. 161). Rector of Great Stanway, Essex, pres. 21 April 1366 (G. Hennessy, ed., *Novum repertorium parochiale Londinense* (London, 1898), p. clxxvi). See Trowell, p. 69.

Nicholas Hungerford (Nicholaus . . . de Vado Famelico)
Styled 'chaplain' of the Black Prince on 10 December 1365 (*CPL: Petitions*, I, p. 509). Clerk and 'familiaris' of Simon Langham Archbishop of Canterbury, cardinal priest of San Sixto, by 1369. Abroad by November 1367, possibly serving as Langham's representative at the Curia; prevented from using (as prior) the assets of the Priory of St Frideswide, Oxford, as security for debts incurred overseas (see above, nn. 64, 66). Died at the papal court, at Viterbo or Rome, between 24 September and 20 November 1369 (Appendix 1, Document 7; *Urbain: LC*, VIII, p. 21 (23121); IX, pp. 336 (26949), 516 (27776)).

Prior of St Frideswide's, Oxford, elected 15 May 1349; until death (*VCH, Oxon.*, II, pp. 98, 100). Attempted exch. with John de Dodeford for 'a certain vicarage', before 10 December 1365, but deprived on a charge of simony;

reinstated at the petition of the Black Prince (*CPL: Petitions*, I, p. 509). See above pp. 152–3 and nn. 64, 66; Trowell, pp. 72–3.

John Ipswich (Episwich, J.)

Clerk of the household chapel of the Black Prince by 10 November 1357 (probably by 12 June 1355); joined the prince's expedition to France, 1355–7 (*BPR*, IV, p. 227; C 61/67, m. 8). Died probably by 24 December 1358 (*BPR*, II, p. 151). Given a hood of 'grys' by 10 November 1357. Probably held a grant from the prince's steward in Cornwall (*BPR*, II, p. 152).

Ord. subdeacon by the Bishop of Winchester, 15 March 1348, at Southwark (*Reg. Edington*, II, p. 128). Rector of Blisland, Cornwall, pres. 12 June 1347; vac. by 14 March 1354 (*BPR*, I, p. 86; II, p. 59). Dean of the Free Chapel in Wallingford Castle, pres. 20 December 1351; probably until death (*BPR*, IV, pp. 36, 54, 320). Rector of Sancreed, Cornwall, pres. by 13 February 1354; vac. by 25 June 1356 (*BPR*, II, pp. 57, 98; IV, p. 188). Rector of Lanteglos, Cornwall, pres. 25 June 1356; vac. by 24 December 1358, probably *post mortem* (*BPR*, IV, p. 188; II, p. 151). See Trowell, p. 72.

Edmund Mirescough (E. de Murisco)

Clerk of the household chapel of the Black Prince by 10 November 1357 (*BPR*, IV, p. 227). Died by 20 July 1394 (A. H. Thompson, 'The Registers of the Archdeaconry of Richmond, 1361–1442', *The Yorkshire Archaeological Journal*, 25 (1920), p. 194). Given 100s., 18 May 1358, 'a son aler vers son pays' (E 36/278, fol. 143^v; see also *BPR*, IV, p. 251).

Rector of Bentham, York diocese, pres. 2 December 1357; until death. Obtained licences for non-residence for two periods of three years, 17 March 1359 and 8 October 1376; cited before the Archdeacon of Richmond for non-residence, 25 September 1376 (*CPR 1354–1358*, p. 641; Thompson, 'The Registers', pp. 183, 194). See Trowell, p. 73.

William Mugge (G. Mughe)

Chaplain of the royal household chapel from summer 1340; still on 24 November 1347, and probably until presentation to St George's Chapel, Windsor (list a; E 101/389/8, m. 8; E 101/390/12, fol. 28). Died between 14 January and 24 February 1381 (*Fasti*, X, p. 34; *CPR 1377–1381*, p. 601). Will of 15 April 1380 (Reg. Courtenay, fols. 201^v–202) mentions a noted missal formerly owned by Stephen de Gravesend, Bishop of London 1318–38, and a bequest to Mugge's 'camerarius . . . in curia romana'; will of Thomas Lynton, dean of the royal household chapel (Reg. Courtenay, fol. 225^v), 1387, mentions a *ciphum* received from Mugge's executors. With Edward III's expeditions to the Netherlands and France in 1340 and to Brittany in 1342–3, and the Crécy–Calais campaign (E 36/204, fol. 108; E 101/389/8,

m. 14; E 101/390/12, fols. 13, 28; E 101/391/9, fol. 4). Paid 40s. for a new horse 16 April 1341; received wages of war at 18d. per day for 98 days in 1340 (E 101/389/8, mm. 8, 14). Paid 56s. 5d. by the Black Prince's treasurer, 11 November 1342, for covers for 'arblasts, coffres et autres instrumentz' (E 101/388/13, m. 3). Paid 100s. 5d. on 8 July 1350, owing on 23 July 1349 from the treasurership of Thomas Clopton (E 404/489/4). Given a tun of wine by the Black Prince, between Mich. 1352 and Mich. 1353 (*BPR*, IV, p. 108). Paid 66s. 8d. on 5 March 1354 for robes, owing at the end of the first treasurership of William de Retford, on 23 February 1353, styled 'capellano capelle' (E 404/494/654; E 403/372/2, m. 1). Cloth and fur for his robe 'de la suite des clercs de nostre chapelle' allowed for Christmas 1364 in the account of the Great Wardrobe (Appendix 1, Document 5); robes for 1361 also allowed in the Great Wardrobe account (E 101/393/15, m. 13; E 361/4, m. 4d). Paid 60s. for a grey horse given to the king's avener for the cart of Walter Clench, 26 December 1366 (E 101/396/2, fols. 42^v–43). Granted a dispensation to absent himself from St George's Chapel, Windsor, for up to 60 days p.a., 15 December 1363 (*CPL: Petitions*, I, p. 474). Goods sequestrated, *post mortem*, by the Bishop of Exeter (*Reg. Brantingham*, I, p. 447). Mugge granted his manor of Killebury, Devon, to the king on 1 June 1356, and lands in Datchet to St George's Chapel, Windsor, on 20 March 1356 (*CCR 1354–1360*, p. 314; Windsor Aerary, x.1.3). A fourteenth-century cartulary of Mugge family lands in Devon is London, British Library, Add. Roll 28722. For other transactions see Windsor Aerary xv.44.116, xv.32.22 and xv.58.B.6.

Rector of Hartfield, Chichester diocese, pres. 29 October 1344; vac. by 3 August 1349 (*CPR 1343–1345*, p. 361; *CPR 1348–1350*, p. 360). Prov. to a canonry at Lichfield with the expectation of a prebend, 27 September 1348, and again 14 January 1357 (*CPL: Petitions*, I, pp. 139, 291). Rector of Weston, Norwich diocese, pres. (in the first instance possibly without success) 8 June 1348; exch. with John Derby for archdeaconry of Barnstaple, 2 September 1358; this post held probably until 1367 (*CPR 1348–1350*, p. 307; *CPL: Petitions*, I, pp. 309, 332; *CPR 1358–1361*, p. 191; *Fasti*, IX, p. 20). Appointed dean of St George's Chapel, Windsor, 18 June 1349; until death (*CPR 1348–1350*, p. 325). Canon of Exeter Cathedral from 1351 until death; treasurer 20 September 1367 to *c.* 5 June 1377, when exch. with Robert Broke for the rectory of Crewkerne (*Fasti*, IX, pp. 11, 20, 34, 67; *CPR 1374–1377*, p. 476). Commissioner for presentations in the diocese of Exeter, appointed 20 June 1370 (*Reg. Brantingham*, I, pp. 140, 182; see also p. 43). See Trowell, pp. 71–2.

William Oxwick (Oxwich, G.)
Dean of the household chapel of the Black Prince by 6 June 1357 (*BPR*, IV, p. 205). Given robes by 10 November 1357 (*ibid.*, p. 227). From 6 June 1357, and until after 22 February 1361, he received the costs of the prince's oblations for a period beginning 1 July 1355 (*BPR*, IV, pp. 205, 139, 379). Possibly the 'dominus Guillelmus capellani domini principis' who dined in the household of the Archbishop of Bordeaux, July 1355, and who was given grain for the prince's household by the archbishop's *granarius* (Bordeaux, Archives Départementales de la Gironde, G. 238, fols. 41, 39; see also *Archives Historiques du Département de la Gironde*, 21 (1881), pp. 242, 236).

Rector of Hartest, Norwich diocese, pres. 1346; still on 31 August 1363 (C. Morley, 'Catalogue of Beneficed Clergy of Suffolk, 1086–1550', *Proceedings of the Suffolk Institute of Archaeology*, 22 (1934–6), p. 67). Prebendary of London by 31 August 1363. Prov. to canonry at York Cathedral with the expectation of a prebend 31 August 1363, notwithstanding the London prebend (*Urbain: LC*, I, p. 479 (4249); *CPL: Petitions*, I, p. 454). See Trowell, p. 72.

William Tiddeswell (G. de Horarum Fonte)
Clerk of the royal household chapel by Michaelmas 1352, and chaplain by 15 February 1359; until death (lists b, c; E 404/494/108; E 404/494/439). Died between 16 December 1363 and 17 July 1364 (Appendix 1, Documents 3–4). With Edward III's expedition to Rheims and the Ile-de-France, 1359–60 (paid 8 September–2 June; E 101/393/11, fol. 89), and possibly with the 1355 expedition to Calais and France. Owed £11 on 23 February 1353, at the end of the first treasurership of William de Retford, for robes and a new horse; this sum was paid on 16 July 1353, in part by an assignment of £6 on the proffers of the Sheriff of Lincoln, of which 19s. 4½d. was received in cash that year (E 404/494/108; E 403/368, m. 18; E 372/198, Lincoln rot. 2 dorse). Paid £7 13s. 4d., owing on 1 July 1356 from the treasurership of John de Buckingham (23 February 1353–25 February 1357) for robes and a new horse (E 404/488/103). Paid £6 2s. on 9 February 1358, owing on 20 January from Buckingham's treasurership, for war wages and robes (E 404/486/231). Paid £7 6s. 8d. on 11 February 1359, owing on 15 December 1358 from Retford's second treasurership, for robes and a new horse (E 404/494/439, E 403/394, m. 28). Paid £27 9s. 9d. for transport of a horse, for the 1359–60 expedition in instalments on 16 December 1363 and, *post mortem*, 17 July 1364; executors paid 55s. 5d. owing from 1358–9 on 17 July 1364 (see Appendix 1, Documents 3–4). Appointed John de Saxton, dean of the royal household chapel, and John Waddworth on 18 August 1360 as his attorneys in England for one year while abroad (*CPR 1358–1361*, p. 253).

Granted pension, due to a royal clerk from the Abbot of Romsey, Hants, by reason of his new election, 24 May 1349 (*CCR 1349–1354*, p. 82). Ord. subdeacon by the Bishop of Winchester at Southwark on 20 February 1350, deacon 13 March 1350 and priest 27 March 1350 (*Reg. Edington*, II, pp. 153, 155, 157). Rector of Houghton-by-Wragby, Lincolnshire, pres. 23 July 1349; vac. by 13 December 1361 (*CPR 1348–1350*, p. 359; Reg. Gynwell, fol. 151ᵛ). Canon of St Stephen's, Westminster, pres. 20 July 1356; vac. by 15 October 1361 (*CPR 1354–1358*, p. 417; *CPR 1362–1364*, p. 85). See Trowell, p. 73.

Early Music History (1989) Volume 9

ROB C. WEGMAN

MUSIC AND MUSICIANS AT THE GUILD OF OUR LADY IN BERGEN OP ZOOM, C. 1470–1510*

Marian guilds and confraternities proliferated in fifteenth-century Brabant. They gave expression to the pride, devoutness and community spirit of the urban middle classes. Their chapels were invested with all the riches their members could afford: altarpieces, stained-glass windows, painted statues, silk and velvet cloth, gold and silverware, and other expensive ornaments. But the jewel in the crown for every confraternity was polyphony. Prestigious Marian confraternities such as those at 's-Hertogenbosch, Bergen op Zoom and Antwerp were among the major musical establishments of the Low Countries.[1] They employed some of the best-known composers

*I should like to thank David Fallows, Chris Maas, Barbara Haggh, Willem Elders, Leeman Perkins, Jaap van Benthem and Reinhard Strohm for reading the first draft of this article and offering valuable suggestions. I also acknowledge the kind help I received from Mr de Bakker and Mr Verraes of the City Archive of Bergen op Zoom.

In order to facilitate comparison, all prices in non-Brabant currencies and in Brabant pounds and shillings are converted into Brabant groats in the English translations and in Appendix 2. Unless specified otherwise, 'groat' means 'Brabant groat'. The following coins are mentioned in the Middle Dutch texts: Brabant pound (lb.) = 12 scellingen (sc.) = 240 Brabant groats (gr./den.); braspenning (brasp.)=3.75 groats; stuver (st.)=3 groats; oortken=0.75 groat.

In the footnotes the following abbreviations are used:

BOZ City Archive, Bergen op Zoom
 SA Stadsarchief (Archive of the City of Bergen op Zoom), containing:
  SR Stadsrekeningen (City accounts)
  OLV Rekeningen van het Onze Lieve Vrouwe Gilde (Accounts of the Guild of Our Lady)
 R Rechterlijk archief (Judicial archive)
 ARR Archief van de Raad en Rekenkamer van de Markiezen van Bergen op Zoom (Archive of the Council and Audit Chamber of the Marquises of Bergen op Zoom) (transferred in 1949 from the Algemeen Rijksarchief, The Hague, where it was stored in the Eerste afdeling, Commissie van Breda)

[1] For music at Antwerp, see J. du Saar, *Het leven en de composities van Jacobus Barbireau* (Utrecht, 1946), pp. 5–21; J. Van den Nieuwenhuizen, 'De koralen, de zangers en de zangmeesters van de Antwerpse O.-L.-Vrouwekerk tijdens de 15e eeuw', *Gouden jubileum*

Rob C. Wegman

of their time: Jacob Obrecht, Pierre de la Rue, Johannes Ghiselin, Jacobus Barbireau, Matthaeus Pipelare, Nicasius and Jheronimus de Clibano, Paulus de Roda and Hermannus de Atrio.[2] Other Marian confraternities in Brabant are also known to have cultivated polyphony, though probably on a lesser scale, for instance Brussels and Diest.[3] And many town archives in the Netherlands and

gedenkboek van de viering van 50 jaar heropgericht knapenkoor van de Onze-Lieve-Vrouwekatedraal te Antwerpen (Antwerp, 1978), pp. 29–72; K. K. Forney, 'Music, Ritual and Patronage at the Church of Our Lady, Antwerp', *Early Music History*, 7 (1987), pp. 1–57. The pay records of the Illustrious Confraternity of Our Lady at 's-Hertogenbosch provide a wealth of information on music and musical life in this establishment, and were published in transcription by W. F. H. Oldewelt, *Rekeningen van de Illustere Lieve Vrouwe Broederschap (1330–1375)* ('s-Hertogenbosch, 1925); A. Smijers, *De Illustre Lieve Vrouwe Broederschap te 's-Hertogenbosch* (Amsterdam, 1932), covering the period 1330–1500; A. Smijers, 'De Illustre Lieve Vrouwe Broederschap 's-Hertogenbosch', *Tijdschrift van de Vereeniging voor Nederlandsche Muziekgeschiedenis*, 15 (1935), pp. 1–105 [covering the period 1500–25]; 16 (1946), pp. 63–106 [1525–35] and 216 [1460–1]; 17 (1955), pp. 195–230 [1535–41]; M. A. Vente, 'De Illustre Lieve Vrouwe Broederschap te 's-Hertogenbosch', *Tijdschrift van de Vereeniging voor Nederlandse Muziekgeschiedenis*, 19 (1960–3), pp. 32–43 and 163–72. For general discussions on music at the confraternity in 's-Hertogenbosch, see A. Smijers, 'Meerstemmige muziek van de Illustre Lieve Vrouwe Broederschap te 's-Hertogenbosch, 1541–1615', *Tijdschrift van de Vereeniging voor Nederlandsche Muziekgeschiedenis*, 16 (1946), pp. 1–30; G. C. M. van Dijck, *De Bossche optimaten: Geschiedenis van de Illustre Lieve Vrouwebroederschap te 's-Hertogenbosch, 1318–1973*, Bijdragen tot de Geschiedenis van het Zuiden van Nederland 27 (Tilburg, 1973), pp. 51–3, 106–12 and 146–62. For music at the Confraternity of Our Lady at Bergen op Zoom, see A. Piscaer, 'De zangers van het Onze Lieve Vrouwe Gilde te Bergen op Zoom', *Land van mijn hart*, ed. L. G. J. Verberne and A. Weynen (Tilburg, 1952), pp. 70–81; K. (C. J. F.) Slootmans, 'De Hoge Lieve Vrouw van Bergen op Zoom', [*Jaarboek van de*] *Oudheidkundige kring 'De Ghulden Roos'*, Roosendaal, 24 (1964), pp. 20–48; 25 (1965), pp. 193–233; 26 (1966), pp. 161–84.

2 For Jacob Obrecht, Johannes Ghiselin and Paulus de Roda, see below. For Jheronimus and Nicasius de Clibano, see Smijers, *De Illustre Lieve Vrouwe Broederschap*, pp. 116–56; R. Woodley, 'Iohannes Tinctoris: A Review of the Documentary Biographical Evidence', *Journal of the American Musicological Society*, 34 (1981), p. 230; R. Strohm, *Music in Late Medieval Bruges* (Oxford, 1985), pp. 50 and 183; Forney, 'Music, Ritual and Patronage', pp. 37–8. For Hermannus de Atrio, who worked in 's-Hertogenbosch from 1493–4 to 1513–14, see R. Loyan, 'Hermannus de Atrio', *The New Grove Dictionary of Music and Musicians*, ed. S. Sadie, 20 vols. (London, 1980), VIII, p. 509, and F. A. D'Accone, 'The Singers of San Giovanni in Florence during the 15th Century', *Journal of the American Musicological Society*, 14 (1961), pp. 343–5 (perhaps related to the singers Jaspar de Atrio of Bruges and Johannes de Atrio of Rheims: see Strohm *op. cit.*, p. 182, and A. Pirro, 'Obrecht à Cambrai', *Tijdschrift van de Vereeniging voor Nederlandsche Muziekgeschiedenis*, 12 (1927), p. 80). For Jacobus Barbireau, see du Saar, *op. cit.*, Van den Nieuwenhuizen, *op. cit.*, Forney, *op. cit.*, and E. Kooiman, 'The Biography of Jacob Barbireau (1455–1491) Reviewed', *Tijdschrift van de Vereniging voor Nederlandse Muziekgeschiedenis*, 38 (1988), pp. 36–58. Pierre de la Rue worked in 's-Hertogenbosch 1489/90–1491/2; see Smijers, *De Illustre Lieve Vrouwe Broederschap*, pp. 187–92 ('heer Peteren van Straten ons tenorist'). Matthaeus Pipelare worked in Antwerp and was *sangmeester* in 's-Hertogenbosch in 1498–1500 (see Smijers, *De Illustre Lieve Vrouwe Broederschap*, pp. 206–14). The priest Symon Britonis who worked as a 'bovensenger' in 's-Hertogenbosch in 1482–3 and 1483–4 (*ibid.*) is not to be identified with the singer and composer Simon le Breton, since the latter died in 1473 (cf. D. Fallows, 'Simon', *The New Grove Dictionary*, XVII, pp. 323–4).

3 For Brussels, see B. Haggh, 'Music, Liturgy, and Ceremony in Brussels, 1350–1500'

Belgium must possess documentation on the use of polyphony in still other guilds and confraternities.

Contacts and cross-influences between the musical establishments of Brabant were close and frequent. The pay records of Antwerp, 's-Hertogenbosch and Bergen op Zoom, for instance, tell us repeatedly of reciprocal visits of singers and choirmasters, exchanges of repertory, and mutual assistance in the recruitment of musicians. Moreover, singers moved easily from one confraternity to another: the associations were, after all, identical with respect to organisation, sources of income and musico-liturgical practice. Musical life in Brabant was homogeneous and closely integrated. It thus provides a good basis for direct comparisons between different centres.

Such comparisons are important for two reasons. First, they may help us to explain the extraordinary mobility of fifteenth-century musicians, who drifted freely in and out of various institutions, 'living from day to day like the birds on the branches', as one contemporary put it.[4] The key to that phenomenon must surely lie in the recruitment policy and patronage exerted by the musical centres,[5] which brings us to the second reason. The relative status and importance of centres depended on the funds they could extract to carry out an effective recruitment policy. Competition was fierce; good singers were easily cajoled into working elsewhere. But how did the confraternities spend their money? Were the richest establishments also the most successful ones? To answer these and similar questions one must make precisely the sorts of comparison that musical life in Brabant affords.

The Guild of Our Lady at Bergen op Zoom highlights many of the problems of patronage that musical centres in Brabant had to face. Founded as a minor musical establishment in 1470, it developed

(Ph.D. dissertation, University of Illinois at Urbana-Champaign, 1988). I am indebted to Prof. Haggh for sending me the portions of her thesis that are relevant to Bergen op Zoom. The payment records of 1498–9 of the confraternity at 's-Hertogenbosch mention 'the choirmaster of Diest, two choristers and another priest, also a singer' ('[den] sangmeester van Diest, twee coralen ende enen anderen her, oic senger') who had come from Diest; see Smijers, *De Illustre Lieve Vrouwe Broederschap*, p. 209.

[4] This was Ercole I d'Este of Ferrara in a letter of 1476, see D. Fallows, 'The Contenance angloise: English Influence on Continental Composers of the Fifteenth Century', *Renaissance Studies*, 1 (1987), p. 189.

[5] See, for instance, C. Wright, 'Antoine Brumel and Patronage at Paris', *Music in Medieval and Early Modern Europe: Patronage, Sources and Texts*, ed. I. Fenlon (Cambridge, 1981), pp. 55–6.

within three decades into an institution of international stature, challenging even the ducal chapel of Philip the Fair. How was the guild able to achieve such prominence so rapidly? Financial data derived from its pay records, if compared with those of other Brabant confraternities, may help to answer that question. The guild of Bergen op Zoom is interesting also because of its importance for Jacob Obrecht. Obrecht's international reputation rose rapidly in the 1480s and 1490s, culminating in his appointment as *maestro di cappella* at the court of Ferrara. His career, and the development of the Bergen op Zoom guild, went their own independent ways but intersected three times. The different terms under which the composer was employed each time tell us as much about him as they do about the guild.

This article describes the foundation and early development of the Guild of Our Lady at Bergen op Zoom as a musical institution, and re-examines Obrecht's association with the guild. The first and third sections deal with musical life during the periods 1470–94 and 1494–1510; the second concerns Obrecht's relationship with Bergen op Zoom.

THE CREATION OF A MUSICAL CENTRE UNDER
JOHN II OF GLYMES: 1470–1494

On several counts one would not expect Bergen op Zoom to have developed into an important musical centre in the late fifteenth century. In 1496 the town numbered only about 8000 inhabitants, against around 16,000 inhabitants in 's-Hertogenbosch and some 30,000 in Antwerp. It possessed only four religious establishments, the parish church of St Gertrude and three monasteries, whereas 's-Hertogenbosch counted, apart from the parish church of St John, eighteen monasteries and twelve chapels, and Antwerp could boast forty-two ecclesiastical institutions, five of which were parish churches.

Yet Bergen op Zoom, strategically placed outside the Scheldt estuary, became increasingly prosperous in the course of the fifteenth century thanks to the international fairs that were held there each year, around Easter and the feast of St Martin (11 November).[6]

---

[6] C. J. F. Slootmans, *Paas- en Koudemarkten te Bergen op Zoom, 1365–1565*, Bijdragen tot de Geschiedenis van het Zuiden van Nederland 64 (Tilburg, 1985), 3 vols.

Already in the fourteenth century the lords of Bergen op Zoom had bargained with other feudal overlords to secure safe-conducts for merchants attending the fairs. Consequently Bergen op Zoom became an important meeting-place for merchants from all over the Low Countries, Germany, northern France, Scotland and England.[7]

In the fifteenth century, the increasing revenues from the fairs enabled John II of Glymes (1417–94), lord of Bergen op Zoom, to carry out an extensive rebuilding programme in the parish church of St Gertrude – lasting from 1443 to 1470. The relations between the lords of Bergen op Zoom and St Gertrude's during the fifteenth century were very close, though not always without considerable friction. It was with the financial support of the lord and the city of Bergen op Zoom that St Gertrude's had been raised to the dignity of a collegiate church in 1428 (formally ratified by Pope Eugenius IV on 7 July 1442). In return John and his successors acquired the right of patronage over the church, and the chapter had to render account to him and the city for its financial management.[8] John II was prepared to pay considerable sums of money in order to enhance the prestige of 'his' church. Plans to expand the fourteenth-century building date back to as early as 1443, when the Antwerp master builder Evert van der Veeweyden, *alias* Spoorwater, was commissioned to design a new choir aisle. The first stone of this aisle was laid in the same year.[9] However, when the church was severely damaged in the city fire of 1444, Spoorwater made a design for a much larger building, containing transepts, aisles and radiating chapels, which was erected under his supervision during the following twenty-six years (see Figure 1). As part of this extensive rebuilding, a chapel of the Holy Virgin was constructed at the north side of the choir, presumably in the 1460s.[10] After the church was completed, in 1470, it was further enriched

---

[7] It is interesting to note that Bergen op Zoom was also visited by William Caxton in the early 1470s. In the City Accounts of 1474–5 (BOZ SA 245.2), I have found a payment to '*meester* William Caxton, as delegate of the King of England' ('meester Willeme Kaxton als gecommitteirde vanden Coninge van Ingelant'; fol. 70[r], January or February 1475) and in the City Accounts of 1475–6 again to 'William Caxton and other delegates of the King of England' ('Willeme Caxtone ende anderen gedeputeirden vanden coninge van Ingelant'; BOZ SA 245.3, fol. 123[v], 8 April 1475).

[8] C. J. F. Slootmans, *Jan metten Lippen, zijn familie en zijn stad: Een geschiedenis der Bergen-op-Zoomsche heeren van Glymes* (Rotterdam, 1945), pp. 14–15, 87–9.

[9] R. de Kind, 'De plaats van de Sint-Gertrudiskerk in het werk van Evert Spoorwater', *Bergen op Zoom gebouwd en beschouwd* (Alphen aan den Rijn, 1987), pp. 138–57.

[10] Slootmans, 'De Hoge Lieve Vrouw' (1964), pp. 21 and 34 n. 9.

with a large organ (built by Daniel van der Distelen of Mechlin), lofts and choir stalls, all of which were finished by 1477.[11]

There can be little doubt that it was an integral part of John II's plans to provide funds for polyphony. It is certain that there was already an ensemble comprising at least one adult master and a group of boys by the late 1460s, when the new building was nearing its completion. Unfortunately, we possess almost no documentation on the cultivation of polyphonic music prior to 1470; this is mainly because no city accounts from the period 1452–70 survive and the accounts of the church itself all seem to be lost.[12] The earliest surviving reference to the cultivation of polyphony in Bergen op Zoom comes from a letter by the local schoolmaster Jan van den Veren, dated September 1465, in which he offers his position to an unnamed colleague working at St Gilles in Bruges. The letter is interesting because it provides an insight into the incentives for fifteenth-century scholars and clergymen to seek employment elsewhere:[13]

Besides, the [schoolmaster's] income from the choir is estimated at over 480 groats, and, as concerns the singing, you will be in charge only of Gregorian chant, even though you are familiar with the Boethian formulas. Discant and the scales will be taught by somebody else, who adorns the choir with his art [i.e. the choirmaster]. You will marvel at the state and the ceremonies of the church of Bergen. Everywhere you will find the place agreeable, both inside and out (as you perhaps well know). There are two markets, one in the winter and one around Easter, both drawing huge numbers of merchants. Many people from Bruges often come to Bergen and *vice versa*. The passage is easy, both inwards and outwards, and there are

---

[11] See M. A. Vente, *Bouwstoffen tot de geschiedenis van het Nederlandse orgel in de 16e eeuw* (Amsterdam, 1942).

[12] For what is left of the chapter accounts, see M. A. Vente and C. Vlam, eds., *Bouwstenen voor een geschiedenis der toonkunst in de Nederlanden*, 4 vols., II (Amsterdam, 1971), pp. 49–50 (covering the periods 1510/11–1518/19 and 1560/1–1569/70).

[13] 'Preterea accidentia in choro pluris quam duabis libris grossis estimantur, neque aliquid onus cantus nisi gregoriani tibi dabitur, tametsi boeticus modulos nosti. Discantui et coklibus docendis alius preest qui chorum sua arte decorat. Statum autem et cerimonias ecclesie Bergensis tute miraberis. Locum per omnia amenum intus et foris sicut forte bene nosti offendes. Bine apud nos nundine sunt: une hiemales, altere paschalis, mercatorum confluxus non modicus. Multi multotiens Brugenses Bergis adveniunt et e contra. Facilis ultro citroque transitus est, navium copia non deest, si fortassis navigandum tibi foret vel navigio aliquid aut adducendum aut reducendum. Denique de annona aut penu quid scribam? Omnia parvo emuntur.'; G. G. Meersseman, 'L'épistolaire de Jean van den Veren et le début de l'humanisme en Flandre', *Humanistica Lovaniensa*, 19 (1970), pp. 179–80. (I am indebted to Reinhard Strohm for drawing my attention to this letter, and to Eddie Vetter for helping me with the interpretation of the Latin text.)

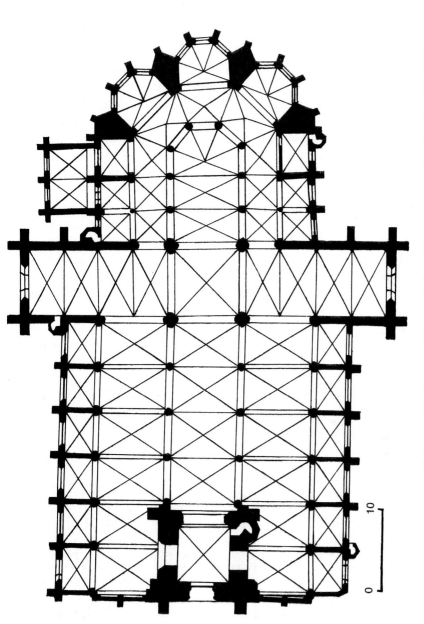

Figure 1   The church of St Gertrude in Bergen op Zoom in the later fifteenth century (based on R. de Kind, 'De plaats van de Sint-Gertrudiskerk in het werk van Evert Spoorwater', *Bergen op Zoom gebouwd en beschouwd* [Alphen aan den Rijn, 1987], pp. 140–1). The Chapel of Our Lady was sited presumably at the north side of the choir.

many ships (in case you have to travel, or to forward something by boat). What should I finally write about food and provisions? Everything is cheap.

From legal documents we know that as early as 1467 a *meester* Willem [de] Brouwer *alias* Scotelaer was 'sancmeester inder kerken van berghen' (choirmaster in the church of Bergen) and 'voight vanden chorailen' (guardian of the choristers).[14] There is no evidence that adult singers were employed at St Gertrude's prior to 1470. The choirmaster, Willem de Brouwer, may be the composer of the Middle Dutch song *So lanc so meer* in El Escorial, Biblioteca del Monasterio, MS iv.a.24 (*c.* 1470), which is attributed in this source to 'W. Braxatoris', a Latin corruption of the French word for 'brouwer' (=brewer), 'brassart'.[15] No compositions seem to have survived under his sobriquet Scotelaer. By 1486 his wife, Margriet vanden Ghoir, is mentioned as a widow in legal documents of Bergen op Zoom.[16] Willem de Brouwer died presumably before 1480, for by this year his position had been taken over by Jacob Obrecht.

From 1470 onwards, the accounts of the town council of Bergen op Zoom survive, and they give specific information on the services sponsored by the city. We learn that there was a trade guild of St Anthony in Bergen op Zoom, which celebrated the feast-day of the saint (17 January) with an annual procession followed by a banquet at the town hall. As part of the festivities, a polyphonic Mass was sung at the altar of St Anthony in the church of Bergen op Zoom. One of the more specific descriptions of this service is to be found in the city accounts for 1472–3:[17]

---

[14] Slootmans, 'De Hoge Lieve Vrouw' (1965), p. 213 n. 7. The documents are: BOZ R 285 fol. 125ʳ (16 June 1467), R 285 fol. 165ʳ (18 February 1468), and R 214 fol. 57ᵛ (2 March 1470).

[15] Edited in: P. Gülke, ed., *Johannes Pullois: opera omnia*, Corpus Mensurabilis Musicae 41 (n.p., 1967), p. 43; M. K. Hanen, ed., *The Chansonnier El Escorial iv. a. 24*, 3 vols. (Henryville, Ottawa and Binningen, 1983), iii, pp. 382–4 (see also i, pp. 94–5). The chanson is ascribed to Jean Pullois in Trent, Museo Provinciale d'Arte, MS 90, fol. 344ᵛ (*So lang si mir in meinem synn*). For the identification of 'Braxator[is]' as 'Brauwere', see Strohm, *Music in Late Medieval Bruges*, p. 137. See also the accounts for 1450 of the Burgundian chapel, where Johannes Brevere is called 'dit Brassatoris' (J. Marix, *Histoire de la musique et des musiciens de la cour de Bourgogne sous le règne de Philippe le Bon* (Strasbourg, 1939), p. 250).

[16] BOZ R 301, fol. 44ʳ (11 May 1486).

[17] 'Vander missen op sente anthonis dach te solempniseren met discante, welke misse in sente anthonis choir voer de hootmisse gedaen waert; betailt den priestere die de misse celebreerde: vj groten; meestere willeme den sanghmeester met sijnen choralen: xviij groten; den organist metten blaser vij½ groten. Van luydene xviij groten mitgaders der stad pijpers voir sente anthonis spelen xij groten, maict tsamen v sc. j½ den.br.'; BOZ SA 244 (SR 1472–3), fol. 39ᵛ.

For celebrating the Mass on St Anthony's day with polyphony, which Mass was done in the chapel of St Anthony before High Mass; paid to the priest who celebrated the Mass: 6 groats; to *meester* Willeme the choirmaster with his choristers: 18 groats; to the organist with the bellows pumper: 7.5 groats; for the ringing [of the church bells]: 18 groats; and to the city pipers for the plays of St Anthony: 12 groats; together: 61.5 groats.

A few years later it became customary to celebrate all services on St Anthony's day with polyphony; these latter services, too, were financed by the city of Bergen op Zoom. One may assume that similar celebrations of the other major feast-days were financed by the chapter of St Gertrude's: this is certainly true of the feast of the Finding of the Cross (3 May, the high point of the liturgical year in Bergen op Zoom), Christmas and Easter, and very probably also of the six Marian feasts.

An important musical establishment was created when John of Glymes and the city council of Bergen op Zoom founded the Guild of Our Lady, in or shortly before 1470. This guild was based in the Chapel of the Holy Virgin, which had just been completed. In the chapel was erected a richly decorated statue of Mary, which was venerated by the members of the guild and very probably also by the citizens of Bergen op Zoom. The statue was carried in procession each year on 'ommeganck dach' or 'processie dach' (*litaniis maior*, 23 April; Holy Cross procession, 3 May), and on the feast of the Assumption (15 August). The number of (lay) members of the guild fluctuated between about 750 and 1100. Their entrance fees, gifts and bequests (often estates and immovables, which yielded annual levies and interests) were an important source of income for the guild.[18]

On 24 December 1470, a daily polyphonic *Lof* service in the Chapel of Our Lady was established in the following ordinance (cf. Appendix 1):

Concerning the *Lof* of Our Lady, and how much the choirmaster and the singers etc. shall receive.

Anno [14]70, on the 24th day of December, [was] commissioned and decreed concerning the foundation and the observance of the *Lof* of Our Lady and all that pertains to it, by my dear lord of Bergen, [in his capacity as] head of the Guild of Our Lady in the church of Bergen, [with] the burgomaster and the aldermen:

---

[18] Slootmans, 'De Hoge Lieve Vrouw' (1966), pp. 161–3.

Figure 2 Map of Bergen op Zoom in the early sixteenth century; from Guicciardini, *Beschrijvinghe der gantser Nederlanden* (Amsterdam 1618) (Bergen op Zoom, City Archive)

[1] First, that *meester* Willem *de sanckmeester* will from now on be obliged to come to the church every evening and sing the *Lof* of Our Lady with the children, for which he shall receive six rheinguldens for his own part, and four rheinguldens for the children, each [rheingulden] equalling twenty stivers [=60 groats].

[2] Also he will be obliged to divide and distribute among his fellow singers the *loten* [tokens]; each [singer] shall be given a *loot* representing the appointed fee at which the rulers of the same guild desire him [to sing].

[3] *Item*, the *opperste tenoriste* [highest tenor] shall receive, for each time he appears at this same *Lof*, one groat; and each of the other singers – up to the maximum of five [singers] agreed by the chapter [of St Gertrude's] – [shall receive], for each time he appears, one *oortken* [=0.75 groat].

[4] And for this [reward], all the aforementioned persons will be obliged to sing at all the Masses of Our Lady, at the same rate of payment as each receives for the *Lof* in the evening.

[5] *Item*, certain *loten* will be made and [on each *loot*] shall be written the appointed value of the coins that each [singer] earns for his service; the rulers are obliged to take over the *loten* from the singers four times per year, and then to pay each his due.

[6] *Item*, my lord had consented that his followers will pay one *loot* of one *oortken* to each of the choirmasters coming from elsewhere for each time they come and sing the *Lof* of Our Lady; and the rulers will immediately exchange this same [*loot*] for money . . .

[8] *Item*, the lords of the chapter [of St Gertrude's] have consented and declared that they shall have the bells rung [every] evening after the *Lof*, without charging [the Guild of] Our Lady for this.

The *Lof* or *Salve* was a non-liturgical, devotional service usually held after Vespers or Compline. It featured the singing of antiphons and hymns (often accompanied by, or alternating with, the organ), the saying of prayers, and the ringing of church bells. The *Lof* enjoyed great popularity in the Low Countries, particularly with the lay confraternities. The services could be simple or as elaborate as the funds of the confraternities allowed, ranging from modest devotional meetings that did not involve polyphony to splendid and sumptuous 'concerts' for the musical entertainment of citizens and visitors. The foundation document of the *Lof* service in Bergen op Zoom indicates that a regular polyphonic practice had been established by 1470. This must obviously have raised the prestige of the guild; yet a comparison with the foundation document of the *Lof* service at the Confraternity of Our Lady in Antwerp (1479)[19] indicates that

---

[19]   Forney, 'Music, Ritual and Patronage', pp. 10 and 52–4.

Table 1 *Budgets reserved for polyphony in the foundation documents of the Lof services at the Guilds of Our Lady at Bergen op Zoom and Antwerp*

Employees	Bergen op Zoom (1470) 365 *Loven*+6 Marian Masses	Antwerp (1479)[a] 365 *Loven*
Priests	—	720
		720
Choirmaster	360	960
Choristers	240	480
Singers	371 (*opperste tenoriste*)	365
	278.25	365
	278.25	365
	278.25	365
	278.25	
	278.25	
Organist	—	960
Bellringer	—	480
Carilloneur	—	360
Total	2362.25	6140

[a]Based on K. K. Forney, 'Music, Ritual and Patronage at the Church of Our Lady, Antwerp', *Early Music History*, 7 (1987), pp.10 and 52–4.

the budget reserved for polyphonic music was still rather modest (Table 1).

Although in Bergen op Zoom the choir consisted of six adult singers (as against four in Antwerp; excluding the choirmaster), there was as yet no priest or organist involved in the services (an organ was built in St Gertrude's only in 1472–7). Moreover, the musicians' fees were generally lower than those in Antwerp: in Bergen op Zoom only the highest tenor (*opperste tenoriste*) received the same salary as his colleagues in Antwerp: one groat per *loot*; his fellow singers had to content themselves with *loten* of 0.75 groat. And the *sangmeester* of Bergen op Zoom was salaried very poorly indeed, compared with his colleague in Antwerp. For his services he received an annual stipend of only 360 groats (as against 960 in Antwerp), while his duties included more: in addition to the *Lof* he was obliged to sing at Mass on each of the six Marian feasts of the liturgical year.

In comparison with the wealthy confraternity of 's-Hertogen-bosch, where there had been a continuous polyphonic tradition from the fourteenth century onwards, both Antwerp and Bergen op Zoom were low-budget establishments: in 1470–1 the annual salary of even the lowest-paid singer at 's-Hertogenbosch was 13 rheinguldens (780 groats), about twice as much as that of his colleagues in the other two establishments.[20] Around 1470, the budget reserved for musicians' salaries in 's-Hertogenbosch was about 10,000 groats.

In such circumstances it must have been extremely difficult for the Guild of Our Lady at Bergen op Zoom to attract and to keep singers of sufficient quality.[21] However, thanks to the patronage of John of Glymes, this situation was soon to change radically. On 31 December 1474 the lord of Bergen op Zoom and the city government renounced their right to levy stallage at the twice-yearly Bergen op Zoom fairs to the Guild of Our Lady.[22] Through this generous gesture, the annual revenues of the guild nearly doubled, with an increase of over 15,000 groats. The dean and jurors of the guild were obliged to submit each year on the Feast of the Assumption (15 August) a detailed account of their receipts and expenditure, which was then to be approved by the lord and the city government. From 1480–1 onwards, virtually all these accounts survive.[23] Fortunately they are itemised, and in each one of them there is a separate section listing the expenditure on the polyphonic services.

A brief glance at the accounts of the first two decades (see

[20] This was *heer* Mathijs van Bergen, apparently a native of Bergen op Zoom; see Smijers, *De Illustre Lieve Vrouwe Broederschap*, p. 144 (accounts of 1470–1).

[21] One reference to the payment of singers, in 1472–3, is in the accounts of the steward of the territory of Bergen op Zoom (BOZ ARR 648.3, fol. 23ᵛ): '*Item* at the command of my lord [to] the countess's son [?] for singing the *Lof* of Our Lady, paid for the *loten* he had earned, 114 groats; and to the other singers from elsewhere to whom my dear lord himself gives the *loten*, paid in the last year 33 groats' ('Item ten bevele mijns heeren gravinnen soen van onser liever vrouwen loeve te singene na tloet dat hij gewonnen hadde betaelt ix sc. vj den.br. / den anderen sangers van buytten dien mijn lief heer tloet selve doet geven ende betaelt bynnen desen jaer betaelt noch. betaelt ij sc. ix den.gr.br.'). F. Caland, 'Bergen op Zoom van 1412 tot 1613 (plus 1716)', *Bouwsteenen: Jaarboek der Vereeniging voor Noord-Nederlandsch Muziekgeschiedenis*, 2 (1872–4), pp. 189–93, a collection of extracts from the Bergen op Zoom city accounts, includes one from the now lost accounts of 1471–2: 'Paid to *meester* Willem the choirmaster with his choristers, 18 groats; to the organist with the bellows pumper, and Jan van Oudenhoven, the cantor, 7.5 groats' ('Bet. mr. Willem de sangmeestere met sijnen choralen xviij gr.; de orghaniste metten blasere ende Jan van Oudenhoven den cantoer, vijꜝ gr.', p. 190). Jan van Oudenhoven was still active as a singer in 1474–5, when he was inscribed as a member of the Confraternity of Our Lady at 's-Hertogenbosch: 'Item heer Jan van Andehoven, canonic ende senger te Bergen opten Zoeme'; Smijers, *De Illustre Lieve Vrouwe Broederschap*, p. 155).

[22] Slootmans, *Paas- en Koudemarkten*, I, pp. 272–3. The ordinance of 31 December 1474 is transcribed in Slootmans, 'De Hoge Lieve Vrouw' (1964), p. 43.

[23] BOZ SA, inv. nos. 861.1–861.89 (OLV, covering the period 1480/1–1575/6; accounts of 1484–5, 1497–8, 1508/9–1510/11, 1512–13, 1532–3, and 1545–6 are missing).

Rob C. Wegman

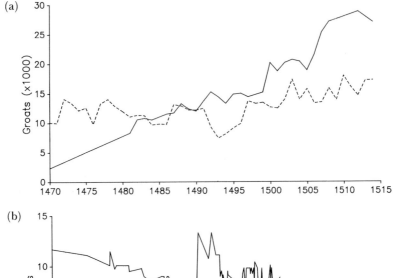

Figure 3 (a) Expenditure on musicians' salaries at the Guild of Our Lady in Bergen op Zoom (solid line) and the Illustrious Confraternity in 's-Hertogenbosch (broken line) during the period 1470–1515 (in thousands of Brabant groats). Figures for 's-Hertogenbosch are based on A. Smijers, *De Illustre Lieve Vrouwe Broederschap te 's-Hertogenbosch* (Amsterdam, 1932), and A. Smijers, 'De Illustre Lieve Vrouwe Broederschap te 's-Hertogenbosch', *Tijdschrift van de Vereeniging voor Neder-landsche Muziekgeschiedenis*, 15 (1935), pp. 1–105. (b) Relative value of the Brabant groat (indicated in numbers of Venetian ducats that could be purchased with 1000 Brabant groats), based on P. Spufford, with W. Wilkinson and S. Tolley, eds., *Handbook of Medieval Exchange*, Royal Historical Society Guides and Handbooks 13 (London, 1986), pp. 217–23 (see n. 24).

Appendix 2) is sufficient to show that much had changed since 1470. By 1480–1, expenditure on music had increased by a factor of approximately 3.5 in relation to the budget estimated in the ordinance of 1470; in the next years this figure rose quickly to about 4.5 (1481–2 and 1482–3), 5 (1486–7), 5.5 (1487–8) and 6 (1491–2) (see the solid line in Figure 3a).

Naturally, such figures need interpreting with caution, particularly in view of the sharp inflation which the Brabant groat suffered during the late fifteenth century. Yet the funds for the polyphonic services were increasing in real terms. Figure 3b indicates the relative value of the groat in Venetian ducats (one of Europe's most stable currencies; it was struck from pure gold).[24] The groat devalued considerably in the 1470s and 1480s, until Maximilian of Habsburg took deliberate measures to curb the inflation in his ordinance of Christmas Eve 1489.[25] After 1489, however, the groat still kept devaluing. The abrupt adjustment of the exchange rate in 1489 is not in any way reflected in the line representing the expenditure on music at Bergen op Zoom. The reason for this is that the salaries of musicians remained stable nominally; that is, the musicians kept rendering the same services for the same nominal amount of money, regardless of spending power. This is illustrated by the account of the Guild of Our Lady of 1489–90. This account consists of two sections, divided by the date of Maximilian's ordinance of 1489: one section 'in lichten ghelde' (devalued money, running from 15 August to 24 December 1489) and one 'in zwaren ghelde' (revalued money, running from 25 December 1489 to 15 August 1490).[26] In spite of the revaluation, the musicians received the same amount of groats for each *loot* both before and after the ordinance. Thus the inflation affected the standard of living of the musicians, but not the quality of the polyphonic services.[27]

[24] Based on P. Spufford, with W. Wilkinson and S. Tolley, eds., *Handbook of Medieval Exchange*, Royal Historical Society Guides and Handbooks 13 (London, 1986), pp. 217–23, where the values of the Venetian ducat are given in Flemish groats for the period 1370–1500. After the unification of the coinages of the Burgundian Netherlands in 1433–5 the Brabant groat was tied to the Flemish groat in a fixed relationship of 3 Brabant groats=2 Flemish groats. Hence, in order to arrive at the values in Figure 3b, all values in the *Handbook of Medieval Exchange*, pp. 222–3, have been multiplied by 1.5. The expenditure on music in 's-Hertogenbosch (Figure 3b), which is recorded in the accounts in rheinguldens, has been converted into Brabant currency at the fixed rate of 1 rheingulden=60 Brabant groats. Although by 1467 the rheingulden had officially become worth 63 Brabant groats, and by 1488 135 Brabant groats, 'gulden' still remained in use, into the sixteenth century, as the name of the pound of 40 Flemish groats (=60 Brabant groats), and it was treated as such in the accounts of both Bergen op Zoom and 's-Hertogenbosch.

[25] In his ordinance of 1489, Maximilian ordered new groats, stivers etc. to be struck whose intrinsic value (silver content) was three times that of the old ones (which had greatly devalued mainly as a result of Maximilian's own debasements in the 1480s). The silver content of the Brabant groat at once nearly trebled, from *c.* 0.167 to 0.499 grammes (cf. E. Scholliers, *Loonarbeid en honger: De levensstandaard in de XVe en XVIe eeuw te Antwerpen* (Antwerp, 1960), pp. 221–2) and so did its value expressed in Venetian ducats (see Figure 3b).

[26] The accounts of 1489–90 of the Confraternity of Our Lady at 's-Hertogenbosch are also divided into two sections, corresponding to the different values of the coinage, cf. Smijers, *De Illustre Lieve Vrouwe Broederschap*, pp. 187–9.

[27] The effects of inflation (and revaluation) were of course particularly felt in the prices of

The broken line in Figure 3a represents the annual expenditure on musicians' salaries at the Confraternity of Our Lady at 's-Hertogenbosch. It shows that Bergen op Zoom was overtaking 's-Hertogenbosch's position as the best-funded musical establishment of Brabant by 1490. Unfortunately, the accounts of the Guild of Our Lady at Antwerp are not structured in such a way as to allow us to establish the total annual expenditure on music. However, several indications in these accounts suggest that, financially speaking, Antwerp lagged far behind the other two cities.

As already indicated, the cause for Bergen op Zoom's spectacular rise as a musical centre in the 1480s and 1490s lies in the revenues from the twice-yearly fairs. Between 1480 and 1498 these revenues nearly doubled; they then remained stable until 1530, when economic decline set in as a result of the severe floodings of Zuid Beveland.[28] As Figure 3a shows, the expenditure on music at the Guild of Our Lady also nearly doubled between 1480 and 1498. After 1494 the guild was able to pay quite substantial salaries to some of its musicians, as will be discussed later.

For the first seven years after 1480–1 the accounts of the Guild of Our Lady in Bergen op Zoom record only the total sum paid to each singer and in most cases also the monetary value of the *loten*. On the basis of these data the number of *loten* cashed by each singer can be easily reconstructed; from 1491–2 onwards, this number is always specified in the accounts. The nominal monetary value of the *loten* under John II of Glymes ranged from 1 to 3.75 groats. It is obvious that by differentiating between the fees of singers – no doubt in appreciation of their artistic competence – the guild was able to attract some of the finest composers and singers of Brabant and the surrounding area. Indeed, from an analysis of the accounts from the period 1480/1–1493/4 it appears that the main cause for the steady increase in spending on music (apart from pay rises) lies in recruitment policy: when new singers were employed, they were generally appointed at higher fees than their predecessors who had left the previous year.[29] This indicates that there was a deliberate effort to

goods imported from countries with strong, stable currencies, especially Italy. However, the standard of living was also falling in general in Brabant after *c.* 1475 (cf. Scholliers, *Loonarbeid en honger*, pp. 124–6).

[28] See the graph in Slootmans, *Paas- en Koudemarkten*, I, pp. 286–7, which indicates the revenues of the Bergen op Zoom fairs, and the numbers of merchants attending the fairs, for the period 1481–1543.

[29] See Appendix 3 below, which indicates the average value of the *loten* distributed each year.

improve the quality of the choir gradually by employing better singers.

Appendix 2 shows that the maximum number of *loten* that a singer could accumulate in a year lies generally between about 420 and 440. If we subtract the 365 *loten* of the daily *Lof* services, this leaves between fifty-five and seventy-five *loten* for various other services in the course of the liturgical year. It is certain that these other services were Masses, since the titles heading the chapters listing expenditure on music read in all the accounts: 'Other expenses, for Masses for Our Lady, held with singers, choristers and the organist, as well as for the *Lof* of Our Lady every evening, and all that pertains to it' ('Ander uutgheven van missen voer onser liever vrouwen te doen doene metten sangheren coralen ende organiste midtsgaders oic van onser liever vrouwen love alle avonde ende des daeraen cleeft'). It is difficult to establish precisely which Masses were celebrated with polyphony. We do, however, get an impression by looking at the services which were held at the Confraternity of Our Lady in 's-Hertogenbosch: here at least sixty-nine polyphonic Mass services were held in addition to the daily *Loven*: seven Marian feasts, six feasts of various saints, four quarterly Requiems for deceased members, and fifty-two weekly Wednesday Masses.[30] In the accounts of the Bergen op Zoom guild, the revenues of the collections held during the services are listed in a separate chapter, and are specified by feast-day: these feast-days include the six Marian feasts, All Saints, Christmas, Easter, Whitsunday, and the feasts of the Holy Cross and St Catharine. One may assume that some of these were among the major feasts at the guild, and that they were duly celebrated with polyphony. An entry in the city accounts of 1487–8 shows that the triplex feasts, in the church proper, always included polyphony:

To the same lords [of the chapter of St Gertrude's] with whom it has been agreed on behalf of the city that they will celebrate all hours of St Anthony from the first to the second Vespers inclusive with the organ and polyphony, *in the same manner as is done on the triplex feasts and days* [my italics], paid now as in the other, previous, accounts, 300 groats.[31]

[30] Van Dijck, *De Bossche optimaten*, pp. 107–8.
[31] 'Den selven heeren metten welken is overcomen vanden statweghen dat zy den dienst van sente anthoenis vanden yersten vesperen totten tweeden toe inclux tot allen getiden houden zullen met orghelen ende discante geliic men doet in anderen triplicen feesten ende hoochtijden betailt nu als in anderen voirgaenden rekeningen – xxv sc.'; BOZ SA 250.1 (SR 1487–8), fol. 73v.

There is evidence that a weekly Mass of Our Lady was solemnly celebrated on Saturdays in the church of Bergen op Zoom.[32] Together with the feasts mentioned earlier, and possible commemorative Masses requested by donors, this would add up to more than sixty Masses per year.

The above data indicate that the fifty-five to seventy-five additional Masses were probably fairly evenly divided over the liturgical year. Hence, the maximum number of *loten* that could be accumulated by a singer in a month or a season probably remained stable regardless of the time of year. With this knowledge in mind, it becomes possible to make a number of useful calculations. For instance, if a singer was appointed or discharged in the course of the financial year, the number of *loten* he had collected allows us to calculate the minimum number of days he must have been in service during that year. In the financial year 15 August 1496–15 August 1497, for example, Jacob Obrecht cashed fifty-two *loten*. The following sum allows us to conclude that he must have worked in Bergen op Zoom for at least forty-three days, and hence that he was almost certainly appointed as a singer before 3 July 1497:

$$\frac{52\ loten}{420\text{–}40\ loten}\times 365 \text{ days}=c.\ 43\text{–}5 \text{ days}$$

It is known that Obrecht was still working as a choirmaster in Antwerp on 23 April 1497 (when 'meester Jacobe den sangmeester van Antwerpen' was mentioned in the city accounts of Bergen op Zoom).[33] Since the accounts of the Guild of Our Lady at Antwerp record the payment of the full annual salary to 'den sangmeester' on 24 June 1497 (the last day of the financial year 1496–7 in Antwerp),[34] it can be concluded that Obrecht went to Bergen op Zoom between 24 June and 3 July 1497.

[32] Slootmans, 'De Hoge Lieve Vrouw' (1965), p. 218 n. 83.
[33] 'On the same [procession] day, given to *meestere* Jacobe the choirmaster of Antwerp, six *gelten* Rhine wine [=c. 16.5 litres] at the same price as above [i.e. 12 groats per *gelte*] makes 72 groats' ('Opten selven [ommeganck] dach geschoncken meestere Jacobe den sangmeestere van Antwerpen zesse ghelten rjns wijns ten prijse als voerscreven, facit vj sc.'; BOZ SA 253 (SR 1 March 1497–1 March 1498), fol. 38[r]).
[34] 'Paid to the choirmaster his wage for this year, according to custom: 1080 groats' ('Betaelt den sangmeester van zijnen loen vander jare nader costumen iiij lb. x sc.'; Antwerp, Cathedral Archive, Rekeningen van het Gilde van het Onze Lieve Vrouwelof, 1487–1527, fol. 89[r]).

To take the reverse approach, the accounts of the Guild of Our Lady at Bergen op Zoom tell us that the singer Symon of Amerode received a pay rise, from 1.5 to 2.25 groats per *loot*, on Maundy Thursday (23 March) 1486, and that his total income between 15 August 1485 and 15 August 1486 was 685.5 groats. So Symon received *x loten* of 1.5 groats in period A (219 days), and *y loten* of 2.25 groats in period B (146 days).

The maximum number of *loten* that Symon could have earned in period A is $(219 \div 365) \times c. 440 = 264$ *loten* of 1.5 groats ($= 396$ groats). This leaves $685.5 - 396 = 289.5$ groats for period B, equalling $289.5 \div 2.25 = c. 129$ *loten*. Together, this adds up to $264 + 129 = 393$ *loten*.

Conversely, the maximum number of *loten* that Symon could have earned in period B is $(146 \div 365) \times c. 440 = 176$ *loten* of 2.25 groats ($= 396$ groats). This leaves $685.5 - 396 = 289.5$ groats for period A, equalling $289.5 \div 1.5 = 193$ *loten*. Together this adds up to 369 *loten*.

Therefore we can be almost certain that Symon of Amerode earned between 369 and 393 *loten* in 1485–6.

It is partly with the help of such calculations that we are able to calculate the total annual number of *loten* distributed among the singers and the choirmaster (see Appendix 3). During the period 1482/3–1496/7, and again after 1506–7, this number fluctuated between *c.* 2750 and *c.* 3300; in the period 1498/9–1505/6 it generally fluctuated between *c.* 2000 and *c.* 2500. With an average number of services per year of *c.* 420–40, this means that the average number of musicians involved in each service (including the choirmaster, but excluding the organist) was between six and eight in the period 1482/3–1496/7, between four and six in the period 1498/9–1505/6, and again between six and eight after 1506–7. We may conclude that the choral force of one choirmaster and six singers described in the foundation document of 1470 was never much exceeded, even though the actual number of singers associated with the guild in one year could be as high as thirteen. It seems very likely that a fixed number of *loten* was reserved for each service, and that every day the singers decided among themselves who was to participate and who was to wait his turn (or have the day off).

How was the music performed at the Guild of Our Lady? We have already observed that the average service in the 1480s and early 1490s involved one choirmaster, six or seven adult singers, an unspecified number of choirboys, and one organist. Unfortunately

Rob C. Wegman

the accounts from these years give practically no indication of the voice-types (as, for example, those at 's-Hertogenbosch do), but it seems likely that there was, as everywhere else, a relatively even, standard distribution of 'tenoristen', 'contratenoristen', 'hogencon-ters' (or 'hoechtenoristen') and 'bovensangers'.[35] The organist was certainly involved in all polyphonic services. His duties seem to have consisted mainly of providing accompaniment to the singers, although in some services no accompaniment was required: an ordinance concerning the payment of the organist Trudo le Hardy, dated 13 January 1506, states 'that the same Trudo shall from now on, in all Masses in which no organ is required, share and receive payment with the singers, but only as long as he sings with them, and not otherwise'.[36] Very little is known about the choristers. They lived in the 'choraelhuys' in the Schoolstraat, and they were under the musical supervision of the choirmaster, who received their fees. The city of Bergen op Zoom paid for the annual celebration of Holy Innocents' Day, at which one of the choristers was appointed 'boy bishop'.[37] Evidence of John of Glymes's personal concern for the choristers is provided by a number of payments recorded in the accounts of his household in Oudenbosch.[38]

[35] See, for a study of voice distributions in fifteenth-century choirs, D. Fallows, 'Specific Information on the Ensembles for Composed Polyphony, 1400–1474', *Studies in the Performance of Late Mediaeval Music*, ed. S. Boorman (Cambridge, 1983), pp. 109–59.

[36] 'dat de selve Trudo voertaen in alle missen daer inne men gheen orghele en behoeft soe verre hij mede singhet ende anders nyet participeren zal ende loon hebben metten anderen sanghers' (Slootmans, 'De Hoge Lieve Vrouw' (1965), p. 219).

[37] See, for instance, BOZ SA 248 (SR 1479–80), fol. 47ʳ: 'Paid to the singers here with their bishop of Holy Innocents' Day, at the command of the *borgemeesters* and *scepenen*, 144 groats' ('Den sangers alhier met hueren bisscop van alre kinderen daghe betailt ten bevele van borgemeesters ende scepenen xij sc.br.').

[38] '*Item* paid at the command [of the lord] to Thoenken de Backer, chorister of Bergen [op Zoom], when he went to Zwolle, 60 groats' ('Item thoenken de backer choral te bergen gegeven ten bevele als hy te zwolle wairt toech v sc.br.'); BOZ ARR 1774.10, fol. 105ʳ (29 May 1479).

'Paid at the command etc. to *heer* Janne van Pepingen for having lodged in his house a little chorister, 81 groats' ('Heer Janne van pepingen van te hebben ghehouwen een choraelken tot zijnen huyse gegeven ten bevele etc. vj sc. ix den.'); BOZ ARR 1774.10, fol. 106ʳ (28 June 1479).

'Also on the same day [3 December 1479] paid at the command etc. to Ghyskene the chorister of Diest when he went ill to his [parental] home 120 groats' ('Noch eodem die gegeven ten bevele etc. ghyskene den chorael van dyste als hy sieck thuys toech x sc.br.'); BOZ ARR 1774.11, fol. 118ʳ.

'On 12 January [1480], paid to the mother of Ghyskene the chorister when she brought this same [Ghyskene] back to Bergen [op Zoom] 26 groats' ('xij Januarij der moeder van ghyskene den chorael als zij den selven wederomme te bergen bracht gegeven ij sc. vj den.'); BOZ ARR 1774.11, fol. 119ʳ.

Occasionally the accounts of the guild record payments for new paper choirbooks, for instance in 1481–2: 'and for having used paper for a songbook of Our Lady, 72 groats'.[39] This sum almost certainly corresponds to one *riem* of writing paper (480 sheets).[40] Since the sheets were folded in gatherings, it is easy to see that the amount of paper purchased in Bergen op Zoom in 1481–2 (probably 480 bifolios, = 960 folios) was sufficient for about four choirbooks of the size of Vatican City, Biblioteca Apostolica Vaticana, MS San Pietro B 80, or seven choirbooks of the size of Brussels, Bibliothèque Royale, MS 5557. Two years later Jacob Obrecht was paid 18 groats 'for paper for his songbooks' and 3 groats for compiling an index.[41] The sum of 18 groats probably corresponds to four or five *boeken* (quires) of writing paper (one *boek*=24 sheets), a total of *c.* 96–120 sheets. The wording of the payment seems to suggest that Obrecht used the paper for making single gatherings which he added to the existing choirbooks. If he had made a new choirbook out of the paper, it would have been somewhat smaller than San Pietro B 80. In 1496–7 *meester* Nanno was paid 12 groats 'for writing the Mass of the Name of Jesus in the book of Our Lady'.[42] This was very probably a

'Paid to *meester* Rombout, surgeon at Bergen [op Zoom], at the command etc., for having lodged [and treated?] Ghyskene the chorister of Diest for six months, 480 groats' ('Meester Rombout cyrurgijn te Bergen ten bevele etc. van des de selve gehouwen heeft in zijner cost ghyskene den choral van dyeste een half jair ende bat betaelt ij lb.br.'); BOZ ARR 1774.11, fol. 124ʳ (October 1480).

39 'ende van pampier verbesicht voer eenen sangbouc voer onse vrouwen vj sc.' (BOZ SA 861.2 (OLV 1481–2), fol. 4ᵛ).

40 In Bergen op Zoom the price of one *riem* of paper was 69 groats in 1478–9 and 1479–80, and probably also in 1480–1 (BOZ ARR 1774.10, fol. 102ᵛ, and ARR 1774.11, fol. 118ʳ; ARR 649.1, fol. 36ᵛ). In April 1480 the price had fallen slightly, to 68.5 groats (BOZ ARR 1774.11, fol. 120ᵛ). In 1486–7, however, it had risen to 89 groats per *riem* (BOZ ARR 649.4, fol. 39ʳ), probably because of the inflation, since paper was generally bought from French paper manufacturers and hence was paid in French currency (cf. n. 27 above). In 1489–90 the price of one *riem* of paper was 180 groats in devalued money and 60 groats in revalued money (ARR 649.5, fol. 39ᵛ). In Antwerp the price of one *riem* of paper was 72 groats in 1485–6, and 66 groats in 1484–5 and 1486–7 (C. Verlinden and J. Craeybeckx, eds., *Dokumenten voor de geschiedenis van prijzen en lonen in Vlaanderen en Brabant* (xve–xviiie eeuw) (Bruges, 1959), p. 361).

41 '*Meester* Jacob the choirmaster for paper for his songbooks, paid 18 groats. And for compiling an index, 3 groats' ('Meester Jacobe de sangmeester om papier tot zijnen sangboecken betailt xviij gr. Noch van eenen register te besien iij gr.'); BOZ SA 861.4 (OLV 1483–4), fol. 6ʳ. The price of one *boek* of paper was usually 4.5 groats.

42 '*Item* paid to *meester* Nanno for copying the Mass of the Name of Jesus in the book of Our Lady 12 groats' ('Item meester nanno vander missen vanden naem Jhesus in onser vrouwen boeck te scriven betaelt xij gr.br.'); BOZ SA 861.15 (OLV 1496–7), fol. 16ᵛ. This mass may have been composed by Jacob Obrecht, who worked at the Guild of Our Lady from between 24 June and 3 July 1497 onwards. Perhaps this was the *Missa In nomine Yhesu* (based on the Introit *In nomine Jesu omne genuflectatur* of the feast of the Holy Name of

polyphonic setting written for the private endowment of a 'missen vanden name Jhesus' that had been made by the Bergen op Zoom *wijntavernier* Dierick de Clerck in 1487.[43]

Since the contacts between Bergen op Zoom, Antwerp and 's-Hertogenbosch were intensive, and since the three centres were closely related in their musico-liturgical practice, there can be little doubt that there was much exchange of polyphonic music, and that the centres shared by and large the same repertory. A direct indication of this is the following payment in the 's-Hertogenbosch accounts of 1498–9: '*item* for fetching in Bergen [op Zoom] a mass in polyphony for the singers: 24 groats'.[44] Since in 1498–9 the internationally famous Jacob Obrecht was working in Bergen op Zoom, and since no one of his fellow singers around this time is known to have written polyphonic music, it would seem very likely that the mass in question was a newly composed cycle by Obrecht. An important centre of music distribution for Flanders and Brabant was Petrus Alamire's scriptorium at Mechlin. The accounts of both Antwerp and 's-Hertogenbosch repeatedly mention payments for the purchase of choirbooks from 'meester Petter Alamyre sangshriffer'. There can be no doubt that the Guild of Bergen op Zoom, too, bought some of its manuscripts from Alamire: the accounts of 1525–6, for instance, record the payment of 48 groats to the painter Ole Jacobssone 'for fetching the songbook of Our Lady at Mechlin'.[45] There is thus considerable likelihood that a substantial portion of the repertory in the surviving Alamire manuscripts was known and performed at Bergen op Zoom.

In order to determine the social status of the singers during the period 1470–94 I have made comparisons with the annual salaries of musicians working in other institutions and artisans working in

Jesus:) mentioned in two letters or Ercole d'Este's Milanese agent Manfredus de Manfredis dated 9 and 12 June 1504. See M. Staehelin, 'Obrechtiana', *Tijdschrift van de Vereniging voor Nederlandse Muziekgeschiedenis*, 25 (1975), p. 15. The 'Jacomo' mentioned in the letter was not the composer of the mass, but the scribe Jacopo Dini; see M. Staehelin, 'Berichtigung und Ergänzung zu "Obrechtiana"', *Tijdschrift van de Vereniging voor Nederlandse Muziekgeschiedenis*, 26 (1976), pp. 41–2.

[43] BOZ R 302, fol. 32ʳ (10 April 1487). The mass was funded by a portion of the interest of four homesteads in Bergen op Zoom, of which Dierick de Clerck had been the proprietor. No polyphony was specified in the bequest, but the endowment was large enough for a regular polyphonic service.

[44] 'item omme te doen haelen tot Bergen een misse in dietscante voir die sengeren 8 st.' (Smijers, *De Illustre Lieve Vrouwe Broederschap*, p. 209).

[45] 'betaelt ole jacobssone schildere van onser liever vrouwen sangboeck te Mechelen te doen halene iv sc.br.' (BOZ SA 861.39 (OLV 1525–6), fol. 24ᵛ).

Table 2 *Annual incomes in Brabant in the late fifteenth century (in Brabant groats)*

Estimated annual salaries at Bergen op Zoom 1480–1500	
Guild of Our Lady (based on 420 *loten* per year):	
Lowest-paid singers (1 Brabant groat per *loot*)	420
Highest-paid singers (3.75 Brabant groats per *loot*)	1575
Choirmaster (3.75 Brabant groats per *loot* plus Holy Cross *lof*)	1635
City of Bergen op Zoom:	
City trumpeters	1980
Musicians in other institutions	
Jacobus Barbireau (Guild of O.L., Antwerp, until 1491)	720
Jacob Obrecht (Guild of O.L., Antwerp, 1491–7)	1080
Jacob Obrecht (Guild of O.L., Antwerp, 1503)	1560
Nicasius de Clibano ('s-Hertogenbosch, 1480s and 1490s)	2028
Artisans in Antwerp (1480s and 1490s)[a]	
Hodmen	*c.* 1700
Stonecutters	*c.* 2350
Masons	*c.* 2950
Carpenters	*c.* 2950
Minimum annual costs of living in Brabant in the late fifteenth century[b]	
Single adult	*c.* 550
Family of 5 persons (2 parents and 3 non-working children)	*c.* 1400

[a]Based on E. Scholliers, *Loonarbeid en honger: De levensstandaard in de XVe en XVIe eeuw te Antwerpen* (Antwerp, 1960), pp. 65–101.

[b]Based on data presented in Scholliers, *Loonarbeid en honger*, pp. 168–76.

Antwerp (Table 2). It goes without saying that these figures present an incomplete picture: musicians could augment their incomes substantially by rendering irregular services (copying music, singing at extra-liturgical occasions, composing, teaching, etc.) or – if they were priests – by obtaining benefices. Yet the general impression is that even good singers or choirmasters in Brabant (particularly laymen) had to work very hard in order to earn more than unskilled hodmen in Antwerp. Comparison with salaries elsewhere – Cambrai, Bruges, Paris, Ferrara, Milan, Rome, Naples – might bring this impression into relief.[46] A telling figure, for instance, is the salary offered to Brumel by Duke Alfonso d'Este of Ferrara in 1506 (as part

[46] A comprehensive study of the expenditure on music at the various musical institutions in Europe in the fifteenth century is very much needed, and would considerably add to our understanding of musical life in general, and certain aspects (e.g. the mobility of musicians) in particular. See, for a pioneering attempt, L. Lockwood, *Music in Renaissance Ferrara 1400–1505* (Oxford, 1984), pp. 173–95.

of a package also containing benefices, travel allowance and housing), which was 100 Venetian gold ducats, equivalent around this time to *c.* 11,000–12,000 groats.[47] By Brabant standards this was an astronomic figure, and it is easy to see why composers of international stature, such as Jacob Obrecht, left for Italy as soon as they saw an opportunity.

JACOB OBRECHT AT BERGEN OP ZOOM

In the course of his restless and in a sense perhaps tragic life Jacob Obrecht worked at the Guild of Our Lady in Bergen op Zoom three times, first as a choirmaster in 1480–4 and then as a singer in 1488 and 1497–8.[48]

The first question that must be dealt with is whether Obrecht was born in Bergen op Zoom, as a number of writers have maintained. Since several families with the name Obrecht (or Oebrecht, Hobrecht, Obrechs, Obert, etc.) are known to have lived in the counties of Holland, Brabant and Flanders,[49] it seems likely that the composer's family also came from the south-west Dutch-speaking parts of the Low Countries. Nearly four centuries after Obrecht's birth an arbitrary borderline was drawn through this area as a result of the independence of Belgium (1830), and it is difficult to avoid the

[47] Wright, 'Antoine Brumel', p. 56.

[48] For literature on Jacob Obrecht at Bergen op Zoom, see J. Asberg, 'Obrecht te Bergen op Zoom', *Taxandria: Tijdschrift voor Noordbrabantsche Geschiedenis en Volkskunde*, 35 (1928), pp. 71–5; E. H. G. C. A. Juten, 'Jacob Obrecht', *Annales du Congrès d'Anvers 1930*, ed. P. Rolland, 2 vols., Fédération Archéologique et Historique de Belgique, 7th ser., 77 (Antwerp, 1930–1), II, pp. 441–51; A. Piscaer, 'Jacob Obrecht', *Sinte Geertruydtsbronne: Driemaandelijks Tijdschrift Gewijd aan de Geschiedenis en Volkskunde van West-Brabant en Omgeving*, 15 (1938), pp. 1–15; A. J. L. Juten, 'Nog eens over Jacob Obrecht, de "sangmeester"', *Taxandria: Tijdschrift voor Noordbrabantsche Geschiedenis en Volkskunde*, 48 (1941), pp. 263–9; A. Piscaer, 'Jacob Obrecht: Geboortedatum en andere bijzonderheden', *Mens en Melodie*, 7 (1952), pp. 329–33; L. G. van Hoorn, *Jacob Obrecht* (The Hague, 1968), pp. 32–68.

[49] For Obrecht at The Hague, see: A. M. J. de Haan, comp., *Inventaris van het archief van de Heilige Geest en het Heilige Geesthofje te 's-Gravenhage* (The Hague, 1969), Regesten 5, 6, 24, 40, 43, 101, 143, 189, 225; Inventaris 786; J. G. M. Sanders, comp., *Inventaris van het archief van het Karthuiserklooster Het Hollandse Huis bij Geertruidenberg*, Inventarisreeks 34 ('s-Hertogenbosch, 1984), Regesten 81, 298, 343, 395–6, 470, 681, 724, 799, 815, 816, 865, p. 81; C. Lingbeek-Schalekamp, *Overheid en muziek in Holland tot 1672* (Poortugaal, 1984), p. 212. For Delft, see D. P. Oosterbaan, *De Oude Kerk te Delft gedurende de Middeleeuwen* (The Hague, 1973), pp. 52 and 98 n. 120. For Gouda, see Oosterbaan, *op. cit.*, p. 336 n. 2. For Bergen op Zoom, see Piscaer, 'Jacob Obrecht' (1938), pp. 14–15. For Ghent, see B. de Keyzer, 'Jacob Obrecht en zijn vader Willem: De Gentse relaties', *Mens en Melodie*, 8 (1953), p. 318. For Ostend, see E. van der Straeten, *La musique aux Pays-Bas avant le XIXe siècle*, 8 vols., III (Brussels, 1875), p. 182. For Louvain, see Slootmans, 'De Hoge Lieve Vrouw' (1965), pp. 197 and 213 n. 9; E. Houtman, *Inventaris van het oud archief van de stad Aalst* (Brussels, 1974), p. 202.

impression that the zeal of early twentieth-century Dutch writers to prove that the composer was born in Bergen op Zoom was partly inspired by their wish to save at least one 'national' medieval composer for the Netherlands, after all the others were lost to Belgium. The case for Bergen op Zoom as Jacob Obrecht's birthplace is, however, weak. It rests on the following premises:[50]

1. In his motet *Mille quingentis*, Jacob Obrecht states that his father Willem Obrecht begot (*generavit*) a son Jacobus on St Cecilia's day (22 November), while he was crossing (*peragravit*) Sicily. Since Jacob Obrecht was to celebrate his first Mass on 23 April 1480 (see below), he must have been about thirty years old by this time and was therefore probably born around 1450. In that year, the lord of Bergen op Zoom, John of Glymes, made a pilgrimage to Jerusalem, accompanied by a small group of prominent citizens from Bergen op Zoom. Willem Obrecht may have been among the pilgrims, and his son Jacob could have been born just when Willem was on his way through Sicily.

2. In contemporary sources, the composer's surname is often spelt 'Hobrecht' instead of 'Obrecht'. This pronunciation is believed to be typical of West Brabant, particularly of Bergen op Zoom.

There is no evidence that Jacob's father was ever associated with Bergen op Zoom. The name Willem Obrecht occurs in several fifteenth-century documents,[51] only one of which can be stated with certainty to refer to the composer's father. He was the trumpeter Willem [H]oebrecht who lived and worked in Ghent from 1452 to his death in 1488.[52] The assumption that this Willem was among the prominent followers of John of Glymes during his pilgrimage to Jerusalem is highly implausible. First, in 1452 Willem Obrecht was appointed a city trumpeter in Ghent at the rather modest annual salary of 720 Flemish groats (= 1080 Brabant groats), indicating that

[50] Piscaer, 'Jacob Obrecht: Geboortedatum en andere bijzonderheden'.
[51] A Willem Obrecht lived in The Hague in 1367–87 (De Haan, *op. cit.*, Regesten 24, 40 and 43; Sanders, *op. cit.*, p. 81 and Regest 298). Anny Piscaer has traced a Willem Obrecht in Bergen op Zoom in 1401 (Piscaer, 'Jacob Obrecht' (1938), p. 14). Another Willem Obrecht in Bergen op Zoom was traced by Korneel Slootmans in documents of 1458 and 1464 (Slootmans, 'De Hoge Lieve Vrouw' (1965), pp. 197 and 214 n. 11). A Willem Obrecht was commissioner for Holland of the Jubilee Indulgence of 1450, and was prior of the monastery of Sion, near Delft, in 1450–75 (Oosterbaan, *op. cit.*, pp. 52 and 98 n. 120). Another Willem Obrecht of Delft studied at the University of Bologna in 1507 (Juten, 'Nog eens over Jacob Obrecht', pp. 265–9; A. Smijers, 'Het motet "Mille quingentis" van Jacob Hobrecht', *Tijdschrift van de Vereeniging voor Nederlandsche Muziekgeschiedenis*, 16 (1941), pp. 213–14). At Gouda, a Willem Obrecht was rector of the local convent in 1460 (Oosterbaan, *op. cit.*, pp. 321 and 336 n. 2). In 's-Hertogenbosch, a Willem Hubrecht was singer at the Illustrious Confraternity of Our Lady in 1511/12–1513/14 (Smijers, 'De Illustre Lieve Vrouwe Broederschap' (1935), pp. 75–80). For Willem Obrecht of Ghent, the composer's father, see n. 52 below.   [52] De Keyzer, *op. cit.*, pp. 317–19.

his social position was by this time relatively low.[53] Second, even though pilgrims to the Holy Land often travelled through Sicily, there is no evidence that John of Glymes did so, too. Third, it is very unlikely that any one of the pilgrims would have brought along his wife to Jerusalem, let alone an expectant mother. Finally, if Jacob was born in Bergen op Zoom while his father was on pilgrimage, he would have needed to have access to a logbook when he wrote *Mille quingentis*, in 1488, in order to know where Willem happened to be at the precise time of his birth.[54] In sum, the assumption that Willem Obrecht accompanied John of Glymes on his pilgrimage to the Holy Land is not only speculative but lacks credibility. The second argument is likewise rather weak. In documents of Bergen op Zoom, Jacob Obrecht's surname (and that of his namesake, the Louvain priest Jacobe Obrechts, who was proprietor of the house 'De vier heemskinderen' in Bergen op Zoom[55]) is never spelt 'Hobrecht'. This particular spelling is, however, found in documents of Ghent (1488: 'her Jacob Hobrecht priestre'), Bruges (1488, 1490, 1491, 1500: 'magister Jacobus Hobrecht') and Antwerp (1501: 'Hobrecht').[56] In view of these considerations, the assumption that the composer was born in Bergen op Zoom must be rejected.[57]

Returning to the motet *Mille quingentis*, the obvious implication of its text is surely that Jacob Obrecht was born in Sicily; there is no reason to prefer the less obvious reading that Willem was not present

[53] *Ibid.*, p. 318. It is true, as Reinhard Strohm has pointed out to me, that noblemen were occasionally accompanied by trumpeters on pilgrimages to the Holy Land (see, for instance, F. Ll. Harrison, *Music in Medieval Britain* (London, 1958), p. 222), but John of Glymes's retinue was very small and included only prominent citizens of Bergen op Zoom (Slootmans, *Jan metten Lippen*, p. 20).

[54] One may perhaps assume poetic licence in view of the pun 'Cecilie ad festum que ceciliam peragravit' in the motet text.

[55] This is the Jacob Obrecht who was enrolled at Louvain University in 1470, and who was formerly believed to be the composer (further documentation on him is provided by Slootmans, 'De Hoge Lieve Vrouw' (1965), pp. 213–14 n. 9).

[56] See the survey in B. Murray, 'Jacob Obrecht's Connection with the Church of Our Lady in Antwerp', *Revue Belge de Musicologie*, 11 (1957), pp. 130–3. Phonological research has revealed that the prothesis of *h* in words beginning with vowels was a uniquely Flemish habit; it occurs sporadically in Brabant sources, but only when these come from centres bordering on Flanders (e.g. Antwerp). See A. Berteloot, *Bijdrage tot een klankatlas van het dertiende-eeuwse middelnederlands* (Lengerich, 1983), p. 96 and map 141; A. van Loey, *Middelnederlandse spraakkunst*, 2 vols., II (7th edn, Groningen, 1976), pp.108–9 and 124–5.

[57] One argument that could perhaps be advanced in favour of origin in the region around Bergen op Zoom, however, is that Obrecht said his first Mass – or at least was paid for it – in Oudenbosch (see n. 63 below), since it seems to have been usual for priests to say their first Masses in the places where they were born (I thank Willem Elders for pointing out this to me).

at his son's birth: 'On the feast of St Cecilia, when he [Willem] was crossing Sicily, he begot Jacob before Orpheus and the Muses'.[58] If one combines the facts (a) that Willem Obrecht was employed as a city trumpeter in Ghent from 1452 onwards, (b) that he must have been in Sicily around 1450, and (c) that Ghent accounts of 1451 mention 'een trompetter van Cycilien',[59] it becomes reasonable to develop the hypothesis that Willem had lived and worked as a trumpeter in Sicily for some time (perhaps at the Aragonese court of Sicily), that his son Jacob was born there during his tenure, and that he went to Ghent around 1451. Confirmation of this hypothesis may eventually be found among documents preserved in Sicilian archives. For now, Sicily must remain the place where Obrecht is most likely to have been born.

Jacob Obrecht was choirmaster of the Guild of Our Lady at Bergen op Zoom from (at least) 1480 until late August 1484, when he departed for Cambrai. Documents from Bergen op Zoom speak only of 'meestere Jacobe den sangmeester' during this period, and do not specify his surname. The basis for the identification with the composer is provided by a later entry in the chapter accounts of the Cathedral at Cambrai, dating from 28 July 1484, where the newly appointed master of the choristers Jacob Obrecht is called 'de Bergis'.[60]

The earliest surviving account of the guild at Bergen op Zoom runs from 15 August 1480 to 15 August 1481. References to 'meester Jacobe den sangmeester' dating from before 15 August 1480 are to be found in the accounts of the steward of Oudenbosch and its environs.[61] These are accounts of the household of John of Glymes at

---

[58] 'Cecilie ad festum que ceciliam peragravit/[c]oram idem orphei cum musis Jacobum generavit'; since 'coram' governs the ablative, it would seem that it cannot be referring to the genitive of 'Orpheus'. However, Eddie Vetter has drawn my attention to the fact that in late medieval Latin 'coram' governed both the genitive and the ablative (see J. W. Fuchs, O. Weijers and M. Gumbert, *Lexicon latinitatis neerlandicae medii aevii/Woordenboek van het Middeleeuws Latijn van de Noordelijke Nederlanden*, II (Leyden, 1981), col. c1191, where an example of 'coram' taking the genitive [Zwolle, 1491] is quoted).

[59] De Keyzer, *op. cit.*, p. 318.

[60] Pirro, 'Obrecht à Cambrai', p. 78. Bergen op Zoom in Latin was 'Bergae (ad Somam)'; the Latin form of Bergen (Mons) in Hainaut was 'Montes'. According to Reinhard Strohm, 'Bergae' may also apply to Bergues-St-Winnoc in French Flanders (Strohm, *Music in Late Medieval Bruges*, p. 152 n. 28). Other fifteenth-century musicians called 'de Bergis' were Rubertinus de Bergis (Strohm, *op. cit.*, p. 182) and the composer Cornelis Rigo de Bergis (L. Kessels, 'The Brussels/Tournai-Partbooks: Structure, Illumination, and Flemish Repertory', *Tijdschrift van de Vereniging voor Nederlandse Muziekgeschiedenis*, 37 (1987), pp. 97–100).

[61] BOZ ARR 1774.1–1774.11 (covering the period 1461/2–1479/80). This manuscript was

Oudenbosch (about 20 km north-east of Bergen op Zoom), where the lord of Bergen op Zoom spent much of his time probably because his mistress Mayken Sanders lived there.[62] The day-to-day expenses paint a vivid picture of household life: we find payments for items such as paper, besoms, cheese, wine, beer, and also for 'viij methalen pispotten', 'eenen padden steene' (a toadstone), 'vuergewerk' (fireworks, purchased, appropriately, two weeks before New Year's Day 1479), and for 'eenen boecke gheheeten Nycolaus de lyra' ('a book called *Nycolaus de Lyra*'). There are also expenses for Masses, which are divided into two categories: payments 'van eender missen' (usually 6 groats) and 'van eender singender missen' (36 groats). Perhaps this distinction is synonymous with the still existing liturgical distinction between the *missa lecta* and the *missa in cantu*. On the other hand, the 36 groats for the 'singing Mass' would have been quite sufficient for a polyphonic service (considering the fact that the price of one *loot* normally varied from 1 to 3.75 groats). In addition to the expenses for Masses we find payments to singers. The singer Michelet (also called Michiele van Bastoengnen) was repeatedly sent to Antwerp to purchase parchment. The barber-surgeon Jannes Greefkens ('Jannes de barbier'), who sang at the Guild of Our Lady in 1480–1 and 1481–2, was paid 6 groats for bloodletting the diseased shoeing-smith on 5 August 1479. On 6 July of the same year he was given 'eenen sangboecxken' ('a small songbook') worth 30 groats.

Jacob Obrecht is first mentioned in a payment of 23 April 1480: 'On the twenty-third of the same month, paid at the command etc. to *meestere* Jacop the choirmaster on his first Mass: 240 Brabant groats'.[63] Since other priests are known to have received much less than Obrecht on their first Masses,[64] one might perhaps conclude that the lord of Bergen op Zoom held the composer in special esteem. Another payment to Obrecht in 1480, hitherto unpublished, is recorded on the following page: 'Paid to *meester* Jacop the choir-

---

kept until 1949 in The Hague, Algemeen Rijksarchief, Eerste afdeling, Commissie van Breda (no. 473). See W. A. van Ham, *Inventaris van de archieven van de raad en rekenkamer van de markiezen van Bergen op Zoom*, Inventarisreeks 25, 5 vols. ('s-Hertogenbosch, 1980), II, p. 315.

[62] Slootmans, *Jan metten Lippen*, p. 68.

[63] 'xxiij eqd. M. Jacop den sangmeestere gegeven op zijn yeeste misse ten bevele etc. xx sc.br.' (BOZ ARR 1774.11, fol. 121ʳ).

[64] On 23 May 1479 *heer* Willeme van Nyspen received 156 groats on his first Mass (BOZ ARR 1774.10, fol. 105ʳ). *Meester* Anthoenis Peck received 87 groats on his first Mass on 16 April 1480, just one week before Obrecht received his 240 groats (BOZ ARR 1774.11, fol. 120ᵛ).

master for having sung four Masses on Whitsunday [21 May]: 144 groats'.[65] It is unlikely that 'de misse singen' (to sing Mass) here refers to the singing of polyphony, since in other contexts this same wording appears to be synonymous with 'de misse celebreeren' (to celebrate Mass).[66] On the other hand, 36 groats per Mass was an unusually high fee for an officiant: the usual fee for the priest who 'sang' Mass was 6 or 12 groats.[67]

These payments indicate that Jacob Obrecht must have become choirmaster of the Guild of Our Lady at Bergen op Zoom before 15 August 1480. There is no evidence that he already held this post in 1479, as is sometimes assumed.[68] Unfortunately the domain accounts of Oudenbosch from the period 1481–1526 are lost, and as a result very little is known of Jacob Obrecht's later relations with the lord of Bergen op Zoom. Information concerning his activities in Bergen op Zoom during the period 15 August 1480–15 August 1484 derives entirely from the accounts of the Guild of Our Lady. This information can be summarised as follows:

1. In 1480–1 and 1481–2 Jacob Obrecht received an annual salary of 720 groats, twice as much as the salary reserved in 1470 for his predecessor Willem de Brouwer (see Table 1 above). On 24 June 1482 the rulers of the guild agreed that Obrecht could take part, like his fellow singers, in the distribution of the *loten*.[69] Obrecht's *loten* were worth 3 groats (less than the

[65] 'Meester Jacop den sangmeestere van iiij missen te hebben gesongen inde sinxen daghe betaelt xij sc.br.' (BOZ ARR 1774.11, fol. 121ᵛ).

[66] Compare, for instance, the following payment for the celebration of St Anthony's day in the city accounts of 1474–5, with the one of 1472–3 quoted in note 17 above: 'Vander missen opten voirscreven sente anthonis dach te doen ende te solempniseren met discante welke misse in sente anthonis choir voer de hootmisse gedaen wordt betailt voir *den priester die die [misse] gesongen* heeft [in 1472/3: den priestere die die misse celebreerde], voer den sangeren choralen voer den organiste metten blaser tsamen iiij sc. j½ gr. Ende den tromper opten voirscreven dach van siinen arbeyde betailt xij gr. facit tsamen – v sc. j½ gr.br.' (my italics); BOZ SA 245.2 (SR 1474–5), fol. 93ʳ.

[67] See note 17 above; see also e.g. BOZ SA 248 (SR 1479–80), fol. 47ᵛ ('uutgenomen mijnen heren den deken ende den priestere de hoomisse zingende elken xij gr.'), and BOZ SA 250.2 (SR 1488–9), fol. 195ʳ ('den priester die de misse zanck vj gr.').

[68] This assumption goes back to the paper of 1930 of E. H. G. C. A. Juten ('Jacob Obrecht', p. 445), who stated that the various expenses for choirboys in BOZ ARR 1774.10 and 1774.11 (see n. 38 above) gave him reason to suspect the presence of a choirmaster (and hence of Obrecht) in Bergen op Zoom as early as 1479. Now that it is known that Willem de Brouwer was choirmaster of the guild before Obrecht, there is no longer a basis for Juten's assumption.

[69] '*Meester* Jacobe the choirmaster to whom *loten* are also granted, besides the 720 groats which he had [earned], which are separated from his earnings after [the feast of] St John, when the [new] payment started, each *loot* 3 groats, [together] makes 117 groats' ('Meester Jacobe den sangmeester die oic loot geconsenteert is voer de iij lb. die hij hadde die afgesneden zijn by hem verdient post Johannis dat zijn wedde verscheen elc loot iij gr. facit ix sc. ix den.br.'); BOZ SA 861.2 (OLV 1481–2), fol. 3ʳ.

3.75 groats per *loot* earned by the best-paid singers, Michiele Cramer and Cornelise Zwagers). Between 24 June 1482 and 15 August 1483 the composer participated, on average, in three out of every four services. This should not necessarily be interpreted as a sign of neglectfulness, although it is true that the record of attendance of his successors was better (nearly every year more than 90% of the services).

2. During his tenure in 1480–4 Jacob Obrecht was in charge of the copying of polyphonic music in new gatherings and choirbooks with a total size of at least 575 sheets (=1150 folios, or 2300 pages; see above). It is likely that a substantial portion of these books and gatherings were filled with works by Obrecht himself, since there are several indications later in his life that he was a quick and prolific composer.[70] One of the masses which Obrecht composed during these years found its way in 1484 to Ferrara, where it was received 'molto volontiera' by Duke Ercole I d'Este.[71] This may just possibly have been the *Missa Beata viscera*, which was copied in Siena, Biblioteca Comunale degli Intronati, MS K.I.2 in 1481,[72] and which is based on the Communion at Mass for the Blessed Virgin Mary.

3. In 1483–4 Jacob Obrecht lived with Reijnier *metten bulten* (Reijnier 'with the hunch') who also sang in the services of the Guild of Our Lady and was paid, like Obrecht, *loten* of 3 groats. Together, Jacob and Reijnier earned 637 *loten* in 1483–4, pointing to an average attendance for both singers of around 75% of the services.

After having worked as a choirmaster in Bergen op Zoom for more than four years, Jacob Obrecht became *magister puerorum* at Cambrai

---

[70] During his brief tenure at Cambrai (September 1484–October 1485), for instance, Obrecht had already written enough 'books of music which he is said to have compiled' ('libris cantus quos composuisse asseritur'), for the chapter of the cathedral to accept them, *faute de mieux*, as a settlement of his debts (Pirro, 'Obrecht à Cambrai', p. 79). And in 1501–2, the Guild of Our Lady at Antwerp bought four quires of paper 'which *meester* Jacob the choirmaster needs for writing masses in' (Forney, 'Music, Ritual and Patronage', p. 39 n. 98). Since four quires contain 96 sheets (192 folios), Obrecht could have copied at least twelve (and probably copied more) masses in them. And one can only wonder of what size and importance the 'sangboek in discante' must have been for which the same guild paid him a sum equalling one annual salary (1440 groats), later in the same year (*ibid.*). In his *Dodekachordon* (Basel, 1542), Heinrich Glarean twice pointed to Obrecht's extraordinary productivity as a composer (my translation): 'Which composer has not sometime attempted [to write] the Salutation of the Holy Virgin in the [Dorian] mode, and this frequently in competition with others? In this type of contest Jacob Obrecht gladly competed, for in productivity he surpassed all the singers of his generation – which he seems to have wanted to demonstrate in the *Missa Hercules Dux Ferrarie* [*sic*] – for whatever [material] he tried to set, it became a composition, as he said' (p. 296); 'Moreover, he is said to have possessed such quickness of invention and abundance of creativity, that he composed in one night an excellent mass, at which [feat] learned men were astonished' (p. 456).

[71] Lockwood, *Music in Renaissance Ferrara*, pp. 162–3.

[72] Edited in C. J. Maas, gen. ed., *New Obrecht Edition*, vol. 2 (Utrecht, 1984), pp. 1–31. For the date of MS K.I.2, see F. A. D'Accone, 'A Late 15th-Century Sienese Sacred Repertory: MS K.I.2 of the Biblioteca Comunale, Siena', *Musica Disciplina*, 37 (1983), pp. 121–70, esp. p. 146.

in 1484.[73] He was appointed on 26 July of that year, but took up his duties only on 6 September, three weeks after the financial year in Bergen op Zoom had ended. Eleven months later, in October 1485, Obrecht was discharged from his office,[74] and after some difficulties concerning unpaid debts he went to Bruges to become *succentor* at the church of St Donatian, a post for which a friend of his had interceded on his behalf several months before.[75]

In 1487–8, events were to bring Obrecht back again to Bergen op Zoom, albeit by way of Ferrara. In September 1487 Duke Ercole I d'Este sent his singer Cornelius di Lorenzo to Bruges, armed with letters asking the chapter of St Donatian to give leave to Obrecht to come and visit the duke for a few months.[76] These letters were discussed by the chapter on 2 October 1487, and it was decided that Obrecht could absent himself for six months beginning on the next festival of St Donatian (14 October). Immediately after Obrecht's arrival in Italy, around the beginning of December, Ercole started energetic attempts to obtain benefices for him, evidently in order to persuade him (or to comply with his wish) to become a singer in his chapel. This strategy must have failed unexpectedly at a relatively

---

[73] Cf. Pirro, 'Obrecht à Cambrai'.

[74] The chapter accounts say that Obrecht resigned ('recedat'), but do not indicate whether he was actually forced to resign. The composer had already accepted the post of *succentor* at St Donatian in Bruges by 23 June 1485 (when the chapter of that church asked Aliamus de Groote to fill the post until the arrival of Obrecht, who had promised to leave Cambrai soon; cf. E. H. G. C. A. Juten, 'Jacob Obrecht', p. 446; further details in Strohm, *Music in Late Medieval Bruges*, pp. 38–9). A month later, on 27 July 1485, the Cambrai accounts give evidence of discontent with Obrecht's work as *magister puerorum*: the choristers had contracted scabies, 'which is not otherwise seen', and the chapter instructed the composer to look after them better. Obrecht's resignation followed three months later; it was only after the discharge that the chapter found out that he had embezzled funds (Pirro, 'Obrecht à Cambrai', p. 79). Although the composer was clearly a disappointment as master of the choristers, it is difficult to conclude from the available evidence that he was actually dismissed.

[75] E. H. G. C. A. Juten, 'Jacob Obrecht', p. 446; Strohm, *Music in Late Medieval Bruges*, pp. 38–41.

[76] For this and what follows, see B. Murray, 'New Light on Jacob Obrecht's Development: A Biographical Study', *The Musical Quarterly*, 43 (1957), pp. 500–16; Van Hoorn, *Jacob Obrecht*, pp. 69–106; L. Lockwood, 'Music at Ferrara in the Period of Ercole I d'Este', *Studi Musicali*, 1 (1972), pp. 112–13 and 127–9; Lockwood, *Music in Renaissance Ferrara*, pp. 163–4. Obrecht first met Duke Ercole I d'Este of Ferrara at Godÿ (almost certainly Goito, *c.* 15 km north-west of Mantua), from which place Ercole wrote the letter of 1 December 1487 to his wife (printed in Murray, 'New Light', p. 510). Obrecht and Ercole left Godÿ for Mantua on 2 December 1487 and planned to arrive in Ferrara on 5 December. From Mantua Ercole sent the first letter concerning Obrecht's benefices to his papal agent Bonfrancesco Arlotti (Lockwood, 'Music at Ferrara', p. 112). On the letters from Bergen op Zoom to Bruges and *vice versa*, see E. H. G. C. A. Juten, 'Jacob Obrecht', p. 447.

late stage, for when Obrecht finally returned to the north, he had already considerably overstayed his leave of absence.

Meanwhile political events in Flanders had taken a turn for the worse. In January 1488, just when Ercole's papal agent was discussing the matter of Obrecht's benefices with Pope Innocent VIII, the mounting irritation of the Flemish towns over Maximilian of Habsburg's repeated attempts to re-conquer territories lost to France in the Treaty of Arras (1482) led to open revolt. Maximilian quickly convened the Estates of Flanders in Bruges, but was taken prisoner by the town on 2 February, only to regain his freedom on 16 May 1488 by swearing an oath that he would defer to a newly forged treaty limiting his powers. Once freed, Maximilian broke his oath and prepared for a punitive expedition with his father's army, which had been drawn together at Louvain. The experience of previous urban risings in Flanders now boded bloodshed, deprivation of civic privileges, and huge payments in reparation to Maximilian.

Obrecht, returning from the south in early June, evidently decided to wait in Bergen op Zoom – one of Maximilian's most loyal towns – until the storm had passed. From here he exchanged several letters with the chapter of St Donatian, explaining that he could not return 'propter pericula viarum'. The chapter grudgingly accepted this excuse, but insisted that he be back in Bruges by 15 August. While Bergen op Zoom was now preparing to assist Maximilian in his war against Flanders, Obrecht received permission from the *borghemeesters* and *scepenen* to work temporarily as a singer at the Guild of Our Lady for 3.75 groats per *loot*. The guild accounts for 1487–8 record the payment of 180 groats, equalling forty-eight *loten*, to the composer: '*Item* to *meester* Jacop the choirmaster, who had come here, paid [at the command] of the *borghemeesters* and *scepenen* a certain number of *loten* of 3.75 groats, [together] makes 180 groats'.[77] The number of *loten*, forty-eight, points to a stay of at least forty days. Assuming that Obrecht wrote his first letter to Bruges, which arrived there on 12 June, upon his arrival at Bergen op Zoom, we may conclude that he stayed in the town from 8 or 9 June to at least 17 or 18 July (letters from Bergen op Zoom usually arrived in Bruges in two or three days). Between the latter dates and 15 August Obrecht

---

[77] 'Item meestere Jacop de sangmeestere die hier ghecomen was ghegeven bij borghemeesters ende scepenen sekere loet van .i. brasp. elck stuck facit vij sc. vj den.'; BOZ SA 861.6 (OLV 1487–8), fol. 5^r.

must have left for Bruges, despite the fact that the tensions between Maximilian and Flanders which had earlier deterred him were still unresolved.

Jacob Obrecht was discharged by the chapter of St Donatian on 22 January 1491.[78] After this date there is a gap in the composer's biography of about a year. On 7 August 1491 the post of choirmaster at the Confraternity of Our Lady at Antwerp became vacant because of the death of Jacobus Barbireau. After an interim choirmaster had filled the post, Obrecht was appointed in 1492 (or perhaps in late 1491) at an annual salary of 1080 groats, one and a half times that of Barbireau.[79] It is likely that the composer maintained good relations with Bergen op Zoom, which was after all only 30 km north of Antwerp and could be visited in one day. As we have seen, he was in the town on 23 April 1497, and it was presumably on this date that he agreed with the lord of Bergen op Zoom to become a singer in the choir of the Guild of Our Lady.

Much had changed since Obrecht had last worked in Bergen op Zoom: John II of Glymes had died in 1494, and his son John III introduced an entirely new recruitment policy, the details of which will be described below. In order to persuade the composer to come to Bergen op Zoom John III offered him a fee of 6 groats per *loot*, which meant that if Obrecht attended all services he could earn as

---

[78] Obrecht was forced by the chapter to resign, but the reasons are unclear: 'it was decided that the *succentor* Jacobus Obrecht was to be given his leave if he would not ask his leave himself. . . And that Father de Hoya should persuade him that, for the sake of his honesty and honour, he had better come to the chapter to ask his leave, rather than being told so by the lords [of the chapter]' ('conclusum fuit quod succentor Jacobus Obrecht licentiaretur nisi de se ipso licentiam capiat et petat . . . Et quod pater de Hoya inducat magistrum Jacobum ut potius veniat in capitulo et licentiam capiat et petat propter honestatem et honorem suum quam quidem licentiaretur a dominis'; chapter acts of St Donatian, 26 May 1490. I am indebted to Reinhard Strohm for providing me with a transcription of the account.

[79] Murray, 'Jacob Obrecht's Connection'; Forney, 'Music, Ritual and Patronage', pp. 42–4. Elly Kooiman assumes that there were two, possibly three, interim choirmasters between Barbireau and Obrecht in 1491–2 ('The Biography of Jacob Barbireau', pp. 39–41), but this seems unlikely. Barbireau died on 7 August 1491, more than six weeks after the beginning of the financial year 1491–2 (24 June 1491). Hence, unless poor health prevented him from working, he must have held the post during this six-week period (being the first of the three choirmasters for whom payment was recorded on 24 June 1492). Barbireau was apparently still in good health by 24 June 1491, when he received his full annual salary for the preceding financial year. Since he died relatively young (at the age of thirty-five or thirty-six) it seems likely that his death was due to an accident or a sudden disease. The third of the three choirmasters of 1491–2 was probably Obrecht, as Kooiman observes: on 24 June 1492 he was described as 'the present choirmaster' ('de sanghmester dye nu is'; *ibid.*, p. 41). This leaves only one interim choirmaster.

much as *c.* 2500–2600 groats per annum. On his arrival at Bergen op Zoom, between 24 June and 3 July 1497, he was given a bonus of 75 groats, at the personal command of John III.[80] The figure of fifty-two *loten* recorded in the accounts of 1496–7 indicates that in the following seven or so weeks, up to the end of the financial year, he must have attended nearly all the services. A number of these services were carried out together with the singers of the chapel of Philip the Fair, who visited Bergen op Zoom in late July 1497.[81] Jacob Obrecht almost certainly met Pierre de la Rue on this occasion.

Unfortunately the accounts of 1497–8 of the Guild of Our Lady are lost.[82] The accounts of the next year, 1498–9, tell us that Jacob Obrecht received 144 *loten* of 6 groats, together equalling 864 groats.[83] With the help of the calculation described earlier it can be established that the minimum period in which 144 *loten* could be earned was *c.* 119–25 days. Since the accounts of 1498–9 started on 15 August 1498, it can be concluded that Obrecht must have stayed in Bergen op Zoom until at least 12–18 December 1498. This is just

[80]   'Ende uut bevele vanden heeren tsijnen aencomen hem gegeven eenen davits gulden facit vj sc. iij den.'; BOZ SA 861.15 (OLV 1496–7), fol. 12ᵛ.

[81]   The city accounts of 1 March 1497–1 March 1498 record the payment of two *amen* Rhine wine (*c.* 275 litres) to 'Eertshertoghe Philipse' on 24 July 1497 (BOZ SA 253, fol. 39ʳ). Two days later the following payment was recorded: 'On the same day [26 July 1497], given to the singers of Duke Philip's chapel nine *gelten* Rhine wine [*c.* 24.75 litres] at the same price as above, 108 groats' ('Opten selven dach geschoncken den sangeren van hertoghe philips capelle ix gelten ryns wyns ten prijse als voeren ix sc.'); BOZ SA 253, fol. 39ᵛ. The accounts of the Guild of Our Lady of 1496–7 contain the following entry: 'And also at the [same] command as above [i.e. of the *borgemeesters* and *scepenen*], paid to the singers of Duke Philip because they helped sing the *Lof*, together 97.5 groats' ('Ende desgelijcx uut bevele als voeren hertoghe philips sangeren om dat sy dloff mede halpen singen geschoncken tsamen viij sc. j½ den.'); BOZ SA 816.15 (OLV 1496–7), fol. 13ʳ. Philip the Fair also visited Bergen op Zoom on 26 October 1496, for a meeting of the Order of the Golden Fleece (Slootmans, *Jan metten Lippen*, p. 115).

[82]   There is, however, a curious payment to Obrecht in the city accounts of 1498–9, dating 3 May 1498, which on the face of it seems to suggest that the composer was absent for some time in 1498: 'On the same day [3 May 1498], given to *meestere* Jacobe Obrechts with a certain singer from elsewhere six *gelten* Rhine wine [*c.* 16.5 litres], makes 72 groats' ('Opten zelven dach geschoncken meestere jacobe obrechts met sekeren sangheren van buyten zesse gelten ryns wyns facit vj sc.'); BOZ SA 254 (SR 1498–9), fol. 36ᵛ. If this payment was made in reward of services rendered on the Holy Cross procession, as seems likely, it is curious that Obrecht is mentioned separately in the chapter containing miscellaneous payments (and not, as are the regular participants, in the chapter 'Vanden Cruyscosten', which contains the expenses for the feast of the Holy Cross). Also, the fact that the payment was made to Obrecht *together* with a foreign singer suggests that the two musicians came from elsewhere.

[83]   'Item meestere jacobe obrechts voer syn loot tot c xliiij looten toe elck loot vj gr. facit iij lb. xij sc.br.'; BOZ SA 861.16 (OLV 1498–9), fol. 12ʳ.

Figure 4 View of Bergen op Zoom, dominated by the church of St Gertrude; drawing (c. 1500) by Albrecht Dürer (Bergen op Zoom, City Archive)

two or three weeks before his appointment as *succentor* at the church of St Donatian in Bruges, 31 December 1498.[84] Our previous impression that the composer attended nearly all the services is thus confirmed.[85]

From the discussion so far a clear pattern emerges: Jacob Obrecht was evidently not the kind of musician who regarded a position, once obtained, as permanent. As *magister puerorum* in Cambrai he applied for the post of *succentor* in Bruges within nine months of his appointment; and he accepted the *succentor*-ship before 23 June 1485 – that is, more than a month before the chapter acts of Cambrai record the first irregularities which are believed to have led to his discharge.[86] Once in Bruges, Obrecht seems to have set his sights on a position in Italy: his motet *Inter praeclarissimas virtutes*, written in italianate style but preserved in a manuscript which draws its repertory directly from Flanders, is a musical letter of application comparable to Bach's *Musikalisches Opfer*.[87] If it was intended for Duke Ercole I d'Este of Ferrara, as is likely, it is not difficult to understand why the latter invited Obrecht to come and visit him in Italy in 1487. In a sense, the 1490s seem to have been the critical decade for Obrecht.

[84] See the entry of 31 December 1498 in the chapter acts of St Donatian, Van der Straeten, *op. cit.*, p. 185.

[85] Hence there is no reason to suppose that Obrecht suffered from poor health in 1497–8. The first concrete evidence of severe illness dates from September 1500, when the composer is described in the chapter acts of St Donatian as 'gravi aegritudine laborante' (Van der Straeten, *op. cit.*, pp. 185–7). According to Piscaer, Obrecht also suffered from poor health in Antwerp in 1492–7 ('Jacob Obrecht' (1938), pp. 11–12), but the evidence she adduces is not conclusive.   [86] See n. 74 above.

[87] Segovia, Archivo Capitular de la Catedral, MS s.s., fols. 78ᵛ–81ʳ. See A. Smijers, 'Twee onbekende Motetteksten van Jacob Hobrecht', *Tijdschrift van de Vereeniging voor Nederlandsche Muziekgeschiedenis*, 16 (1941), pp. 130–3; Murray, 'Jacob Obrecht's Connection', p. 129; A. Dunning, *Die Staatsmotette 1480–1555* (Utrecht, 1970), pp. 14–17; M. E. Nagle, 'The Structural Role of the Cantus Firmus in the Motets of Jacob Obrecht' (Ph.D. dissertation, University of Michigan, 1972), pp. 152–87. The character of a letter of application is especially marked in the second and third sections of the motet, which in Nagle's translation run as follows (*op. cit.*, p. 155; emended here after the original text): 'Well then, because of your fatherliness which is so great, I always sound forth [your] praises in my songs, jubilating, not as I should, but as I am able to. And I humbly offer *this present page*, put together in a crude style of harmony, for the praise of God and your comfort. For *what else I can give you now as a service, I do not know*. You have no need of money, and you are rich in insight and understanding. You enjoy prosperity and joy; you rejoice in tranquillity and peace; you are being praised among those who honour dignity. Be strong in your fight. Therefore *accept this present musical song, and me, Jacob Obrecht, your very humble servant, benevolently and with good will*. Command and rule happily and long.' I suggest that Obrecht wrote *Inter praeclarissimas virtutes* in 1487, after hearing of the reputation which he enjoyed with Duke Ercole I d'Este, and that he sent it to him in an attempt to obtain a position in Ferrara. The motet is immediately followed in Segovia s.s. by *Mille quingentis* of 1488.

He was forced to resign by the chapter of St Donatian in Bruges on 22 January 1491. After a gap of a year, we find him working in Antwerp in 1492 for the modest annual salary of 1080 groats, only 24 groats more than he had earned ten years before in Bergen op Zoom. In 1497, Obrecht was one of the first musicians to profit from the more generous patronage of John III of Glymes in Bergen op Zoom, and there are strong indications that he worked very hard in the eighteen months that he stayed here. For inexplicable reasons, however, he left this prospering musical centre for Bruges, which in the 1490s was already beginning to decline. Illness forced him to go back again to Antwerp, where he worked for 1080 groats per annum in 1501–2, and, from 1503, at an annual salary of 1560 groats. It is perhaps indicative of Obrecht's despair that in 1504 he was prepared to move to a city infested with plague – despite his poor health – finally to obtain the position consonant with his international reputation: the post of *maestro di cappella* in Ferrara, vacant because of Josquin's departure, at a salary of 100 ducats per annum (*c.* 11,000–12,000 Brabant groats). Subsequent strokes of misfortune quickly drew Obrecht's life to a close: after six months in Ferrara he suddenly found himself without a position when his employer Ercole I d'Este died (January 1505); a last attempt to obtain a position in Mantua failed (May 1505); and finally the composer contracted the dreaded plague himself, of which he died in late July 1505.[88]

Considering Obrecht's career as a whole it is interesting to see a development in his association with Bergen op Zoom. As a young and promising composer he held his first responsible post in 1480–4 at the Guild of Our Lady, then still a relatively modest musical centre. The reasons for his brief return in 1488, when his reputation was rising and his future looked bright, were of a political nature: his

[88] Lockwood, *Music in Renaissance Ferrara*, pp. 207–10. Richard Sherr (private communication, 1 August 1989) has discovered that Obrecht died before 1 August 1505, the date of two supplications, preserved in the Vatican Archives, for benefices that had become vacant on the composer's death. Two other supplications, dated 30 September 1505, imply that Obrecht may have been a member of the chapel of Pope Julius II, probably between November 1503 and September 1504. I am indebted to Prof. Sherr for sharing this material with me in advance of its publication. A 'Jacobus Obrechs' is mentioned in an obituary of St Goedele, Brussels, in 1507 (Haggh, 'Music, Liturgy, and Ceremony', p. 640). In a private communication dated 25 February 1989, Prof. Haggh wrote to me: 'It is always possible that the composer had some association with the church that is not mentioned by the documents and that he endowed an obit in Brussels, but I did see most of the documents from that period in the St Goedele archives and did not find any other mention of Obrechs.' Possibly, as Prof. Haggh adds, his name will, in due course, turn up in one of the more than ten thousand Brussels charters from this period.

participation as a singer in the services of the guild was now merely a matter of convenience. In the following decade, Bergen op Zoom's status as a musical centre rose quickly, while Obrecht somehow failed to turn the promises of his extraordinary musical talent to full profit. The cause for his return to Bergen op Zoom in 1497–8 lay in the new patronage and recruitment policy exerted by Lord John III of Glymes. Considering the later development of Bergen op Zoom as a musical centre – within a few years Obrecht could have earned more than 3000 groats per year – it would probably have been wisest for him to stay there rather than go to Bruges or Antwerp, let alone plague-infested Ferrara. It is true that Obrecht did not have the benefit of hindsight. Still, it is hard to avoid the impression that he found it difficult to settle for less than what his talent and stature entitled him to. Obrecht was born to be a second Josquin, and in the end he staked his life to become one.

MUSIC AT THE GUILD OF OUR LADY
UNDER JOHN III OF GLYMES

On 7 September 1494 Lord John II of Glymes died at the age of 77, having ruled Bergen op Zoom and its domains for more than half a century. Ten days later, on 17 September, his son John of Walhain was inaugurated lord of Bergen op Zoom, a ceremony on which a 'missen van den heyligen gheest' (Mass of the Holy Ghost) was performed by the singers of the church of St Gertrude.[89]

John III of Glymes was in many respects a more internationally oriented, cosmopolitan figure than his father (Figure 5). He had been made a knight of the Order of the Golden Fleece in 1481, was appointed 'yersten camerlinc' (first chamberlain) of Maximilian of Habsburg in 1485, and later became ambassador to Emperor Charles V. Thanks to his political and diplomatic skills he developed into one of the most powerful and influential noblemen of the

---

[89] 'On the twenty-first day of September [1494], given to the singers of the church [of St Gertrude] for the Mass of the Holy Ghost, which they sang when my lord was to be inaugurated, 6 *gelten*, makes 90 groats' ('Opten xxien dach septembris gesconcken den zangers van der kerken van der missen van den heyligen gheest die zij zongen als men mijnen heer hulden soude vj gelten maict vij sc. vj den.'); BOZ SA 252 (SR 1494–5), fol. 186ʳ. At the meetings of the Order of the Golden Fleece polyphonic Masses of the Holy Ghost were also performed; see W. F. Prizer, 'Music and Ceremonial in the Low Countries: Philip the Fair and the Order of the Golden Fleece', *Early Music History*, 5 (1985), pp. 113–52.

Figure 5   John and Henry of Glymes with their patron saints; left panel from an anonymous triptych (*c.* 1480). Left: John (1452–1532), who became Lord of Bergen op Zoom in 1494, with his patron saint John the Evangelist. Right: his brother Henry (1449–1502), who became Bishop of Cambrai in 1480, with his patron saint Henry (Emperor Heinrich II of the Holy Roman Empire). John and Henry were respectively knight and chancellor of the Order of the Golden Fleece. (Bergen op Zoom, City Archive)

Burgundian Netherlands.[90] John III's involvement in international affairs, however, prevented him from devoting as much energy to the government of his domains as his father had given. It has been estimated that he spent only about 130–40 days each year in Bergen

90   See John III's biography in Slootmans, *Jan metten Lippen*, pp. 48–56 and 107–309.

213

op Zoom.[91] Nevertheless, during his reign Bergen op Zoom prospered more than ever before. Its increasing importance as a market town was in fact one of the main contributory causes of the decline of the Bruges staple market after 1500. An indication of Bergen op Zoom's wealth and confidence in the last decades of the fifteenth century is provided by the fact that the city started to rebuild the church of St Gertrude completely in 1489, barely twenty years after Spoorwater's building had been completed.[92] If the new church had been finished it would have been almost as big as the church of Our Lady at Antwerp.

Bergen op Zoom now took its place on the international political stage. For the reception of important visitors, such as Philip the Fair (1497), Emperor Maximilian I (1508) and the knights of the Order of the Golden Fleece (1496), as well as of various ambassadors, officials, princes and noblemen, it needed a representative musical establishment equal in quality and splendour to the finest chapels of north-western Europe. Before John III became lord of Bergen op Zoom, he had had ample opportunity to become acquainted with famous household chapels, such as that of Charles the Bold (when he participated in the siege of Neuss and the battle of Nancy) and, in his capacity of first chamberlain, with the chapels of Maximilian of Habsburg and Philip the Fair. From now on these latter chapels, rather than the choirs of other confraternities in Brabant, were to provide the model for the Guild of Our Lady.

As we have seen, under John II of Glymes the choir of the Guild of Our Lady underwent a steady but slow rise in quality, mainly because most of the new singers were appointed at fees above the average level. In spite of the continuous increase in spending on music, however, the period 1480–94 had been very much a time of stability. The choir of the guild consisted of a nucleus comprising the choirmaster and six permanent singers (singers 2, 3, 4, 5, 6 and 7 in Appendix 4 below), and a varying number of 'hangers-on', who usually participated in the services on a less regular basis. The top fee was fixed at 3.75 groats per *loot*, and this ceiling was not raised even for a well-regarded singer like Michiele Cramer, whom the guild was so very anxious to retain in 1485 when he was invited to

---

[91] *Ibid.*, p. 201.
[92] C. J. A. C. Peeters, 'Het Nieuwe Werk als het bijna mogelijke', *Bergen op Zoom gebouwd en beschouwd*, pp. 157–69.

become a singer in Maximilian of Habsburg's chapel.[93] On the whole, the accounts of 1480–94 give the impression that there was not an active, energetic recruitment policy. Indeed, one might rather say that this period was characterised by a more or less perfunctory management of the available funds, aimed primarily at keeping up the existing standard. The fact that this standard was in fact gradually rising seems to have been a fortuitous consequence of the increasing market revenues rather than the result of a deliberate policy.

All this was to change radically after 1494. The first sign of a change of policy is in the accounts of 1494–5, where a new singer, Lucas of Brussels, is mentioned as receiving the unprecedented fee of 6 groats per *loot*. Two years later, in 1496–7, two other new singers, Willeme Jacobssone from The Hague and Jacob Obrecht, were appointed at fees of 4.5 and 6 groats respectively. But the real breakthrough came in 1498–9, when the guild employed two singers at 6 groats per *loot*, three at 7.5 groats per *loot*, and one at 9 groats per *loot* – all appointed after 1494. Of the singers who had worked at the guild during the last year of John II's reign (1493–4), only two were now left: Michiele Cramer, once the guild's best singer, now with his fee of 3.75 groats the next to lowest-paid musician; and the 'old and slow' Willeme van Hondswijck, who apparently was allowed to stay at the guild for reasons of charity (at a fee of 2.25 groats per *loot*).

The trend was now towards employing fewer, but better-paid, singers. This is illustrated by Appendix 3, in which for each financial year the average value of the *loten* and the average number of singers per service are given. It can be easily observed that the average value of the *loten*, which had stayed between 2 and 3 groats during the period 1480–94, rose quickly from about 3 to 7 groats in 1494–1508. At the same time, the average number of singers per service fell from between six and nine in 1480–94 to between four and six in 1494–1508. It is instructive to compare Appendix 3 with Figure 3a above. The graph shows that during the period 1470–1510 the total amount of money spent on musicians' salaries at the Guild of Our Lady was rising continuously, but it gives no sign of any change around 1494. The Appendix, on the other hand, tells us *how* the amounts were actually spent, and indicates a significant change in the pattern of spending in the mid-1490s.

[93] See Piscaer, 'De Zangers van het Onze Lieve Vrouwe Gilde', pp. 74–5 and 149.

The Guild of Our Lady was now looking for singers of high quality. What it could offer them, if they attended all services, was annual salaries of *c*. 2500–2600 groats (at 6 groats per *loot*), *c*. 3100–3300 (at 7.5 groats per *loot*), or even *c*. 3700–3900 (at 9 groats per *loot*). One need only compare these figures with the ones given in Table 2 to realise that within five years (1494–9) a veritable turnaround had taken place at the guild. However, singers of high quality were not only scarce and expensive, but also much favoured by other musical centres. Bergen op Zoom now entered a labour market characterised by fierce competition, and it comes as no surprise that the stability which had prevailed during the period 1480–94 now gave way to rapid turnover: none of the singers appointed in the period 1494–1510 stayed at the guild for more than four or five years. Some singers were able to make a good living in this system of tough competition, but others – Jacob Obrecht was a notable example – failed. A good example of a successful singer was Henricke Haudijn of Diest, who worked at the Guild of Our Lady in 1506 and 1507 at a fee of 9 groats per *loot*. In April 1507 the choirmaster of 's-Hertogenbosch, Claessen Craen, died, and Haudijn was asked to become his successor. In order to get him, the 's-Hertogenbosch confraternity had to raise its top weekly wage from 14 stivers (=2184 groats *per annum*) to 20 stivers (=3120 groats *per annum*).[94] In spite of this financial sacrifice, 's-Hertogenbosch eventually lost the competition for Haudijn with Bergen op Zoom: in 1510 he became choirmaster at the Guild of Our Lady at a fee of 12 groats per *loot*, earning a salary of more than 5000 groats *per annum*. With Henricke Haudijn's appointment as choirmaster in 1510 a new period in the history of the guild started, which however will not be dealt with in the present study. Other famous singers were Clause of Lier, who worked irregularly at the guild in 1499–1503 and is also found listed as one of Philip the Fair's singers in 1492–1502,[95] and Johannes Ghiselin *alias* Verbonnet, who already had an international career behind him when he became the guild's best-paid singer in 1507.[96]

There are also musical innovations which may perhaps be connec-

---

[94]   Smijers, 'De Illustre Lieve Vrouwe Broederschap' (1935), pp. 66–73.
[95]   Van der Straeten, *op. cit.*, vii (Brussels, 1885), pp. 107–8, 144–5, 151, 153, 156, 178, 268–9 and 496–7; Prizer, *op. cit.*, p. 126.
[96]   C. Gottwald, *Johannes Ghiselin – Johannes Verbonnet* (Wiesbaden, 1962).

ted with John III's patronage. From 1494–5 onwards, for instance, the choirmaster was paid an extra 360 groats per year 'for singing the *Ave Maria* with the choristers, when the bells are ringing during the *Lof*.'[97] And four years later we find the first mention of an annual service in which all the available musical resources of Bergen op Zoom were drawn together in a sumptuous celebration: the 'generael processie avont'. The accounts for 1499–1500 describe this service as follows:[98] 'And on Procession-General Eve, when the singers, the organist and the city pipers sang and played certain motets in the night, together with carillon-playing and bell-ringing, to which [service] the [chapter of St Gertrude's] church does not contribute, paid 48 groats.' No doubt this display of musical splendour was partly designed to impress the thousands of merchants who stayed at Bergen op Zoom during the Easter fairs. As early as 1399 it had been stipulated that the Procession of the Holy Cross (around 3 May) was to conclude the Easter fair in a festive climax.[99] Unfortunately it is not possible to extract more specific information from the accounts on the cultivation of polyphony under John III of Glymes. It seems very likely, though, that with respect to performance practice and choice of repertory there was much more continuity with the previous period than there was with respect to recruitment policy.

The unsettledness of the period 1494–1510 was to give way to new stability after 1510. After a gap of three years in the accounts (1508/9–1510/11) the choir of the guild appears to have been almost entirely restaffed in 1511–12, and most of the new members were to remain in more or less permanent service during the 1510s. From 1518–19 onwards, two (later three) trumpeters also participated in the services. These later developments, however, will be dealt with in detail in a separate study.

This article has focused on the creation and early development of Bergen op Zoom as a musical centre. Within forty years of its foundation the Guild of Our Lady became one of the most important

---

[97] 'Also to the same [choirmaster] for singing the *Ave Maria* with the choristers when the bell is ringing during the *Lof*, 360 groats' ('noch den selven voer ave maria metten coralen te singene als de clocke int loff clipt xxx sc.br.'); BOZ SA 861.13 (OLV 1494–5), fol. 10ʳ.

[98] 'Ende opten generael processie avont als de sangeren organiste ende stadtpijpers sekere motetten inden nacht songen ende speelden met beyarden ende luyen sonder dat de kerke daertoe oic geeft betaelt iiij sc.br.'; BOZ SA 861.17 (OLV 1499–1500), fol. 13ʳ.

[99] Slootmans, *Paas- en Koudemarkten*, I, p. 14.

musical establishments of the Low Countries, surpassing the venerable Illustrious Confraternity of Our Lady at 's-Hertogenbosch and rivalling the chapels of Maximilian of Habsburg and Philip the Fair. The rapid growth of the guild was mainly the result of John II of Glymes's decision, in 1474, to renounce to it the revenues of the twice-yearly Bergen op Zoom fairs. Those revenues were to rise dramatically in the decades following his decision. However, we have also observed that the relative importance of Bergen op Zoom as a musical centre depended not only on the funds themselves, but also on the ways they were spent. While John II created the guild and provided the resources for its further growth, it was his son and successor John III who turned these resources to full advantage.

It may seem odd to assess the musical life of a medieval institution on the basis of purely financial criteria, rather than musical data such as manuscripts and compositions or the presence of famous musicians and composers. On the other hand, compositions and sources have been very unevenly preserved, and therefore tend to give a distorted picture of musical life in fifteenth-century Europe. And it is difficult to tell what makes a musician 'famous', particularly if he was not a composer. The first criterion one would think of is the musical centres in which he worked: everyone would agree that a musician who worked, for instance, at the Burgundian chapel or the chapel of Duke Ercole I d'Este of Ferrara must have possessed outstanding qualities. But obviously it would be circular to establish the quality of musicians on the basis of the centres where they worked, and the importance of musical centres on the basis of the singers they employed.

The advantage of financial criteria, then, seems to be that they are objective, and that financial data of different musical centres can be directly compared. In particular, musical life in the Burgundian Netherlands lends itself to direct comparison, because the exchange rates between the various coinages were fixed (since 1433) and the standards of living in the larger towns were more or less commensurable. Comparisons between the Low Countries and Italy may be more difficult, since one may have to allow for differences in the costs of living. But by attempting to relate musicians' salaries to the basic costs of living (see Table 2 above) it might be possible to overcome such difficulties. Comparisons between the standards of living of musicians in different countries might help us to understand and interpret, at least in part, their extraordinary mobility. Of course it would be one-sided to consider fifteenth-century musicians as workers driven merely by the impulse to earn more, no matter where their travels would lead them (the 'birds on the branches'). Yet an understanding of the large-scale economic processes, and their effects on the demand for a luxury like polyphonic music, could help us to explain at least some of the changing patterns of migration. To establish this link between economic history and music still remains a task for the future.

University of Amsterdam

APPENDIX 1

Foundation document of *Lof* service of the Guild of Our Lady, 24 December 1470 (Bergen op Zoom, City Archive, Stadsarchief inv. no. 157 (La.G), fols. 16[r-v]; previously published in Slootmans, 'De Hoge Lieve Vrouw' (1964), pp. 42–3).

Van onser vrouwen love ende hoe vele men den sancmeester ende sangeren etc. gheven zal.

Anno lxx opten xxiiij[ten] dach decembris overdreghen ende geordoneert by mynen lieven heer van berghen burgemeesters ende scepenen als overste van onser liever vrouwen gulde binnen der kercken van berghen ter erectien ende onderhoudinghe van onser vrouwen loove ende des daer ane cleeft.

[1] Inden eersten dat meester willem de sanckmeester nu synde gehouden syn sel te comen alle avonde onder [*sic*] kercken ende aldaer singhen metten kinderen onser vrouwen lof daer voer hy voer hem selve hebben sel zesse rynsche guldens ende voer de kinderen vier der selven rynsche guldenen twintich stuvers voer tstuck gerekent.

[2] Des sel hy oick gehouden syn den anderen mede sangeren te deylene ende te disterbuerenne tloot dat men daer toe ordineren sel gegeven te wordenne elcken naer sinen loon by alsoe dat de regeerders vander selver gulden op hem begheren.

[3] Item sel de opperste tenoriste hebben telker reysen dat hy ter selver loove comparaten sel enen brabantschen groten ende elken vanden anderen sangheren biden capittel geadmitteert tot vive toe telker reysen dat sy compareren selen elken een oortken.

[4] Ende midts desen sullen alle de voirg[escreven] personen ende elck van hen gehouden syn sel te singhenne alle onser vrouwen missen eck op de

verboorte van alsoe vele als elck inden loove comende des avonts winnen soude.

[5] Item datmen zekere looden maken ende doen maken ende daerop teijkenne de waerde vanden penninghen die elck in tsinen verdienen ende toegeordineert syn boven welke looden de regeerders gehouden syn selen te overtenemenne vanden sangeren vier reysen tsiaers ende hem daer voer te gheven gelt elcken naer tsine.

[6] Item heeft voort myn heer geconsenteert vanden sinen te worden betaelt elken vanden sangheren meesteren van buyten comende telken dat sy comen sullen singhen onser vrouwen lof een loot van enen oortkenne ende dat sullen den selven de regeerderen ter stont wisselen ende gelt voer gheven.

[7] Is oick geordineert dat alle de stuvers die vanden guldebroeders tot misse gelt sullen worden gegeven to wetenne vanden ghenen daer af onse vrouwe egenen koste af en heeft van spyse noch van drancke tot onser vrouwen dienste sullen worden geappliceert sonder daer af yet inde koste ende maeltyt te applicerenne ende te voegenne ende alsoe sullen de regeerders voirscreven vanden selven stuvers in hare rekeninge bisonder rekeninge ende bewys doen van jaer tot jaer.

[8] Item hebben de heeren vanden capittele geconsenteert ende geseedt dat men tsavonts clocke clippen naden loove sonder onser vrouwen kost.

[9] Item sel de maeltyt opten kersnacht voerde sanghers in tgeheele afgesneden wesen ende oick alle maeltiiden noch en selmen oick voer de selve maeltiiden egene penninghen gheven des is hier ine uytgenomen de groote maeltyt te half oexst.

APPENDIX 2

Expenditure on music at the Guild of Our Lady 1480/1–1507/8

In order to save space, the accounts are not presented in transcription but are given in summary. The original spelling has been retained. All sums are given in Brabant groats. If the number of *loten* indicated in the account does not correspond with the total salary of the musician divided by the value of one *loot*, the correct number is given, followed by the incorrect number between brackets, e.g.: 157 (160). If the total salary is not exactly divisible by the value of one *loot*, the quotient is rounded down and followed by a question mark between brackets: e.g. Cornelise Zwagers's salary in 1486–7 was 1474.5 Brabant groats, and each *loot* was worth 3.75 groats. This gives 393.2 *loten*, indicated below as 393(?) *loten*. The numbers in square brackets refer to the list of singers (Appendix 4).

1480–1481

Heer Anthuenise de Rouck (officiant)		1440
The *sangmeester* [1]	annual salary	720
	Holy Cross *lof*	60
Organist		
annual salary (960), reduced by 60 because of temporary absence		900
Choristers	Holy Cross *lof* and other services	300
Heer Michele [2]	[66 *loten* of 3 gr.?]	198
Heer Cornelise [3]	[113 *loten* of 3 gr.?]	339
Meester Willeme van Hondswijc [4]	422 *loten* of 1.5 gr.	633
Heer Symon van Amerode *cantor* [5]	[248 *loten* of 1.5 gr.?]	372
Heer Henrick Malecourt [6]	[301 *loten* of 1.5 gr.?]	451.5
Michelet [7]	[346 *loten* of 1.5 gr.?]	519
Heer Peter de Coster [8]		366
Heer Cornelise Both [9]		154.5
Meester Janne Mol [10]		477
Johannes Greefken [11]		436.5
	allowance from the dean of the previous year	90
Heer Janne de Greve [12]		83.25
Aubertijne [13]		345
Bellringers		432
Total		8316.75

1481–1482

Heer Anthuenise de Rouc (officiant)		1440
Meestere Jacobe *den sangmeester* [1]	annual salary	720
	Holy Cross *lof*	60
	earned after 24 June 1482: 39 *loten* of 3 gr.	117
Organist	salary	960
	reimbursement for purchase of bonnet	30
Choristers	services of Our Lady	240
	Holy Cross *lof*	60
Heer Michiele [2]	336–420 *loten* of 3 and 3.75 gr.	1260
Heer Cornelise [3]	[329–411 *loten* of 3 and 3.75 gr.?]	1234.5
Meester Willeme van Hondswijc [4]	432 *loten* of 1.5 gr.	648
Heer Symone [5]	392 *loten* of 1.5 gr.	588
Heer Henricke Mailcourt [6]	424 *loten* of 1.5 gr.	636
The young *heer* Michiele [7]	456 *loten* of 1.5 gr.	684

Meester Gielise [14]	76 *loten* of 1.5 gr.	114
Heer Quintene [15]	105 *loten* of 1 gr.	105
Meester Janne Mol [10]		57
Jannes *de barbier* [11]		31.5
Aubertine [13]		791.25
Bellringers		792
Total		10,568.25

1482–1483

Heer Anthuenise de Rouck (officiant)		1260
The *sangmeester* [1]	332 *loten* of 3 gr.	996
	Holy Cross *lof*	60
Denise the organist	salary (until his death)	840
Janne van Steenberghen		
	for keeping the organs after Denise's death	150
Choristers	services of Our Lady	210
	Holy Cross *lof*	60
Heer Michiele [2]	480(?) *loten* of 3.75 gr.	1803.5
	reimbursement for purchase of tabard	360
Heer Cornelise [3]	434 *loten* of 3.75 gr.	1627.5
Meester Gielise [14]	288–430 *loten* of 1.5 and 2.25 gr.	646
Meester Willeme van Hondswijck [4]	248 *loten* of 1.5 gr.	372
Heer Symon *de canter* [5]	320 *loten* of 1.5 gr.	480
Heer Henrike Mailcourt [6]	384 *loten* of 1.5 gr.	576
The young *heer* Michiele [7]	406 *loten* of 1.5 gr.	609
Heer Quintijne [15]	342 *loten* of 1 gr.	342
Bellringers		420
Total		10,812

1483–1484

Heer Anthuenise de Rouck (officiant)		1440
Meester Jacobe *den sangmeester* [1] and Reijnier 'with the hunch, who was living with him' [16]	637 *loten* of 3 gr.	1911
To the *sangmeester* [1] alone	Holy Cross *lof*	60
Organist	salary	1231.5
Choristers	salary	240
	Holy Cross *lof*	60
Heer Michiele [2]	393 *loten* of 3.75 gr.	1473.75
	reimbursement for purchase of tabard	360
Heer Cornelise van Scietdamme [3]	90 *loten* of 3.75 gr.	337.5

Heer Cornelise uuten Hage [17]	103(?) *loten* of 2.25 gr.	232.25
Meester Willem van Hondswijck [4]	390 *loten* of 1.5 gr.	585
Heer Symon *de cantor* [5]	364 *loten* of 1.5 gr.	546
Heer Henric Mailcourt [6]	416 *loten* of 1.5 gr.	624
The young *heer* Michiele [7]	389 *loten* of 1.5 gr.	583.5
Heer Quintijn [15]	318 *loten* of 1 gr.	318
Bellringers		522
Total		10,524.5

1484–1485

Lost

1485–1486

Heer Anthuenise de Rouck *priester* (officiant)		1440
Den sangmeestere meestere Pauwelse van Rode [18]		
	432(?) *loten* of 3.75 gr.	1621.5
	Holy Cross *lof*	60
Organist	salary	1440
Choristers		360
Heer Michiele Cramer *tenoriste* [2]	417(?) *loten* of 3.75 gr.	1566
	bonus from *burgemeester* and *schepenen*	540
Heer Cornelise Zwagers [3]	438(?) *loten* of 3.75 gr.	1645.25
Heer Symon van Amerode *priestere ende cantere* [5]		
	c. 369–93 *loten* of 1.5 gr. and 2.25 gr.	685.5
Meester Willeme van Honswijck [4]	308 *loten* of 1.5 gr.	462
Heer Henricke van Maelcourt *tenoriste* [6]	360 *loten* of 1.5 gr.	540
Heer Michiel van Bastoengen *alias* Michelet [7]		
	381 *loten* of 1.5 gr.	571.5
Heer Alairde Henricxsone *priestere* [19]	[24 *loten* of 1.5 gr.?]	36
Bellringers		546
Total		11,513.75
Total in account		11,514.25

1486–1487

Heer Anthuenise de Rouck *priestere* (officiant)		1440
Den sangmeester meestere Pauwelse van Rode [18]		
	307(?) *loten* of 3.75 gr.	1153.5
	Holy Cross *lof*	60
Organist	salary	1440
Choristers		360

Heere Michiele Cramer *tenoriste* [2]	430 *loten* of 3.75 gr.	1612.5
bonus from *burgemeester* and *schepenen*		540
Heere Cornelise Zwaghere [3]	393(?) *loten* of 3.75 gr.	1474.5
Heere Michiele van Bastoingnen *alias* Michelet [7]		
181 *loten* of 1.5 gr. until 10 Jan 1487		271.5
210 *loten* of 1.75 gr. from 11 Jan to 19 Aug 1487		367.5
Meester Willem van Honswijck [4]	285 *loten* of 1.5 gr.	427.5
Heere Symon van Amerode *priestere ende cantere* [5]		
463 *loten* of 2.25 gr.		1041.75
Heere Henricke van Malencourt *tenoriste* [6]	594 *loten* of 1.5 gr.	891
Heere Alaerde Henricxsone *priestere* [19]	60 *loten* of 1.5 gr.	90
Bellringers		546
Total		11,715.75

1487–1488

Heer Anthoenis de Ruck *priestere* (officiant)		1440
Den sangmeester meester Pauwelse van Rode [18]		
461(?) *loten* of 3.75 gr. (incl. 64 *loten* of the previous year)		1730.25
	Holy Cross *lof*	60
Organist	salary	1440
Choristers		—
Meester Jacop *den sangmeester* [1]	48 *loten* of 3.75 gr.	180
Heere Maghiel Cramer *tenoriste* [2]	416 *loten* of 3.75 gr.	1560
bonus from *burgemeester* and *schepenen*		540
Heer Cornelise Zwagher [3]		
460 *loten* of 3.75 gr. (including a number of *loten* from the previous year)		1725
Heer Maghiel van Bastoengien [7]	416 *loten* of 1.875 gr.	780
Meester Willem van Hontswijck [4]	309 *loten* of 1.5 gr.	463.5
Heer Symoen van Ameroede *priester ende cantoer* [5]		
422 *loten* of 2.25 gr.		949.5
Heer Hendric van Maelcoert *tenorijste* [6]	414 *loten* of 1.5 gr.	621
Heer Alert Heyndricss *priester* [19]	474 *loten* of 1.5 gr.	711
Bellringers		546
Total		13,286.25

1488–1489

Heere Anthuenise de Rouck *priestere* (officiant)		1440
additional reward for having served longer than 8(?) years		183

Den sangmeester meester Pauwelse van Rode [18]

	420 *loten* of 3.75 gr.	1575
	Holy Cross *lof*	60
Choristers		240
Meestere Adriane *den organist*	salary	1440
Heere Michiele Cramere *tenoriste* [2]	432 *loten* of 3.75 gr.	1620
	bonus from *burgemeester* and *schepenen*	540
Heere Cornelise Zwaghere [3]	246 *loten* of 3.75 gr.	922.5
Heer Symone van Amerode *priestere ende cantoer* [5]		
	420 *loten* of 2.25 gr.	945
Heere Michiele van Bastoengien *alias* Michilet [7]		
	449(?) *loten* of 1.875 gr.	843
Meester Willeme van Hondswijck [4]	378 *loten* of 1.5 gr.	567
Heere Henricke van Maelcoert *tenoriste* [6]	398 *loten* of 1.5 gr.	597
Heere Alaerde Henricxsone *priester* [19]	389 *loten* of 1.5 gr.	583.5
Heer Janne (replaced Zwaghere) [20]	[94 *loten* of 1.5 gr.?]	141
Bellringers		654
Total		12,351

1489–1490

(before Maximilian's ordinance of 24 December 1489)

Various priests (officiants)		36
Meestere Pauwelse van Rode *de sangmeester* [18], and *meestere* Thomase [21], who came in his stead, together 171 *loten* of		
	3.75 gr.	644.25
	Holy Cross *lof*	60
Choristers		120
Organist		600
Heere Michiele Cramer *priester* [2]	157 (160) *loten* of 3.75 gr.	588.75
	bonus from *burgemeester* and *schepenen*	270
Heere Janne Holtken [22]	141 *loten* of 3 gr.	423
Heere Symone van Ammerode *de cantere* [5]		
	138(?) *loten* of 1 lelyaert*	430.5
Heere Michiele van Bastoengnen [7]	144 *loten* of 1.875 gr.	270
Meester Willeme van Honswijck [4]	112 *loten* of 1.5 gr.	168
Heere Henricke van Waelcourt [6]	151 *loten* of 1.5 gr.	226.5
Heere Alaerde Henricxssone [19]	146 (144) *loten* of 1.5 gr.	219
Bellringers		261
Total		4317

*Coin of unknown value

(after Maximilian's ordinance of 24 December 1489)

Heer Adam vander Craenleyden *priester ende canonic*, and other various priests (officiants)		1353.75
Heer Thomase *den sangmeester* [21]	253 *loten* of 3.75 gr.	948.75
	Holy Cross *lof*	60
Choristers		120
Organist		840
Heere Michiele Cramer *priester ende tenoriste* [2]		
	256 *loten* of 3.75 gr.	960
	bonus from *burgemeester* and *schepenen*	270
Heere Jan Holtken *priester* [22]	265 *loten* of 3 gr.	795
Heere Symone van Ammerode *cantere* [5]	277 *loten* of 2.25 gr.	623.25
Heere Michiele van Bastoengnen [7]	228 *loten* of 2.25 gr.	513
Heer Willem van Honswijck [4]	180 *loten* of 1.5 gr.	270
Heere Henricke van Maelcourt [6]	230 *loten* of 1.5 gr.	345
Heere Alaerde Henricxzone [19]	240 *loten* of 1.5 gr.	360
Bellringers		213
Total		7671.75
Sum total of 1489–90		11,988.75

1490–1491

Various priests (officiants)		1404
Anthoenise de Rouck (officiant)		180
Meestere Thomase *de sangmeester* [21]	415 *loten* of 3.75 gr.	1556.25
	Holy Cross *lof*	60
Organist	salary	1440
Choristers	440 *loten* of 1.5 gr.	660
Heere Michiele Cramer [2]	406 *loten* of 3.75 gr.	1522.5
	additional bonus	540
Heere Servase van Maestricht [23]	105 *loten* of 3.75 gr.	393.75
Heere Janne van Gheele *alias* Holtken [22]	384 *loten* of 3 gr.	1152
Heere Cornelise Zwaghere [3]	145(?) *loten* of 2.25 gr.	326.75
Heere Symone van Ammerode [5]	408(?) *loten* of 2.25 gr.	918.25
Heere Michiele van Bastoingnen [7]	421(?) *loten* of 1.875 gr.	790.5
Heer Willeme van Honswijck [4]	369 *loten* of 1.5 gr.	553.5
Heere Henricke Maelcourt *priester* [6]	405 *loten* of 1.5 gr.	607.5
Heer Alaerde Henricxss [19]	351 *loten* of 1.5 gr.	526.5
Heer Janne *des dekens capellaen* [20]	370 *loten* of 1.5 gr.	555
Bellringers		522
Total		13,708.5

1491–1492

Heer Anthoenise de Rouck *priester ende canonick* (officiant)		1440
Meestere Thomase *den sangmeestere* [21]	420 *loten* of 3.75 gr.	1575
	Holy Cross *lof*	120
Meestere Jacobe the organist	salary	1440
Choristers	422 *loten* of 1.5 gr.	633
Heere Michiele Cramer *tenoriste* [2]	420 *loten* of 3.75 gr.	1575
	additional bonus	540
Heere Cornelise Zwagere [3]	420 *loten* of 3.75 gr.	1575
Heere Servase van Maestricht [23]	416 *loten* of 3.75 gr.	1560
Heere Janne van Gheele *alias* Holtken [22]	85 *loten* of 3 gr.	255
Woutere *de tenoriste* [24]	182 *loten* of 3 gr.	546
Heere Symone van Amerode *cantere* [5]	402 *loten* of 2.25 gr.	904.5
Heere Michiele van Bastoingene [7]	420 *loten* of 1.875 gr.	787.5
Heere Willeme van Hondswijck [4]	320 *loten* of 1.5 gr.	480
Heere Henricke van Maelcourt *priestere* [6]	365 *loten* of 1.5 gr.	547.5
Heere Alaerde Henricxss [19]	229 *loten* of 1.5 gr.	343.5
stocking-cloth (at the command of the *burgemeester* and *scepenen*)		72
Heere Janne *des dekens capellaen* [20]	232 *loten* of 1.5 gr.	348
Bellringers		522
Total		15,264

1492–1493

Heere Anthoenise de Rouck *priestere ende canonic* (officiant)		1680
Meestere Thomase *den sangmeestere* [21]	380 *loten* of 3.75 gr.	1425
	Holy Cross *lof*	120
Meester Karel *de sangmeester* [25]		
33 *loten* of 3.75 gr. (appointed July 1493)		123.75
Meestere Jacobe the organist	salary	1440
Choristers	422 *loten* of 1.5 gr.	633
Heere Michiele Cramer [2]		
420 *loten* (and 24 old *loten*) of 3.75 gr.		1665
	additional bonus	540
Heere Cornelise Swaghere [3]	351 (352) *loten* of 3.75 gr.	1316.25
Heere Servase van Maestricht [23]	372 *loten* of 3.75 gr.	1395
Wouter *den sanger* [24]	235 *loten* of 3 gr.	705
Heere Symone van Amerode *cantere* [5]	400 *loten* of 2.25 gr.	900
Heere Adriane Bouckeel [26]	72 *loten* of 2.25 gr.	162
Heere Michiele van Bastoengien [7]		
374(?) (372) *loten* of 1.875 gr.		702

Meestere Willeme van Honswijck [4]	305 *loten* of 1.5 gr.	457.5
Heere Henricke van Maelcourt *priestere* [6]	412 *loten* of 1.5 gr.	618
Bellringers		522
Total		14,404.5

1493–1494

Heere Anthoenise de Rouck *priestere ende canonick* (officiant)		1680
Meestere Kaerlen *den sangmeester* [25]	413 *loten* of 3.75 gr.	1551
	Holy Cross *lof*	120
Meestere Jacobe the organist	salary	1440
Choristers	422 *loten* of 1.5 gr.	633
Heere Michiele Cramer [2]	412 *loten* of 3.75 gr.	1545
	aditional bonus	540
Heere Janne Stevens [27]	331 *loten* of 3.75 gr.	1241.25
Heere Symone van Amerode *de cantere* [5]	406 *loten* of 2.25 gr.	913.5
Heere Janne Blockeel [28]	115(?) (132) *loten* of 2.25 gr.	259.5
Heere Willeme van Honswijck [4]	230 *loten* of 1.5 gr.	345
	163 (162) *loten* of 2.25 gr.	366.75
Jacobe van Alckemair [29]	84 *loten* of 1.5 gr.	126
	303 *loten* of 2.25 gr.	681.75
Heere Michiele van Bastoingnen [7]	366 *loten* of 1.875 gr.	668.25
Heere Henricke van Maelcourt [6]	413 *loten* of 1.5 gr.	619.5
Bellringers		582
Total		13,312.5

1494–1495

Heere Anthoenise de Roeck *priestere ende canonick* (officiant)		1680
Meestere Kaerle *den sangmeester* [25]	413 *loten* of 3.75 gr.	1551
	Holy Cross *lof*	120
'for singing the *Ave Maria* with the choristers, when the bells are ringing during the *Lof*'		360
Meestere Jacobe the organist	salary	1440
Choristers	422 *loten* of 1.5 gr.	633
Heere Lucas van Bruessele [30]	63 *loten* of 6 gr.	378
Heere Michiele Cramer [2]	420 *loten* of 3.75 gr.	1575
	additional bonus	540
Wouter *de tenoriste* [24]	71 *loten* of 3.75 gr.	266.25
Heere Janne van Nyeupoort [27]	408 *loten* of 3.75 gr.	1530
Jacobe van Alckemaer *tenoriste* [29]	74 *loten* of 2.25 gr.	166.5
	166 *loten* of 3.75 gr.	622.5

Meestere Willeme van Honswijck [4]	397 *loten* of 2.25 gr.	893.25
Heere Symone van Amerode *de cantere* [5]	383 *loten* of 2.25 gr.	861.75
Heere Michiele van Bastoingnen [7]	411 *loten* of 1.875 gr.	770.79
Heere Henricke van Maelcourt *tenoriste* [6]	421 *loten* of 1.5 gr.	631.5
Bellringers		852
Total		14,871.54

1495–1496

Heere Anthuenise de Rouck *priestere ende canonick* (officiant)		1680
Meestere Kaerle *de sangmeester* [25]	244 *loten* of 3.75 gr.	915
	Holy Cross *lof*	120
	Ave Maria	360
Meestere Peter *den sangmeester* [31]	124 *loten* of 3.75 gr.	465
Meestere Jacobe the organist	salary	1440
Choristers	422 *loten* of 1.5 gr.	633
Heere Lucas van Bruessele [30]	238 *loten* of 6 gr.	1428
Heere Michiele de Cramer [2]	409 *loten* of 3.75 gr.	1533.75
	additional bonus	540
Woutere *de tenoriste* [24]	45(?) *loten* of 3.75 gr.	169
Heere Janne van Nyeupoort [27]	426 *loten* of 3.75 gr.	1597.5
Heere Quintene [15]	132 *loten* of 3 gr.	396
Meestere Willeme van Honswijck [4]	437(?) *loten* of 2.25 gr.	984
Heere Symone *de cantere* [5]	deceased	—
Jacobe van Alckemaer [29]	139(?) *loten* of 2.25 gr.	313.25
Heere Michiele van Bastoingnen [7]	341(?) *loten* of 1.875 gr.	639.38
Heere Henricke van Maelcourt [6]	432 *loten* of 1.5 gr.	648
Willeme van Honswijck (junior) [32]	202 *loten* of 1.5 gr.	303
Bellringers		852
Total		15,016.88

1496–1497

Heere Anthuenise de Rouck *priestere ende canonick* (officiant)		1680
Meestere Petere *den sangmeestere* [31]	422 *loten* of 3.75 gr.	1582.5
	Holy Cross *lof*	120
	Ave Maria	360
Meestere Jacobe the organist	salary	1440
Choristers	422 *loten* of 1.5 gr.	633
Meestere Jacobe Obrechts [1]	52 *loten* of 6 gr.	312
bonus on his arrival, at the command of the lord of Bergen op Zoom		75

Willeme Jacobss *uuten Haghe* [33]	21 *loten* of 4.5 gr.	94.5
Heere Michiele Cramere [2]	417 *loten* of 3.75 gr.	1563.75
	additional bonus	540
Heeren Janne van Nyeupoort [27]	175 *loten* of 3.75 gr.	656.25
Heere Ghysbrechte Pieterss *hoeghcontere* [34]	73 *loten* of 3.75 gr.	273.75
Heere Govaerde *hooghcontere* [35]	173 *loten* of 3.75 gr.	648.75
Heere Quintene [15]	280 *loten* of 3 gr.	840
Meestere Willeme van Honswijck [4]	426 *loten* of 2.25 gr.	958.5

additional bonus, at the command of the *burgemeester* and *scepenen*, 'because he became old and slow, and is an old singer' 120

Heere Jacobe van Alckemaer [29]	316 *loten* of 2.25 gr.	711
Heere Henricke Maelcourt [6]	138 *loten* of 1.5 gr.	207
Willeme [32], son of Willeme van Honswijck		
	405 *loten* of 1.5 gr.	607.5

'Paid to certain foreign singers, who helped sing on Procession Day and in the [following] weeks, at the command of the *burgemeester* and *scepenen*' 117

'Also paid, at the same command as above, to the singers of Duke Philip [the Fair], because they helped sing the *Lof* 97.5

Bellringers	762
Total	14,400

1497–1498

Lost

1498–1499

Heere Anthuenise de Rouck *priestere ende canonick* (officiant)		1680
Meestere Petere den sangmeester [31]	419 *loten* of 3.75 gr.	1571.25
	Holy Cross *lof*	120
	Ave Maria	360
Meestere Jacobe the organist	salary	1440
Choristers	422 *loten* of 1.5 gr.	633
Dominicus *den tenoriste* [36]	88 *loten* of 9 gr.	792
Meester Janne Slijper *tenoriste* [37]	176 *loten* of 7.5 gr.	1320
Gommare van Lyere [38]	104 *loten* of 7.5 gr.	780
Gielise [van Lyere] *svoirsc. Gommaers broeder* [39]		
	99 *loten* of 7.5 gr.	742.5
Meestere Jacobe Obrechts [1]	144 *loten* of 6 gr.	864
Heeren Willeme van Sinte Mertens dijcke [40]	187 *loten* of 6 gr.	1122

Heere Michiele Cramer [2]	335 *loten* of 3.75 gr.	1256.25
	additional bonus	666
Meestere Willeme van Honswijck [4]	425 *loten* of 2.25	956.25
	additional bonus	120
Bellringers		762
Total		15,185.25

1499–1500

Heere Anthuenise de Rouck *priestere ende canonick* (officiant)		1680
Meestere Petere *den sangmeester* [31]	424 *loten* of 3.75 gr.	1590
	Holy Cross *lof*	120
	Ave Maria	360
Meestere Jacobe the organist	salary	1440
Choristers	422 *loten* of 1.5 gr.	633
Gommare van Lyere [38]	420 *loten* of 7.5 gr.	3150
Gielise *svoirs. Gommaers broeder* [39]	420 *loten* of 7.5 gr.	3150
Heere Clause van Lyere [41]	74 *loten* of 7.5 gr.	555
Johannes *de basconter* [42]	424 *loten* of 7.5 gr.	3180
Heere Willeme *uuten Haghe* [33]	405 *loten* of 6 gr.	2430
Meestere Willeme van Honswijck [4]	422 *loten* of 2.25 gr.	949.5
	additional bonus	120
Bellringers		762
Service of Procession-General Eve		48
Total		20,167.5

1500–1501

Heere Anthuenise de Rouck *priestere ende canonick* (officiant)		1680
Meestere Peter *de sangmeester* [31] 341(?) (339) *loten* of 3.75 gr.		1278.25
	77 *loten* of 7.5 gr.	577.5
	Holy Cross *lof*	120
	Ave Maria	360
Meester Jacobe the organist	salary	1440
Choristers	422 *loten* of 1.5 gr.	633
Dominicus *den tenoriste* [36]	134 *loten* of 9 gr.	1206
A messenger, for summoning *heere* Dominicus		30
Heere Clause van Lyere [41]	28 *loten* of 7.5 gr.	210
	74 *loten* of 9 gr.	666
Jannes *den tenoriste vanden Bossche* [37]	259 *loten* of 7.5 gr.	1942.5
Gommare *den sanghere* [38]	420 *loten* of 7.5 gr.	3150

Gielken *den bovensanghere* [39]	159 *loten* of 7.5 gr.	1192.5
Heeren Willeme van Sinte Mertensdijcke [40]	379 *loten* of 6 gr.	2274
Meestere Willeme van Honswijck [4]	434 *loten* of 2.25 gr.	976
	additional bonus	120
A foreign singer, paid at the command of the *burgemeester* and		
	scepenen	72
Bellringers		762
Service of Procession-General Eve		60
Total		18,749.75

1501–1502

Heere Anthuenise de Roeck *priestere ende canonic* (officiant)		1680
Meestere Petere Vinelo *sangmeester* [31]	420 *loten* of 7.5 gr.	3150
	Holy Cross *lof*	120
	Ave Maria	360
Meestere Jacobe the organist	salary	1440
Choristers	422 *loten* of 1.5 gr.	633
Heere Dominicus [36]	350 (352) *loten* of 9 gr.	3150
Meestere Clause van Lyere [41]	57 *loten* of 9 gr.	513
Gommare van Lyere [38]	407 *loten* of 7.5 gr.	3052.5
Heeren Willeme van Sinte Mertensdijcke [40]		
	421 (420) *loten* of 6 gr.	2526
Petere van Breeda [43]	254 *loten* of 6 gr.	1524
Meestere Willeme van Honswijck [4]	426 *loten* of 2.25 gr.	958.5
	additional bonus	120
A singer from Utrecht		120
Bellringers		762
Service of Procession-General Eve		60
Total		20,169

1502–1503

Heere Anthuenise de Rouck *priestere ende canonick* (officiant)		1680
'for having held *memorie* for my lord the bailiff'		180
Meestere Petere Vineloo *sangmeestere* [31]	426 *loten* of 7.5 gr.	3195
	Holy Cross *lof*	120
	Ave Maria	360
Meestere Jacobe the organist	salary	1440
Choristers	422 *loten* of 1.5 gr.	633
Heere Clause van Lyere [41]	126 *loten* of 9 gr.	1134

Leeuwen *den tenoriste* [44]	297 *loten* of 9 gr.	2673
Gommare van Lyere *de sanghere* [38]	84 *loten* of 7.5 gr.	630
	paid when he left	150
	for singing during the Easter Fairs	240
Aernde Thuenissone [45]	112 *loten* of 7.5 gr.	840
Heere Willeme *uuten Haghe* [33]	422 *loten* of 6 gr.	2532
Petere van Breeda *sanghere* [43]	416 *loten* of 6 gr.	2496
Meestere Willeme van Honswijck [4]	429 *loten* of 2.25 gr.	965.25
	additional bonus	120
Heer Quintene *de sanghere* [15]	273 *loten* of 1 gr.	273
Willeme, son of *meester* Willeme van Honswijc [32]		
for singing during the Easter Fairs		120
Other foreign singers		96
Bellringers		762
Service on Procession-General Eve		60
Total		20,699.25

1503–1504

Heere Anthuenise de Rouck *priestere ende canonick* (officiant)		1680
Meestere Petere Vineloo *sangmeester* [31], 'and the other		
[choirmasters] who came in his place'	408 *loten* of 7.5 gr.	3060
	Holy Cross *lof*	120
	Ave Maria	360
Meestere Jacobe the organist	salary	1440
Choristers	422 *loten* of 1.5 gr.	633
Leeuwe *den tenoriste* [44]	400(?) (407) *loten* of 9 gr.	3603
Aernde *uuten Haghe* [45]	296 *loten* of 7.5 gr.	2220
Heere Willeme van Sinte Mertensdijcke [40]	32 *loten* of 6 gr.	192
Petere van Breeda *sanghere* [43]	415 *loten* of 6 gr.	2490
Franchoyse *de sanghere* [46]	210 *loten* of 6 gr.	1260
Berthelmeeuse *de sanghere* [47]	214 *loten* of 6 gr.	1284
Daniele *de sanghere* [48]	143 *loten* of 3 gr.	429
Heere Willeme van Honswijck [4]	64 *loten* of 2.25 gr.	144
additional bonus (for half a year, until his death)		60
Meestere Clause van Lyere [41] 'for having served for a while'		240
A singer from England	*item*	225
Gielise *de sanghere* [39]		
'for having sung during the St Martin Fairs'		144
Bellringers		762
Service of Procession-General Eve		60
Total		20,406

1504–1505

Heere Anthuenise de Roeck *priestere* and other priests (officiants)		1650
Meestere Jaspare *de sangmeestere* [49], 'and the other [choir-		
masters] who had worked in his place'	420 *loten* of 7.5 gr.	3150
	Holy Cross *lof*	120
	Ave Maria	360
Meestere Jacobe the organist	salary	1440
Choristers	422 *loten* of 1.5 gr.	633
Leeuwe *den tenoriste* [44]		
	9 *loten* of 9 gr. from 18 to 26 Aug 1504	81
Constantiinen *den tenoriste* [50]		
	351 *loten* of 7.5 gr. from 2 Sept 1504 to 11 July 1505	2631.5
Petere van Breeda [43]		
	369 *loten* of 6 gr. from 18 Aug 1504 to 30 June 1505	2214
	61 *loten* of 7.5 gr. from 30 June to 18 Aug 1505	457.5
Heere Cornelise *uuten Hage priester* [17]		
	160 *loten* of 6 gr. from 2 April to 18 Aug 1505	960
Berthelmeeuse *de sanghere* [47]		
	55 *loten* of 6 gr. from 18 Aug to 9 Sept 1504	330
	paid after 9 Oct 1504	30
Franchoyse *den sanghere* [46]		
	349 *loten* of 6 gr. from 18 Aug 1504 to 30 June 1505	2094
	61 *loten* of 7.5 gr. from 30 June to 18 Aug 1505	457.5
Daniele *den sangere* [48]		
	226 *loten* of 3 gr. from 18 Aug 1504 to 21 March 1505	678
Heer Adriane Peterss van Dort *priester* [51]		
	250 *loten* of 3 gr. after 23 Aug. 1504	750
Heere Mertene Moelenbergh [52]		
	26 *loten* of 1.5 gr. from 27 July to 18 Aug 1505	39
Bellringers		762
Service of Procession-General Eve		60
Total		18,897.5

1505–1506

Heere Andriese *priester ende capellaen* (officiant)		1680
Meestere Jaspare *den sangmeester* [49]	418 *loten* of 7.5 gr.	3135
	Holy Cross *lof*	120
	Ave Maria	360
Meester Trudo the organist	salary	1620

Choristers	422 *loten* of 1.5 gr.	633
Meester Henricke van Diest [53]	124 *loten* of 9 gr.	1116
Petere van Breeda [43]	398 *loten* of 7.5 gr.	2985
Franchoyse *den sanghere* [46]	412 *loten* of 7.5 gr.	3090
Johannes vanden Bossche *tenoriste* [37]	381 *loten* of 7.5 gr.	2857.5
Heere Cornelise *uuten Haghe* [17]	404 *loten* of 6 gr.	2424
Heere Adriane van Dort [51]	42 *loten* of 3 gr.	126
Heere Mertene Moelenbergh [52]	386 *loten* of 1.5 gr.	579
Bellringers		762
Service of Procession-General Eve		60
Total		21,547.5

1506–1507

Heere Andriese *priestere ende capellaen* (officiant)		1989
Meestere Jaspare *den sangmeester* [49]	426 *loten* of 7.5 gr.	3195
	Holy Cross *lof*	120
	Ave Maria	360
Meestere Trudo the organist		1800
Choristers	422 *loten* of 1.5 gr.	633
Henricke van Diest [53]	356 *loten* of 9 gr.	3204
Franchoyse *de sanghere* [46]	426 *loten* of 7.5 gr.	3195
Johannese *de tenoriste* [37]	427 *loten* of 7.5 gr.	3202.5
Willeme *de sanghere* [54]	75 *loten* of 7.5 gr.	562.5
Petere Bonte [55]	427 *loten* of 7.5 gr.	3202.5
Heere Cornelise *de sanghere* [17]	424 *loten* of 6 gr.	2544
Heere Mertene Moelenbergh *cantere* [52]	349 *loten* of 1.5 gr.	523.5
Bellringers and bellows-pumper		762
Service of Procession-General Eve		60
Total		25,353

1507–1508

Various priests (officiants)		1500
Meestere Jaspare *de sangmeester* [49]	346 *loten* of 7.5 gr.	2595
	Holy Cross *lof*	120
	Ave Maria	360
Meestere Kaerle *den sanghere* [25], came in the place of *meestere*		
Jaspare on 24 June 1508	47 *loten* of 7.5 gr.	352.5
Meestere Trudo the organist	salary	1800
Choristers	422 *loten* of 1.5 gr.	633

Meestere Janne Verbonet [56]	402 *loten* of 9 gr.	3618
Franchoyse *den sanghere* [46]	388 (385) *loten* of 7.5 gr.	2910
Johannese *den tenoriste* [37]	427 *loten* of 7.5 gr.	3202.5
Willeme *den sanghere* [54]	422 *loten* of 7.5 gr.	3165
Heere Bouwene *den sangere* [57]	283 *loten* of 7.5 gr.	2122.5
Heere Cornelise *de sanghere* [17]	324 *loten* of 6 gr.	1944
	99 *loten* of 7.5 gr.	742.5
Diericke *den sanghere* [58]	68 *loten* of 6 gr.	408
Heere Mertene Moelenberch *cantere* [52]	412 *loten* of 3 gr.	1236
Bellringers and bellows-pumper		402
Service of Procession-General Eve		60
Total		27,171

1508–1509

Lost

1509–1510

Lost

APPENDIX 3

Financial year	Total number of *loten*	Average value of the *loten* (Brabant groats)	Average number of singers per service (*c.* 430 services)
1480–1	?	?	?
1481–2	?	?	?
1482–3	3234–376	2.21–2.30	7.5–7.9
1483–4	3100	2.13	7.2
1484–5	—		—
1485–6	2729–53	2.59–2.61	6.3–6.4
1486–7	2987	2.45	6.9
1487–8	3356	2.53	7.8
1488–9	3226	2.42	7.5
1489–90	3089	2.52	7.2
1490–1	3779	2.36	8.8
1491–2	3911	2.68	9.1
1492–3	3354	2.82	7.8
1493–4	3236	2.57	7.5
1494–5	3227	2.87	7.5
1495–6	3169	2.96	7.4
1496–7	2898	2.92	6.7
1497–8	—	—	—
1498–9	1977	4.76	4.6
1499–1500	2589	5.80	6.0
1500–1	2305	5.85	5.4
1501–2	2335	6.37	5.4
1502–3	2585	5.70	6.0
1503–4	2182	6.37	5.1
1504–5	2337	5.92	5.4
1505–6	2565	6.36	6.0
1506–7	2910	6.75	6.8
1507–8	3218	6.93	7.5
1508–9	—	—	—
1509–10	—	—	—

APPENDIX 4

Singers employed at the Guild of Our Lady at Bergen op Zoom, 1480–1510
Fees per *loot* are given between square brackets (in chronological order) and
indicate the relative quality of the singer. Literature cited is abbreviated as
follows:

Bouwstenen	C. G. Vlam and M. A. Vente, eds., *Bouwstenen voor een geschiedenis der toonkunst in de Nederlanden*, 4 vols., II (Amsterdam, 1971); III (Amsterdam, 1980)
DoorM	G. van Doorslaer, 'La chapelle musicale de Philippe le Beau', *Revue Belge d'Archéologie et d'Histoire de l'Art*, 4 (1934),' pp. 21–57 and 139–65
GottJGV	C. Gottwald, *Johannes Ghiselin – Johannes Verbonnet* (Wiesbaden, 1962)
HagghM	B. Haggh, 'Music, Liturgy, and Ceremony in Brussels, 1350–1500' (Ph.D. dissertation, University of Illinois at Urbana-Champaign, 1988)
JutenPV	E. H. G. C. A. Juten, 'Petrus Vineloo', *Taxandria: Tijdschrift voor Noordbrabantsche Geschiedenis en Volkskunde*, 36 (1929) p. 68
LockF	L. Lockwood, *Music in Renaissance Ferrara 1400–1505* (Oxford, 1984)
LockM	L. Lockwood, ' "Messer Gossino" and Josquin Desprez', *Studies in Renaissance and Baroque Music in Honor of Arthur Mendel*, ed. R. L. Marshall (Kassel, 1974), pp. 15–24
NieuwK	J. van den Nieuwenhuizen, 'De koralen, de zangers en de zangmeesters van de Antwerpse O.-L.-Vrouwekerk tijdens de 15e eeuw', *Gouden jubileum gedenkboek van de viering van 50 jaar heropgericht knapenkoor van de Onze-Lieve-Vrouwekatedraal te Antwerpen* (Antwerp, 1978), pp. 29–72
NobPR	T. Noblitt, 'Additional Compositions by Paulus de Rhoda?', *Tijdschrift van de Vereniging voor Nederlandse Muziekgeschiedenis*, 37 (1987), pp. 49–63
PiscOLV	A. Piscaer, 'De zangers van het Onze Lieve Vrouw Gilde te Bergen op Zoom', *Land van mijn hart*, ed. L. G. J. Verberne and A. Weynen (Tilburg, 1952), pp. 70–81
PiscPV	A. Piscaer, 'Petrus Vineloo te Bergen-op-Zoom', *Tijdschrift van de Vereeniging voor Nederlandsche Muziekgeschiedenis*, 13 (1929), pp. 17–19
PrizMC	W. F. Prizer, 'Music and Ceremonial in the Low Countries:

Philip the Fair and the Order of the Golden Fleece', *Early Music History*, 5 (1985), pp. 113–53

SartJ   C. Sartori, 'Josquin des Prés cantore del Duomo di Milano (1459–1472)', *Annales Musicologiques*, 4 (1956), pp. 55–83

SeayD   A. Seay, 'The *Dialogus Johannis Ottobi Anglici in arte musica*', *Journal of the American Musicological Society*, 8 (1955), pp. 86–100

SlootHLV   K. (C. J. F.) Slootmans, 'De Hoge Lieve Vrouw van Bergen op Zoom', *[Jaarboek van de] Oudheidkundige kring 'De Ghulden Roos'*, Roosendaal, 25 (1965), pp. 193–233

SmijH i   A. Smijers, *De Illustre Lieve Vrouwe Broederschap te 's-Hertogenbosch* (Amsterdam, 1932); reprint of a series of articles in *Tijdschrift van de Vereeniging voor Nederlandsche Muziekgeschiedenis*, 11–14 (1925–32)

SmijH ii, iii   A. Smijers, 'De Illustre Lieve Vrouwe Broederschap te 's-Hertogenbosch', *Tijdschrift van de Vereeniging voor Nederlandsche Muziekgeschiedenis*, 15 (1935), pp. 1–105 [ii]; 16 (1946), pp. 63–106 [iii]

StraM   E. van der Straeten, *La musique aux Pays-Bas avant le XIXe siècle*, 8 vols. (Brussels, 1867–88)

StrohmB   R. Strohm, *Music in Late Medieval Bruges* (Oxford, 1985)

1. Jacob Obrecht [3, 3.75, 6]

See main text.

2. Michiele Cramer [3, 3.75]

Clericus singer (tenorist) 1480–1 (or earlier) to 1498–9. In 1485 Cramer was invited by Maximilian of Habsburg to become a singer in his chapel; the guild retained him by promising him an annual bonus of 540 Brabant groats, and a pension of 960 Brabant groats in case of incapacity. (PiscOLV 74–5 and 149; SlootHLV 200–1)

3. Cornelise Zwagers of Schiedam [3, 3.75, 2.25, 3.75]

Clericus singer 1480–1 (or earlier) to 1492–3 (absent in 1489–90). Zwagers had worked in the chapel of Duke Galeazzo Maria Sforza of Milan in 1474–5 ('Cornelio Svagher di Fiandra'; SartJ 64–5). Around 1503 he worked as a *contra alto* in Antwerp, and was later recruited there for Ferrara (StraM vi, 72–4; PiscOLV 81; LockM 15–17). Van der Straeten mentions an unpublished note by Léon de Burbure according to which Zwagers was also called Cornelis de Hulst (StraM vi, 73). If this was the case, Zwagers's absence in 1489–90 might be explained partly by the fact that a tenorist Cornelis Hulst was working for two weeks in 's-Hertogenbosch in 1489–90 (SmijH i, 188). This is presumably the tenorist Cornelis of Hulst who was associated with Antwerp Cathedral in 1497–1503 (NieuwK 42).

4. Willeme van Hondswijck [1.5, 2.25]

(Clericus?) singer (master's degree) 1480–1 (or earlier) to 1503–4. Died in early 1504. From 1496–7 onwards Hondswijck received an annual bonus of 120 Brabant groats because of his old age. His son Willeme van Hondswijck [32] also worked as a singer at the guild.

5. Symon of Amerode [1.5, 2.25]

Clericus singer (cantor) 1480–1 (or earlier) to 1494–5. Died in 1495.

6. Hendrick Malecourt [1.5]

Clericus singer (tenorist) 1480–1 (or earlier) to 1496–7. Since accounts of 1497–8 are lost, he may have worked at the guild until 1498. Possibly the composer of *Malheur me bat* (attributed to 'Malcort' in Rome, Biblioteca Casanatense, MS 2856), but two other Malcourts are known to have worked in Brussels around this time (HagghM 627).

7. Michiel of Bastogne *alias* Michelet [1.5, 1.75, 1.875, 2.25, 1.875]

Clericus singer 1480–1 (or earlier) to 1495–6. Described as 'young' until 1484. Possibly the composer Michelet. A 'Micheleth' is mentioned in Hothby's *Dialogus* (SeayD 95). Michiel of Bastogne is not identical with Michiel Berruyer of Lessines in Hainaut, since the latter worked in the chapel of Maximilian I in 1492–3, when Michelet was in Bergen op Zoom (StraM III, 213; SmijH I, 193; for Berruyer, see also NieuwK 42). (See also main text, p. 202).

8. Peter de Coster (or Peter the sexton?) [—]

Clericus singer 1480–1 (and perhaps earlier). May have gone to 's-Hertogenbosch (see under 13 below), in which case he could be identical with Peteren the 'new tenorist', who worked there from around 1 August 1482 onwards (SmijH I, 175).

9. Cornelise Both [—]

Clericus singer 1480–1 (and perhaps earlier).

10. Janne Mol [—]

Singer (master's degree) 1480/1–1481/2 (and perhaps earlier). Probably identical with the Johannes de Mol who was active in Brussels from 1482 until his death in 1495 (HagghM 633–4). A Giovanni Molli, or Johannes de Molis, was appointed *maestro di cappella* at the Duomo of Milan on 1 September 1477 (SartJ 76).

11. Johannes Greefken [—]

Singer and barber-surgeon 1480–1 (or earlier) to 1481–2. See also main text, p. 202.

12. Janne de Greve [—]

Clericus singer 1480–1 (and perhaps earlier).

13. Aubertijne [—]

Singer 1480–1 (or earlier) to 1481–2. A tenorist Abertijne is found in documents from St Goedele at Brussels dated 1474–7, 1490–3 and 1518–19

(HagghM 535); this singer is probably identical with the tenorist Albertinus Malcourt who was in continuous service at St Goedele in 1474–1519 (HagghM 627). An Obertijn was *bovensenger* at the Confraternity of Our Lady at 's-Hertogenbosch from around 1 September 1481 (paid on 24 June 1482 for having worked 42½ weeks) to around 23 September 1482 (SmijH I, 172–5). If Obertijn was identical with Aubertijne, as Piscaer assumes (PiscOLV 77), he must have returned to Bergen op Zoom for some time, since he earned 791.25 Brabant groats in 1481–2 (i.e. after 15 August 1481). The 's-Hertogenbosch accounts tell us that three singers were recruited in Bergen op Zoom between 24 June 1481 and 24 June 1482 (SmijH I, 171). This entry may apply to singers 8, 9, 10, 12, 14 and to Aubertijne.

14. Gielise [1.5, 2.25]
Singer (master's degree) 1481/2–1482/3.

15. Quintijne [1, 3, 1]
Clericus singer 1481/2–1483/4 (since the accounts of 1484–5 are lost, he may have continued to work at the guild for some time after 15 August 1484). Returned 1495/6–1496/7 and 1502–3. A soprano Quintijn (from Nieuwpoort) was employed at the confraternity in 's-Hertogenbosch in 1471–2 (SmijH I, 146–52).

16. Reijnier 'with the hunch' [3]
Singer 1483–4. Lived with Jacob Obrecht. A Reynerus was a singer in 's-Hertogenbosch in 1473 (SmijH I, 150–4).

17. Cornelis from The Hague [2.25, 6, 7.5]
Clericus singer 1483–4 and 1504/5–1507/8.

18. Paulus de Roda [3.75]
Choirmaster (master's degree) 1485–6 (but presumably already in 1484) to 1489–90. Left the guild between 15 August and 24 December 1489. Composer (cf. NobPR 49–63; composed a polyphonic Requiem around 1496 or 1497, see SmijH I, 202). Was a member of the Confraternity of Our Lady at 's-Hertogenbosch, and was regularly involved from 1471 in fetching new musicians for that confraternity (cf. SmijH I and II). Died September 1514 (SmijH II, 82).

19. Alairde Hendrickssone [1.5]
Clericus singer 1485–6 (but possibly as early as 1484) to 1491–2.

20. Janne [1.5]
Clericus singer 1488–9 (filled in Zwagers's place during the latter's absence) and 1490/1–1491/2. Called 'the deans' chaplain' in the accounts.

21. Thomase [3.75]
Choirmaster (master's degree) 1489/90–1492/3. Became choirmaster between 15 August and 24 December 1489, and left Bergen op Zoom in

June 1493. Possibly identical with the *meester* Thomas who was choirmaster at the Grote Kerk in Dordrecht in 1506 (Bouwstenen II, 80).

22. Janne van Gheele *alias* Holtken [3]
Clericus singer 1489/90–1491/2.

23. Servase of Maastricht [3.75]
Clericus singer 1490/1–1492/3.

24. Woutere [3]
Singer (tenorist) 1491/2–1495/6 (absent in 1493–4). Worked irregularly at the guild. Presumably identical with the tenorist Wouter who worked irregularly in 's-Hertogenbosch in 1496 and 1497 (SmijH I, 199–203; PiscOLV 81).

25. Kaerle [3.75, 7.5]
Choirmaster (master's degree) from July 1493 to 1495–6. Became a member of the Confraternity of Our Lady at 's-Hertogenbosch between 24 June 1495 and 24 June 1496 (SmijH I, 198). Perhaps he was the 'Carlo de Fiandra compositore de chantij' who worked in Ferrara in 1503 (LockF 327). Appointed choirmaster again on 24 June 1508, and may have held this position until 1510.

26. Adriane Bouckeel [2.25]
Clericus singer 1492–3.

27. Janne Stevens of Nieuwpoort [3.75]
Clericus singer 1493/4–1496/7 (since accounts of 1497–8 are lost, he may have worked for some time after 15 August 1497).

28. Janne Blockeel [2.25]
Clericus singer 1493–4.

29. Jacobe of Alkmaar [2.25, 3.75, 2.25]
(Clericus?) singer (tenorist) 1493/4–1496/7 (since accounts of 1497–8 are lost, he may have worked until 1498).

30. Lucas of Brussels [6]
Clericus singer 1494/5–1495/6. Barbara Haggh kindly informed me that a possible candidate for identification with Lucas of Brussels is Lucas de Thimo, who worked at St Pieter in Brussels in 1488–9 (private communication, 28 January 1989; see HagghM 674).

31. Peter Vineloo [3.75, 7.5]
Choirmaster (master's degree) 1495/6–1503/4. Came from Sluis, where he had been choirmaster in 1488. Appointed *magister cantus chori* at St Saviour in Bruges on 12 January 1495; was admonished there on 21 December 1495 to instruct his boys more diligently. Became choirmaster at Bergen op Zoom around 1 May 1496. Succentor of St Donatian in Bruges from 1504 until his death in 1507. (JutenPV; PiscPV; StrohmB 55 and 189)

32. Willeme van Hondswijck (junior) [1.5]
Singer 1495/6–1496/7 (since accounts of 1497–8 are lost, he may have

worked for some time after 15 August 1497) and 1502/3. Son of *meestere* Willeme van Hondswijck (see under 4 above).

33. Willeme Jacobssone from The Hague [4.5, 6]
Clericus singer 1496–7 (and probably 1497–8), 1499–1500 and 1502–3. Almost certainly identical with Willeme of St Maartensdijk (see under 40 below).

34. Ghysbrechte Pieterssone [3.75]
Clericus singer (*hoeghcontere*) 1496–7. Was appointed choirmaster in the Grote Kerk at Goes (27 km west of Bergen op Zoom) on 16 November 1496. Left Goes without permission, before 9 December 1497 (Bouwstenen, II, 102–3).

35. Govaerde [3.75]
Clericus singer (*hooghcontere*) 1496–7.

36. Dominicus Janssoen van Grafft [9]
Clericus singer (tenorist) 1498–9 (but almost certainly also in 1497–8), and 1500/1–1501/2. Was appointed as tenorist by the Bergen op Zoom city council on 2 August 1497 (BOZ R 308, fol. 130ᵛ): 'Dominicus Janssoen van Grafft has been appointed as tenorist by the *burgermeesters* and *scepenen* of this town with the stipulation that he be paid 3 stivers [=9 Brabant groats] per *loot*. His employment will start as soon as he has returned from Haarlem. The same Dominicus has tied himself to serve this town and to stay in its service for one year following his arrival, on penalty of 10 pounds [=2400 Brabant groats] to be paid to the town of Bergen [op Zoom]' (translated from SlootHLV 214 n. 22). Was appointed singer at the confraternity at 's-Hertogenbosch on 1 November 1498, and worked there irregularly until 1500 or 1501 (SmijH I, 209–14; SmijH II, 50; PiscOLV 78; SlootHLV 201 and 214).

37. Janne Slijper [7.5]
Singer (tenorist; master's degree) 1498–9 (and possibly in 1497–8) and 1500–1 (when he is called 'from 's-Hertogenbosch'). Almost certainly identical with the tenorist Jannen of Oirschot, who worked for four weeks in 's-Hertogenbosch between 24 June 1498 and 24 June 1499, nine weeks in 1500–1 (between the same dates) and permanently in 's-Hertogenbosch from 24 June 1501 until he left in 1505 (SmijH I, 210; SmijH II, 49–62). In 1505–6 he was again in Bergen op Zoom, where he stayed until 1507–8 (but, since accounts of 1508/9–1510/11 are lost, he may have stayed until 1511).

38. Gommare van Morteltere of Lier [7.5]
Singer (*hooghconter*) 1498–9 (but perhaps also 1497–8) to 1502–3. Worked irregularly at the confraternity in 's-Hertogenbosch in 1500–4, until he was appointed there on 2 October 1504. Became gravely ill in 1504–5, but worked regularly at the 's-Hertogenbosch confraternity from 1505 to January or February 1508 (SmijH II, 49–67; PiscOLV 79–80). Went

apparently to the county of Holland (SmijH II, 87) but returned several times to 's-Hertogenbosch in the period 1509/10–1517/18 (*ibid.*, 72, 74, 79, 86–7, 89). Attempted to obtain a permanent position at 's-Hertogenbosch in 1520, 1522, and 1523 (*ibid.*, 94, 98, 102), but was refused each time. Later in the 1520s seems to have worked at the Nieuwe Kerk in Delft, where a *hooghconter* Gommaer Claesz. of Lier is mentioned between 1 May 1524 and 1 February 1531 (Bouwstenen III, 90; cf. SmijH III, 102). Renewed attempts in 1526–9 to obtain a position at 's-Hertogenbosch failed (SmijH III, 66, 69, 70, 72, 74), but he was finally appointed in 1529. Remained at the confraternity of 's-Hertogenbosch until 1550–1. Brother of Gielise van Morteltere (under 39 below). Had a son Franchoyse (Gommaerssone van Liere), who worked as a singer in Bergen op Zoom from 1524–5 to 1529–30.

39. Gielise van Morteltere of Lier [7.5]

Singer (*bovensanghere*) 1498–9 (but perhaps also 1497–8) to 1500–1. Appointed as singer in 's-Hertogenbosch on 1 January 1501, and worked there until 1503–4 (SmijH II, 49–57; PiscOLV 80).

40. Willeme of St Maartensdijk [6]

Clericus singer 1498–9 (and probably 1497–8), 1500–1 and 1501–2, and 1503–4. Almost certainly identical with Willeme from The Hague (see under 33 above).

41. Clause of Lier [7.5, 9]

Clericus singer (master's degree) 1499/1500–1503/4. Worked irregularly at the guild during this period, since he was also employed at the chapel of Philip the Fair, where he was listed in 1492–5, 1499, 1500, 1501 and 1502 (StraM VII, 107–8, 144–5, 151, 153, 156, 178, 268–9, 496–7; DoorM 148; PiscOLV 79; PrizMC 126). On 12 January 1501, Duke Philip the Fair had a letter sent to 'mess. Claes van Liere, étant à Berg-op-Zoom' asking him to sing at the meeting of the Order of the Golden Fleece at Brussels on 14–18 January (DoorM 40).

42. Johannes [7.5]

Singer (*basconter*) 1499–1500. Perhaps identical with the 'Johannes de basconter' who worked in 's-Hertogenbosch from 1509–10 to 1518–19 (SmijH II, 70–97). He is mentioned in the chapter accounts of St Gertrude in 1510 (Bouwstenen II, 49).

43. Peter of Breda [6, 7.5]

Singer 1501/2–1505/6. Perhaps identical with Peter Bonte (see under 55 below).

44. Leeuwe (Leon?) [9]

Singer (tenorist) 1502–3 to 26 August 1504.

45. Aernde Thuenissone from The Hague [7.5]

Singer 1502/3–1503/4.

46. Franchoyse [6, 7.5]
Singer 1503/4–1507/8 (since accounts of 1508/9–1510/11 are lost, he may have stayed in Bergen op Zoom until 1511). Possibly identical with the *heere* Franchoyse Bertrant who worked in Bergen op Zoom from 1511–12 to 1521–2.

47. Berthelmeeuse [6]
Singer 1503/4–1504/5. Earned only five *loten* after 9 October 1504.

48. Daniele [3]
Singer 1503–4 to 21 March 1505.

49. Jaspare [7.5]
Choirmaster (master's degree) 1504 to 1508.

50. Constantijnen [7.5]
Singer (tenorist) from 2 September 1504 to 11 July 1505.

51. Adriane Peterssone of Dordrecht [3]
Clericus singer from 23 August 1504 to around October 1505.

52. Mertene Moelenbergh [1.5, 3]
Clericus singer (cantor) from 27 July 1505 to 1507–8 (since accounts of 1508/9–1510/11 are lost, he may have stayed in Bergen op Zoom until 1511). He is not mentioned in accounts of the Guild of Our Lady from after 1507–8, but he apparently remained cantor of St Gertrude until 1517 (Bouwstenen II, 49).

53. Henricke Haudijn of Diest [9]
Singer (master's degree) 1505/6–1506/7. Became choirmaster in 's-Hertogenbosch before 24 June 1507, and stayed there until June 1510 (he may have worked in 's-Hertogenbosch as early as 1477, when he was apparently still a boy; see SmijH I, 165). Was choirmaster in Bergen op Zoom from 1511–12 (but probably 1510–11) to 20 June 1542.

54. Willeme [7.5]
Singer 1506/7–1507/8 (since accounts of 1508/9–1510/11 are lost, he may have stayed in Bergen op Zoom until 1511).

55. Petere Bonte [7.5]
Singer 1506–7. Presumably identical with Peter of Breda (see under 43 above).

56. Johannes Ghiselin *alias* Verbonnet [9]
Singer (master's degree) 1507–8 (since accounts of 1508/9–1510/11 are lost, he may have stayed in Bergen op Zoom until 1511). Composer (GottJGV; LockF 202).

57. Bouwene [7.5]
Clericus singer 1507–8 (since accounts of 1508/9–1510/11 are lost, he may have stayed in Bergen op Zoom until 1511). Piscaer's identification with Noel Bauldewyn is presumably erroneous (PiscOLV 78).

58. Diericke [6]

Singer 1507–8 (since accounts of 1508/9–1510/11 are lost, he may have stayed in Bergen op Zoom until 1511). Probably identical with Diericke of Namen, who worked at the guild from 1511–12 (or earlier) to 1516–17.

APPENDIX 5

Alphabetical index of musicians

Unless specified otherwise, numbers are those under which musicians are listed in Appendix 4.

1. First names:

Adriane Bouckeel, 26

Adriane Peterssone of Dordrecht, 51

Aernde Thuenissone from The Hague, 45

Alairde Hendrickssone, 19

Aubertijne, 13

Berthelmeeuse, 47

Bouwene, 57

Clause of Lier, 41

Constantijnen, 50

Cornelise Both, 9

Cornelis from The Hague, 17

Cornelise Zwagers, 3

Daniele, 48

Diericke, 58

Dominicus Janssoen van Grafft, 36

Franchoyse, 46

Ghysbrechte Pieterssone, 34

Ghyskene of Diest, chorister, main text pp. 194–5, note 38

Gielise, 14

Gielise van Morteltere of Lier, 39

Gommare van Morteltere of Lier, 38

Govaerde, 35

Hendrick Malecourt, 6

Henricke Haudijn of Diest, 53

Jacobe of Alkmaar, 29

Jacob Obrecht, 1

Janne, 20

Janne Blockeel, 28

Holtken, Janne van Gheele *alias*, 22
Michelet, Michiel of Bastogne *alias*, 7
Scotelaer, Willem de Brouwer *alias*, main text p. 182
Verbonnet, Johannes Ghiselin *alias*, 56.

3. Patronymics:
Hendrickssone, Alairde, 19
Jacobssone, Willeme – from The Hague, 33
Janssoen, Dominicus – van Grafft, 36
Peterssone, Adriane – of Dordrecht, 51
Pieterssone, Ghysbrechte, 34
Thuenissone, Aernde – from The Hague, 45

4. Surnames:
Backer, Thoenken de, chorister, main text p. 194, note 38
Blockeel, Janne, 28
Bonte, Petere, 55
Both, Cornelise, 9
Bouckeel, Adriane, 26
Brouwer, Willem de – *alias* Scotelaer, main text p. 182
Coster, Peter de, 8
Cramer, Michiele, 2
Gheele, Janne van – *alias* Holtken, 22
Ghiselin, Johannes – *alias* Verbonnet, 56
Grafft, Dominicus Janssoen van, 36
Greefken, Johannes, 11
Greve, Janne de, 12
Haudijn, Henricke – of Diest, 53
Hondswijck, Willeme van – (senior), 4
Hondswijck, Willeme van – (junior), 32
Malecourt, Hendrick, 6
Moelenbergh, Mertene, 52
Mol, Janne, 10
Morteltere, Gielise van – of Lier, 39
Morteltere, Gommare van – of Lier, 38
Obrecht, Jacob, 1
Oudenhoven, Jan van, main text p. 187, note 21
Roda, Paulus de, 18
Slijper, Janne – of 's-Hertogenbosch, 37
Stevens, Janne – of Nieuwpoort, 27
Vineloo, Peter, 31
Zwagers, Cornelise, 3

5. Names after place of origin:
Alkmaar, Jacobe of, 29
Amerode, Symon of, 5
Bastogne, Michiel of – *alias* Michelet, 7
Breda, Peter of, 43
Brussels, Lucas of, 30
Diest, Ghyskene of, chorister, main text pp. 194–5, note 38
Diest, Henricke Haudijn of, 53
Dordrecht, Adriane Peterssone of, 51
Lier, Clause of, 41
Lier, Gielise van Morteltere of, 39
Lier, Gommare van Morteltere of, 38
Maastricht, Servase of, 23
Nieuwpoort, Janne Stevens of, 27
Schiedam, Cornelise Zwagers of, 3
's-Hertogenbosch, Janne Slijper of, 37
St Maartensdijk, Willeme of, 40
The Hague, Aernde Thuenissone from, 45
The Hague, Cornelis from, 17
The Hague, Willeme Jacobssone from, 33

6. Unnamed singers:
England, singer from, 1503–4
Singers of unknown origin, 1496–7, 1500–1, 1502–3, see also main text, p. 187, note 21
Singers of Philip the Fair, 1496–7
Utrecht, singer from, 1501–2

7. Organists:
Adriane, 1488–9
Denise, 1482–3
Jacobe, 1491–1505
Janne van Steenberghen, 1482–3
Trudo le Hardy, 1505–54, see also main text, p. 194, note 36

REVIEWS

BONNIE J. BLACKBURN, *Music for Treviso Cathedral in the Late Sixteenth Century: A Reconstruction of the Lost Manuscripts 29 and 30.* London, Royal Musical Association, 1987. vi+162 pp.

On 7 April 1944, twenty-five manuscripts of polyphonic music written before 1630 and a large number of musical prints, all in the possession of the Biblioteca Capitolare of Treviso, were destroyed in an Allied raid over the city. Of the manuscripts, no. 3 was subsequently recovered in the form of photographs owned by the American musicologist Laurence Feininger; thanks to the research of Bonnie J. Blackburn, these photographs are now joined by the reproductions of two motets from the lost manuscripts 29 and 30, originally in the possession of Father J. de Bruijn of Houten, Holland. On the basis of these discoveries (and the consequent recovery of a visual image of an unusual lost source), local archival sources, the complete thematic index of the manuscripts of pre-1630 polyphonic music in Treviso Cathedral compiled by Mgr Giovanni D'Alessi (now housed in the Archivio Capitolare) and D'Alessi's invaluable study,[1] Professor Blackburn sets out to unravel not only the mystery of the contents of the lost manuscripts 29 and 30 but also the complex musical reality of the city, its cathedral, its churches and its confraternities.

Analysis of the contents of MS 29 as listed in D'Alessi's thematic index reveals a total of five unica and sixty contrafacta in which music by several of the leading composers of the day, including Palestrina, Contino, Rore, Willaert, Jachet and Gombert, is adapted to locally specific texts, most probably at the hands of the manuscript's compiler and owner Pietro Varisco, a priest at Treviso

[1] *La cappella musicale del Duomo di Treviso (1300–1633)* (Vedelago [Treviso], 1954).

Cathedral. The presence in MS 29 of an extraordinarily large number of contrafacta leads Blackburn to raise the difficult question of their place and exact function in local liturgical usage. Treviso Cathedral, like many other institutions, retained a certain autonomy regarding the commemoration of local saints in the aftermath of the Tridentine reforms. Much has been written on the subject of the sixteenth-century motet, but rarely has it been analysed in the context of its specific relationship to liturgy and ceremonial, largely because of the almost complete lack of precise information in sources of the time. Blackburn unites what scanty contemporary evidence has survived with information gleaned from seventeenth-century archival material (not infrequently the only means of shedding light on the situation of the sixteenth-century motet) and, in particular, with the products of recent research on the musical and liturgical practices of the Sistine Chapel, the Roman oratories, St Mark's, Venice, the Venetian Scuole Grandi and the confraternities of Treviso. In this wider context, the analysis of musical practices at Treviso Cathedral assumes an altogether broader significance.

The final chapters of this study are devoted to physical descriptions of the manuscripts, and to the presentation and discussion of two newly discovered motets: *Tu es vas electionis* (MS 29), a contrafactum of Dominique Phinot's *Tua est potentia*, and *Suscipe verbum* (MS 30) by Ghiselin Danckerts. (Only two motets by Danckerts were previously known.) Blackburn's meticulous reconstruction and description of both manuscripts and motets, exemplary of its kind, can now be confirmed and expanded through the medium of a microfilm made prior to World War II by the Danish musicologist Knud Jeppesen. Jeppesen, a friend of D'Alessi, was no stranger to Treviso, and several times had occasion to consult the manuscripts of the cathedral archive. At his request, the materials assembled during his many years of dedicated research were deposited after his death with the Statsbiblioteket at Århus, where I was fortunate to come across the present microfilm. Originally this contained a selection of motets from MSS 3, 4, 5, 7, 8, 24, 29, 30 and 36, but its quality has now deteriorated and, despite careful restoration, only the items from MSS 4, 5, 7, 8, 24 and 29 are even remotely legible, though even here the effects of oxidation are considerable. The microfilm contains the following five-part motets from MS 29 (in all cases, the *quinta pars* is inexplicably absent, and all attempts at reconstruction on the basis of canon techniques have been of no avail): *O magnum mysterium* by Francesco Patavino *alias* Santa Croce (no. 1), *Senex puerum portabat* by Henri Schaffen (no. 10), *Hodie beata virgo* by Giovanni Battista Corvus (no. 11), *Accepto evangelio* (*secunda pars* of the motet *Beatissimus Marcus*) by Gioseffo Zarlino (no. 21), the contrafactum *Ave confessor gloriose Liberalis* by Philippe Verdelot (no. 22), *Hic est dies egregius sanctissimi Liberalis* – (2 p.) *Hodie beatum Liberalem* by Innocenzo Alberti (no. 23) and *Tanto tempore* by Dominique Phinot (no. 24).

The recovery of Jeppesen's microfilm provides confirmation of the physical description of MS 29 as given by D'Alessi and now amplified by Blackburn. The margins, cropped in the photographs presented by Blackburn, are here plainly visible. As for the contents, no fewer than three of the seven compositions are unica. I shall discuss them in turn.

O magnum mysterium by Francesco Patavino was copied into MS 29 from MS 30. Perhaps for this reason it is not included by Blackburn among the many unica of MS 29, yet to all intents and purposes the destruction of MS 30 renders the later copy unique. Beside this piece, on the left-hand page, is what appears to be the final section of a list, which unfortunately cannot be deciphered, of the contents of the volume. The music of Patavino is legible, though not without some difficulty; the words are largely blurred but can be reconstructed through reference to liturgical sources. It is in any case fortunate that the Archivio Capitolare in Treviso possesses a transcription of this composition by D'Alessi (shelf-mark: sala 2, scaffale 1-E-2, scatola 11), which is almost certainly based on the more authoritative and legible MS 30 (beside the title of the composition, D'Alessi has added the figures '5' and '9', respectively the numbers of the composition and of its folio in MS 30).

A second unicum in MS 29 is the motet *Senex puerum portabat* by the Flemish composer Henri Schaffen. Here the legibility of Jeppesen's reproduction is marred by a number of blemishes; the words are again badly focused but, as in the case of *O magnum mysterium*, they can be reconstructed from liturgical sources. As with the first motet, the music draws heavily on the technique of imitative counterpoint in the Flemish style. Present in the same photograph is *Hodie beata virgo* by Giovanni Battista Corvus, presumably copied from the author's *Motettorum quinque vocum, liber primus* (Venice, 1555).

Of notable interest is the third unicum, *Hic est dies egregius sanctissimi Liberalis* – (2 p.) *Hodie beatum Liberalem* by Innocenzo Alberti, a native of Treviso employed in the *cappella* of Duke Alfonso II d'Este at Ferrara. Above the music, the following words can be read with difficulty: 'In festo sanctissimi Liberalis confessoris tarvisinae civitatis protectoris'; the incipit, as transcribed by D'Alessi (on the photograph, the words are practically illegible), pays homage to St Liberalis, patron saint of Treviso. The photographic reproduction is of sufficient quality to permit a reading of the music without undue difficulty; the problems, if any, concern what seem to be a number of copyist's errors. The style is characterised by a general simplification of earlier contrapuntal style that is quite in keeping with Alberti's generation of north Italian composers.

Jeppesen's microfilm, together with the photographs of Father de Bruijn, thus accounts for four of the five unica present in MS 29 (only *Gaude et laetare* by Jachet de Berchem still defies recognition). It also contains the contrafactum *Ave confessor gloriose Liberalis* (based on *Educes me de laqueo*, part 2 of Verdelot's *In te Domine speravi*), thus providing a second example of the work of the probable 'arranger' Pietro Varisco, whose activities are well illustrated by Blackburn in her discussion of Phinot's *Tua est potentia* and its arrangement as *Tu es vas electionis*. (She is, however, unable to explain the transformation not only of the text but also of the attribution: in MS 29, the motet is ascribed not to Phinot but to 'Gislinus Danckerts'). Unlike the music of Phinot, which is subjected to a series of cuts, the original structure of Verdelot's motet undergoes little change, though the new version is peppered with syncopations and other rhythmic modifications, and Verdelot's final melismas (to the words 'redemisti me Domine Deus veritatis') are set to a reiterated 'Alleluia'. Despite this, as Blackburn observes of *Tu es vas electionis* (and the other contrafacta, for which incipits are provided by D'Alessi), Varisco is careful to maintain as far as possible the rhythms of the opening phrase; apart from the division of a *longa* into two breves in Verdelot's *bassus secundus*, roughly a quarter of the composition is completely unchanged. Of the final two motets from MS 29 which appear on Jeppesen's microfilm, the presence of Zarlino's *Accepto evangelio* (2 p. of *Beatissimus Marcus*) seems fortuitous, in so far as it appears on the same opening as the above-cited compositions by Verdelot and (in part) Alberti. As in the case of Phinot's *Tanto tempore*, this composition has evidently been copied from an earlier print.

Besides MS 29, Jeppesen's microfilm contains a number of reproductions of motets from two further manuscripts destroyed on the fateful night of 7 April 1944: nos. 4 and 5. MS 4 is described in Francesco Veretoni's sixteenth-century catalogue (likewise destroyed, but transcribed by D'Alessi on pp. 181–2 of the above-mentioned study) as a 'libro mezan da motetti' (i.e. a book of 'average' dimensions) with cover 'de parmore' (from *parmula*, a little board), and must thus have resembled closely the recently restored MSS 7, 8, 9 and 10. It was probably bound in wooden covers with a leather spine. D'Alessi comments that a number of manuscripts, among them no. 4, 'had suffered the effects of ink corrosion and the unsuitable conditions in which they had been stored during the nineteenth century'. On the basis of D'Alessi's thematic index and other materials reflecting a first-hand knowledge of the source, the compilation of MS 4 can be dated between 1559 and 1569; it was lacking fols. 73–7. The motets contained in the manuscript, intended for the use of the *cappella* of Treviso Cathedral, cover the feasts of the *proprium sanctorum* from 4 August (St Dominic) to 26 December (St Stephen). Five of the seventy-five compositions in the manuscript (of which twenty-seven are anonymous) are contained on Jeppesen's microfilm: the four-part *Dum sacrum mysterium* by Francesco Lupino, *Quasi stella matutina* by Costanzo Festa and *Praecamur te Pater* by Francesco Patavino, and the five-part *Cum pervenisset Beatus Andreas* and *Congregati sunt* by Benedetto Menchini of Pistoia.

Of these, *Dum sacrum mysterium* is the antiphon at the Magnificat for first Vespers *in festo S. Michaelis* (29 September); the motet has been copied from Lupino's *Primo libro di motetti a quattro voci* (Venice: Antonio Gardano, 1549). *Quasi stella matutina*, proper to the feast of St Jerome (30 September), has a concordance in Vatican City, Biblioteca Apostolica Vaticana, Cappella Sistina MS 17 which presents numerous variants in all the parts. Francesco Patavino's four-part motet *Praecamur te Pater* has already been transcribed by D'Alessi as part of the musical appendix of his study of music at Treviso Cathedral. (Although his thematic index gives the following information: 'Indication of the bars appears in arabic numerals above the parts (the hand appears to be later)', the microfilm does not permit confirmation of this annotation.) Patavino's text is a prayer on behalf of the Serenissima and its possessions ('populum istum tuum

Venetiarum') for liberation from enemy invasions, plague, famine and, in general, 'ab omni malo'.

Practically nothing is known of Benedetto Menchini, the composer of two five-part motets in MS 4, although a collection of his motets, the *Sacrae cantiones Benedicti Menchini pistoiensis chori opidi Danielis magistri, quinque vocibus: liber secundus*, was published in Venice in 1594 (no copies are known of the *liber primus*). Given the date of compilation of MS 4, it is clear that Menchini's pieces must date back to several decades before 1594, and the possibility cannot be excluded that they were copied from the earlier motet publication (of which they would thus provide the only known trace). The *Indice alfabetico de' maestri dei quali esistono opere nell'archivio musicale del Rev.mo Capitolo di Treviso compilato da D. Jacopo Campion fu maestro di cappella e mansionario di questa cattedrale l'anno 1845*, which fortunately survived the raid of 1944, contains the following entry for Benedetto Menchini: 'Mottetti, p. 118, n. 17, anno 1560', and under the rubric 'Benedetto Nanchini', the author lists an unspecified number of masses ('p. 4, n. 128') and motets ('p. 124, n. 45'). Stylistically, both *Cum pervenisset Beatus Andreas* and *Congregati sunt* display some naïvety of part-writing leading at times to a distinct structural weakness.

In all probability, MS 5 was similar in appearance to MS 4; in any case, it is also cited in the list of books of average dimensions 'coverti de parmore'. Originally it contained fifty-two motets (thirty-six of which were anonymous) for the use of the *cappella* on a limited number of liturgical occasions. Among these is a group of five anonymous compositions for first Vespers *in festo Corporis Domini*, whose texts and *cantus firmi* (contained in the lowest part) correspond exactly to those of a fourteenth-century Gregorian manuscript which still survives in the Archivio Capitolare. These five compositions, *Sacerdos in aeternum* (fol. 29), *Misereatur Dominus* (fol. 30), *Calicem salutaris* (fol. 30), *Sicut novellae olivarum* (fol. 30) and *Qui pacem* (fol. 30), appear to constitute a unified cycle, probably the work of a single composer who may tentatively be identified as Antonio Spalenza, documented as *maestro di cappella* at Treviso Cathedral from 1573 to 1577. Spalenza is further represented in MS 5 by another *Corpus Domini* motet, *Panis quem ego dabo* (fol. 35), whose text is also found in the Treviso liturgical source. D'Alessi's transcription of the cycle, itself an unicum, is also presented in the Archivio Capitolare (shelfmark: sala 2, scaffale 1-E-2, scatola 8). MS 5 was presumably

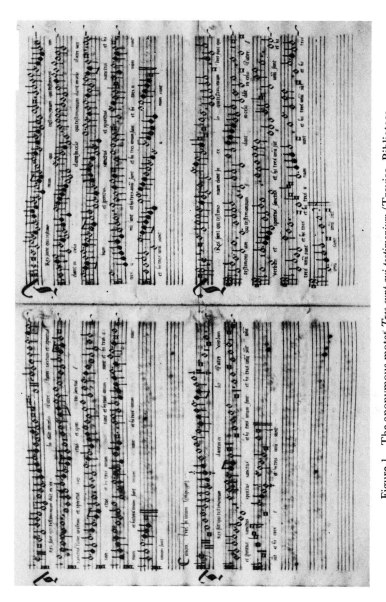

Figure 1 The anonymous motet *Tres sunt qui testimonium* (Treviso, Biblioteca Capitolare, MS 5, fols. 32ᵛ–33ʳ [destroyed]: reproduced from microfilm copy in Århus, Statsbiblioteket)

compiled between 1559 and 1572, since this date is given in D'Alessi's card catalogue below the incipit of the motet *Panis quem ego dabo* ('at the end of the bass part, there is the annotation *24 September 1572*'). On the basis of this information, it is perhaps reasonable to suppose that Spalenza was working at Treviso Cathedral at least as early as this.

The appearance of MS 5 itself may be judged from that of two motets in Jeppesen's microfilm: the anonymous six-part *Tres sunt qui testimonium* (Figure 1) and Costanzo Festa's four-part *Sancta Trinitas*. The first of these draws its text from the verset to the responsory *Quo seraphin clamabat*, proper to the feast of Holy Trinity and again present on fol. 23 of the Treviso liturgical manuscript; the musical structure is based on a symbolic triple canon at the unison, indicated above the tenor part by the words 'Canon. Tres in unum Congregatj'. To date, all attempts to trace concordances for Costanzo Festa's *Sancta Trinitas* have proved unsuccessful, and it seems possible that MS 5 represents the unique source.

The recovery of a partial photographic record of a series of manuscripts once considered irredeemably lost, the discovery of the music of a considerable number of unica and the acquisition of new information about the lives and work of three musicians (Innocenzo Alberti, Benedetto Menchini and Francesco Patavino) are the principal benefits of the identification of Jeppesen's microfilm. And, in general, the recovery of a second, highly significant photographic reproduction of motets from the lost manuscripts of Treviso Cathedral, together with D'Alessi's unpublished transcription of one otherwise lost motet, promps the obvious question of how much more of this material has been preserved through the work of many musicologists who visited Treviso and its archives in the period before World War II. In the wake of Professor Blackburn's excellent example, it can only be hoped that further research along these lines will yield more results of even greater significance.

Michele Pozzobon
Treviso

POSTSCRIPT

The present volume was already in press when I had the fortune to make a number of important discoveries at the Biblioteca Capitolare, Treviso. Of particular interest among a large number of prints and manuscripts of sixteenth- and seventeenth-century polyphony and liturgical chant, whose loss during the raid of 7 April 1944 has long been taken for granted, is MS 29, together with sizable fragments of four further manuscripts of polyphonic music. MS 29 is badly charred around the edges, but the music is still legible through the burns; careful restoration, and the use of appropriate photographic techniques, should permit the contents of the manuscript (if not the manuscript itself) to be consulted in their entirety. The same is true of many of the prints (of which the basso continuo partbook of Viadana's *Cento concerti* of 1614, RISM V1402, represents the sole surviving documentation). The other manuscripts show signs of considerable damage due to humidity; here restoration will necessarily yield more limited results.

The coordination of a long-term project of restoration and study of the newly recovered material has been undertaken by the Fondazione Benetton of Treviso, in the context of a series of research initiatives on local cultural and artistic traditions.

Anthony F. Carver, *Cori spezzati*. 2 vols., Cambridge, Cambridge University Press, 1988. Vol. i, xvi+282 pp.; vol. ii (music), vi+162 pp.

This study sets out to trace the origins, development and interaction of the numerous strands of musical composition which, in their various sixteenth- and seventeenth-century manifestations, are known as 'cori spezzati'. As the Preface informs us, it 'makes no claim to completeness as a history of polychoral music. This is ruled out by the sheer quantity of extant sources dating from the 1570s onwards'. After a comprehensive account of the stylistic antecedents of polychoral music and some of its earliest surviving manifestations, in particular the liturgical psalms of north Italian composers of the period *c.* 1530–50 and the large-scale 'political' repertory of the *Novus thesaurus musicus* (1568) (all but a handful of whose contents are by composers who were in the employment of the Habsburgs), the author proceeds to investigate the dissemination, aggrandisement and, ultimately, the decline of the phenomenon. This part of the discussion considers the music of a selection of 'composers whose outputs in this area seem significant', including Lassus (some of whose polychoral compositions, however, precede the appearance of the *Novus thesaurus musicus*), Andrea and Giovanni Gabrieli and their Venetian contemporaries, the most prolific of those late sixteenth-century composers who were active elsewhere in northern Italy, Palestrina, Victoria and some of their Roman and Spanish con-temporaries, and the most representative masters of polychoral music in Germany where the Gabrielian style remained in vogue long after its popularity had waned in Italy. Two appendices reproduce key readings about *cori spezzati* by Vicentino, Zarlino and Massimo Troiano (his description of the Bavarian royal wedding of 1568), and an inventory of four choirbooks (Vienna, Österreichische Nationalbibliothek, MSS 16702, 16703, 16707, 16708) which are almost entirely made up of polychoral music representing part of the repertory in use at the court chapel of Graz in the early seventeenth century. The bibliography devotes separate sections to a checklist of manuscripts and early prints containing polychoral music, but is restricted to those 'of which the author has first-hand experience'; its utility would have been greatly increased if it had also referred to some of the bibliographies of sixteenth- and seventeenth-century sacred music currently in preparation.[1]

Carver's major preoccupation throughout is with compositional style, 'the glorious sonority and fascinating formal patterns which first drew me to the subject', though his declared aim is also 'to incorporate where appropriate the latest findings of those involved in archival research'. This latter concern enables him to draw a usefully clear distinction between, on the one hand, Adrian Willaert's double-choir liturgical psalm settings and, on the other, the ceremonial polychoral motets of Andrea Gabrieli, whose role is now redefined in the light of the Habsburg 'political' repertory as 'founder of the colourful Venetian school of the late sixteenth and early seventeenth centuries'. Thus while the performance of Willaert's double-choir psalms required neither a large number of singers (one choir, indeed, sang one to a part) nor the distancing of the two groups of performers, the large-scale *concerti* of Andrea and Giovanni Gabrieli frequently gave rise to the employment of extra voices flanked by instrumentalists and also involved the physical division of the performing forces. For the most part, however, Carver's references to archival materials are brief and general, and are frequently used to shed light on matters of pure chronology rather than performance. The following is a characteristic example:

Documentation of polychoral performances in Rome ... begins in the 1570s. In 1573 Victoria's *Super flumina Babylonis* à 8 was performed at a ceremony marking the separation of the Collegium Romanum and the Collegium Germanicum (Collet 1914: 56–7). From 1576 at the Seminario Romano Vespers and Compline were sung 'a due chori' on principal feasts; extra singers were brought in from outside for the purpose (Casimiri 1935: 12–14). Recent research by Noel O'Regan and Graham Dixon shows that polychoral music became popular in Rome from the late sixteenth century onwards, particularly with confraternities. (pp. 4–5: one of the more detailed archivally based discussions)

Is not this apparent 'popularity' the dubious consequence of the fact that at Rome systematic archival research for the period in question began with precisely these institutions?

It is indeed unfortunate that no real attempt is made to treat organically the many questions of performance practice which

[1] Cf. the bibliographies of Anne Schnoebelen (printed music for the Mass, 1600–1700), Jeffrey Kurtzman (printed music for the Office, 1540–*c.* 1725), Graham Dixon and Jerome Roche (the Italian motet repertory, 1600–50).

together exert a decisive influence on the musical 'text' as heard, not merely as transmitted on the written page. If the study of performance practice is important in the context of early music as a whole, it is doubly so in the case of a repertory which, in so many cases, seems to have served above all as an adjunct to ceremonial pomp on the greatest occasions of church and state: a sonorous 'image' of grandeur, an agent of propaganda with regard both to other institutions and to the public at large. Typical of Carver's approach is his treatment of the question of scoring. Here, he makes few attempts to investigate the composition (and differences in composition) of both the regular and ad hoc instrumental bands employed in the performance of large-scale music through reference to pay records and descriptions of actual performances (though he does unwittingly suggest the possibility of regional divergences when, in his description of Philippe Rogier's twelve-part motet *Verbum caro factum est*, he notes the original specification of an 'arpa' as the *basso seguente* instrument for the high Choir 1; Venetian church archives of the sixteenth and early seventeenth centuries make no references whatever to this instrument, which was however used in contemporary Spanish-controlled Naples. Instead, we are treated to a series of perfunctory and somewhat disjointed discussions of, for example, the use of voices and instruments in the performance of polychoral music during the Bavarian royal wedding festivities of 1568 (p. 4, another of the more specific documentary references in the volume); a general reference to the employment of both voices and instruments for the performance of polychoral music in Habsburg lands, Munich and Venice before the early seventeenth century, at which time composers begin to offer concrete suggestions for scoring (p. 16); a further glance at the use of voices and instruments in the Bavarian festivities of 1568 (pp. 75–7); a speculation, based on the supposed 'particular fondness for instrumental participation in church music in some [unspecified] Spanish cathedrals', on the possible use of instruments to double the voices in Choirs 2 and 3 of Victoria's polychoral compositions while Choir 1 is generally supplied with an organ part (p. 123); some general remarks about scoring in Giovanni Gabrieli's *Sacrae symphoniae* of 1597 (pp. 146–7) and about implied and specified scoring in Gabrieli's *Symphoniae sacrae* of 1615 (pp. 164–6) and, finally, the scoring of large-scale works as discussed in Michael Praetorius's *Syntagma musicum* of 1619 (pp. 218–20). This fragmentary approach to what was surely a fundamental aspect of the 'sound' of much polychoral music is confusing in its own right. On occasion, that confusion is compounded by remarks such as those (p. 218) where 'Gabrieli's normal use' of the term *cappella* is defined as 'synonymous with Praetorius's *chorus vocalis*' – itself, says Carver, used by Praetorius 'without making it clear whether it is a solo or ripieno group'; only on turning to p. 147 (no cross-reference is supplied) do we learn that *cappella*, in the works of Giovanni Gabrieli, 'is a ripieno chorus of "normal" vocal range'. The issue of spatial separation in performance, again treated in a series of individual paragraphs or individual sentences with little or no attempt at overall organisation, is largely reduced to the question of the harmonic self-sufficiency of the various choirs, it being supposed, not unreasonably, that the clear separation of groups of performers requires each to be harmonically complete. Two objections remain. First, the tutti sections of Willaert's double-choir *salmi* are characterised throughout by the harmonic self-sufficiency of the two groups of performers, although, as we know, these compositions were conceived especially for St Mark's where they were performed without hint of spatial separation. (Indeed, their texts are drawn not from the 'Gallican' psalter, which was widely used throughout Europe, but from the so-called 'Roman' psalter in use only at St Mark's and in a handful of other centres.) Secondly, the only architectural environments to receive any discussion whatever are the ducal chapels of Munich and Venice, and even here the descriptions are cursory and incomplete.

The fragmentation which results from this treatment of the questions of scoring and the spatial separation of choirs is exacerbated by the frequent insertion of paragraphs on themes which are themselves fundamentally extraneous to any discussion of the technique of *cori spezzati*. Nothing in the section devoted to the parody masses of Palestrina (pp. 116–18), for example, would suggest that the use of parody technique in the compositions for *cori spezzati* is in any way different from its application in other repertories, and this in turn raises the question of whether Carver's study of polychoral techniques is, in essence, an open-ended examination of various aspects of style in those works which happen to be polychoral. However, at first glance this problem of overall organisation is not apparent. The articulation of chapter headings by geographical division ('The early Italian contribution', 'The Franco-Flemish tradition', 'Double-choir music at the Munich court', 'Polychoral music in Rome and Spain', 'Venice: the grand climax', 'Across the Alps: the German craze') seems plausible, if rather too general. And within this framework the discussion, in the opening chapters, of the techniques of dialogue, psalmody, voice-pairing, double-choir canon and 'flexible antiphony', all of which can be regarded to some degree as either precursors or ingredients of true double-choir music, augurs well. Yet later on the author returns intermittently to two of these categories, dialogue and psalmody, in the music of a variety of composers including Bonardo, Lassus, Andrea and Giovanni Gabrieli, Merulo, Handl and Schein. As he does so, the façade of geographical cum thematic organisation soon crumbles to reveal the rather more banal reality of a structure articulated by a series of composers loosely grouped in schools. Thus Animuccia, Palestrina, Victoria, later Roman composers, Rogier, Andrea and Giovanni Gabrieli, Merulo, Donato, Croce, Bassano, Porta, Chamaterò, Asola, Monte, Handl, Hans Leo Hassler, Hieronymus Praetorius, Michael Praetorius, Schein, Scheidt and Schütz follow each other in what seems an almost interminable succession, seldom with any real attempt to establish concrete connections (or even draw parallels) between them, whether in terms of exclusively musical analysis or with reference to the liturgical, ceremonial and (hence) musical traditions of the institutions where these musicians were employed. One typically inaccurate diagnosis occurs in the section devoted to the polychoral output of 'Giovanni Croce' (pp. 173–81), *maestro di cappella* at the ducal chapel of Venice from 1603 to 1609, whose three volumes of double-choir psalm settings for Compline (.1591), Terce (1596) and Vespers (1597), two volumes of eight-part motets (1594, 1595) and one collection of eight-part settings of the Ordinary (1596) are discussed in close succession. On the 1591 publication Carver writes:

The overriding impression in the psalms is of adherence to the Willaert tradition (Croce was a protégé of Zarlino), especially in the texture and the utilisation of the cadential structure of the psalm tone. Some verses are given entirely to one choir, but choirs are sometimes exchanged at the half-verse and sparing use is made of antiphonal repetition and tutti where it is appropriate to the text.

Croce may well have been a protégé of Zarlino, who was himself responsible for the famous codification of Willaert's style of *cori spezzati* (*Le istitutioni harmoniche*, 1558, part III, ch. 66). But the style of Croce's psalms is determined less by any personal affiliations than by liturgical tradition. Willaert himself based the structure of his double-choir psalms, which are characterised by strict alternation of the choirs every verse or half-verse, thoroughgoing use of the Gregorian psalm tone, and a largely homophonic declamatory style, on a specific liturgical practice; their manner of performance in St Mark's (one choir with one singer to a part, the other with the remainder of the *cappella*) is clearly derived from earlier plainsong usages in the basilica. Interestingly, psalms in the Willaert style for St Mark's were written a full two centuries later by no less an heir to the tradition than Baldassare Galuppi.

In the purely musical domain, Carver's technique of comparing two or more settings by different composers of a single text rarely yields more than a series of rather fortuitous divergences, and even when parallels do seem to exist, as in the hint of a 'thematic quotation' of Andrea Gabrieli's eight-part *Quem vidistis pastores* in Giovanni Gabrieli's fourteen-part motet of the same name, it is difficult to draw conclusions which go beyond the mere observation of facts. Similarly, the detailed descriptions of individual compositions which fill much of the volume, while interesting as an introduction to a repertory which is still largely unknown, are hard to justify in methodological terms. Not atypical is the case of the Flemish composer Philippe Rogier (pp. 125–8), *maestro di cappella* at the court of Philip II of Spain from 1586 to his death ten years later. *Laudate Dominum in sanctis eius* 'is a conventional psalm-motet, mostly homophonic after an imitative opening for the first choir' (end of description). The eight-part *Regina caeli* 'is very sectional, with a fermata after each "Alleluia". After the first section in fairly broad imitative style (with hints of the chant), "Resurrexit sicut dixit" comes as a shock in *note nere* with dotted rhythms, though Choir 1 reintroduces white notes'. And so on, through the *Missa Domine in virtute tua* and *Missa Domine Dominus noster*. Here as elsewhere, even in terms of Carver's self-imposed parameters of compositional practice, the results are unsatisfactory: some attempt at generalisation is required, even if limited to statistical analysis.

In short, after the opening chapters, which undoubtedly provide the most comprehensive account yet available of the musical development of *cori spezzati* before *c.* 1570, this study rapidly deterio-rates into a series of descriptions of the polychoral compositions of individual composers. These pieces are often described as the 'best' of their kind (the volume is peppered with such generalised value judgments), and are pursued with reference to a series of standard categories of compositional techniques such as repetitive and non-repetitive antiphony, dialogue, psalmodic antiphony, thematic unity, contrapuntal technique and harmonic self-sufficiency of individual choirs. As an investigation of style, it will provide a reference tool for future studies addressed to the many other issues including the questions of liturgical and ceremonial function, archi-tectural environments and choir sizes which determined specific compositional and performance practices. In this sense Carver's book, for all its methodological shortcomings, must be welcomed.

David Bryant
Fondazione Giorgio Cini, Venice

CAMBRIDGE
Opera
JOURNAL

A new approach to opera

Cambridge Opera Journal provides a new forum for the exchange of views and ideas from a variety of disciplines, attracting authors eager to communicate to a wider audience.

Cambridge Opera Journal addresses audiences from a wide variety of disciplines from musicology to literature, theatre and history, avoiding narrowly musicological or philological modes of enquiry.

Coverage
Coverage is broad. The journal is comprehensible to non-musicologists and is written for academics and scholars of related disciplines, as well as the serious opera lover.

Early issues consider *Madam Butterfly* in Japan, singers of Italian opera and their patrons and constructions of gender in Monteverdi's dramatic music.

Forthcoming Articles
The buffa aria in Mozart's Vienna, *John Platoff*
Liszt, Wagner and Heinrich Dorn's *Die Nibelungen, Adelyn Peck Leverett*
'Twisted relations'. Method and meaning in Britten's *Billy Budd*,
Arnold Whittall

Subscriptions 1990, Volume 2, March, July and November: £18 for individual subscribers; £32 for institutions; airmail £9.50 per year extra
ISSN 0954-5867

To **subscribe**, or for **further information**, please contact:
Journals Publicity Department,
Cambridge University Press,
*FREEPOST, The Edinburgh Building,
Shaftesbury Road, Cambridge CB2 1BR,
England
(*No postage required if posted in the UK)

Cambridge Journals

British Journal of Music Education

Editors: **John Paynter**, University of York;
Keith Swanwick, University of London Institute of Education

The principal concern of the journal is to develop debate about issues in music education and to do so without restriction of style, method, or specialism. A large proportion of contributors are practising teachers. An important part of the journal's production is the annual cassette tape with music examples related to articles published during the year.

The range of subjects covered is wide:

● classroom music teaching ● individual instrumental teaching and group teaching ● music in higher education ● international comparative music education and the development of literature in this field.

Subscriptions 1990, Volume 7, March, July and November: £19.00 for individuals; £29.00 for UK institutions; £33.00 for institutions elsewhere; £12.00 for single parts; airmail £9.50 per year extra
ISSN 0265-0517

───── Also from Cambridge ─────

Popular Music

Popular Music is a multi-disciplinary journal which covers all aspects of popular music broadly defined – from Abba to zydeco, from broadside ballads to hip-hop. It presents the results of scholarly work in an accessible form, while at the same time responding to current events. Each issue contains substantial articles, shorter topical pieces, news, correspondence and reviews.

Subscriptions 1990, Volume 9: January, May and October: £22.00 for individuals; £40.00 for institutions; £15.00 for single parts; airmail £9.50 per year extra   ISSN 0261-1430

To **subscribe**, or **for further information**, please contact:
Journals Publicity Department,
Cambridge University Press, *FREEPOST,
The Edinburgh Building, Shaftesbury Road,
Cambridge CB2 1BR, England
(*No postage required if posted in the UK)

Cambridge Journals